Building Family, School, and Community Partnerships

THIRD EDITION

Kay Wright
EASTERN KENTUCKY UNIVERSITY

Dolores A. Stegelin
CLEMSON UNIVERSITY

Lynn Hartle
UNIVERSITY OF CENTRAL FLORIDA

PEARSON

Merrill
Prentice Hall

Upper Saddle River, New Jersey
Columbus, Ohio

Library of Congress Cataloging-in-Publication Data

Wright, Kay.
    Building family, school, and community partnerships / Kay Wright, Dolores A. Stegelin, Lynn Hartle.—3rd ed.
        p.   cm.
    Rev. ed. of: Building school and community partnerships through parent involvement.
    Includes bibliographical references and index.
    ISBN 0-13-188622-3
        1. Home and school—United States.   2. Parent-teacher relationships—United States.   3. Community and school—United States.   4. Education—Parent participation—United States.   I. Stegelin, Dolores.   II. Hartle, Lynn
III. Wright, Kay Building school and community partnerships through parent involvement.   IV. Title.

LC225.3.W75 2007
371.19'2—dc22
                                                                                                    2005036340

Vice President and Executive Publisher: Jeffery W. Johnston
Publisher: Kevin M. Davis
Acquisitions Editor: Julie Peters
Editorial Assistant: Michelle Girgis
Senior Production Editor: Linda Hillis Bayma
Production Coordination: Thistle Hill Publishing Services, LLC
Design Coordinator: Diane C. Lorenzo
Cover Designer: Kristina Holmes
Cover image: SuperStock
Production Manager: Laura Messerly
Director of Marketing: David Gesell
Marketing Manager: Amy Judd
Marketing Coordinator: Brian Mounts

This book was set in Janson Text by Integra Software Services. It was printed and bound by R.R. Donnelley & Sons Company. The cover was printed by R.R. Donnelley & Sons Company.

Photo Credits: Dolores Stegelin, pp. 3, 4 (*top*), 5, 6, 12, 14, 15, 68, 73, 81, 138, 140, 142, 153, 165, 170, 184, 196, 199, 200, 206, 306, 307 (*both*), 308, 321 (*both*), 322, 331; Paul Riccomini, p. 4 (*bottom*); Kay Wright, pp. 36, 38, 52, 58, 62, 97, 106, 115, 121, 220, 232, 235, 242, 251, 273, 277, 279, 289, 295, 296, 297; Lynn Hartle, pp. 49, 101, 110, 223, 288.

Pearson Education Ltd.
Pearson Education Singapore Pte. Ltd.
Pearson Education Canada, Ltd.
Pearson Education—Japan

Pearson Education Australia Pty. Limited
Pearson Education North Asia Ltd.
Pearson Educación de Mexico, S.A. de C.V.
Pearson Education Malaysia Pte. Ltd.

10 9 8 7 6 5 4 3 2 1
ISBN: 0-13-188622-3

This book is affectionately dedicated to
Matthew and Michael Springate,
Forrest, Amber, Steve, Heather, Cory, and Caleb Stegelin,
Dolores Hartle, and Kelsey, John, Betty, and
Murdo MacLeod

Kay Wright, EdD, is Professor of Child and Family Studies in the Department of Family and Consumer Sciences at Eastern Kentucky University. During the past 26 years of work in the field of early childhood education, she has been a preschool and kindergarten teacher, a consultant with the Kentucky Department of Education, Director of the Child Development Center at Eastern, and an early childhood teacher educator. She was instrumental in the founding of Ecumenical Preschool and served on its board for several years. Most recently, Dr. Wright has been involved in the implementation of the Interdisciplinary Early Childhood Education Certificate for teachers preparing to work with children from birth to primary school in Kentucky. She has served as the president of the Kentucky Association for Children Under Six and has served in a variety of service capacities through professional organizations. She has also coordinated several state training grants and written numerous publications for the Kentucky Department of Education. Dr. Wright has conducted many workshops at the state, local, and national levels and has authored publications in the field of early childhood education. Her professional interests include emergent curriculum, literacy and families, and exploring the ongoing needs of families through the lifespan.

Dolores (Dee) Stegelin, PhD, is Professor and Program Coordinator of Early Childhood Education in the Eugene T. Moore School of Education, College of Health, Education, and Human Development, at Clemson University. Dr. Stegelin's research interests are in early childhood advocacy and policy, early literacy, parent education, public school early childhood programs, and inclusion of children with special needs. She is the author of three textbooks (*Early Childhood Education: Policy Issues for the 1990s; Changing Kindergarten: Four Success Stories;* and *Building School and Community Partnerships Through Parent Involvement*). She has published in professional journals including *Young Children, Journal of Early Childhood Teacher Education, Early Education & Development, Journal of Children's Health, Early Childhood Education Journal,* and the *Australian Journal of Early Childhood.* Dr. Stegelin is the co-director of the Early Childhood Longitudinal Study Project at Clemson University, an interdisciplinary initiative utilizing the National Center for Educational Statistics ECKL-S database. She is public policy chair for the South Carolina Association for the Education of Young Children; serves on the research committee of the Association of Childhood Education International (ACEI) and on the conference committee for the National Association of Early Childhood

Teacher Educators (NAECTE) and is active in the National Association for the Education of Young Children (NAEYC).

Lynn Hartle, PhD, is an Associate Professor in Early Childhood Education in the Department of Child, Family, and Community Sciences at the University of Central Florida. After 10 years as a Montessori preprimary directress, her career in higher education spans 20 years at five universities, where she has taught more than 14 different graduate and undergraduate courses, many online. Each class is taught with consideration of the role of technology in teaching and her research interest—how to differentiate learning experiences for children typically developing and those with special needs from culturally and linguistically diverse families. She has also been involved in grant-funded projects, the most recent of which is the U.S. Department of Education 2005 Early Childhood Educator Professional Development (ECEPD) Program Grant. These teaching experiences grounded in research are synthesized in her first co-authored book, *The Successful Teacher's Guide to Frequently Asked Questions*, and in various journals, including *Young Children*, *Early Childhood Education*, and the *Journal of Research in Childhood Education*. She is a frequent speaker at national conferences and holds board positions on Readiness Coalitions and the National Association for Early Childhood Teacher Educators. She is currently the president of the National Association for the Education of Young Children, Technology and Young Children Interest Forum.

The need for parent involvement in school and early care settings has never been greater. Traditionally, American early childhood settings have invited and included parents at some level. We believe wholeheartedly that parents should be full partners in the classroom, modeled by international programs such as the Reggio Emilia schools of Italy.

PURPOSE OF THIS TEXT

This textbook is designed to be practical, useful, and informative for teachers, students, and many different professionals who develop professional programs and implement them with children and their families. We have designed the book to be logical and forthright in its presentation style.

This text focuses on the changing family forms that are reflected in the makeup of contemporary early childhood classrooms and child-care settings. Because family structures are changing so rapidly, teachers are challenged to find effective ways to communicate with parents, grandparents, foster parents, and other caring adults. Teachers will encounter not only traditional family forms but also single-parent households, gay- and lesbian-parent households, households headed by grandparents or other relatives, foster-parent families, and families with multicultural and language differences. Both teachers and parents need the emotional and affective support of one another, and young children need the guidance and affection of both their parents and their classroom teachers.

Each chapter includes guiding questions, key terms, critical concepts, summary statements, classroom strategies for teachers, advocacy ideas to implement, resources for the teacher and student, references, and in-class research-to-practice activities and applications.

ORGANIZATION OF THIS TEXT

We have created three distinct sections to this book. Part I provides a detailed overview of contemporary American families and schools. Chapter 1 focuses on the importance and rationale for family–school connections and provides an overview of family and child issues in contemporary American families. Specific themes are identified and create the justification for the critical role of parents in the early childhood setting. Chapter 2 features a mosaic of parent involvement over time. The history of parent involvement is described from A.D. 1 through 2000, along with the importance of establishing and maintaining home and school partnerships and preparing teachers to build partnerships with families. Chapter 3 provides an overview of child and family advocacy and gives the classroom teacher many strategies for becoming an effective advocate and involving parents in the advocacy process.

Part II of the text focuses on the kinds of families that represent contemporary American culture. Chapter 4 addresses cross-cultural issues involving families and the community. The journey of growth and development within the context of cultures in our near and far environments is presented. Chapter 5 targets the unique needs of parents and families of children with disabilities and special needs. Included are discussions of typical reactions of parents to a child with special needs, a description of special needs, and suggestions for parent involvement and advocacy for special needs. Chapter 6 centers on the growing trend of divorce and blended families in the United States. Stages of adjustment to divorce are discussed as well as classroom strategies for teachers to use when working with children and parents in divorced and blended family situations. Chapter 7 focuses on families and children of adoption, a growing phenomenon in our country. Suggestions for responding to the adopted child's needs as well as involving adoptive parents in the classroom are presented. Chapter 8 features the nontraditional family makeup, including alternative lifestyles, homosexuality, and cultural issues and effects of gay- and lesbian-parent households.

Part III is an important application component of the textbook that includes two significant chapters. Chapter 9 details specific strategies for working with parents and families from a multicultural and technology perspective. Chapter 10 provides information and concrete strategies for assessing the parent involvement component of the early childhood classroom. This textbook concludes with important applications for classroom teachers, directors, and administrators.

ACKNOWLEDGMENTS

We gratefully acknowledge the contributions of our reviewers for their valuable insights and suggestions: Susan Matoba Adler, University of Illinois, Urbana-Champaign; Ann Barbour, California State University, Los Angeles; Jane Christine Catalani, San Antonio College; and Patricia Clark, University of Maine.

DISCOVER THE COMPANION WEBSITE ACCOMPANYING THIS BOOK

The Prentice Hall Companion Website: A Virtual Learning Environment

Technology is a constantly growing and changing aspect of our field that is creating a need for content and resources. To address this emerging need, Prentice Hall has developed an online learning environment for students and professors alike—Companion Websites—to support our textbooks.

In creating a Companion Website, our goal is to build on and enhance what the textbook already offers. For this reason, the content for each user-friendly website is organized by topic and provides the professor and student with a variety of meaningful resources. Common features of a Companion Website include:

- **Introduction**—General information about the topic and how it will be covered in the website.
- **Web Links**—A variety of websites related to topic areas.
- **Timely Articles**—Links to online articles that enable you to become more aware of important issues in early childhood.
- **Learn by Doing**—Put concepts into action, participate in activities, examine strategies, and more.
- **Visit a School**—Visit a school's website to see concepts, theories, and strategies in action.
- **For Teachers/Practitioners**—Access information you will need to know as an educator, including information on materials, activities, and lessons.
- **Observation Tools**—A collection of checklists and forms to print and use when observing and assessing children's development.
- **Current Policies and Standards**—Find out the latest early childhood policies from the government and various organizations, and view state, federal, and curriculum standards.
- **Resources and Organizations**—Discover tools to help you plan your classroom or center and organizations to provide current information and standards for each topic.

■ **Electronic Bluebook**—Paperless method of completing homework or essays assigned by a professor. Finished work can be sent to the professor via email.

To take advantage of these and other resources, please visit Merrill Education's **Early Childhood Education Resources Website**. Go to **www.prenhall.com/wright**, click on the book cover, and then click on "Enter" at the bottom of the next screen.

TEACHER PREP

MERRILL
PRENTICE HALL

TEACHER PREPARATION CLASSROOM

See a demo at
www.prenhall.com/teacherprep/demo

Your Class. Their Careers. Our Future. Will your students be prepared?

We invite you to explore our new, innovative and engaging website and all that it has to offer you, your course, and tomorrow's educators! Organized around the major courses pre-service teachers take, the Teacher Preparation site provides media, student/teacher artifacts, strategies, research articles, and other resources to equip your students with the quality tools needed to excel in their courses and prepare them for their first classroom.

This ultimate on-line education resource is available at no cost, when packaged with a Merrill text, and will provide you and your students access to:

Online Video Library. More than 150 video clips—each tied to a course topic and framed by learning goals and Praxis-type questions—capture real teachers and students working in real classrooms, as well as in-depth interviews with both students and educators.

Student and Teacher Artifacts. More than 200 student and teacher classroom artifacts—each tied to a course topic and framed by learning goals and application questions—provide a wealth of materials and experiences to help make your study to become a professional teacher more concrete and hands-on.

Research Articles. Over 500 articles from ASCD's renowned journal *Educational Leadership*. The site also includes Research Navigator, a searchable database of additional educational journals.

Teaching Strategies. Over 500 strategies and lesson plans for you to use when you become a practicing professional.

Licensure and Career Tools. Resources devoted to helping you pass your licensure exam; learn standards, law, and public policies; plan a teaching portfolio; and succeed in your first year of teaching.

How to ORDER *Teacher Prep* for you and your students:

For students to receive a *Teacher Prep* Access Code with this text, instructors **must** provide a special value pack ISBN number on their textbook order form. To receive this special ISBN, please email: **Merrill.marketing@pearsoned.com** and provide the following information:

- Name and Affiliation
- Author/Title/Edition of Merrill text

Upon ordering *Teacher Prep* for their students, instructors will be given a lifetime *Teacher Prep* Access Code.

BRIEF CONTENTS

CONTENTS

PART III EFFECTIVE STRATEGIES FOR PARENT INVOLVEMENT AND ASSESSMENT OF PARENT INVOLVEMENT

Note: Every effort has been made to provide accurate and current Internet information in this book. However, the Internet and information posted on it are constantly changing, so it is inevitable that some of the Internet addresses listed in this textbook will change.

CHAPTER 1

The Parent–School Connection

Serving Families in a Contemporary Context

Lesson 6: Take parenting and family life seriously and insist that those you work for and who represent you do.

EDELMAN, 1992, P. 43

High quality child care and early education are critical to the success of two national priorities: Helping families work and ensuring that every child enters school ready to succeed.

CHILDREN'S DEFENSE FUND, 2005

KEY TERMS

Bronfenbrenner's ecological model	domestic violence	maternal employment rates	Reggio Emilia programs
child poverty rate	family of origin	one-way strategies	two-way strategies

GUIDING QUESTIONS

1. Why is the parent–school connection important?
2. How is Bronfenbrenner's ecological model helpful in explaining parent–school relationships?
3. What are critical forces impacting contemporary American families?
4. What is the role of extended families, and why is the "typical American family" a myth?
5. How does multiculturalism influence parent–teacher interactions?
6. Why do teachers still struggle to connect with parents?
7. What factors should teachers consider when developing effective parent–school strategies?

he preceding quotations echo a growing belief by educators in the United States that parent involvement in schools and the quality of family life for young students should be associated with more positive educational outcomes. What remains elusive, however, are the types of programs offered by schools to encourage parent involvement and the most effective parent involvement strategies that can be used with the increasingly diverse parent population (Zellman & Waterman, 1998). This text is dedicated to uncovering this information so that future teachers and parents might better understand the critical connection among parents, schools, children, and positive educational outcomes.

Marian Wright Edelman, founder and president of the Children's Defense Fund (CDF) and one of America's greatest child advocates, is the author of an inspirational book that provides readers with 25 lessons for life. Entitled *The Measure of Our Success: A Letter to My Children and Yours* (1992), these 25 lessons include suggestions and admonitions for working hard, setting goals, taking risks, valuing family relationships, being honest, persevering, being confident, always learning, remembering your roots, taking charge of your attitude, and being faithful. Lesson 6 reflects the notion that all of us spend so much time in our lives involved in careers and daily living prerequisites that we must critically evaluate our relationships with supervisors, colleagues, and other significant individuals *as to their priority for families and quality parent–child relationships*. Edelman urges us to take the role of parents and families very seriously and to spend time only with those who do.

Many books have been written about families and schools. Indeed, the importance of parent involvement in children's schools has been a persistent theme in the research and school reform efforts of the last three decades (Bronfenbrenner, 1979; Comer, 1990; Epstein, 1988; Finn & Petrilli, 1998; Gonzalez-Mena, 2002; Rockwell & Kniepkamp, 2003; Sullivan, 1998; Zellman & Waterman, 1998). Thus, the topic of families and schools is certainly not a new one.

Why, then, is it important to look once again at the parent–school–community connection? What new variables affect today's families? Why are schools still struggling to understand their child populations better? What makes many teachers excited and inspired by today's children and families and other teachers seemingly overwhelmed and discouraged by their interactions with parents and children? What do parents really *want* and *expect* from schools and community agencies, and how does that differ in the new millennium? How do parents prefer to interface with teachers, administrators, and other school professionals, and how is that influenced by linguistic and economic diversity as well as family form and makeup?

The need for the parent–school connection has never been greater. The complexity of contemporary American classrooms continues to challenge both teachers and parents. This growing complexity stems from several key forces such as linguistic and cultural diversity, inclusion, changing family forms, and challenges to basic societal expectations for safety and security. From Columbine High School in Colorado to quiet and unassuming elementary school settings, school violence and classroom complexity have caused all of us to pause and ask critical questions about

Family forms are constantly changing in our contemporary society.

the students in today's classrooms. Teacher education programs across the United States have the challenging responsibility to prepare new teachers to embrace this classroom diversity and to recognize and utilize the many resources available to them, including parents, home situations and resources, and family strengths. Home, family, school, neighborhood, and society shape the contours of childhood and adolescence (Bronfenbrenner, 1979; Edwards & Young, 1992; Goffin & Stegelin, 1992; Gonzalez-Mena, 2002).

Chapter 1 provides the reader with the following key themes and foci:

Theme 1. *Today's families are changing in many ways.* A description and profile of contemporary American families and children are provided, making more clear to future teachers why their classrooms are indeed so much more complex developmentally, linguistically, and economically.

Theme 2. *The parent–school–student connection is critical,* as is the rationale for continuing to build effective, long-lasting, and vital home–school linkages. Teachers should spend time early in the school year assessing parental needs and attitudes. Teachers and administrators must strive to understand the increasing challenges of communicating with contemporary families and collaborate with parents to find effective ways to share information and meet the needs of the child.

Theme 3. *There are several basic communication strategies for teachers and parents.* Provided here is a brief overview of communication avenues for parents, teachers, administrators, counselors and psychologists, special education teachers, and other service-related personnel; in-depth coverage is given in another chapter. Communication strategies today are different, and the role of technology in promoting, strengthening, and easing the communication between parents and school professionals is growing.

Theme 4. *The authors dedicate this textbook effort to building partnerships among schools, parents, and communities.* An overview of the content of this textbook is provided as a guide for the use of the textbook as a tool to help future teachers become better prepared.

Contemporary fathers spend quality time with their children.

To understand the young child, we must first understand the family of origin.

Specifically, chapter 1 addresses the following topics as a part of the listed themes:

- The current status and profile of American families, providing statistics on the emerging patterns of "new" family forms. *What new patterns are teachers seeing today?*
- Current demographics on the contemporary American child with the goal of helping future teachers better understand the internal and external dynamics in the lives of children today. *Why do more children seem tired, preoccupied, and less prepared for the everyday demands of the classroom?*
- The importance of forming collaborative partnerships in fostering the growth and development of the child. *What does the research reflect in terms of quality of shared relationships and resulting child outcomes?*
  - Contemporary lifestyle and "real" issues that affect families and schools in their efforts to nurture young children. *Why are parenting and teaching so complex today?*
  - The individual roles of the school, the family, and the community in engaging in partnerships. *How does this collaboration work? How are roles defined and by whom?*
  - The emerging needs of the family and how they impact schools, teachers, and classrooms. *What is different about the demands and needs of contemporary families versus those of only a decade ago?*
  - Strategies for involving families in decision making, classroom activities, parent-oriented activities, and parent–child activities in the home. *How can teachers engage parents more deeply in the heart of teaching, curricular decisions, and home–school activities?*

With these themes in mind, let us now begin a journey to redefine and rediscover the American family and the important issues and avenues that professionals should understand to meet the needs of America's increasingly diverse young children and their families. In this chapter, the term *schools* is used to denote early childhood programs and child-care arrangements, both public and private, providing care and education for children from birth through age 8 (National Association for the Education of Young Children [NAEYC], 1986). Also targeted are individuals within the schools and centers who provide care and education: administrators, teachers, caregivers, and support personnel. Teachers and administrators are not adequately prepared to address the range of children's social and psychological needs. They know what ought to be done, but not how to do it (Edwards & Young, 1992, p. 85).

UNDERSTANDING TODAY'S FAMILIES

To interface effectively with children and their parents, it is essential to better understand the American family. Technology, world violence, changing family forms, and linguistic and developmental diversity all combine to define the American family in the 21st century. *Strategies that worked 10 to 15 years ago do not work today* (Wallach, 1993). How are contemporary American families changing? How do these changes affect the communication patterns and interaction strategies that are successful or unsuccessful?

To understand better the complex needs of the individual child within the school and community setting, we must first understand the child's **family of origin**. This section provides information on the American family, how it is changing, and how these changes affect the quality and quantity of interactions among the child, the family, the school, and the community.

To understand the complex needs of the child, we must first understand the child's family of origin.

Maternal Employment

The employment of so many mothers in today's workforce is one of the most important factors in the changing face of the American family. New mothers in the United States return to work very quickly by international standards. A third of new mothers in the United States return to work within 3 months of giving birth (Berger, Hill, & Waldfogel, 2005; Klerman & Leibowitz, 1999; Smith & Bachu, 1999). By comparison, only about 5 percent of new mothers in other industrialized nations such as Germany, Sweden, and the United Kingdom return to work within the same time frame. Although female employment has grown steadily, the needed systems to support the young child and the family have not. This factor alone accounts for many stressors encountered by children, their parents, and subsequently the schools that serve them. Whether the family is a

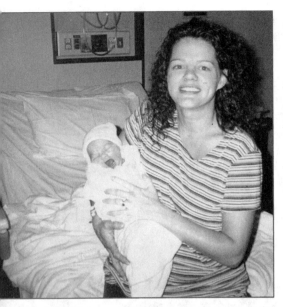

Over 50 percent of mothers of infants are in the labor force.

dual-earner or single-headed household, employment of the mother affects the dynamics of the family system dramatically. Sixty-five percent of mothers with children under age 6 and 79 percent of mothers with children ages 6 to 13 are in the labor force (Bureau of Labor Statistics, 2001). According to Olmstead (1992), more than 66 percent of children under age 6 have mothers in the labor force. The proportion of single mothers with jobs, after remaining steady at around 58 percent from 1986 to 1993, increased sharply to 71.5 percent in 1999 (Pear, 2000). Although a substantial number are not working full-time, it is clear that many more mothers than ever before are leaving their infants and toddlers in out-of-home care provided by non-family members. The need for after-school care and transitional child-care options has also increased dramatically. Whether this employment situation and subsequent child-care need is through choice or necessity, it contributes to family stress.

In addition, welfare reform programs are designed to help mothers participate in the workforce in new and creative ways. Welfare reform accounts for the addition of some low-income women to the already growing list of employed mothers. Although requiring parents on welfare to work and to be gainfully employed does make sense from an economic and political perspective, it has added another dimension of stress for these families. Child care is now necessary for families who are working to get off welfare; these families are seeking many diverse avenues of before- and after-school care, as well as care for their infants, toddlers, and preschoolers. Financial restraints may prevent them from securing quality, consistent child care in homes or centers; often, children are left to fend for themselves or with unwilling neighbors or relatives.

The need for quality child care to accommodate this societal trend of maternal employment continues to challenge early childhood professionals and policy makers. According to the CDF (2005), every day, 12 million preschoolers—including 6 million infants and toddlers—are in child care. At least 40 percent of all care and 75 percent of family child care in the United States is entirely unregulated and thus may not meet even minimal standards of health and safety; Ryan (1992) reported that 80 percent to 90 percent of child-care settings are unlicensed. More than 10 million children under the age of 6 have mothers in the workforce; of these, 35.6 percent are in family child care or are cared for in a relative's or sitter's home; 24.3 percent are in organized child-care programs; and the remaining 10.2 percent are in either kindergarten or other forms of child care (Hoyt & Schoonmaker, 1991). The research is clear that the quality of child care has a lasting impact on children's well-being and ability to learn (Carnegie, 1994). Children in poor-quality child care have been found to be delayed in language and reading skills and display more aggression toward other children and adults (Phillips, 1995). As **maternal employment rates** continue to escalate, the challenge of providing quality, safe, and developmentally appropriate child care remains one of the greatest issues for America's early childhood teachers and administrators, as well as for legislators and other decision makers.

Extended Family, Grandparents, and "New" Family Forms

Another major force in the lives of young children is the changing face and definition of the family. This is an important fact for teachers and administrators to realize, as children are being parented by a more diverse family unit than in the past. Members of the extended family are assuming more parenting responsibilities than in the past because of the financial, social, and emotional issues young parents may be coping with. Grandparents are providing the primary parenting and nurturing processes for many young children. The rise in grandparent involvement in direct parenting responsibilities is occurring for many reasons, and grandparents are assuming more financial and physical responsibility for younger children at a time when their own resources may be more limited.

Why is this important for teachers to understand? Communication patterns with older adults will be different from those with younger adults. Grandparents may be limited in their physical capacity to visit the child's classroom, attend school events, or respond to a teacher's requests for individual child conferences. In addition, financial restraints may limit the older adults' ability to afford to maintain a vehicle or pay for gasoline. Use of the Internet for communication may not be as feasible for the grandparent, for a variety of reasons. Teachers, however, can rely on the grandparent to provide accurate and comprehensive information about the overall well-being of the child, establish predictable homework routines, and be responsible for disciplining and nurturing the child. The teacher should assess each child's individual resources at the beginning of the school year. Realizing the potential capacity of the grandparent or other older adult relative as a substitute parent figure for the child will strengthen and optimize the developing communication patterns for that teacher and child for the school year.

Ruby J. Jones: A Case Study of a Grandmother's Parenting Role

In the fall of 2003, Ruby J. Jones, 75, of Savannah, Georgia, became the primary guardian and parent for her young grandchildren, Eric, age 7, and Mandy, age 4. Ruby's single daughter and only child, Samantha, 36, was severely injured in a car accident in January of that year, and she had to be placed in an assisted living center to receive continuous medical care. Samantha suffered a traumatic brain injury in the accident and was left in a comatose state. Because Samantha had not married, and the father of Eric and Mandy had not been involved in the care and upbringing of the children, Ruby was the only living relative who could assume the parenting role for Eric and Mandy. Samantha's long-term prognosis is not good, and doctors do not foresee her being able to live an independent life or to assume responsibility for Eric and Mandy. Ruby's husband, Howard, passed away in 1997, and Ruby

(Continued)

(Continued)

had been retired from teaching for more than 20 years when she became the children's primary legal guardian and parent.

Ruby's new role has been a major adjustment for her. While relatively healthy and active, Ruby had settled into a quiet life of retirement and was financially comfortable with her teacher's retirement pension and a portion of her husband's pension and Social Security. However, she lived in a small house that was suited to her lifestyle. When Eric and Mandy came to live with her, the house became more crowded, and Ruby had to put many of her items in storage to make room for Eric and Mandy's furniture, toys, and clothes. Ruby loves her grandchildren and stays actively involved in their classrooms. Mandy is in a state-funded preschool program at the same elementary school that Eric attends as a second grader. Ruby doesn't like to drive and frequently takes a taxi to the school for conferences with Eric's and Mandy's teachers or to attend a parent meeting. Mandy's and Eric's teachers have worked to establish good rapport with Ruby and to understand her lifestyle and physical limitations. Both teachers made home visits during September of this year to better understand the home situation. When they learned that she did not have a computer, they were able to locate one through a faith-based foundation in the community. Now Ruby is able to check e-mail messages from the children's teachers and to log on to the Web site that Eric's teacher has established. Ruby's budget is tight but manageable, and she looks forward to meetings with the children's teachers and conversations with other parents at the school. She does worry about the future and how she will be able to meet the needs of the children as they all grow older. But for now, she is committed to being the best parent she can be, and she has no regrets at assuming this major responsibility so late in her life.

Divorce, Separation, and Remarriage

The good news is that there has been a leveling off of divorce rates in the United States, noted in the late 1990s (Goldstein, 1999). The important message for teachers and schools, however, is that divorce and remarriage have become a common phenomenon in our society. Teachers and schools confront daily the issues involving divorce, separation, and remarriage. These trends explain a great deal of the growing complexity of the family. Teachers and school administrators must decide how to interface with custodial and noncustodial parents; how to communicate with parents, stepparents, and other caretakers; and how to scaffold the young child who is going through multiple transitions in his or her family of origin.

Substantial changes have occurred in the marital status and living arrangements of Americans (Saluter, 1989). One of the most noted changes in American families is the increase in the single population, reflected in the delay of marriage and in the dissolution of marriage. More than half of all first marriages result in divorce, and the rate is even higher for subsequent marriages (Darden & Zimmerman, 1992; Walsh, 1992). Divorce rates are associated with such demographics as age at marriage, and teenagers who marry face the highest divorce rate. Schools deal with this phenomenon as they enroll more and more young children who are the product of teenage marriages or teenage pregnancies. The crisis of the absent father is being addressed by child advocacy groups; approximately 25 percent of U.S. children have little or no contact with their fathers (Louv, 1993). Early childhood teachers and caregivers interact daily with children who have little contact with a father figure in their lives.

Divorce may be the best option for some couples, and the emotional reprieve it provides the family may be in the best interests of all, including the children. However, divorce places an inordinate amount of stress on the family financially and emotionally, at least for a transitional period. Children of all stages of development, from preschool through the adolescent years, must somehow negotiate the difficult and emotional terrain of their parents' separation and divorce (Wallerstein & Blakeslee, 1995). Often overcome with their own emotional needs and issues, parents may not have the emotional resources to address their children's anxieties. Children frequently blame themselves for the divorce, unable to understand the complexity of adult relationships. Thus, children find themselves in a maze of home–school–community existence, greatly in need of emotional support from adults. The issues concerning divorce, remarriage, and stepfamilies are discussed more fully in chapter 6.

Economic Uncertainty for the American Family

As the world shrinks, events in one country directly impact the well-being of other countries. Growing world violence and terrorism have made the world feel even more uncertain. The worldwide economy reflects this uncertainty, and the U.S. economy mirrors an up-and-down cycle that impacts American families. Unemployment continues to be a real issue for many families, and today's young children necessarily must feel the effects of and deal with some of that family stress. The workplace and job demands contribute considerable anxiety to American families. Work sites are usually separate from other areas of people's lives, making it more difficult for people to do the shopping, transport the children to and from child care, and visit with extended families and supportive neighbors. Thus, for most American families, fragmentation occurs because of the emphasis on the importance of work and careers but without sufficient support for the general fabric of the family.

Job change and transition have become more commonplace. Gone are the days when mother or father could make a long-term, 20- or 30-year commitment to a place of employment and count on its security until retirement. Transformations in urban economies have limited the kinds of jobs available to high school graduates and dropouts (Edwards & Young, 1992). Although many new occupations have emerged in the areas of service and technology, U.S. workers of all educational and income levels face much less job security. Corporations are downsizing, outsourcing work to foreign countries, moving to managed health care programs, and looking for comprehensive ways to cut costs. Workers who have been loyal to the same employer for many years are finding themselves unemployed and needing to retool. Even higher education, a traditional bastion for job security, is scrutinizing tenure and questioning the long-term employment commitment to its highly educated workforce. Children whose parents are experiencing workplace stress are also anxious and uncertain. "If Daddy's job ends, what will that mean?" "If Mommy's company relocates to Atlanta, will I have to move and give up all my friends?" These are typical concerns and anxieties of children today, and teachers recognize and deal with these issues daily.

In addition to increasing job insecurity, American parents work in settings that frequently are not family-friendly. Some successful efforts have been made to identify and publicly reward those corporations that provide benefits and support mechanisms for employees and their families. Such benefits as child care on-site or through vouchers, parental leave for childbirth and neonatal care, sick leave for parents with children who are ill, and tax-deferred benefits related to parent and child care needs all contribute to a sense of well-being for American parents who work. Unfortunately, changes in this progressive direction are slow and frustrating.

Child Poverty and Homelessness

One of the striking ironies in the United States is the rate of child poverty. One of every four children in the United States lives in a family whose income is below—often far below—the poverty level, and that **child poverty rate** doubles among Blacks and Latinos (CDF 2005). Although poverty rates seem to rise and fall for the overall American population, children remain the most impoverished age group, and obstacles to their well-being continue to mount. Child poverty brings with it a host of other related family issues such as lack of quality child-care options, inadequate health care and insurance, immunization needs, poor nutrition, inadequate housing, HIV/AIDS, substance abuse, and chronic violence (Edwards & Young, 1992). One of the major struggles for low-income parents is the challenge of attaining quality child care. According to the CDF (2005), full-day child care can easily cost between $4,000 and $10,000 per year—at least as much as college tuition at a public university. Yet one quarter of America's families with young children earn less than $25,000 a year, and a family with both parents working full-time at the minimum wage earns only $21,400 a year (Shulman, 2000).

Child poverty reflects family poverty and other complicated family issues such as drug use. The crack epidemic is touching every corner of low-income African American communities (Drug Enforcement Agency [DEA], 1996; Edwards & Young, 1992), as well as rural and suburban areas. The effects of crack are reflected in the school-age population in the United States, and American teachers in early childhood settings must deal not only with the care and education of these children but also with the needs of parents.

In addition to crack and cocaine, the use of heroin has escalated significantly during the past decade. The availability of higher purity heroin has meant that users now can snort or smoke the narcotic. Evidence suggests that heroin snorting is widespread or increasing in areas where high-purity heroin is available, generally in the northeastern United States (DEA, 1996).

Violence, the American Family, and the Schools

Contemporary American teachers and parents are true partners in meeting the needs of the younger child. One of the issues that requires close collaboration is violence. Violence comes in several noted forms: school violence, community violence, and world violence. Without becoming paralyzed by the current statistics on violence, teachers and schools must move forward to create learning environments that recognize the need for caution but that also encourage the child to feel secure and creative.

How serious is violence in the United States? Consider these statistics: Every day, 10 American children are murdered, 16 die from gunshot wounds, 316 are arrested for crimes of violence, and 8,042 are reported abused or neglected (CDF, 1997). In 1996, more than 3 million children were reported as victims of child abuse and neglect to child protective agencies in the United States (National Committee to Prevent Child Abuse, 1998). The effects of violence on young children are documented in the literature. Even before a child is born, violence can have a profound effect on the child's life. Shaken baby syndrome, the shaking of an infant or child by the arms, legs, or shoulders, can be devastating and result in irreversible brain damage, blindness, cerebral palsy, hearing loss, spinal cord injury, seizures, learning disabilities, and even death (Poussaint & Linn, 1997).

Violent children usually come from violent homes, where parents model violence as a means of resolving conflict and handling stress. Some of the psychological outcomes of early violence include lack of bonding and feelings of emotional insecurity and mistrust. "Children who grow up in violent communities are at risk for pathological development because being in a constant state of apprehension makes it difficult for them to establish trust, autonomy, and social competence" (Wallach, 1993, p. 4).

Research also shows that chronic exposure to violence adversely affects a child's ability to learn (Prothrow-Stith & Quaday, 1995; Shores, 1992). Teachers in school settings for young children frequently speak of their concern for the children they teach and the emerging patterns of violence and transitions that children experience within the home and community. According to the CDF (1996), more than 50,000 children have been killed in the United States since 1979 by guns in the home, school, and neighborhood. For many inner-city children, violence has become a way of life. A study of more than 1,000 children in Chicago found that 74 percent of them had witnessed a murder, shooting, stabbing, or robbery. Violence is witnessed through child abuse, domestic abuse, gangs, drug dealers, drive-by shootings, and other criminal activity in the neighborhoods (Wallach, 1993).

Concern about the rising rates of violence resulted in the establishing of a special panel by the NAEYC to provide recommendations on how to respond to the manifestations of violence in the lives of children and to develop position statements that identify appropriate guidelines (Slaby, Roedell, Arezzo, & Hendrix, 1995). Researchers and practitioners alike are acknowledging a growing awareness of the repeated witnessing by young children of violent assaults against others. These events include preschoolers observing shootings firsthand (Dubrow & Garbarino, 1989) and witnessing stabbings in their immediate neighborhoods (Bell & Jenkins, 1993). In addition, parents often underestimate the amount of violence their children are experiencing, as well as the amount of potentially damaging emotional distress that can result (Richters & Martinez, 1993). Research indicates that one in four secondary students in the United States believes that his or her school's efforts to address violence are not adequate (Everett & Price, 1995; Slaby et al., 1995).

Effects of Violence on the Child and Family.

The immediate and long-term effects of violence on the development of the child are still being determined. For infants and toddlers, exposure to violence threatens the development of trust—trust in the care-giving environment and eventually in the children themselves (Wallach, 1993). When families live in a constant state of anxiety or fear, it is difficult for them to provide a safe, consistent, and trusting environment in which their young children can grow and develop. Infants and toddlers, who are in the preoperational stage of cognitive development, must explore their environment and learn about relationships between objects and people to grow cognitively and emotionally. When parents cannot allow their children to explore the immediate and surrounding environments, opportunities for this development are hampered.

Preschoolers, who are also in the preoperational stage of cognitive development, need safe spaces and environments in which to explore. If preschoolers live in dangerous neighborhoods where home and child-care environments and economic resources are very limited, then their cognitive and emotional growth is stymied. Drive-by shootings, gang violence, and other random criminal acts have created unsafe neighborhoods in both low- and middle-income areas. Children today are more likely to live a passive, less physically active existence simply because parents are more fearful of the immediate neighborhood than in the past; they don't let their children stray very far from home and may not even let the children play outdoors at all.

Domestic abuse is another form of violence that negatively affects young children. This type of abuse can take several forms but usually involves some kind of child abuse (emotional, verbal, physical, or sexual) or abuse between parents. When children are subjected to both **domestic violence** and neighborhood violence, the overall negative effects are much greater (Wallach, 1993). When children must defend themselves both within the home and within the immediate neighborhood, basic developmental tasks such as developing a sense of trust and feelings of self-worth are affected. Preoperational children are especially vulnerable to blaming themselves for the pain they see and experience in their families. In turn, children who have feelings of low self-esteem are not as confident in their own abilities at school. Teachers see these children in the classroom on a daily basis, and they are complex to understand and teach. Teachers

Contemporary schools can be a hub of activities for children and families.

FIGURE 1.1   Teacher Strategies to Confront the Effects of Violence

- Give children consistent love and attention—every child needs a strong, loving relationship with a caring adult to feel safe and secure and to develop a sense of trust.

- Ensure that children are supervised and guided—they learn important social skills by interacting with others in well-supervised activities. Unsupervised children often have behavioral problems that can lead to violence.

- Model appropriate behaviors—children learn by example. Discuss problems with them, and help them to learn nonviolent solutions to conflict and problems.

- Be consistent with rules and discipline—children need structure for their behavior, including clearly stated, logical consequences for not following the rules.

- Try to keep children from seeing too much violence in the media—limit television viewing time and talk with children about the violence they see in movies, on TV, and in video games. Help them to understand how painful violence is in real life and discuss its serious consequences.

- Offer parenting classes that deal with effective parenting and child development.

- Send home tip sheets or include tips in family newsletters that deal with topics related to violence prevention, stress prevention, and communication.

- Teach children at an early age that feelings are normal—even feelings of anger or hurt—but that violence is not an acceptable method for expressing anger, frustration, and other negative feelings.

- Be a vigilant, positive role model. (Massey, 1998)

must understand the ramifications of violence in the lives of young children if they are to intervene effectively on the children's behalf in the classroom. See Figure 1.1 for teacher strategies to confront the effects of violence. The trauma of violence leaves a long-lasting effect on children, and the major effect during childhood is usually regression (Wallach, 1993).

Early childhood teachers also play a crucial role in helping to identify children who may be the target of such violence as child abuse or neglect. By documenting their observations, early childhood teachers can play a pivotal role in confronting the issue of violence in the personal lives of the children they teach. Through modeling of appropriate child management and discipline methods, teachers demonstrate to parents more effective ways of communicating with and managing their children. Finally, violence is of such concern to most parents today that teachers will find a ready audience for parent education meetings and may have a relatively easy time finding resource people in the community and targeting violence as a major issue or theme in their parent education programs. Key points for teachers to remember are listed in Figure 1.2.

> ## FIGURE 1.2   Key Points for Teachers to Remember About Violence Prevention
>
> - Model disciplinary methods to children that discourage violence.
> - Analyze your own feelings, attitudes, and experiences about violence.
> - Assist children in identifying kinds of violence and sources of violence in their lives.
> - Be alert to signs of children's trauma related to violence.
> - Be familiar with and follow appropriate guidelines for reporting suspected abuse and neglect to authorities.
> - Support families in their efforts to cope with fears and concerns about violence in their neighborhoods.
>
> *Note.* From *Early Violence Prevention: Tools for Teachers of Young Children* (p. 37), by R. G. Slaby, W. C. Roedell, D. Arezzo, and K. Hendrix, 1995, Washington, DC: National Association for the Education of Young Children.

APPLYING BRONFENBRENNER'S ECOLOGICAL MODEL

This chapter explains the close and interdependent relationships among children, parents, and schools. Bronfenbrenner's ecosystem explanation of the intersecting forces in a child's life helps us to understand this interdependence. In short, the child who functions within the school- or community-based educational setting is a product of his or her immediate environment. As **Bronfenbrenner's** (1979) **ecological model** suggests, no one is an island. Issues that affect parents also affect children; the parent who is stressed has children who are also stressed. Teachers, administrators, counselors, and other professionals in school, child-care, and community settings must be able to observe, record, and evaluate child behavior that reflects stress or developmental concerns or both. As classrooms become more diverse in terms of ethnicity, socioeconomic levels, and developmental ranges, the professional must be prepared and trained to deal with the subsequent complexity of the classroom.

American families reflect fast-paced, hectic, fragmented lifestyles that are focused on economic and emotional survival. These variables seem to apply to all children regardless of socioeconomic level. Emotional stressors may not originate in financial problems for many middle- and upper-income families, but these families are just as vulnerable to the emotional effects of divorce, drug use, unemployment, neighborhood violence, and family-related issues. Perhaps the best way to describe the American family in the early 21st century is weary yet resilient. With

Partnerships among teachers, parents, and children are encouraged by NAEYC.

violence increasing in all neighborhoods, the American family seems to seek a return to basic feelings and needs for survival. This very basic need and instinct must be recognized, acknowledged, and addressed by the school- and community-based professional.

RESILIENT CHILDREN AND FAMILIES

Grandparents, aunts, and uncles all form the village of people who help raise a child.

Teachers can find hope in their interactions with today's children and families. With all the complexity in the lives of American families, children and parents are amazingly resilient. Case studies document children who have survived very difficult and challenging odds. Children who grow up in violence-infested neighborhoods; who are exposed at early ages to drug abuse; who experience the emotional turmoil of families in transition because of divorce, remarriage, mobility, and other reasons; and who otherwise have had to overcome seemingly insurmountable odds can, in fact, develop into productive, hopeful young adults. Research has been focused on the characteristics of the resilient child, who somehow manages to overcome difficult odds to achieve academic and life success.

This resilience of children and families is impressive. Each family has its own goals and paints its own portrait as it interfaces with society and the schools. Teachers who view families from the strength and resilience perspective are most likely to succeed in their interactions with children and parents. This individuality is what each family brings to the parent involvement component of any early childhood setting (Edwards & Young, 1992). It is important for teachers to keep these family variations in mind as they assess, plan, implement, and evaluate parent and family involvement initiatives and programs. "Until schools acknowledge the range in dispositions, backgrounds, experiences, and strengths among families, efforts to establish sound home/school communication and partnerships will falter" (Edwards & Young, 1992, p. 86).

THE STATUS OF CHILDREN IN THE UNITED STATES

The CDF is one of the most visible advocates for the rights and well-being of children in the United States. Its yearbook, *The State of America's Children* (1997), depicts America's young and school-age children as being in peril. Since the 1990s, children have experienced the highest rate of poverty of any segment of the U.S. population. Along with the issue of poverty, violence in the lives of young children has increased dramatically, creating concern for the long-term well-being of America's young children. The policy agenda for the CDF focuses on issues (listed in Figure 1.3) that reflect the daily lives and needs of children.

FIGURE 1.3	Moments in America for Children

- Every 9 seconds — a child drops out of school.
- Every 10 seconds — a child is reported abused or neglected.
- Every 14 seconds — a child is arrested.
- Every 25 seconds — a baby is born to an unmarried mother.
- Every 32 seconds — a baby is born into poverty.
- Every 34 seconds — a baby is born to a mother who did not graduate from high school.
- Every 1 minute — a baby is born to a teenage mother.
- Every 2 minutes — a baby is born at low birth weight.
- Every 3 minutes — a baby is born to a mother who received late or no prenatal care.
- Every 4 minutes — a child is arrested for an alcohol-related offense.
- Every 10 minutes — a baby is born at very low birth weight.
- Every 15 minutes — a baby dies.
- Every 2 hours — a child is killed by a firearm.
- Every 4 hours — a child commits suicide.
- Every 7 hours — a child dies from abuse or neglect.

Note. Adapted from *The State of America's Children,* by CDF, 1996, Washington, DC: Children's Defense Fund.

Legislative Efforts on Behalf of Families

Among the most pressing issues for children in America today are those related to domestic, community, and school violence; access to quality child care and early education; economic support for low-income families; and safe communities in which to live. To address these issues, pending legislation includes bills for expanded and improving Head Start programming, increased child-care assistance, access to comprehensive health insurance coverage at birth, reduced poverty, and provision of safe after-school care for nearly half of all poor 6- to 12-year-olds throughout the United States for the next 5 years (CDF, 2005). Legislation dealing with school and youth violence, set within the context of larger societal violence, is also growing. As these new initiatives are legislated, schools, child-care centers, and community-based programs will become the major avenues for program implementation. For example, expanded Head Start means the creation of new collaboration between Head Start and state-funded preschool programs, usually based in schools, child-care centers, or community-based sites.

With the national effort to balance the budget a high priority, the needs of children over the next 10 years are of concern to advocates for child well-being. In the rush to welfare reform, which certainly can be understood and justified from an economic standpoint, the immediate needs of children may not be adequately assessed and anticipated. With welfare time limits being implemented in many states, women with young children are now pursuing career options, vocational training, or other self-support avenues but without sufficient support for their children's child care or after-school care needs.

The long-term benefits of welfare reform may be worthwhile, but the short-term outcomes for young children whose welfare-dependent parents are riding the turbulent waters of reform and change at both the state and federal levels may make the children the ultimate victims. When financial support systems are withdrawn, reduced, or dramatically altered within a short period of time, teachers, administrators, and other professionals committed to the education and care of children must be aware of these changes and the subsequent behavioral and emotional changes in the children in their classrooms and care centers.

Recent Data on Child Care and Early Education

Following is a description of contemporary early childhood program facts and child-care needs.

- About 12 million children of working parents—including 6 million infants and toddlers—are cared for each month by someone other than a parent (CDF, 2005).
- The challenge of finding decent and affordable child care is a major issue for most working parents.
- The supply of child care is most inadequate in low-income neighborhoods, which tend to lack the necessary economic base to support good child-care programs.
- The average cost of serving one child in a child-care center is $4,940 per year and can easily range up to $10,000 per year (CDF, 2005).
- Only 1 of 7 child-care centers and 1 of 10 family child-care homes are of high enough quality to enhance children's development.
- In 1995, Head Start served 752,000 children—about 36 percent of those eligible.
- Some employers are designing child-care programs to fit the company's work schedules; for example, Toyota Motor Manufacturing in Georgetown, Kentucky.
- Some employers are pooling resources to conduct joint child-care projects, as a consortium of employers in Phoenix and a group of employers in the hotel industry in Atlanta did. (CDF, 1996)

The status of America's children continues to be a concern for early childhood teachers, advocates, and policy makers, and the voices of schoolteachers and child-care providers and administrators will continue to need to be heard (Stegelin, 1992). Professionals who work with children on a daily basis are in the best position to observe, assess, and document the needs of these children. As welfare reform unfolds, economic characteristics will change as reflected in the changing employment arena and escalating rates of divorce and remarriage. As the world continues to move to a multicultural perspective, the young children in America will continue to need support from parents, teachers, and the community.

THE PARENT–SCHOOL–STUDENT CONNECTION: A CRITICAL LINKAGE

Why *should we continue to maximize the effort to communicate, in some way, with every parent in the classroom?* Teachers in early childhood classrooms are given so much responsibility that parent communication and involvement seem overwhelming at times. In addition, the typical American family leads such a complex lifestyle that time and access to communication avenues have become increasingly limited. Unlike in the 1950s and 1960s, when "Father," the kind and gentle Jim Anderson on *Father Knows Best*, was always available to give sound advice and good guidance to his children, today's families operate almost in a tangential way, touching base here and there. These communication patterns are made even more complex with the merging of families into blended families, who frequently function with looser boundaries than do traditional, nuclear families. Not unlike the families popularized back then, families today hold the same common desire to raise healthy and happy children in a safe and comfortable environment. A variety of factors affect families as they work to reach this goal. One is the economic struggle that many families experience as mothers and fathers leave the home each day to go to one or more jobs.

Goals of Contemporary Parents and Schools

In a 1996 Washington, DC, Family Re-Union V Conference, parent panelists indicated a desire (a) to have more time with their children; (b) to be able to provide their children a decent standard of living without sacrificing quality parenting; (c) to know that their children were in nurturing, safe, and healthy environments while the parents were at work or training; and (d) to have employers who understand, value, and respond appropriately to family issues (Daniel, 1996, p. 2). As we study how families use existing resources to meet the economic, educational, and caring needs of individuals within the family, including both the adults and the children, it is important to remember that each individual within the family, regardless of age, is engaged in ongoing development in relation to his or her sociocultural world (Erikson, 1950).

Ecosystems, the School, and the Family

Several constructs can help today's early childhood education teacher gain insight into the complexity of child and family life. Lev Vygotsky's (1962, 1978) *sociocultural theory of child development* and Bronfenbrenner's (1979) *ecological systems theory* continue to serve as an appropriate model to justify and support the home–school connection. The interrelationship of the developmental process and the environment can be seen clearly in the *ecosystem model.* In this approach, Bronfenbrenner sees each person's development as being embedded in a series of environmental systems that are all interrelated.

The *microsystem* consists of those individuals and events closest in one's life; the primary example is the nuclear family, with each person influencing and being influenced by the other. Other microsystems are the child-care setting, the school, the church, and the home of an extended family member. Thus, the school and the child-care setting

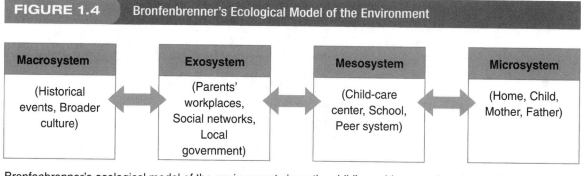

FIGURE 1.4	Bronfenbrenner's Ecological Model of the Environment

Macrosystem	Exosystem	Mesosystem	Microsystem
(Historical events, Broader culture)	(Parents' workplaces, Social networks, Local government)	(Child-care center, School, Peer system)	(Home, Child, Mother, Father)

Bronfenbrenner's ecological model of the environment views the child's world as a series of nested structures. The *microsystem* refers to relationships between the child and the immediate environment, the *mesosystem* to connections among the child's immediate settings, the *exosystem* to settings that affect but do not contain the child, and the *macrosystem* to the broader cultural context in which development takes place.

are immediate resources for the family and fall within the most intimate of connections for families.

Relationships that develop and exist between and among these microsystems are labeled *mesosystems*. Each individual's environment also includes *exosystems*, examples of which are school boards, governmental agencies, the workplace, and other community agencies and institutions. The microsystem, mesosystem, and exosystem all exist within the context of the larger culture, known as the *macrosystem* (see Figure 1.4).

Parents, Schools, and Communities: A Case for Parent Involvement

The family serves as the "cradle" in caring for and nurturing children. The family serves to wrap the child in the kind of security from which the child emerges comfortably to interact with peers and adults in a variety of settings and to take a place in the world. The family knows and loves the child. The title of Hillary Rodham Clinton's (1996) much-debated book borrowed the African proverb "It takes a village to raise a child." Mothers and fathers, brothers and sisters, grandparents, stepparents, foster parents, early childhood teachers, child-care providers, school administrators, neighbors, and other individuals within the community are all a part of this village. As these lives intertwine, each person contributes something of his or her own culture to the growing child. As stated by Lyon (1995),

> Culture rules how we position our bodies, how we touch each other, what we regard as mannerly, how we look at the world, how we think, what we see as art, how we sense time and perceive space, what we think is important, and how we set immediate and lifelong goals. (p. 21)

This textbook focuses on the role that teachers and caregivers can play in empowering families in the care and education of their children; the strategies presented in this chapter (and elaborated on throughout the book) are designed to help teachers enhance their communication and collaboration with families. This process, however, as noted by Bronfenbrenner in his discussion of the mesosystem, is an interaction between and among schools, families, and the community, with all parties responsible for the success of the interaction.

Collaborative Role of the School

What is the appropriate role of the school in the lives of children and families? How involved should the school and the child-care or classroom teacher become in the personal lives of the children whom they teach and care for? How far into the home and the neighborhood should the school's responsibility extend? What forms should these partnerships take?

Because of the complexity of families today, school professionals need to think and behave in terms of interactions with parents and families (Edwards & Young, 1992). Boundaries that separate home, school, and neighborhoods are blurring and thus provide a rich opportunity for teachers to connect with parents and families in new and creative ways. Parents still seek a safe place to go to talk about their children, and families still search for places where they can interact with other families. Schools and teachers must dance on the fine line between providing plenty of support for children and families and intrusion. Schools must do more than just encourage parent involvement that is isolated from the larger social and educational context of the classroom. In short, teachers have become a sort of service broker for children and their families (Edwards & Young, 1992).

Families, schools, and communities have a common goal: to nurture and guide children to adulthood. "Although the process of cultural transmission takes place as the child interacts with the total social environment, in contemporary American society we regard families and schools as being primarily responsible for seeing that preparation for adulthood takes place" (Phillips, 1994, p. 137). Teachers and caregivers, in their actions and in their words, certainly impart values and ideas about how people should treat each other. They set models for children to follow in terms of the importance of education and the value of the family and impart ideas about the children's self-worth. Such enculturation by schools is called "education" (Phillips, 1994, p. 138).

Working with parents has been a critical component of early childhood education (Powell, 1991). In the mid-1960s, the United States addressed the crucial issues of building partnerships with families to meet the needs of their children. As part of a concerted effort to provide equal opportunities for citizens (Economic Opportunity Act of 1964), Project Head Start was conceived. The focus of this program, piloted as a summer project in 1965, was to intervene in the lives of young children in the areas of health and nutritional services, social services, and education. The creators of this program and of subsequent early childhood intervention programs since the 1960s believed that providing these services to economically deprived children and families could prevent young children from entering first grade at a disadvantage, compared with their more affluent peers, and remaining at that disadvantage throughout the school experience. They also recognized that a child is an integral part of a family and that "schooling" does not take place simply within the school. Therefore, the focus became empowering families by involving parents in decision making, in the classroom, in parent-oriented activities, and in home activities with their children (U.S. Department of Health and Human Services [DHHS], 1990, p. 4).

Throughout the years, various organizations representing professionals in the field have continued in this support of the inclusion of families in the care and education of young children by schools. Partnerships are emphasized by the NAEYC in the document *Developmentally Appropriate Practice in Early Childhood Programs Serving Children From Birth Through Age Eight* (Bredekamp, 1987). This work represents the early childhood profession's consensus of developmentally appropriate practice and serves as a guide for the standards used in accrediting early childhood programs. The standards include, but are not limited to, the following:

- Informing parents of the program's philosophy
- Informing parents of operating policies
- Providing an orientation for new children and families
- Communicating about child-rearing practices with parents
- Making parents welcome visitors in the classroom at all times
- Encouraging family-member involvement in the program in various ways, such as by implementing a system to communicate daily happenings to parents; by reporting changes in the child's physical or emotional state to parents; and by conducting conferences to discuss children's needs, progress, and accomplishments
- Informing parents of activities through notes, telephone calls, bulletin boards, newsletters, and so forth

The National Association of State Boards of Education (NASBE) also reported on the critical role of parent involvement and the principle that only through sincere respect for the parents' role can teachers begin to see parents as a source of support for their work. The NASBE report *Right From the Start* (1988, p. 19) indicates that programs serving children in preschool through Grade 3 should do the following:

- Promote an environment in which parents are valued as the primary influences in their children's lives and are essential partners in the education of their children.
- Recognize that the self-esteem of parents is integral to the development of their child and should be enhanced by the parents' positive interaction with the school.
- Include parents in decision making about their own child and on the overall early childhood program.
- Ensure opportunities and access for parents to observe and volunteer in the classroom.
- Promote exchange of information and ideas between parents and teacher that will benefit the child.
- Provide a gradual and supportive transition process from home to school for those young children entering school for the first time.

Collaborative Role of Families

Although family members typically view themselves as deeply involved in the day-to-day care and nurturing of their young child, they are less comfortable with the role of teacher of the young child. In fact, the family serves as the child's first and most important educator. In addition to the physical and emotional care and nurturing the family provides for the young child, the adults within the family model their own commitment to education and learning and the value they place on themselves and on other individuals.

Robert Glaser (1985), in the foreword of *Becoming a Nation of Readers: The Report of the Commission on Reading*, states: "The parent and the home environment teach the child his or her first lessons and they are the first teachers of writing, too" (p. vi). According to Powell (1989), it is the parent's responsibility to determine what is in the best interests of the child. Powell outlines three major premises about families and society that constitute the foundation of most arguments for families and early childhood programs to establish and maintain partnerships: (a) doctrine of parents' rights, (b) family influences on the child, and (c) democratic processes. The *doctrine of parents' rights* reflects the American belief that parents have the right and responsibility to determine what is in the best interests of their child. These premises are also reflected in the earlier work of Head Start policies.

In its first manual of policies and instructions, issued in 1967, four areas of parent participation were outlined for the Head Start program. These areas have been used for the past 30 years and are still being used (DHHS, 1990, p. 4):

1. Parents as decision makers
2. Parents as paid staff, volunteers, or observers in the classroom
3. Parents involved in activities that they themselves have helped develop
4. Parents working at home with their own children in cooperation with Head Start staff to support the child's Head Start experiences

The premises described by Powell are also reflected in current legislation. For example, P.L. 99-457, the Education of the Handicapped Act Amendments of 1986, reinforces this premise by including parent involvement as a significant component of the education process.

Collaborative Role of Communities

As we seek connections between theory and practice, we can look to other countries and communities for helpful models. The concept of community–school–home connection is exemplified through several theories, including Lev Vygotsky's theory that emphasizes the importance of culture and language in child development. Communities have always served a crucial role in the support of child and family development in the United States. Much research has been conducted on the role of the community in the lessening of stressors and the provision of support services for children, parents, and families. Research on the Head Start program as it has evolved over 40 years documents the essential role of the parent in the early childhood classroom. Early intervention in the United States has always respected the parent and the home as the primary teacher, and recent legislative iniatives in early childhood special education continue to mandate and support the role of the parent in the decision making related to services for children with special needs. However, as the United States has grown and evolved from an agricultural society to a densely populated, industrial culture, the feeling among many families is that the nurturing, supportive, and connecting role of the community has somehow been diminished. Much can be learned about the role of the immediate community in the lives of developing young children from models used in other countries.

One of the most interesting contemporary models of community involvement in early childhood programs is found in the schools of Reggio Emilia, a town of 130,000 in northern Italy. In this community, children engage in ongoing project work that involves the collaborative efforts of both adults and children. For example, Edwards, Gandini, and Forman (1993), in their noted book on Reggio Emilia, *The Hundred Languages of Children*, describe successful projects undertaken and completed jointly by young children and their adult teachers, parents, and other community members. One such project, "An Amusement Park for Birds," focused on children working with adults to decide what type of park to build for birds. The project flowed over a period of months as the children's observations and investigations of the lives of birds were facilitated and documented by adults. The "finale" of the project was a wonderful park for birds, complete with feeders and waterwheels and even a sunbathing beach (Forman et al., 1993). Adults from the community contributed both time and materials to this effort.

Another project, wonderfully documented in the traveling Reggio Emilia exhibit, brings a farm family into the school prior to the annual harvest of grapes. The children learn from the farmer what will happen when they visit the farm to assist with the harvest. The children and teachers travel to the farm, where they pick, sort, wash, and mash grapes. These new "farmers" return to the school, where the children and the adults celebrate the harvest with food and grape juice.

The Reggio Emilia approach has made a profound impact on American early childhood programs, in part because of its tremendous valuing and inclusion of the community in the early childhood learning environment. Reggio Emilia has expanded on the Italian principle of community involvement—*gestione sociale*—in early child care and education by engaging parents and other adults in the community in the actual educational "happenings" of the school. Adults attend evening meetings that are open to discussions and that are designed to involve the community in the work of the school. One such experience focuses on "meetings around a theme," wherein parents, teachers, and all others connected with the school are invited to discuss and debate a topic, such as the role of the father or children's fears (Edwards et al., 1993, p. 98).

Perhaps the **Reggio Emilia programs** for early childhood have had such appeal to Americans because they cause Americans to reflect on their own past. Rural, agrarian America resembled Reggio Emilia because of its close connection between the immediate community and the school. Parents knew and cared about other children and served as important role models for them. There was a sense of "shared parenting" and "shared responsibility" not only for one's own child but for the neighbors' children as well. Such is the case in Reggio Emilia: The community embraces warmly the young children and their families, seemingly to invest all the more in the rich culture of northern Italy and to preserve its sense of connectedness over the decades. The authors were reared in rural settings (one author in Kansas, one in Kentucky, and one in Pennsylvania), and we believe that the connection of the school or child-care center to family and community, as reflected in Reggio Emilia, is a vital and essential component that is either missing or greatly diminished in the lives of contemporary young children.

These examples depict the inclusion of families and community members in more than just the fund-raising and carpooling events that sometimes characterize American communities. They exemplify the sense of commitment that adults can demonstrate when the school values their expertise and assistance in the education of their children. According to Loris Malaguzzi, founder of the Reggio Emilia early childhood programs, "We must forge strong alliances with the families of our children" (Phillips, 1994, p. 61). Figure 1.5 lists effective strategies for parent involvement in the classroom.

FIGURE 1.5	Teacher Strategies to Encourage Parent Involvement

1. Do a short needs assessment at the beginning of the school year; include information such as parents' telephone number, e-mail address, other contact information, work place, hours of availability, special interests and skills, and parenting concerns and needs.

2. Invite parents to come for individual conferences to explore specific ways to involve them in your classroom. Be open, flexible, and creative. Consider "new" family forms that may include grandparents, stay-at-home dads, foster parents, and other family forms. Be creative: consider meeting a family at a local restaurant, public library, or other mutually convenient location.

3. Consider making home visits to some or all of the students, especially to those who may have special needs such as health, language/cultural, family distress, and others.

4. Create a parent wall in your classroom and ask for parent volunteers to maintain this space, serve as a liaison between the classroom and other parents, and provide peer leadership for other parents.

5. Assess your classroom at the beginning of the school year and periodically for special issues: cultural and language diversity, special needs, families in distress, common interests among parents.

6. Decide on several forms of communication for this particular group of parents. Take into consideration their income levels, geographic location, access to technology, special talents, and financial considerations.

7. Create a Web site for the classroom and post information for parents and students on a weekly basis. Be sure every parent has access to a computer, including using the public library as a resource for parents who may not have a computer at home.

8. Develop a grid of parent involvement activities for the academic year for your classroom. Invite parents to a pot-luck dinner to discuss and respond to your ideas, and then make revisions based on their feedback.

9. Post the Parent Involvement Plan on the Web site, in your classroom, and in a newsletter that you send home with children on a regular basis.

10. Make important information available to parents in several forms: newsletter, e-mail, Web site, posted in the classroom, and shared with the Parent Peer Leader.

11. Assess the success of your Parent Involvement Plan at the end of the year; assess individual events or activities as they occur and do an overall evaluation at the end of the year. Be honest with yourself: what did work and what did not work, and why. Listen to parents' feedback.

BASIC COMMUNICATION STRATEGIES
FOR TEACHERS AND PARENTS

Over time and through the growing impact of technology, methods of communicating with parents have both increased and improved. Today's avenues for connecting with parents seem sophisticated when compared to those of only a decade ago. Parents, teachers, and caregivers can employ numerous strategies to ensure that communication between home and school remains strong and healthy. These strategies can be classified into two main or basic categories: (a) **one-way strategies** and (b) **two-way strategies**.

One-way strategies are those strategies that originate with the teacher and school setting and are targeted to the parent population. They go from the teacher to the parent or home, with no response required or expected. They are highly informative but are not interactive. *Two-way strategies*, by contrast, allow the parent to engage in verbal and written exchange with the teacher and school setting. Each method serves an important purpose. With e-mail, distance learning, and interactive forms of technology, two-way strategies have improved. Software available to teachers has enhanced the formatting of newsletters and other one-way means of communicating with parents, as well. Thus, both one- and two-way means of communicating with parents are much improved and more diverse. Today's teacher, however, must stay informed and educated on the latest forms of technology to keep up with the growing communication options and the expectations of parents.

Chapter 9 elaborates on these avenues of communication and provides suggestions for their effective use. In selecting and implementing communication strategies, school professionals must be sensitive to parents' work schedules, families with single parents, families who may be homeless, transportation constraints, the need for child care, language barriers, families caring for intergenerational members, and other sensitive issues. They must also listen to the families as they share their strengths and concerns. This can be done formally and informally. Successful home–school communication is based foremost on the unique needs and characteristics of each family involved. The professional who is able to assess informally and formally each family that is represented in his or her classroom will ultimately be successful in communication efforts.

Each individual within a family has his or her own learning style. Just as the professional makes routine judgments about how to interact effectively with individual children in the classroom, the same must be done with respective families. Adults are usually rushed and sensitive to time constraints. If a professional can remember that a parent's schedule may be a confounding factor in successful communication, he or she can work to develop individual family strategies. For example, a family with a newborn will not appreciate telephone calls early in the morning or late at night. The parent in a single-parent household will not appreciate having all parent meetings at night. A family with a child with disabilities or special needs may also have medical issues that complicate their lives. Remembering that individual families have unique profiles will ensure that the professional will experience continuous and successful communication.

As teachers, administrators, caregivers, and other professionals who work with children select and implement strategies for engaging families in work and play with their children at home and at school, it is important to remember that the children are the focus of all communication. If all participants in the communication exchange can remember to stay child focused, then issues will be addressed in an objective, forthright, and efficient way. This means that professionals must gain the trust and respect of their students' parents. Parents will then be comfortable and willing to share necessary information with the professional. Likewise, the professional will be able to share all types of information with the parents because of this mutual trust.

Parent involvement activities should include the range of specific learning styles and talents represented by adults and the general ways that people learn. Most professionals who work with young children are knowledgeable about child development and child learning styles and needs. They need to engage in ongoing efforts to understand adult education and learning styles, and this is the challenge to each professional who desires to establish and maintain a successful parent involvement program. Advocacy ideas for teachers to use with parents to encourage two-way communication are presented in Figure 1.6.

FIGURE 1.6	Advocacy Ideas for Teachers in Developing Communication Strategies with Parents

1. Survey parents to determine accessibility to computers, e-mail systems, and Web-sites. For parents who do not have immediate access to a computer in their homes, arrange for them to open a free account at the local public library.

2. Work with your administrator to establish a computer lab in the school that is accessible to parents, and encourage parents in your classroom to assist with this project.

3. Contact local merchants, service organizations, and church groups about their sponsorship of parents who do not have computers. Actively seek technology sources for parents with low-income, cultural or language limitations, and other lack of resources.

4. Seek parent leadership in your classroom so that peer relationships can develop. Encourage parents to work together to locate resources needed by other parents. For example, one family may have a spare computer at home and be willing to give or donate it to the classroom for use by another family.

5. Identify potential language barriers in your classroom. For example, you may have several Hispanic children in your classroom. Locate a resource person within the school or community to help translate your newsletters into Spanish or another language.

6. Locate community resources and programs for parents who have recently moved to the United States and who are seeking a better understanding of the English language.

7. Encourage parents with limited English Language participate in your classroom in comfortable ways. Having parents in the classroom will help children in your classroom become more accepting of children with different cultural backgrounds.

KEY COMPONENTS OF THIS TEXTBOOK

This textbook serves a distinctive purpose: to provide the prospective early childhood teacher with a useful framework and tool for understanding and working with contemporary American parents and families. Key components of this textbook include the following:

- A description of families and schools in contemporary American society, an overview of the parent–school connection, a description of a mosaic of parent involvement models that have evolved over time, and a description of advocacy strategies for classroom teachers are presented.

- A detailed description and profile of individual families in America as we enter the 21st century. Cross-cultural issues involving families and the community are depicted as American families demonstrate increasing linguistic and ethnic diversity. Children with special needs and their families are also included, as the impact of inclusion grows in today's school settings. Children of divorced and blended families are discussed, as are educational needs that reflect a growing number of young students and their families today. Finally, children who are adopted are discussed, as are alternative and future family forms. The most consistent description of contemporary American families is *change*, and we have strived to depict these changes.

- The important processes of effective communication strategies with parents and families as well as assessing and evaluating parent involvement activitiies and programs are also presented. We believe that Part III of this textbook offers the reader an important perspective on parent–teacher communication and parent involvement that is unique to this textbook. Effective strategies for assessing and evaluating the parent–child dynamic in the school setting are included, as well as the most current avenues for connecting with contemporary and diverse parent populations. Relevant and current sources of information, including Web sites and contemporary sources of research-based information are also included.

Critical Concepts

1. Parents have always been a valued part of early childhood programs in the United States. Historically, we can look to Head Start and the early intervention movement of the 1960s as a beginning point for parent–school–community partnerships.

2. Children live in complex home and community environments that greatly impact their ability to perform in the classroom. Bronfenbrenner's ecosystem model provides a helpful explanation of how these forces interact and affect the child's ability to succeed and reach optimal development.

3. Contemporary American families come in varied forms, and teachers should be flexible and open to these new family forms. Children live in homes impacted by divorce and remarriage, poverty, mobility, grandparents and other relatives, foster care, homelessness, and cultural and language diversity.

4. Family forms are ever changing and are being impacted by other cultural influences,

languages, and societal trends. Teachers must remain open to this constant flux in the definition of the family and seek to design effective parent–school strategies based on the unique profile of their respective classroom.

5. Communicating with parents continues to be a major challenge for teachers. Technology is providing new and innovative ways to communicate with parents at the same time that contemporary American families are confronting complex lifestyle issues that often lessen the time and opportunity to interact with the school and classroom teacher.

6. When developing effective communication strategies, each teacher must assess the profile of the children and families of his or her classroom, taking into consideration such factors as income and education levels of parents; geographic proximity to the school; cultural and language needs; makeup of the family in terms of single-headed, married, divorced, or other form; and parent attitudes and feelings of safety within the school environment.

Summary Statements

✓ Although parent involvement and education have been a traditional part of American education over the years, the needs and complexities of today's families and classrooms have never been greater.

✓ Strategies used in parent–school interactions and program development 10 to 15 years ago are not effective with today's complex family makeup and lifestyles.

✓ Maternal employment is a way of life in the United States; more than 60 percent of mothers are employed and more than 12 million children are in some type of child care. To provide effective parent involvement strategies, schools must be able to recognize child and family needs related to maternal employment.

✓ Divorce, separation, and remarriage occur in more than 50 percent of today's American families, and research reflects that emotional repercussions can be expected for young children through adolescence and even adulthood.

✓ Economic uncertainty contributes to child and family stress and is created through job mobility, outsourcing of work, downsizing of companies, and changing job needs.

✓ Technology and a fast-changing economy have changed the employment options and security for most Americans. Teachers need to be aware of the effects of mobility, job transitions, and income-related stressors on the children in their classrooms.

✓ Ethnic and developmental diversity is projected to increase dramatically in the 21st century, especially with a growing Latino population; parent involvement strategies continue to be shaped by these forces.

✓ The child poverty rate is 25 percent, the highest proportion of poverty in the U.S. population. America's children are the victims of increasing rates of violence, abuse, neglect, teenage pregnancy, AIDS, and poverty, as documented by data from the CDF.

✓ America's families and children are amazingly resilient; teachers should determine the strengths of each child and family and shape programs and interactions around these strengths and assets.

✓ Today's families hold the same desire to raise healthy and happy children in a safe environment as families in the *Leave It to*

Beaver era. But the interrelationships among families, schools, and communities are much more complex now and must be negotiated first.

✓ Violence may be the most changing variable in the lives of young children and their families; violence is redefining the way families, schools, and communities are able to interact with one another.

✓ Bronfenbrenner's ecosystem model provides an accurate portrayal of the interrelationships that exist among the child, family, school, community, and society at large. This model helps the professional see his or her role within the whole spectrum of system dynamics for the young child and the family.

✓ The collaborative role of the school is important because of the positive modeling that can occur within the school setting and by the teachers, administrators, and support personnel in these settings.

✓ The role of the family in educating the child and in serving as the child's first teacher is crucial, and schools must work to encourage and validate that role for the family.

✓ The collaborative role of the community and the many agencies within the community is essential if children and families are to identify and meet the necessary resources for their lives.

✓ The Reggio Emilia early childhood programs of northern Italy are representative of a strong parent involvement model for Americans because of the close and intricate relationships among child, parent, school, and the surrounding community.

✓ Appropriate collaborative strategies for teachers and schools will depend on the individual families in their educational setting. Successful parent involvement strategies depend greatly on the teacher's ability to observe; assess both formally and informally; and then implement and evaluate specific, individualized, and measurable strategies for communication with parents and families.

✓ Parent education and involvement may have been an important part of American education over the years, but contemporary American families seek the traditional goals of security and happiness within much more complex lifestyles. The challenge for today's teachers and schools is to continue to strive for these basic, traditional goals that preserve families while taking into consideration the many forces that affect the child and his or her family.

Research to Practice: Classroom Applications and Activities

1. "It takes a village to raise a child" is an African culture's reflection on how best to bring up a young child. What forces in America today encourage and discourage this concept? List examples and discuss as a class.

2. Violence in American families, schools, and communities is on the increase. Global terrorism and random acts of violence have created a new era for the 21st century. In small groups, discuss (a) incidents of violence that you have witnessed or experienced that have impacted your feelings and attitudes; (b) the impact of contemporary media on children's attitudes toward violence; and (c) what you believe schools of the 21st century will need to do to preserve

the safety and well-being of children, parents, and school personnel.

3. Children's and families' well-being in the United States is closely tied to legislation at both federal and state levels. List five pieces of legislation enacted since 1990 that have affected American families; discuss the impact for each piece of legislation selected.

4. The movie *Terms of Endearment* portrays a family over time. View this movie in class and write an essay that includes (a) a comparison of this plot with the happenings in a typical American family today, (b) a discussion of what has held this family together, and (c) the role a school could play in easing the issues for the children in the movie.

5. Contemporary American families are constantly changing in form and function. Invite a panel of four parents from the community to talk to your class about their individual lifestyles, their hopes and goals for their children, and how they see the role of the teacher and school in meeting those goals. Examples of parents to include are a divorced parent, a single parent, a gay parent, a foster parent, a grandparent or other adult relative, and a parent in a traditional family lifestyle. Develop a list of questions for them to consider before having the panel discussion.

6. Read at least two recent articles on the Reggio Emilia early childhood programs of northern Italy. As a class, compare and contrast this approach with traditional early childhood approaches in the United States; identify those elements of Reggio Emilia that you believe might be most helpful in enhancing programs for children in the United States.

7. Invite a family counselor to class to discuss the following: (a) What are the most common issues that families present today to family counselors? (b) How has the typical family changed during the past 10 years in the United States? (c) What forces seem to be most difficult for the family unit? (d) What strategies for communicating with parents and families have worked best for the therapist?

8. Role-play a meeting between a teacher in a kindergarten classroom and two parents who are currently separated. Identify issues that seem to be most detrimental and difficult for this family and the child. List issues that are creating the greatest impact on the child.

9. Write an essay that contrasts today's American family with the family form of one of your grandparents. Identify such factors as (a) length of marriage, (b) number and spacing of children, (c) schooling and child-care experiences, (d) parenting styles, (e) economic and financial constraints, (f) experiences with the extended family, (g) job and employment experiences, and (h) role of the church and other community agencies and institutions in their daily lives.

Resources for More Information on Child Violence

American Academy of Pediatrics (AAP), & American Psychological Association. (1995). *Raising children to resist violence: What you can do* [Brochure]. Elk Grove Village, IL: AAP. Also available at www.aap.org/family/parents/resist.htm (1998, September 21).

Lorion, R. P., & Saltzman, W. (1993). Children's exposure to community violence: Following a path from concern to research to action. *Psychiatry, 56*(1), 55–65.

National Association for the Education of Young Children. (1993). NAEYC position statement on media violence in children's lives. *Young Children, 45*(5), 18–21.

Page, R. M., Kitchin-Becker, S., Solovan, D., Golec, T. L., & Hebert, D. L. (1992). Interpersonal violence:

A priority issue for health education. *Journal of Health Education, 23*(5), 286–292. EJ 453 766.

Pransky, J. (1991). *Prevention: The critical need.* Springfield, MO: Burrell Foundation & Paradigm Press. (Available from NEHRI Publications, Cabot, VT, phone: 802–563–2730)

Prothrow-Stith, D., & Quaday, S. (1995). *Hidden casualties: The relationship between violence and learning.* Washington, DC: National Health & Education Consortium and National Consortium for African American Children, Inc. ED 39–552.

National Committee to Prevent Child Abuse. (1998, April). *Child abuse and neglect statistics* Available online at www.childabuse.org/facts97.html (1998, September).

Books

Carlsson-Paige, N., & Levin, D. (1990). *Who's calling the shots? How to respond effectively to children's fascination with war play and war toys.* St. Paul, MN: Redleaf.

Heidemann, S., & Hewitt, D. (1992). *Pathways to play: Developing play skills in young children.* St. Paul, MN: Redleaf.

Slaby, R. G., Roedell, W., Arezzo, D., & Hendrix, K. (1995). *Early violence prevention: Tools for teachers of young children.* Washington, DC: National Association for the Education of Young Children (NAEYC).

Curricula and Guides

Cherry, C. (1981). *Think of something quiet:* St. Paul, MN: Redleaf. *Activities for helping children relax.*

Levin, D. (1994). *Teaching young children in violent times.* St. Paul, MN: Redleaf. (Preschool–Grade 3)

Web Site

Center for the Study and Prevention of Violence (www.Colorado.edu/cspv)

CHAPTER 2

A Mosaic of Parent Involvement Across Time

Historical and Current Perspectives

Each child experiences two childhoods—his and that of his parents. Each parent experiences two childhoods—his and that of his child.

CHILDHOOD, *GREAT EXPECTATIONS*, 1991

KEY TERMS

baby boom
CEC
child study movement
chronosystem
Comenius
curriculum enrichment
    model
decision makers
direct and active teachers
exosystems
far environment
Froebel

Goals 2000
Hall
human-built environment
Lanham Act
Locke
macrosystem
mesosystem
microsystem
miniature adults
National Association for
    the Education of Young
    Children (NAEYC)

natural physical–biological
    environment
near environment
No Child Left Behind Act
    of 2001
parent cooperative
paid employees
Pestalozzi
Piaget
P.L. 99-457
protective model
Reformation

Renaissance
Rousseau
school-to-home transition
    model
SECA
sociocultural environment
Spock
volunteers
Vygotsky
Watson
WPA

GUIDING QUESTIONS

1. How did the increasing knowledge about significance of learning, health care, and appropriate practices for young children impact both children's near and far environments?
2. What are some major shifts in families' views of children before the 16th century and after?
3. What were some of the major influences on the views of children in families and society in the 16th to 18th centuries?
4. What was one of the major documents available in the mid-1800s to guide families in their parenting roles?
5. Parents and groups showed interest in more humane child rearing through what types of activities?
6. What major theorists influenced childhood care and education from the 1950s into the year 2000, and how?
7. Why did the NAEYC publish the book *Developmentally Appropriate Practices*?
8. What were some of the Goals 2000 that President George Bush spearheaded and supported into law in 1991?
9. What were some of the goals for the No Child Left Behind legislation that President George W. Bush spearheaded?
10. What are some models for school and home partnerships?

he childhoods that we experience, our own and that of our children, are interrelated. We carry the experiences that we had as children in our homes, at school, and across our communities to the parenting of our own children. To this foundation, we add present-day information about parenting topics, including child-care options, nutrition, discipline, health care, developmental norms, and safety. The history of our childhoods, our strengths and limitations as humans, our experiences, and present-day knowledge about children are all parts of living day to day with our children and other adults in an ever-changing world.

In this chapter, we explore the roles of parents and families in the lives of children across time, events, and places. As you "travel" through the pages of this chapter, common themes will be revealed:

Theme 1. The quality of children's overall growth and development is affected by the nature of their interactions with people, places, and events, in both near and far environments. Urie Bronfenbrenner (1979) called the near and far aspects of our environment the microsystem, mesosystem, exosystem, and chronosystem.

Theme 2. Historical changes in our "worlds" have altered the interactions between children and their family members at different points in time through the history of our world. Political, scientific, and historical events have shaped both the role of parents/families and our view of childhood.

Theme 3. Across time, philosophers and theorists, searching for knowledge about children, prepared a foundation for those working with children and families today. Our teaching and caregiving practices are based on the work of these individuals. In this chapter, you will find information about Rousseau, Locke, Comenius, Pestalozzi, Froebel, Piaget, Vygotsky, and Skinner.

Theme 4. The ways in which parents and families discipline their children reflect cultural, societal, and religious influences. For many families, there has been a shift from "spare the rod and spoil the child" to more humanistic forms of guiding and disciplining children.

Theme 5. Across the 18th, 19th, 20th, and now into the 21st century, the period of early childhood (birth to age 8) became recognized as a critical time in the life of the individual. In the beginning, the focus was on how to help the mother in her role as caregiver and educator of her children. Later, preschools and kindergartens were opened to assist families in educating their children. Socialization of children was of great concern in the beginnings of these programs. More recently, government, social service groups, and health-care agencies have emerged in an effort to serve children and families. Quality indicators are used to determine the quality of child-care programs. These indicators stem from the work of local, regional, national, and international organizations and government agencies.

Theme 6. As child care and education have broadened to include a variety of options in schools, family child-care homes, and child-care centers, parenting has become more complex with the number and beliefs of child-care providers, teachers, and administrators. Time and resources are other important factors. Nevertheless, children and adolescents *must* have their parents or guardians involved in their daily lives at home and at school or care. Communication across all parties involved in the care of the child becomes essential. Strategies for this communication vary according to the families served. Teachers and caregivers must learn to work with families in determining which strategies will be most successful in building and maintaining the family–school partnership.

FAMILIES AND CHILDREN CONNECTING TO THEIR NEAR AND FAR ENVIRONMENTS

The worlds of our childhoods are intertwined. Our children experience the history of our pasts, one unseen to them. Our parenting reflects and sometimes rejects the attitudes, beliefs, and practices that were characteristic of our own parents. Similarly, our children will take into their lives as parents what we have brought from our parents and the beliefs, attitudes, and practices we have given to them as their parents. In many ways, what we do and share with our children today is taken across time into a world that we may never see but in which we will play a role.

The roles that parents have played in our families will continue to travel across time into the centuries ahead. These roles mirror the concerns of societies and communities at large as they work to survive in an ever-changing world. They will carry the effects

A caring adult who is consistent and reliable provides nurturing for the child.

of who we are at a given period in time—our genetics, joys and sorrows, economic securities and uncertainties, societal issues, health status, ignorances, and insights. In this chapter, we explore roles of parents and families in the context of the history of "humanness." Some of these issues are revisited in subsequent chapters.

Perhaps of greatest interest to us is what has transpired during our time—from our great-grandparents to our grandparents, parents, and finally ourselves. As we look back at the 20th century and ahead into the 21st, we will find an interconnectedness between the increasing knowledge we have acquired about the significance of learning, health care, and appropriate practices in the early years and the quality of programs available for children and their families. Our intent is, in part, to enhance the quality of life for families and children and, in part, to foster the optimum development of children so that they can compete in the increasingly technological, global marketplace. The ongoing challenge for the early childhood professional has been and will continue to be the advocacy of those practices that are nurturing and appropriate for the young child while meshing with the demands of a changing world.

To provide a simplistic example of the interrelatedness of families to their worlds, think about the human body and the way it functions as a set of systems. If a person loses use of a limb, the body and the brain adapt by shifting the responsibility to another limb, incorporating new strategies for accomplishing tasks, incorporating an artificial device, or a combination of these. Many body systems will be affected and will need to accommodate this change.

When a parent becomes ill in a family, other family members must make changes to accommodate the loss of that person's contributions and to care for that individual. These accommodations may include increased employment, new tasks, a change in residence, and time spent in a hospital. When a school system changes its hours of operation to times later than when parents typically go to work, families must accommodate by seeking additional child care, changing work schedules, giving added responsibility to the children, or imploring the schools to consider families. For a time, families work to reestablish equilibrium within their households.

Using these examples, we can consider how the family functions as a system that is affected from within and through entities outside the family. Urie Bronfenbrenner (1979) described this as the *human ecological system*. Bronfenbrenner noted five systems that form the context for human growth and development and the functioning of the family. The **microsystem** involves the child's very **near environment**—the family. Other microsystems that will closely affect the child include the school or child-care setting.

Interrelations among the microsystems form a child's **mesosystem**. A family depends on a child-care provider to furnish quality care for the child. If this care does not occur within the child-care microsystem, the family microsystem will be affected. Similarly, a family crisis such as the death of a family member or a divorce could affect the microsystem of the school, with a child's behaviors and performance affected.

Exosystems also affect families. We may not see or be directly involved in exosystems. Perhaps the school system changes its bus schedule and the family is affected. Perhaps the child-care center changes its hours of operation or dramatically increases its fees. Families may have little or no control over these events, but they certainly affect the lives of individuals within families.

The time or **chronosystem** in which we experience life is also a factor in the ways individuals interact with each other within the context of the family setting and community. Technological advances over time provide wonderful examples of changing chronosystems and, consequently, changing methods of interaction. For example, television created a medium that brought us closer to the lives of those in the world about us. In many cases, it also inhibited the verbal communication of individuals within the family as it became the focus of family entertainment in many homes. Computer technology has also connected us to the larger world through information and communication devices. While our knowledge is broadened, face-to-face and "voice-to-voice" communication is lessened as individuals rely on electronic messages. Our ability to access information rapidly and efficiently is enhanced in amazing ways, but this must be tempered with concern for building relationships based on physical presence and oral communication within families and across communities.

Finally, the broadest context in which families function is the **macrosystem**. This includes the political and historical events that affect families. The launch of Sputnik 1 by the Soviets in 1957 thrust Americans into a period of concern for improving the quality of education in the United States. The civil rights movement succeeded in gaining more opportunities for minorities. Recent scientific discoveries in brain research have provided a bounty of public information about the importance of prenatal care and nurturing the young child.

THEME 1   *in practice . . .*

Each of our lives can be represented in the paradigm of Bronfenbrenner's systems. Draw a circle in the center of a sheet of paper. Put your name at the center of that circle. This is your *microsystem.* Surround your name with the names of those individuals who were nearest to you when you were born (include your birth year). Surround that circle with a larger circle. This is your *mesosystem.* Write the names of individuals and institutions in which you interacted across your early years. Make a larger circle around the mesosystem. This represents your *exosystem.* Write the names of institutions, organizations, and so forth with which you did not physically interact, but that affected you and the individuals within your family. Create a larger circle surrounding the existing circles. This is your *macrosystem.* What were the events that shaped life within your family during this time? This is the *chronosystem* representing this time of your life. Examine the circles to see your "roots," for example, the factors and individuals that helped bring you to your life today.

Bronfenbrenner's human ecological system continues to be explored by those who work with families and children. Bubolz and Sontag (1993) viewed the family as an open system with interconnectedness across (a) the natural physical–biological environment, (b) the human-built environment, and (c) the sociocultural environment. In other words, families have functioned throughout time and continue to function today within the context of the natural physical–biological, human-built, and cultural environments.

Predictable routines provide children with a sense of order and security.

The **natural physical–biological environment** includes the natural resources with which we are blessed or that might be threatened. Rain, water sources, land, trees, and climate are among these resources. Although we often take these for granted, we know that they are threatened by human consumption and misuse of the environment. In many parts of the world and across time, these elements have served to enhance or threaten a way of life. For example, the community that has a precious mineral as a resource will profit; the community that lies in the shadow of a great volcano is at unrest. Although our view of parenting focuses on the care and nurturing of the child, the ease and comfort and manner of doing so by a parent will vary with the physical and biological resources that are available.

Coupled with the natural physical—biological environment, humans created a **human-built environment**, which includes rural and urban communities. It also includes systems for health care, schooling, manufacturing, business, government, and religions. Along with the very positive aspects of our civilizations are negative aspects—problems that we have created, including toxic wastes that pollute the land, water, and air and destruction of land and life for the purpose of war. Parents' attitudes toward their role in parenting across time will reflect the current availability of human resources and the attitudes of their society toward the role of the family in the functioning of the community.

Cultural practices, languages, laws, and values characterize the **sociocultural environment**. People within a society must decide what is important for maintaining not only the quality of life for individuals and families but also the functioning of the community and society. Not all individuals, however, have had the same amount of "voice" or power in making and influencing these decisions. Throughout history, the representation of certain groups has been limited, with the lives of those people devalued or targeted for oppression and even extermination. The plight of Jewish families during the Holocaust and the children of African American families during and following the period of slavery in the United States are two prominent examples. Values placed on education, freedom of speech, equality of human life, and preservation of human life are all a part of the sociocultural context within which we live.

Given an understanding of the family living, growing, and functioning in the context of the near environment and the **far environment** (that beyond the family, such as the community and the world), we can begin to look at some events that have affected the role of parents throughout time. We can also look at the role of parents and families as the world experiences the birth and infancy of a new century.

HISTORY OF FAMILIES AND CHILDREN

T he only way to explore the roles of families in the lives of children across time is to investigate and attempt to understand the context in which children were viewed during different times in history. The challenges faced by adults at particular times to ensure survival are reflected in the treatment of children. It is challenging to provide an overview of all cultures in existence across different periods of time. However, our insights about one culture should not be generalized to all cultures. Similarly, all children were not treated the same even within one culture. Over time, we see children killed because of their disability, poor health, or being born female—all signs of weakness and inability to work. Distinctions in class guaranteed that some children would be in trades whereas others would be sent to labor in fields and less desirable work sites. Differences in religious practice meant that some children would be educated and some would be viewed as born with sin and in need of harsh punishment to drive out the sin. Skin color determined that some children were not equal to their White counterparts; these children could be owned and used as slaves and their parents sold away, never to be seen again.

It would be a significant task to represent all aspects and historical moments across time for all cultures. Therefore, Table 2.1 serves as an introduction to our discussion of European parents and children and their descendants by giving an example of the experiences of some children and families across differing historical periods. The work of DeMause (1974) and the excellent compilation of historical moments by Berger (2004) have been utilized in the presentation of historical events affecting the lives of children and their families.

As you read the following narrative, you will note additional items not addressed in Table 2.1. You may also wish to add items from your own study of history and your life. Remember, we each bring our own experiences and beliefs to the study of history and childhood, and these may be reflected in our interpretations.

Ancient Times

"During prehistoric times, just as today, the first teachers—the socializers—were parents and families" (Berger, 2004, p. 37). According to Berger (2004), members of primitive societies educated their children, not in school, but in the context of families and communities gathering and hunting to produce food in ways that could maintain the group. Values and laws of the group were passed on so that children could function as a part of the culture and the culture would continue. In this role, children were highly valued.

Egyptian artwork from ancient times depicts children at play and being held and comforted by adults. Written records indicate that schooling outside the home took place (Osborn, 1991). "Formal systems of education also existed in ancient India, China, and Persia, as well as in the pre-Columbian New World, particularly in the Indian cultures of the Mayas, Aztecs, and Incas" (Berger, 2004, p. 37).

TABLE 2.1	History and Experiences of European Parents and Children	
Chronological time	**Historical time**	**Experiences of children and families**
Ancient times	Ancient Greece and Rome—Plato (427–347 B.C.); Aristotle (384–322 B.C.)	Families were supported by the state in the care and education of children. The focus was on raising good citizens who could maintain and support the state. Infanticide was practiced to eliminate those children unfit for this role.
A.D. 476–1450	Middle Ages (Dark Ages)—time between ancient and modern times	Citizens became a part of the feudal system, with strong class distinctions between serfs and their noble counterparts. Life was very poor and education of children was not a high priority. Children of serfs and peasants worked alongside their parents in maintaining feudal properties. Children of higher social means were sent by the age of 7 to work as apprentices. Childhood disappeared and the term *miniature adult* fell out of use. Power was in the hands of those who could read, most often rulers and church officials.
14th, 15th, and 16th centuries	The Renaissance—the great revival of art, literature, and learning that had its beginning in Italy; marked the transition between the medieval and modern world	Gutenberg's printing press made books, including the Bible, available to an increasing number of people. This improved the quality of family life for many. The notion of original sin was prevalent from the 16th to 18th centuries and often resulted in harsh treatment of children. Children also became more exposed to the classical world.
16th century	The Reformation—religious movement aimed at reforming the Roman Catholic Church and resulting in Protestant churches	Families were encouraged to read to their children, especially the Bible. Martin Luther was a leader in encouraging families. Bishop Comenius worked to inspire families to educate their children.
17th and 18th centuries	Period of early childhood reformers—continuation of revival and Reformation	Noted philosophers and those preceding current-day early childhood theorists, including Rousseau, Pestalozzi, and Froebel, focused on the good of the child and the need for seeing early childhood as a distinct and important part of life. Locke introduced his notion of tabula rasa.
	Beginning of Industrial Revolution—hand tools replaced by machine tools; colonization in the United States	Some families followed the earlier concepts of original sin set forth by religious zealots, believing that to spare the rod was to spoil the child. Children were utilized as workers in both fields and trades in their role of ensuring the survival of themselves, families, and societies.

TABLE 2.1	Contiuned	
Chronological time	**Historical time**	**Experiences of children and families**
19th century	Evolution of early childhood programs in the United States	Care for the unique period of childhood became evident. Elizabeth Peabody established the first English-speaking kindergarten in Boston. Susan Blow established the first public kindergarten in St. Louis.
	Emergence of child study movement	Charles Darwin published the first "baby biography."
	Civil War	Man's inhumanity to man was evident in this war, which pitted family member against family member and highlighted the plight of children and their parents during the time of slavery in the United States.
	Child labor	Children became part of sweat shops or factories where health and safety conditions were horrid and children and families worked for extremely limited wages.
20th century	Child study movement	G. Stanley Hall became the father of the child study movement in the United States.
	Heightened focus on child development and early education	Gesell produced charts for developmental norms. A number of theories emerged, including those of Piaget, Erikson, Vygotsky, Bronfenbrenner, and Skinner.
	Heightened focus on parenting skills and health of children	Dr. Spock published a child-care text for parents. Several "women's" magazines emerged with ideas on parenting and family life.
	Child-care centers opened during World War II	Mothers stepped into the workforce as husbands, fathers, and sons went to war.
	More focus on equality of children and families across religions, races, lifestyles, and disabilities	The civil rights movement created a greater awareness of the plight of children of color and their families. This "fight," led by Martin Luther King, Jr., resulted in the Civil Rights Act and the desegregation of schools.
		The Education of All Handicapped Children Act provided funding and support for families of children with disabilities.
		Society began to realize there are many voices in this country representing cultures, religions, and lifestyles, and a focus on nondiscrimination of children became evident through teacher training, legislation, and school policies.

(Continued)

TABLE 2.1	Continued	
Chronological time	**Historical time**	**Experiences of children and families**
		The National Association for the Education of Young Children published work on "developmentally appropriate practice" designed to assist teachers, caregivers, and parents in providing learning experiences for young children based not on chronological age, but on the child's developmental age. This has been very helpful in meeting individual needs of young children.
	More family–school–community initiatives were formed as the research on the importance of the family on children's achievement grew.	With programs beginning in 1964, Home and School Institute, a nonprofit agency, developed systematic training and materials for total community educational involvement—school districts; federal, state, and local government agencies; corporations; and community organizations. The needs of all students have been fundamental concerns of the institute since its inception.
		The National Coalition for Parent Involvement in Education was founded in 1980, at the initiative of what was then the National School Volunteer Program (now National Association for Partners in Education), with funding from the Ford Foundation and Union Carbide. Participating parent and teacher organizations meet monthly to: monitor legislation, initiate projects, and share information and ideas about research, programs, and policies.
	To achieve better home–school–community relationships, teachers need the time and resources to build relationships with parents.	President George Bush and the governors of all 50 states met at the University of Virginia to set national education goals. One result of this meeting was the release in 1991 of *America 2000: An Education Strategy,* which outlined six educational goals or national standards. These goals became the basis of the Goals 2000: Educate America Act of 1994.
	More emphasis on early childhood as a time for teachers and families to take active roles in building preacademic skills needed for school success. Schools raised	In 1996, the U.S. Department of Education funded a consortium of research universities (University of North Carolina, University of California at Los Angeles, University of Virginia at Charlottesville, and the University of Arkansas at Little Rock) to establish the National Center for Early Development and Learning (NCEDL).

TABLE 2.1	Continued	
Chronological time	**Historical time**	**Experiences of children and families**
	the bar on expectations for entrance to kindergarten and government demanded scientific research–based practices in schools. Family literacy is part of this initiative.	The NCEDL's goals were to generate research, policy, and best practices surrounding the complex variables of the child, family, community, program and schools that interact to influence learning and development of young children. Their first conference in 1998 was focused on the "Transition to Kindergarten." The Harvard Family Research Project (Kreider, 2002)—*Getting parents "ready" for kindergarten: The role of early childhood education*—and other studies added to the knowledge base.
21st century	Parents of children in failing schools have more options to transfer their child to a better performing school. But families and schools also face increased pressures of testing requirements.	The No Child Left Behind Act was launched in 2001 by President George W. Bush with intentions of improving the quality of schools and provide choices for families in neighborhoods with failing schools.
	Young children are spending more time with media—TV, video games, and computers—and less time outside playing with friends or being read to by family members.	The Kaiser Family Foundation released a study by Rideout, Vandewater, and Wartella (2003)—*Zero to Six: Electronic Media in the Lives of Infants, Toddlers, and Preschoolers*—that found children under 6 spend an average of 2 hours a day using screen media, the same amount they play outside, but far less than reading or being read to—only 39 minutes each day!
	Families have largely positive views about young children's use of TV and computers, stating that these mostly help children's learning and social skills.	The study found gender differences in media use do start early: in a typical day, 24 percent of young boys will play video games, whereas only 8 percent of girls will play.
	Overall, although TV is an everpresent companion in many households, families do understand that the content of what children watch is as important as the amount of TV they watch.	

The view of the ancient Greeks and Romans also reflects a concern for family life and the education of children. Note, however, that a primary concern for children and their education was based on the rearing of good citizens who could protect and maintain the culture and civilization. Furthermore, infanticide was a common practice of both the Romans and the Greeks.

In ancient Greece, Plato (ca. 428–347 B.C.) and Aristotle (384–322 B.C.) addressed the rearing of children in such a way that the stability and future of the culture and civilization were continued. Parents could choose to send their children to private schools of their choice. However, an increasing interest in the education of children for the benefit of the state was expressed by leaders of the time, including Plato and Aristotle, who stressed that an event of such importance should not be left to chance (Berger, 2004).

In both Rome and Sparta, education remained in the hands of families. Young children had few rights, and laws forbade the rearing of children who were described as "deformed." Those children who were selected to survive were educated by their parents to be good and productive citizens. Children of primary-school age were already in training to be soldiers for their country.

Even though the plight of children was difficult during this time, with their primary function as citizens of the state, Berger (2004) noted that families were seen as important or first educators of their children. However, "a subsequent decline in the importance of the family occurred during the Middle Ages, and concern for parent involvement did not emerge until many centuries later" (p. 39).

At this point in our discussion, Trawick-Smith's (1997) model will be employed to guide the discussion of children and families through time. As noted later, the value placed on children has been and continues to be affected by the context of the historical events and cultures within which they are reared.

First to Seventeenth Centuries

During the period A.D. 1 to 1600, European history details the period of the Middle Ages, beginning at about 400 and ending at about 1400. This was a period of the feudal system, with clear class distinctions among individuals. Children of serfs and peasants worked alongside their parents in maintaining the properties of the feudal estates. Life was poor and harsh, and education was not a consideration for these children. Their noble counterparts, however, began their education for the life of nobility at an early age. Regardless of their preparation for a skill or for assuming positions of leadership, these children were also without childhoods. By age 7, they were sent to apprentice with other families—the jobs in keeping with their position as nobles or as commoners (Berger, 2004).

The expectation that children would behave and think as **miniature adults** is depicted in early paintings of children in adult clothing and with, understandably, somber faces. Their roles, poor health care, high death rate, and the continued practice of infanticide were all factors that denied them the joy we see in childhood today. Important events that occurred during this period include the Renaissance and the Reformation.

The **Renaissance** marks a time across the 14th, 15th, and 16th centuries, when Europe experienced the revival of art, literature, and learning. This period also marked the end of the medieval world. The **Reformation** was the 16th-century religious movement that aimed at reforming the Roman Catholic Church and resulted in establishing Protestant churches. In 1439, Johannes Gutenberg invented the printing press. Consequently, the production of books, no longer limited to reproduction by hand, increased dramatically. The increased availability of books and knowledge played a significant role in improving the quality of life for families.

Changes in the religious aspects of society also affected family life. "The most important aspect of the Protestant reformation was the concept of a priesthood of believers, in which people were expected to learn to read and study the Bible for themselves and thereby find their own salvation" (Berger, 2004, p. 41). The Bible, made available by the printing press and printed in the language of the people, was the subject of study. Martin Luther urged parents to educate their children.

Seventeenth to Nineteenth Centuries

The concept of *original sin*—that all children are born with sin, which was to be expelled by harsh discipline—was prevalent from 1600 to 1800. Events in Europe were mirrored in communities being established in America. In 1642, the Massachusetts Act, requiring all families to teach their children to read the Bible and laws of the land, was enacted. In 1687, the "old Deluder Satan" Law, requiring communities of more than 100 to establish schools, was put into place (Barbour & Barbour, 1997). In these colonial schools, "the major component of schooling was discipline and moral education based on the prevailing beliefs that to spare the rod was to spoil the child" (Roopnarine & Johnson, 1993, p. 2).

Important philosophers who emerged during this time made lasting contributions to early childhood education and the accompanying role of families. Among them were Comenius, Locke, Rousseau, Pestalozzi, and Froebel. These social thinkers rejected the notion of original sin and viewed children as born innocent of sin (Berger, 2004).

Comenius (1592–1670), born in Moravia, was a member and bishop of the Moravian Brethren. In *Didactica Magna*, Comenius spoke to the importance of education in the early years. The *School of Infancy* addressed the role of the home in the early education of young children. *Orbis Pictus* was the first picture book for children.

John **Locke** (1632–1704) "challenged the beliefs of the medieval church that children were born with a fully formed nature or soul, and thought that, instead, they, like other natural phenomena in the universe, were subject to the effects of the environment" (Roopnarine & Johnson, 1993, p. 3). Locke, an Englishman, is well known for his notion of *tabula rasa*, in which he described the newborn with a mind as a "blank slate" to be molded and shaped by parents and teachers. Locke also supported the concept of *hardening* that was prevalent at the time: It was thought that children subjected to cold baths and other methods of "hardening" would become more resilient to disease (Berger, 2004).

Jean-Jacques **Rousseau** (1712–1778) emerged during this time as yet another significant philosopher affecting the lives of children and families. His book *Emile* encouraged greater freedoms for children and the nurturing of children in the early years by their mothers. This concern for children was an interesting contrast to his treatment of his own five children, who were placed in foundling homes soon after birth (Berger, 2004).

Locke, Rousseau, and Comenius played significant roles in the philosophies of Johann **Pestalozzi** (1746–1827), who was later hailed as the father of parent education. His book *How Gertrude Teaches Her Children* emphasized the role of the mother and gave parents strategies for teaching their children. These strategies included using objects to learn to count and recreation, games, and nutritious snacks (Berger, 2004). A Swiss educator and social activist, Pestalozzi went beyond the work of his predecessors by actually establishing a school, the Education Institute in Bergdorf, Switzerland (1801), which put philosophy to practice. One of his major contributions was the belief that all children, not just those of the upper class, could benefit from education (Roopnarine & Johnson, 1993). In addition, he rejected the notion that punishment should be linked with learning and originated the idea of group instruction.

Friedrich **Froebel** (1782–1852) also advocated for the goodness of children, concern for the early years, and inclusion of the parents in a child's education. This German educator began a "garden for children," now known as kindergarten, employing many of Pestalozzi's strategies. Froebel saw mothers as the first educators of their children and wrote a book, *Mother Play and Nursery Songs With Finger Plays*, as an aid for mothers in the early education of their children at home. Froebel organized his curriculum for kindergarten around the natural unfolding of the child, with the mother as an active participant (Berger, 2004).

Nineteenth to Twentieth Centuries

The lives of Pestalozzi and Froebel extended into the 19th century, as did the work of Locke, Comenius, and Rousseau. In 1851, the German government banned kindergarten education because it "was suspicious of what it believed was an atheistic attitude in Froebel's emphasis on play and the transcendental idea of God as incarnate in humankind" (Roopnarine & Johnson, 1993, p. 9). Froebel's work carried into other parts of the world, however. In 1860, Elizabeth Peabody established the first English-speaking private kindergarten in America in Boston. In 1873, Susan Blow, who had worked with Peabody, opened the first public kindergarten in America in St. Louis.

Documents began to appear to assist parents in their roles. These included magazines, such as *Parents' Magazine* (1840–1850), designed to give parents suggestions for breast-feeding, toilet training, and other useful tips in child rearing (Berger, 2004). Although strides were made in the education of young children and child-rearing support for families, life continued to be difficult for children and families. The 19th century not only was marked by the War of 1812, but also was torn apart by the Civil War. Whereas most of written U.S. history depicts the lives of children of European descent, little is written about the lives of children growing up in slavery or of Native American children who witnessed the death of their families and loss of their homes. Ogbu (1988) detailed the effects on parenting that resulted from the oppression faced by many nondominant cultural groups. The enslaved parent and child's relationship focused on maintaining the family by the child's obeying the parent, being quiet, and listening to instructions. Independent thought and action on the part of the enslaved could result in beatings, being sold away from the family, or even death. Parenting, then, was direct and firm.

Children of all backgrounds engaged in hard labor in factories and on frontiers. Their lives were often harsh and brief. Many were born so that parents might have more laborers, and this was their worth. Being able to work and produce meant a family could survive. Adulthood came early, and many times this, too, was brief.

At the end of the 19th century, pioneers in the field of child study, including Pestalozzi and Charles Darwin (1809–1882), "published biographies of their own children in an attempt to capture milestones of human growth" (Trawick-Smith, 1997, p. 29). The role of parents continued to be highlighted, and concern for their role in the education of their children was reflected in the founding of the Parent Teacher Association (PTA) in 1897 (Berger, 2004).

1900 to 1950

At the turn of the 20th century, the foundation had been created for the acknowledgment of the significance of the early years. This, coupled with an increasing interest in scientific research about human development, fed the growing **child study movement**. G. Stanley **Hall** (1844–1924) was an eminent psychologist who is credited as the founder of the field of child study in the United States. One of his greatest contributions was the integration of the fields of child study and education (Trawick-Smith, 1997).

The concern for establishing developmental norms led to the creation of normative charts by researchers, including Arnold Gesell. A problem with these studies, as noted by Trawick-Smith (1997), is the sole focus on White, middle-class children as the subjects.

During this time, the country demonstrated heightened concern for the welfare of children who continued to be exposed to the cruelties of hard labor, dangerously strict parents, and neglect. The first White House Conference on Care of Dependent Children was called in 1909. The Children's Bureau was created in 1912 as a result of this conference and marked the federal government's first display of concern for children (Berger, 2004).

Parents' interest in how best to rear their children was reflected in the onset of women's magazines with articles addressing the care of the home and children. These magazines included *Good Housekeeping, Ladies' Home Journal,* and *Woman's Home Companion* (Berger, 2004). Government also began to disseminate information relative to strategies for child care. The first *Infant Care* book was distributed by the federal government in 1914. This book and other parenting articles advocated strict schedules for infant feeding and sleeping and forbade such damaging behavior as thumb sucking (Berger, 2004).

Parents' interest in participating in the education of their young children was demonstrated by the establishment of the first **parent cooperative** in the United States. This school, founded by faculty wives at the University of Chicago, followed the work of English nursery schools established by Margaret McMillan in 1911. McMillan was an advocate of parent involvement and education through play: "Parent cooperatives and the growth of the nursery schools in the United States strengthened and promoted parent education" (Berger, 2004, p. 60).

The 1930s and 1940s brought difficult times for children and families in the United States. Just out of World War I, the country found itself in the Great Depression, which left many families without food or shelter. The United States entered World War II in

1941, and countless women were left to raise families, earn a living, and assist in the war effort. These two historical events had lasting effects on the field of early childhood: The Depression brought Works Progress Administration (**WPA**) nurseries, which not only created jobs but also provided women the opportunity to work. World War II brought **Lanham Act** nurseries, which were open 10 to 12 hours per day, 6 days per week, and provided mothers the time to work and participate in the war effort. Following the war, funding for these centers was suspended, and women were encouraged to return to their homes (Roopnarine & Johnson, 1993).

During and following this period, researchers in the child study movement began to focus on the emotional development of children. This would not be surprising, given the grave emotional tasks that had been faced by many families and their children during the years of the Depression and World War II. The work of Sigmund Freud (1856–1939) became the subject of discussion. "Childhood fears and behaviors such as shyness or aggressiveness took on new meanings when applied to the child's unconscious and were carefully recorded by teachers" (Roopnarine & Johnson, 1993, p. 19). Play was seen as therapy. Parents had also been exposed to the behaviorist theories of John B. **Watson** (1878–1958) and were faced with choices about the best methods for addressing the emotional concerns of their young children. A famous publication that became a much-used and much-quoted resource for parents was first published in 1946. In *The Common Sense Book of Baby and Child Care*, Benjamin **Spock**, MD (1903–1998), put to rest the concerns and fears of many parents determined to do their best in rearing their children. In contrast with the strict rules applied to child rearing in the early part of the century, Dr. Spock urged parents to enjoy their children and to enjoy being parents. His book addressed a wide range of concerns for parents, including feeding, toileting, sleeping, illnesses, and discipline. This book continues to influence parenting even today (Berger, 2004).

1950 to 2000

The period from 1950 to 2000 was ushered in by the Korean War. But by 1953, relieved to be at the end of a long period of wars, Americans appeared to relax and enjoy a time of prosperity. Popular television shows depicted the American family as two parents, two or three children, father as a professional, and mother as a loving and ever-tidy housewife. These characteristics prevailed in *Father Knows Best, Leave It to Beaver,* and *The Donna Reed Show*. This was the period of the **baby boom** for the many families who had postponed having children until after the war years. The effects of this great increase in babies continues to be seen in social, political, and economic arenas of our world. In the 1950s, schools in the United States reflected the influences of John Dewey's (1859–1952) progressive movement. Barbour and Barbour (1997) noted that these swings from conservative to more progressive philosophies reflect the perceived needs of the American public at the time. "For example, with new immigrants and a growing urban, industrialized society, a movement emerged in the 1920s and 1930s for more openness in education—with schooling tailored to the needs, interests, and abilities of the children" (p. 29).

"Dewey did more than any other person to redirect the course of education in the United States" (Morrison, 1998, p. 79). His child-centered curriculum reflected the interests of children and focused on children's active participation in learning. He also stressed the usefulness of daily life experiences as learning opportunities. "Teachers who integrate subjects, use thematic units, and encourage problem-solving activities and critical thinking are philosophically indebted to Dewey" (Morrison, 1998, p. 80).

Early childhood educators began to study more about the work of developmental theorists, including Jean **Piaget** (1896–1980) and Lev **Vygotsky** (1896–1934). These theorists believed that children construct knowledge through their interaction with materials, people, and events. Cognitive development was seen as a continuous process of learning through play. Piaget also stressed the unique ways in which young children approached learning situations, as compared with adults, and he outlined an age/stage model of cognitive development.

An important role for families, reading stories at home supports early literacy development and readiness for school.

The launching of the satellite Sputnik 1 by the Soviet Union in 1957 brought a new wave of concern to the United States. Why were the Americans not the first to make this journey into space? Was something wrong with the educational system that put us in second place in the "race for space"? A concern for educational systems that were more academic became prevalent. People had even greater interest in not only how children learn but also how they learn best. At the same time that we as Americans were troubled by the prospect of being second in a space race, we were also troubled about the inequality that we saw about us in economics, education, living conditions, and services. We were concerned about the inequalities between People of Color and people who are White, those who are male and those who are female, those who have disabilities and those who do not. We began to think about our future as being in the hands of our children, and the notion of investing in children as investing in the future emerged.

Educators and policy makers concerned about the quality of education for the nation's children and about meeting the needs of all children seemed to find answers in research addressing the development of intelligence. James McVicker Hunt, in *Intelligence and Experience* (1961), challenged the notion that intelligence is fixed; he said that, rather, intelligence could be enhanced by positive environmental experiences. Jean Piaget's work was cited as a model to be used in the early years, which were emphasized as important years for learning.

Two historical pieces of legislation gave rise to many programs for young children and their families: The *Civil Rights Act* was enacted in 1964 and the *Elementary and Secondary Education Act* in 1965. Project Head Start, Title I, and

Chapter I programs were also implemented in 1965 to begin building a system of equal educational opportunity for all children.

> Particularly during the 1960s, many federal programs were based on the idea of conserving one of the country's greatest resources—its children. Head Start, Follow Through, and child welfare programs are products of this view, which has resulted in a "human capital" or "investment" rationale for child care and other services. (Morrison, 1998, p. 93)

"Following the civil rights movement, social issues were of great concern and again schools were pressured to change to a curriculum more responsive to all children" (Barbour & Barbour, 1997, p. 29). This concern became realized in a dramatic way with the passing of P.L. 94-142, the Education of All Handicapped Children Act, in 1975 (in 1990, it was renamed the Individuals with Disabilities Education Act [IDEA]).

Doors have been opened several times throughout history to look at parents and the home as indicators of how a child will fare in education and in life. The work of Hunt (1961), Bloom's (1964) *Stability and Change in Human Characteristics*, and the desire of a nation to learn what is most important in *every* child's education thrust researchers into the world of children at home and the parents' role in their child's education. Researchers with the Dave (1963) study made the following conclusions with respect to the home environment:

> **Work habits of children and parents.** Children from homes with routines, structure, and shared responsibilities do better in school.
> **Academic guidance and support.** Children need someone at home who will offer them encouragement in their schoolwork, understand their strengths and limitations, and be aware of what they are studying.
> **Stimulation to explore and discuss ideas and events.** Children need someone who provides them opportunities to know about events in the world through print materials at home, trips to libraries, and participation in family hobbies and activities.
> **Language development in the home.** Children need opportunities to see and hear adults use oral and written language in the home.
> **Academic aspirations and expectations.** A child needs an adult at home who will set high but realistic standards for the child's school efforts and encourage the child to aspire to the highest levels of education.

According to Bloom (1981),

> My own speculation is that parents are still the key in the learning of their children because they are likely to be a constant factor in their children's lives. When parents are very effective (or when they can learn to be more effective) in supporting the child's learning, they remain with the child over his or her years of schooling. (p. 90)

Programs such as Head Start responded to these concerns by including parent involvement as a required component. Parents work in classrooms as volunteers, participate on advisory boards, and receive education with respect to such topics as child guidance, health care, and developmentally appropriate activities.

If It Weren't for Head Start . . .

LaToya, age 4, and her mom Crystal get ready quickly because the van is coming to take them to the Head Start policy council meeting. Crystal was elected by her fellow Head Start families to represent them on the local Head Start policy council. LaToya goes with her mom because the council makes child care available for parents who are members. LaToya greets her friends as they enter the building. Crystal drops her off and chats with the child care provider, who is also LaToya's teacher in her 4-year-old class.

As Crystal opens the door and looks in at policy council faces, she pauses and thinks about her life two years ago. Crystal and LaToya were living in subsidized housing in a neighborhood where police sirens were commonly heard. LaToya was born when Crystal was 17 years old. LaToya's dad, Gregory, was a great guy who loved Crystal and LaToya. At first, the family was struggling because Gregory was only doing odd jobs to make ends meet. He joined the military to provide some secutiry for the family, but he was killed in Iraq last year. LaToya became very withdrawn and shy after her father's death. Military benefits are good, but not good enough to pay for Crystal and LaToya to live in a nice part of town. Crystal works as a maid in a local resort hotel part-time, because she decided to work on getting her GED. LaToya was staying in a family child care home with many other children, and sometimes Crystal worried about the children's safety, but that was all she could afford.

One day last year when Crystal was feeling frustrated with all of the cleaning, one of her co-workers told her about Head Start and the great care and education that preschoolers get, in addition to support for the child's family. Once LaToya was enrolled in Head Start, Cyrstal found she enjoyed participating and helping out alongside other families in the program. Crystal also took advantage of some career counseling. When the counselor realized Crystal's talents and interest in the sciences, he told her about a scholarship program for the local community college. Crystal had never dreamed of college.

Now, a year later, instead of daydreaming as she mops the floors in the hotel, Crystal has real dreams of becoming a nurse practitioner. LaToya loves the Head Start program; she has learned about butterfly cycles, how to make friends, and how to write her name. LaToya's teacher says she helps other children who are feeling sad like she did when her dad died.

Crystal realizes that she and LaToya are experiencing some important supports that single parents and other parents with low incomes need to make their child's early learning successful. Crystal wonders what would have happened to their lives if it weren't for these opportunities through Head Start. Family involvement and family well being are key elements in making Head Start the successful program it has been for more than 40 years.

The 1960s and 1970s will be remembered as a time of change. Americans experienced deep wounds of an unresolved war in Vietnam. A concern for social issues brought laws and programs that have prevailed. These changes followed, and were accompanied by, a period of unrest on campuses and in cities across the continent. We lost great political leaders and humanitarians, including President John F. Kennedy; his brother, presidential candidate Robert Kennedy; and Reverend Martin Luther King, Jr., perhaps the greatest civil rights leader of all time, to assassins.

This was a time of free love, flower children, hippies, and love children. The drug culture came into the open. Families were divided by separation and divorce in record numbers. Many mothers began to seek employment outside the home, and the number of child-care arrangements broadened. Awareness of the needs of minority groups was demanded. We hailed parents as the first teachers of their children and began to educate government leaders, educators, parents, and business leaders about the importance of the early years in learning. We also saw families struggle with changes in family structures, including changing gender roles, nuclear families isolated from extended families, divorce, remarriage, and single parents. Families struggled with issues of quality, affordable child care, and the effects on the young child of mothers going to work. These individuals and families were pioneers of issues that remain concerns in our society today.

With programs beginning in 1964, Home and School Institute, a nonprofit agency, developed systematic training and materials for total community educational involvement—school districts; federal, state, and local government agencies; corporations; and community organizations. The needs of all students have been fundamental concerns of the institute since its inception.

The 1980s saw Americans attempt to make sense of what we had learned in the 1960s and 1970s. Many programs for children experienced reduced funding or were eliminated. Head Start, however, has stood the test of time and political skirmishes and remains funded. Organizations and individuals advocated for quality in child care and early childhood programs. The **National Association for the Education of Young Children (NAEYC)** published its first edition of *Developmentally Appropriate Practice in Early Childhood Programs Serving Children From Birth Through Age Eight* (Bredekamp, 1987), which has served as a model for developing and implementing quality programs across the country. The Southern Early Childhood Association (**SECA**), the Division for Early Childhood of the Council for Exceptional Children (**CEC**), and the Association for Childhood Education International (ACEI) are among the professional groups that have advocated for quality services for all young children and for improving the quality of life for all families.

Programs for young children are extensions of their homes, providing warmth, comfort, and security.

The National Coalition for Parent Involvement in Education (NCPIE) was founded in 1980, at the initiative of what was then the National School Volunteer Program (now National Association for Partners in Education), with funding from the Ford Foundation and Union Carbide. Participating parent and teacher organizations meet monthly to monitor legislation; initiate projects; and share information and ideas about research, programs, and policies.

Such advocacy efforts resulted in the passing of **P.L. 99-457** in 1986, which addressed the needs of children with disabilities from birth to age 3 and their families at the federal level, and in the widespread urging for reform at the local level.

One example of this effort was the 1989 ruling by the Kentucky Supreme Court declaring the system of public schools in the state unconstitutional. The massive reform that followed is known as the Kentucky Education Reform Act (KERA) (1990). Among the outcomes of KERA have been public programs for 4-year-olds labeled "at risk" because of income level; Family Resource and Youth Service Centers, which coordinate community services to families; school-based decision-making councils; and revisions in curriculum across all grade levels (Lindle, 1994).

In the 1990s, Americans became increasingly aware of the advanced technological capabilities and marketing strategies of other countries. Japan provides a solid example. While the United States was striving to maintain a strong and effective posture in the global economy and to provide appropriate education for a tapestry of children and families with a variety of needs, the rigor of the U.S. educational system again came under scrutiny.

An important political and educational event occurred in 1989, when President George Bush and the governors of all 50 states met at the University of Virginia to set national education goals. One result of this meeting was the release in 1991 of *America 2000: An Education Strategy,* which outlined six educational goals or national standards (Morrison, 1998, p. 52). These goals became the basis of the Goals 2000: Educate America Act of 1994. The following goals were to be achieved by the year 2000:

1. All children in America will start school ready to learn.
2. The high school graduation rate will increase to at least 90 percent.
3. All students will leave grades four, eight, and twelve having demonstrated competency over challenging subject matter . . . , and [all students will be] prepared for responsible citizenship, further learning, and productive employment.
4. The nation's teaching force will have access to programs for the continued improvement of their professional skills.
5. The United States students will be first in the world in mathematics and science achievement.
6. Every adult in America will be literate.
7. Every school in America will be free of drugs and violence and will offer a disciplined environment conducive to learning.
8. Every school and home will engage in partnerships that will increase parental involvement and participation in promoting the social, emotional, and academic growth of children. (cited in Morrison, 1998, p. 52)

As reflected in **Goals 2000,** Americans are attempting to meet the needs of every child as he or she enters the world and the "schoolhouse" door. It is important to note that, aside from the physical or mental issues some children may be born with, children are ready to learn. They are eager to explore, curious by nature, and open-minded. What happens after that is manipulated by the experiences that they find in their worlds of family, society, community, and schools. Teachers, administrators, caregivers, and family members do not always agree on how to nurture this inborn curiosity. Nevertheless, families know their children and must be given opportunities for ownership in the decision-making process at school and in caregiving situations.

Goal 8 of Goals 2000 is of particular importance to those parents and teachers working to enhance communication between homes and schools. Interestingly, this goal was the last stated goal. It is hoped that no one believes this is the least important goal. Regardless, changing our attitudes about the importance of school–home communication and employing appropriate strategies for doing so have remained elusive.

Time and human resources are clearly important factors in school–home communications. Time must be devoted to the needs of the children, documenting student performance, and continuing education. Teachers also note lack of parental concern, disciplinary issues, communication problems, and lack of parental support as important issues. Similarly, parents cite lack of teacher support, feelings of being devalued as a parent, and communication and transportation problems as issues. If Goal 8 is to be met, each of these factors must be addressed. This begins with providing teachers the time and resources to build relationships with parents, and employer support of parents to become engaged in the lives of their children at school and in the care of others.

Laws alone cannot provide the incentive for family involvement in their children's eduction. Investigations into factors that impact young children's success in school, including family involvement, were needed to design effective programing. In 1996, the U.S. Department of Education funded a consortium of research universities (University of North Calorina, University of California at Los Angles, (UCLA), University of Virginia at Charlottesville, and the University of Arkansas at Little Rock) to establish the National Center for Early Development and Learning (NCEDL). The center's goals were to generate research, policy, and best practices surrounding the complex variables of the child, family, community, program, and schools that interact to influence learning and development of young children. Their first conference in 1998 was focused on the "Transition to Kindergarten" with distribution of these proceedings (Pianta & Cox, 1999). The Harvard Family Research Project (Kreider, 2002)—*Getting Parents "Ready" for Kindergarten: The Role of Early Childhood Education*—and other studies added to the knowledge base.

In spirit of supporting school readiness, though highly debated (Hyun, 2003), 3 days after President George W. Bush took office in January 2001, he launched the **No Child Left Behind Act**, a major reform act to follow the Elementary and Secondary Act. This act changed the ways states were to provide and account for quality education for all children. Provisions of this act include: increasing accountability, more choices for families and students, greater flexibililty for school districts, ensuring every child can read, strengthening teacher quality, and promoting English proficiency (see www.ed.gov H.R. 1, the No Child Left Behind Act).

In the 21st century, while laws and research on best practices for families increased, consumerism and media resources were also on the rise, counterbalancing or taking some of the best efforts for school readiness in new directions. Families had more resources to buy the exploding market of technology games and tools, forever changing the ways young children approach learning but also reducing the amount of family time and reading in some cases. In 2003 (Rideout & Vandewater, 2003), the Kaiser Family Foundation released a study—*Zero to Six: Electronic Media in the Lives of Infants, Toddlers, and Preschoolers*—of families' self-reports through surveys, which found that children under 6 spend an average of 2 hours a day using screen media, the same amount they play outside, but far less than reading or being read to—only 39 minutes each day!

Almost all children under 2 years in the Kaiser Study watch TV every day, and 26 percent have a TV in their room, although the American Academy of Pediatrics urges families to avoid television for children under 2. Half of all children under age 6 have used a computer, and 30 percent have played video games. The study found gender differences in media use do start early—in a typical day, 24 percent of young boys will play video games, whereas only 8 percent of girls will play.

While most experts believe that young children's use of moderate amounts of quality technology resources is appropriate (Theuvenelle & Bewick, 2003), the Kaiser Study provided some results that suggest that while interactive media have become an integral part of children's lives, some families may be relying too heavily on passive forms of media such as TV to entertain. Theuvenelle and Bewick (2003) recommend several more appropriate ways families, schools and communities can utilize technology with young children to actually increase collaborations (see Figure 2.1). One example is for teachers to set up Web sites that families and children can utilize to extend schoolwork with fun activities families and children can do together at home.

FIGURE 2.1	Advocacy Ideas for Teachers to Develop Modern Structures for Family–School Collaboration

1. Survey families regarding the form of communication they would like to receive new updates on school in: find out which families have computers and access to the Internet.

2. Work with families and local community leaders and businesspeople to develop a resource file of all interesting events in the community that families can use for little or no money (make sure to provide bus routes and other forms of transportation information).

3. Locate and arrange with local high schools with students who might want to do community service by providing child care for very young siblings during family nights.

4. Arrange to celebrate a few children each week at school during the lunch hour and invite families to join their children (also contact their places of employment to let them know and request an extended lunchtime that day).

5. Make it a regular (i.e., every 2 weeks or month) routine to contact your local legislator via e-mail to let him/her know your views on topics.

6. Have the children in your class learn to write letters to legislators, helping them to see the value, even at a young age, and realize that they have a voice in government.

7. Get to know people in the press who might be interested in coming to your class or other classes you know are doing some exciting work with children. "Showing off" some of the children's great efforts will enhance the public's perceptions of the importance of the early years.

8. If some of the families in your school want to learn more about appropriate uses of technology and how they can use the Internet and other technology resources with their children, invite some high school groups to work with you to conduct some evening classes with the families and children.

To relate the historical information about children and families to the experiences of your life, think about how your family and others provided child care, education, discipline, health care, nutrition, and socialization for you as a child and adolescent. How were practices in caring for you related to cultural beliefs, government intervention, religious movements, education practices, philosophical movements, and extended family members? Do you believe your parents' own rearing was related to how they cared for you?

THE IMPORTANCE OF ESTABLISHING AND MAINTAINING HOME AND SCHOOL PARTNERSHIPS

Why is it so difficult to build and maintain partnerships across schools and homes? This is a question that has many answers, depending on the respondent. When families and teachers don't understand each other's roles or don't feel that their ideas are valued, sometimes the following is expressed.

Responses of teachers might include:

"Parents don't care."

"Parents are too busy."

"Mothers are more concerned about themselves than their children."

"Couples today are more interested in buying things than in their children."

"Parents get mad when we call them."

"Parents don't discipline their children."

"Parents get in the way."

Responses of parents might include:

"Teachers don't want me there."

"My kids don't want me there."

"I don't have time."

"I'm paying them to take care of my kids."

"Teachers know more than I do."

"I wouldn't know what to do."

"I don't want to bake any more cookies."

"It is the only time I have to do my work."

"It is the only time I have to myself."

"I don't have a babysitter."

"I don't have a car."

"I don't have any days off from work left."

These responses reflect both attitudes and real concerns for teachers as well as families. Both must be addressed for true partnerships to form.

Roles of Parents/Families in Programs for Young Children

THEME 6   *in practice . . .*

Make a list of the ways in which you remember your parents being involved in your child-care/school experiences. Put the list aside while you read the following section.

The roles that parents and families play vary according to the ages of children, the inclusion of teachers, the preparation of adults to work with their children in school efforts, and the cultural disparities across families and schools. Nevertheless, parental involvement that supports children in their learning and positive attitudes toward school appears to have a positive effect on children's attitudes about and success in school (Henderson & Berla, 1994).

While parents and families should be considered a part of the school community, not all parents are prepared to take a role in schooling. Language and cultural barriers, disengagement of family members, educational backgrounds of parents, and attitudes of teachers and administrators are but a few of the factors that play into the concept of schools and families as partners in education. A role that works for one parent may not work for another. A parental role that works for one teacher may not work for another. Over the years, a number of distinct roles within models have emerged.

Ira Gordon provided an early model during the 1970s through his observations of parents and families of young children in the school community. He documented five roles of parents, which he represented as spokes on a wheel. First, and the most common role of parents, was parents as audience, in which they watch the performances and efforts of their children as spectators. Second, parents acted as **direct and active teachers** of their children at home. Third, parents served as **volunteers**. Fourth, parents served as **paid employees**. Finally, parents served as **decision makers.** These roles are not to be viewed in hierarchic order with the notion that parents must assume all these roles to be effective parents. Individual interests, time, and strengths of parents are all factors in any parental role (Gordon & Breivogel, 1976).

Since 1997, the work of Joyce Epstein has been at the forefront of research on parent involvement. Epstein has identified six types of parent involvement in her view of building school–family–community partnerships. These types are designed to assist parents and teachers as they prepare to build partnerships for the benefit of children across age groups:

1. Assisting parents with parenting skills and schools in understanding families
2. Communicating with families about school programs and progress through home-to-school and school-to-home communications
3. Involving families as volunteers and audiences at school and other locations as supporters of student learning
4. Involving families in working with their children in learning at home
5. Including families as decision makers through school councils, parent–teacher organizations, committees, and other parent groups
6. Providing services to the community and coordinating resources and services for families, students, and the school with businesses, agencies, and other community groups. (Epstein, Coates, Salinas, Sanders, &Simon, 1997)

Figure 2.2 provides some strategies to help teachers encourage parent involvement.

Susan Swap (1993) addressed the models of home–school relationships in her book *Developing Home–School Partnerships: From Concepts to Practice.* The models are (a) the protective model, (b) the school-to-home transition model, and (c) the curriculum enrichment model.

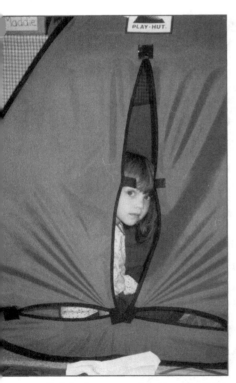

Quiet places provide time to think and be alone . . . so helpful when a child transitions from program(s) to home each day.

Protective Model.

The **protective model** is designed to separate the functions of school and home. Assumptions that characterize this model are as follows (Swap, 1993, p. 28):

- Parents delegate to the school the responsibility of educating their children.
- Parents hold school personnel accountable for the results.
- Educators accept this delegation of responsibility.

Although this model has been characteristic of both public and private school situations, it eliminates the notion that parents are their child's first and most important teachers and that the parents really know their child better than anyone else does. It also represents an example of situations in which parents are very willing to abdicate this aspect of their parenting duties. Some parents will do so because their self-regard in terms of what they think they know about their child is very low, because this was the way of their own parents, or because they are afraid to create or deal with possible conflict. This model would certainly not be advocated for parents seeking care of their young child.

FIGURE 2.2	Teacher Strategies to Encourage Parent Involvement in the 21st Century

1. For each family night, work with the children to decorate the room and set up the event. Excited children who just worked hard on getting the room ready can encourage families to come to family-night events.

2. Because TV is here to stay and there are some good shows on TV, develop a concise guide for parents to know how to utilize the PBS Ready to Learn and other areas of the www.pbs.org Web site and television shows. This will help parents stay in the loop—or as PBS says, in the "triangle" of VIEW, DO, READ—with their children.

3. To help families understand which academics for young children are appropriate and which may not be, send home a note or post on the class Web site one readiness skill the children worked on that day and how that skill is the foundation for other important skills later.

4. At morning circle, ask a few children each day (taking turns) to share something great they did with their families at home the night before. No event is too small or unimportant. This helps children realize the value of being with their families.

5. When children are playing and you notice they might be reenacting some violent movie, video game, or TV show, talk to them about the content and be creative in helping them truly understand the violence as well as alternatives. One teacher asked the children about a movie they were reinacting in the block area. When the children said the movie was too violent, the teacher suggested those 5-year-olds make their own movie (Damian, 2005). See some backstage action here: www.cpsd.us/tobin/directory/Damian/backstagestills/backstage.html and invite families to share in this learning experience.

6. Ask families if they would help you fill your Teachables from Trash box of discarded or unused items from home or their workplace. Collages can be so interesting if made from other families' items.

7. Check out the www.virtualpre-k.org Web site for some great ideas on how to bridge home and school with simple activities that involve everyday items familes have at home.

8. Set up a rotating schedule in which one child per evening is able to call you and talk to you for a few minutes on his or her parent's cell phone (send home notes in advance). Let families know that this is optional and children can call from any phone when it is their turn. Tell children they can also put their parents on the phone, too, especially if it is a speaker phone. This way, teachers are setting the stage for families to feel they can call the teacher as needed.

School-to-Home Transition Model. In the **school-to-home transition model,** parents' efforts in supporting the objectives of the school are encouraged and sought. Assumptions are as follows (Swap, 1993, p. 30):

- Children's achievement is fostered by continuity of expectations and values between home and school.
- School personnel should identify the values and practices outside school that contribute to school success.

- Parents should endorse the importance of schooling, reinforce school expectations at home, provide conditions at home that nurture development and support school success, and ensure that the child meets minimum academic and social requirements.

The role of parents in supporting the school through holding bake sales, building playgrounds, providing class materials, and preparing food for school parties typifies this model. Two-way communication is not actively sought or encouraged (Swap, 1993). Many of these tasks are also suited to those parents who are available, possess certain skills, and have the social know-how to fit into particular groups. This model does not reflect parents as being truly equal partners with school personnel in the care and education of children.

Curriculum Enrichment Model.

The **curriculum enrichment model** is representative of many early childhood programs and certainly of the advocacy works of such groups as NAEYC and SECA. Programs such as Head Start that advocate developmentally appropriate practices for young children and the view of parents as the child's first and most important teachers complete this category. The "logic" that drives this curriculum is that (a) continuity of learning between home and school is of critical importance in encouraging children's learning; (b) the values and cultural histories of many children are omitted from the standard school curriculum, leading to a disruption of this continuity between home and school and often to less motivation, status, and achievement for children in school; and (c) these omissions distort the curriculum, leading to a less accurate and less comprehensive understanding of events and achievements and to a perpetuation of damaging beliefs and attitudes about immigrant and oppressed minorities (Swap, 1993, p. 38).

Assumptions guiding this model are as follows (Swap, 1993, p. 39):

- Parents and educators should work together to enrich curriculum objectives and content.
- Relationships between home and school are based on mutual respect, and both parents and teachers are seen as experts and resources in the process of delivery.

This model provides many opportunities for schools to function "without walls" as parents and community members share their areas of expertise with children and children make sense of what they are learning in school as they see its relation to the outside world. Parents can serve as volunteers within the classroom, reading to children and assisting children in work with manipulatives and physical activities. Parents can play an active role in decision making with respect to services to children via such tools as site-based decision-making councils and policy councils. The child is seen as a part of a family system, with experiences at school affected by experiences at home and vice versa. Finally, this model, representative of the era of the 1960s from which it flourished, speaks to the interconnectedness of humans across and within frames of time and across and within locations of learning, be they home, school, or community.

In their comprehensive review of research addressing parental involvement in schools, Anne Henderson and Nancy Berla (1994) outlined four roles that reflect common themes found in the work of Gordon, Epstein, Swap, and others. Parents' participation in these roles appears to assist children in doing their best in school. These roles are as follows:

1. Parent as teacher creating a home environment that supports children in their learning
2. Parent as supporter contributing knowledge and skills to the schools, enriching the curriculum, and providing services and support to children
3. Parent as advocate negotiating the system for fair treatment and responsiveness of the system to families
4. Parent as decision maker participating in joint problem solving at every level, including councils and committees (Henderson & Berla, 1994)

When parents are enabled to play these key roles in quality school settings, children demonstrate heightened achievement scores, perform better in school, stay in school longer, and attend better schools.

In fact, the most accurate predictor of a student's achievement in school is not income or social status, but the extent to which the student's family is able to:

1. Create a home environment that encourages learning.
2. Express high (but not unrealistic) expectations for their children's achievement and future careers.
3. Become involved in their children's education at school and in the community. (Henderson & Berla, 1994, p. 1)

The rearing and educating of children is a complex task and requires the work of parents, families, teachers, caregivers, community leaders, policy makers, and others. Throughout history, the role of the family in relation to education has been altered by time and events. Since the beginning, however, the parent has been the child's first teacher, and the parent will see the course of the child's education across the school experience.

THEME 6   *in practice . . .*

Review your list of the ways in which you remember your parents being involved in your school experience. Review the roles described by Henderson and Berla and determine those taken by your family. Why do you think they chose those roles, or do you think they even had choices? How do your parents' roles compare with those of your classmates' parents? If someone other than your parents took part in your schooling, consider their roles in the same way. If you are a parent, consider your own roles. Have they changed from those of your parents? Why or why not? If you are a teacher, what expectations do you have of parent participation? Are they different from those of your family? Why or why not?

PREPARING TEACHERS TO BUILD PARTNERSHIPS WITH FAMILIES

T he concern for building partnerships with families has also been expressed by many groups, including state agencies governing the certification of teachers. Kentucky serves as one such example. This concern is reflected in both standards for new teacher and experienced teacher preparation.

New Teacher Standard VI: Collaborates with Colleagues/Parent/Others (Primary—Grade 5). The teacher collaborates with colleagues, parents, and other agencies to design, implement, and support learning programs that develop student abilities to use communication skills, apply core concepts, become self-sufficient individuals, become responsible team members, think and solve problems, and integrate knowledge (Kentucky Education Professional Standards Board, 1999, p. 5).

Interdisciplinary Early Childhood Education Teacher Performance Standards. These standards are very explicit about the extent of collaboration with family and community members, reflecting a broader definition of collaboration and community engagement.

Standard VI: Collaborates with Colleagues/Parents/Others. The early childhood educator shall collaborate and consult with the following to design, implement, and support learning programs for children: staff in a team effort; volunteers; families and primary caregivers; other educational, child care, health, and social services providers in an interagency and interdisciplinary team; and local, state, and federal agencies (Kentucky Education Professional Standards Board, 1995, p. 6).

Professional standards reflect the philosophical need for parent–teacher collaboration. Teachers, administrators, and college teachers talk about the need to include parents and families in the lives of children at school. However, how is philosophy really put into practice? Our greatest evidence is in early childhood programs. Early childhood teachers generally make home visits, work with parents on decision-making councils, hold parent conferences, incorporate parent volunteers into their programs, and engage parents in parent education activities.

Collaboration with families and communities takes thoughtful consideration by all those involved in the process.

Why are early childhood professionals getting the bulk of preparation to work with families? Perhaps it is because of the advocacy work of professional organizations and government agencies. Perhaps it is because of the very young ages and rapid growth changes of the children—that is, infants, toddlers, and preprimary years—and the mutual need for interdependence among families and caregivers/teachers. It certainly relates to the commitment to families and children of those involved in training programs, both on and off campuses. Head Start is a historic example of the focus on parent training and the training of teachers to work with parents. Over 40 years after the creation of Head Start, it remains an exemplary model for us.

As the children become more self-reliant, become dependent on peer interactions, and interact with larger numbers of teachers, parents often become more detached from schooling. Similarly, teachers report decreasing preparation to work with families across increasing grade levels (Wright, Daniel, & Heimelreich, 1999). As early childhood educators/caregivers, we should set the stage for parent involvement in programs for children. This involvement is needed throughout the course of the child's education, including the adolescent years. Teachers will need time and resources at the preservice and staff development levels to build strategies for working with families.

Goals 2000 and the subsequent No Child Left Behind Act of 2001, state standards, professional organization policy documents, and local policies all set a standard for the inclusion of parents, families, and communities in the school and caregiving experience. However, while intentions are worthy and express the concern for collaboration, they are not always carried out in practice. Teacher preparation, communication, attitudes, resources, and time are all factors that must continue to be addressed as we prepare ourselves and help others assist families in their roles with their children and adolescents.

THEME 6   *in practice . . .*

How were your parents involved in your middle and high school years with you? With your teachers? Why do you think most parents become less involved as children move from early childhood to high school? What lessons might other grade levels learn from early childhood programs? In retrospect, what would you have preferred for parent interaction across grade levels? How might you be involved with the schooling of children in your family?

Critical Concepts

1. Bronfenbrenner's human ecological system best describes the family as a system with entities inside and outside of the family.

2. In ancient times, children were taught the customs and rituals in the context of their families and community so they could learn to function as part of that culture and the culture could continue.

3. During the Middle Ages, clear distinctions among individuals emerged with the feudal system, and children were treated as miniature adults.

4. During the 1600s to the 1800s, children were considered to be born with original sin and were made to read the Bible and learn morals.

5. By the early 1800s, some philosophers saw the goodness of children and a reason to teach them important skills.

6. With the growth of agriculture, country children were born to provide more hands on the farm, and many city children labored in factories.

7. It was not until the early 1900s and the advent of the child study movement that children were nurtured.

8. The baby boom and launching of Sputnick in the 1950s sparked an interest in children as individuals with unique learning styles to be fostered by families and schools for more of these creative and scientific breakthroughs.

9. Laws and acts of the late 1990s and into the 21st century provide for the needs of every child, to make sure even those with the least economic means have a good education.

10. Research from the 1960s to the present day revealed some factors that impact children's school success and provided direction for important models for family–school–community collaborations.

Summary Statements

✓ Families operate as systems and are interconnected with other systems, including schools, churches, and other families.

✓ According to Bronfenbrenner, families function across microsystems, mesosystems, exosystems, macrosystems, and chronosystems.

✓ Families operate across environments, including the natural physical–biological environment, the human-built environment, and the sociocultural environment.

✓ A child's experiences with parents, families, and communities reflect the historical events that have occurred across time and the skills and resources that are needed to survive during that period of time.

✓ Across time, families have played a role in the education of their children. The methods of doing so have differed according to the context of the historical situation and the changes in survival strategies of families.

✓ The work of philosophers including Rousseau, Comenius, Pestalozzi, Locke, and Froebel played a significant role in promoting the importance of the early years and the critical role that parents, particularly mothers, played in nurturing their young children.

✓ The field of child study broadened at the turn of the 20th century, with theorists including Pestalozzi and Darwin publishing biographies of their own children.

✓ Disciplinary techniques for children have changed across time for many families. The notion of "original sin" and the harshness toward children to dispel their sinfulness has, in most situations, been replaced by more humanistic child-rearing practices.

✓ Children raised in situations of oppression are likely to be parented in more direct ways to ensure their safety.

✓ Goals 2000, professional standards for teacher certification, and position papers of organizations are examples of public documents that support the involvement of families in schools and caregiving situations.

✓ There is often a gap in philosophical concerns about working with families and the actual practice of engaging families and communities in "schooling."

✓ Programs such as Head Start have historically been involved in parent inclusion and preparation of their teachers and staff members to include parents in a variety of roles.

✓ With changes in family structure and employment, more children are entering child care much earlier in life and decision making regarding rearing of the child is done in collaboration with child-care providers.

✓ More children are attending preschool programs earlier, and families encounter many adults who interact and impact the behavior of their children.

✓ Several models can describe parent involvement roles. These include those suggested by Gordon, Swap, Epstein, and Henderson and Berla.

Research to Practice: Classroom Applications and Activities

1. Divide into small groups. Using chart paper and markers, prepare a timeline that reflects the role of families in the lives of children. Each group may select given centuries so that discussion can be more focused on specific time periods. Discuss reasons that parents may have assumed particular roles during this time. Be prepared to share your beliefs with the other groups.

2. Review the information about how families function as systems within the context of other systems. Think about your family. List the entities that affect the functioning and well-being of your family. Group those according to whether they are representative of the natural physical–biological, human-built, or sociocultural environment. Share your findings with other members of your class to note similarities and differences and issues that you may have overlooked.

3. Discuss the perceived role of children during the time of the ancient Greeks and Romans. Do any examples in today's world seem to replicate in any way the use of children for the benefit of a group? Discuss your thoughts with fellow classmates.

4. Describe evidence of children being viewed or expected to act as miniature adults today. Consider their care, the media, fashion, discipline, and so forth.

5. Do library research on the practice of infanticide. Do any countries practice infanticide today? If so, what is the role of the parent or family in this practice?

6. Do library research on world events during the time of World War II. These

might include the funding of child-care centers in the United States, the Holocaust in Germany, and the going to war by fathers across the world. What effects might these events have had on the role of parents at that time, and what possible lasting effects could they have had on parenting today?

7. Visit a local Head Start program. List the ways in which the curriculum enrichment model of parent involvement is implemented.

CHAPTER 3

Parent and Child Advocacy

The Role of the School and the Early Childhood Professional

Effective public policy advocacy work requires intentionality, which in turn requires organization. If all of us work independently without a well-defined vision and capacity to act and react to changing political, social and economic contexts, we will not make the progress that is needed. If we work together strategically, we can cause the changes that we seek for children, families, and professionals in the field.

NAEYC AFFILIATE PUBLIC POLICY TOOL KIT, 2004, P. 4

KEY TERMS

Americans with Disabilities Act (ADA)

barriers to advocacy

child advocacy

Child Development Associate

child poverty rates

collaboration

DAP

deficit model

early childhood education (ECE)

early intervention

family advocacy

family policy

The First Sixty Months

four Cs

Great Society

Head Start

NAEYC

NASBE

National Governors Association

parent activist group

parent interest group

P.L. 99-457

P.L. 101-476

P.L. 102-119

policy process

project approach

PTA/PTO

public choice theory

Reggio Emilia approach

Right From the Start

zeitgeist

GUIDING QUESTIONS

1. What are definitions of advocacy and public choice theory?
2. Why are parents and teachers sometimes reluctant to become involved in advocacy efforts, and what are common barriers to advocacy involvement?
3. When did child advocacy first evolve in the United States?
4. What were key events of the pre–World War II and post–World War II eras?
5. How has the definition of the child changed in the United States over the past 200 years?
6. What are key steps to the policy process, according to Dye?
7. What are parent interest groups and why are they key to effective child advocacy in school settings?

A t no other time in American history has the need for child and family advocacy been greater, and schools are assuming a greater responsibility for this critical role. The complex issues facing schools and communities, such as changing family forms and transitions, racial and linguistic diversity, societal and domestic violence, threats to security, and terrorism from abroad, require schools to assume a proactive stance.

In terms of advocacy, the rationale for the natural linkages between school and family is strong. The most widely recommended "solution" to the problems that confront American society is more and better schooling (Dye, 1992, p. 162). Social science research also suggests that when children perceive that the school is an extension of or substitute for their families, academic performance is enhanced. In addition, parents' choices among schools and school options not only improve academic achievement but also increase parents' satisfaction and teacher morale (Dye, 1992).

Providing an opportunity for parents to voice their concerns and issues in a constructive and organized manner is an important advocacy role for schools that serve young children. From a policy perspective, the issues that affect parents, families, and children have never been more significant or visible. The evolution of child and family policy to the forefront of both state and federal legislative agendas is unprecedented (Kagan, 1989, 1992; Stegelin, 1992; Weikart, 1989). We have already discussed significant pieces of legislation that affect the well-being of children with special needs and their families (see P.L. 99-457 and the IDEA legislation in chapter 5). In addition, the emergence of the Reggio Emilia approach to **early childhood education (ECE)** is providing convincing evidence of the power of parent involvement and the significant contributions parents can make to the curriculum and quality of their children's daily school lives.

Justifying the school's role in supporting advocacy efforts is not difficult, because considerable documentation establishes a clear relation between successful experiences during the early childhood years and subsequent adult development (Lazar, Darlington, Murray,

From a policy perspective, the issues that affect parents, families, and children have never been more significant.

Royce, & Snipper, 1982; Schweinhart & Weikart, 1986, 1992). Add to this research documentation the U.S. demographic data reflecting increased maternal employment; higher divorce rates, **child poverty rates**, and at-risk status; increased incidence of HIV/AIDS and drug-related cases; and the changing welfare scenario, and the result is a growing need for parents and children to be supported and empowered through effective advocacy.

This chapter addresses the role of the school and the early childhood professional in collaborating with parents and families to ensure that the voice of the child and his or her parents and family will be heard. Decision makers who develop, implement, and evaluate child and family policy, particularly as it relates to the care and education of young children, need to be informed about the pressing issues of contemporary families and schools. Included are the following themes:

Theme 1. Advocacy issues for children and families are increasingly complex because of societal trends related to domestic and community violence, changing family forms, and increasing cultural and linguistic diversity.

Theme 2. Child and family advocacy themes have developed over time. Knowing common definitions of advocacy terms and themes will facilitate becoming an effective child advocate.

Theme 3. Effective advocacy strategies for early childhood settings require an understanding of the special issues that exist for children and families and how to match strategies to those issues and needs.

Theme 4. Schools have become active in child advocacy, and several examples of recent successful advocacy initiatives are described.

Theme 5. Collaboration among families, schools, and the community is essential for effective advocacy to take place. Understanding this important collaborative role will facilitate the development of new advocacy efforts.

> Never before have so many different individuals, child populations, interest groups and agencies been involved in the early childhood movement. . . . There is a wide window of opportunity for parents, teachers, school officials, and state education officials to impact directly the policy process on behalf of young children. (Stegelin, 1992, p. x)

THE EVOLUTION OF CHILD AND FAMILY ADVOCACY OVER TIME

B eing able to advocate freely for child and family issues within a political arena is a relatively new phenomenon in the United States. Only in recent years have politicians found it advantageous to talk about the very real and personal issues of child care, maternal and paternal leave, and other sensitive family issues:

> For as long as I can remember, Americans have found it very difficult to talk about family policy as a political issue. I think that is largely because we are a country that has (as one of its foremost values) the importance of individualism, the importance of individual families, and the idea that the government ought not to reach into individual or

family life any more than is absolutely necessary. Furthermore, I think that whenever we talk about family policy as a political issue, we can't help bringing to bear our own experiences and our own understandings. Sometimes, that can be very painful, and it is always very personal. (Clinton, 1992, p. 21)

Definitions

Advocacy, according to *Merriam-Webster's New Collegiate Dictionary* (2003), is "the act or process of advocating or supporting a cause or proposal" (p. 19). The term *advocacy* is used in this text to refer to organized efforts and initiatives whose goal or cause is to improve services and programs for young children, their parents, or their families. **Child advocacy** refers to focused initiatives to improve services for children in general or a target group of children with defined needs. **Family advocacy** refers to advocacy initiatives designed to better the lives of all families or families with specific or defined needs.

Advocacy is also used in a broad manner to include both formal and informal efforts to seek needed services, enhancements, visibility, and innovations related to meeting the needs of young children and their families. Advocacy and policy are surely related; focused, well-organized advocacy initiatives can result in policy changes.

Formal advocacy efforts are sometimes associated with official policy-making efforts. James Buchanan, the Nobel Prize–winning economist and leading scholar in modern **public choice theory**, argues that individuals come together in the political process for their own mutual benefit. Public choice theory assumes that all political actors—parents, teachers, voters, taxpayers, interest groups, and other constituents—seek to maximize their personal benefits in politics, as well as in the marketplace (Dye, 1992).

Within the school setting, the roles of individuals related to child and family advocacy can range from very informal efforts at the local, grassroots level to moderately formalized efforts at the regional level to more formal and organized efforts that may lead directly to new legislation, change, or revision in existing law or other formal outcomes. Most parents and teachers of young children are engaged in less formal advocacy efforts, such as voting on educational options within a local school district, serving as assistants at the voting booths during elections, or actively engaging in a campaign effort for a local candidate who embraces a new idea or notion that will result in a desired educational outcome.

Some parents and teachers, however, are engaged actively in formalized advocacy efforts that lead directly to new legislation or policy changes within school settings. These individuals may hold offices in decision-making groups that effect change within the educational community, serve as representatives for a local or state jurisdiction, or vote directly on legislative initiatives. Thus, the range of involvement in advocacy efforts varies greatly in most school settings.

Barriers to Advocacy Efforts

According to Lombardi (1986, p. 65), individuals such as early childhood teachers and parents of young children are frequently hesitant to become involved in advocacy or policy-related efforts on behalf of children and families. Common **barriers to advocacy** include the following:

- Feelings of powerlessness to change anything
- Lack of knowledge regarding government regulations
- Fear of the political process
- Lack of confidence in their own expertise
- Lack of time

THEME 1   *in practice . . .*

Spring View Elementary School has an active parent-teacher organization. There is a growing number of Hispanic families in the school district, and the parent-teacher group has decided to advocate for a more defined and effective bilingual education program in Spanish. A small group of Asian parents is objecting to the focus on just Spanish. What are possible solutions?

As an example of the difficulty and challenge of making educational change in early childhood education, Schultz (1992) assessed the complexity of integrating developmentally appropriate practice **(DAP)** in early childhood school settings and identified the following six inhibitors to its quick and universal implementation:

1. The size and complexity of the educational system
2. The complexity of decision making
3. The scope of changes required in implementing DAP
4. The current policy focus on accountability
5. The shifting, never-ending demands placed on the educational system, making it difficult for schools to focus on any one agenda
6. The competing ideas and "packages of curriculum" promoted for early childhood education

In short, the advocacy process for teachers and parents within a school setting can be viewed as a series of political processes and activities that involves problem identification, formulation, legitimating, implementation, and evaluation (Dye, 1992). Advocacy, as used in this text, refers to more informal political processes on behalf of children and their families. But as the steps just described suggest, advocacy efforts can become, with time and organizational commitments, very real and effective political activities and processes. Figure 3.1 describes types of advocacy roles.

Parents who function within school systems today are more informed and consumer oriented than their predecessors were. They, with the support of informed and supportive teachers, can make a difference for children and families because they are in a position to identify salient issues as a consumer and then to organize, collaborate,

FIGURE 3.1	Types of Advocate Roles

- **Leaders:** People who provide vision and keep the advocacy effort on track.
- **Advisors:** People who are willing to share their special expertise with advocates and the policy makers that advocates are trying to influence.
- **Researchers:** People who can collect data and synthesize research reports into issue briefs and background papers.
- **Contributors:** Those who are willing to roll up their sleeves and participate in the nuts-and-bolts work of advocacy, from making phone calls to stuffing letters or marching in front of the state capitol.
- **Friends:** People who do not have the time or resources to participate in every aspect of the planning and implementation of advocacy, yet who care and can always be counted on to help when a push is needed.

Note. Adapted from *NAEYC Affiliate Public Policy Toolkit*, NAEYC, 2004, p. 14.

and communicate with decision makers so that services and programs for young children continuously improve.

> When schools were an integral part of stable communities, teachers quite naturally reinforced parental and community values. At school, children easily formed bonds with adults and experienced a sense of continuity and stability, conditions that were highly conducive to learning. (Comer, 1990, p. 23)

History of Advocacy for Children and Families

Pre–World War II Era. Child and family policy has evolved primarily through the outcomes of wars and national crises. During these times, families had to rely on extraordinary means to meet the demands of child care and family support (Stegelin, 1992). The earliest efforts to advocate for children and families can be found in the initiatives to establish child-care services for families in the 1800s. Child care began in the 1800s as a charitable function for women who worked outside the home only out of economic necessity, usually widows or wives of incapacitated husbands (Farnum, 1987). One of the first real national crises that resulted in expanded child-care needs was the Civil War. According to Farnum (1987), in the aftermath of the Civil War, churches and communities in some Eastern cities developed children's charities that cared for children while their mothers worked. These early initiatives at establishing child care were more like orphanages than today's developmentally appropriate child-care settings but are significant because they were the first vestiges of systematic child care in the United States.

The Depression brought about a few child-care centers that provided meals, play, and parent education. It was World War II, however, that brought government into the child-care business in a major way. Large centers for child care were developed in areas where many women were employed in munitions plants, shipyards, and other war-related industries. The growth of the child development movement in the United States during the 1920s also raised awareness of the well-being of the young child. University laboratory schools were established across the country and were used primarily as a means of studying young children (Irwin & Bushnell, 1980) and observing and recording their typical and atypical growth and development. Although it would take 50 years, until the 1970s, before child advocacy and active prochild legislation would come to fruition, the establishment of this network of laboratory schools serves as an important benchmark in the history of child development and child advocacy.

The 1960s brought about the Great Society and new programs for young children, such as Head Start.

Post–World War II Era. The era after World War II served as a transitional period. American families were changing rapidly, and child care was emerging as a growing need for these families. The persistent efforts of such states as California were responsible for maintaining the momentum toward national child-care concern and public policy.

THEME 2   *in practice . . .*

Susan King is a second-grade teacher in an inner city elementary school. There are many needs related to the language and cultural diversity of this school. Ms. King decides to form a parent advocacy group and to provide parent workshops on how to advocate for their children's educational needs. She develops a manual for parents that includes current terms related to advocacy, published in both English and Spanish. Discuss whether this is an appropriate role for a primary teacher.

In the 1960s, the research focus on children grew dramatically. Coupled with the child-focused initiatives of President Lyndon Johnson's **Great Society**, this research focus began to address such issues as the disadvantaged and at-risk child. The 1960s saw a renaissance of interest in ECE as a means of addressing issues related to child and family poverty (Schweinhart & Weikart, 1986). A clear link between the positive outcomes of early childhood programs for children from low-income families and longitudinal research findings was also established. The **early intervention** movement began to emerge, couched primarily within a **deficit model**. At that time, early childhood intervention represented the main early childhood initiative. As a result, federal and state funds began to be used for programs for young children before they entered public school settings. Kindergarten programs expanded, and the Head Start program was born. Thus, the 1960s marked a significant passage for early childhood policy. The field began to be defined as more than child care, and in its place came the concept of ECE as being a comprehensive, developmental focus on young children, ages birth to 8 years, with special attention to youngsters with special needs (Stegelin, 1992).

The 1970s was a decade of expansion of programs and initiatives for young children and their families. Teacher training programs proliferated in the areas of child development and ECE. The federally sponsored **Child Development Associate** program was born in an effort to make available competency-based training programs for individuals who desired to work with younger children. Research methods became more refined and collaborative. Such fields as education, sociology, psychology, medicine, and related areas began to conduct interdisciplinary research on children and families. Parent education became an important and noted part of educational settings for young children. Children began to be viewed as complex, evolving individuals who have very special developmental needs in four distinct areas: social, cognitive, emotional, and psychomotor.

The New Era. The 1980s marked an escalation in policy efforts for young children. For example, the **National Governors Association** focused on children's issues and hosted a national conference and final report entitled *The First Sixty Months* (National Governors Association & Center for Policy Research, 1987). Then Governor Richard Riley of South Carolina urged governors to continue playing expanding roles in the development of legislation to support ECE programs (Riley, 1986). More than half the states adopted new legislation that expanded programs for young children (Schweinhart & Weikart, 1986), and New York City's prekindergarten program was established for more than 100,000 4-year-olds (McCormick, 1986). **Head Start** continued to expand at the federal level, and a general awareness of early childhood education developed in both federal and state policy arenas. By the end of the 1980s, 3 of every 10 U.S. children under the age of 5 were enrolled in child-care homes, child-care centers, or nursery schools (Schweinhart, 1992). The 100th Congress introduced more than 100 child- and family-related bills, many with bipartisan sponsorship (Kagan, 1989). In 1988, **NASBE** released a comprehensive task force report entitled *Right From the Start*, which advocated a clear and defined role and responsibility of the public schools in the development of futuristic ECE programs for young children and their families. During the 1980s, state departments of education also established new divisions of ECE that were designed to strengthen both the research and practice components of the public school's involvement with young children.

During the 1990s, policy on behalf of children and families came full circle. Once an uncomfortable issue, **family policy** came into its own during this decade as political candidates embraced platforms that openly addressed such issues as family medical leave, maternity and paternity leave, child-care vouchers, services for special needs children, and advocacy rights of parents and families. Presidential candidates' campaigns featured young children and their parents' needs and concerns related to accessible, affordable, and appropriate child care, as well as government-sponsored school programs for younger children, both typical and atypical in their development.

Toffler, in *The Third Wave* (1981), stated, "A powerful tide is surging across much of the world today creating a new, often bizarre, environment in which to work, play, marry, raise children or retire" (p. 1). Innovative school–business partnerships continued to develop during the 1990s as corporate America awakened to the crucial needs of working parents and young children in a variety of ways. School–business partnerships focused on providing more child-care options for employees, as well as on forming formal working relations between corporations and specific schools for the purposes of financial assistance and innovative program development. Corporations came to be more concerned about the well-being of young children and the skill levels of American school children in the areas of literacy and mathematics. Quality ECE programs came to be seen as a wise investment in the future workforce and as a guarantee that the baby boomer generation would be supported adequately by a well-prepared and well-educated younger generation of workers.

THEME 3   *in practice . . .*

Centerview Elementary has a 90% rate of free and reduced lunches for its child population, and childhood obesity is a growing problem. The administration decides to develop new guidelines for food served at the school. Teachers are encouraged to create more physically active teaching strategies and to work closely with parents to improve food selection and increase physical activity at home. Is this an appropriate form of child advocacy for this particular school? What issues related to multiculturalism should be considered?

The Changing Definition of the Child.   The evolution of policy for young children mirrors a changing definition of the child in U.S. culture. As the 1990s began to unfold in the United States, the ways that Americans viewed the child reflected deeply rooted changes in the fabric of society (Stegelin, 1992). The deficit model associated with the early intervention movement begun in the 1960s gave way to a more comprehensive and holistic view of the child as part of a functioning, vital family constellation. As a result of 7 decades of building a policy agenda in support of the young child and her or his family, the term *early childhood education* has come to have a collective meaning that includes child care, early intervention, at-risk children, preschool, kindergarten, and a host of family support and parent education programs.

It is politically correct to act on behalf of young children, their parents, and their families. With the arrival of the new millennium, the need to provide a rationale and argument for quality programs for children and families has evolved into a need to develop new and innovative state and federal policies that combine existing resources so that collaborative programs for children and parents are an integral part of our educational system. Kagan (1989) described this evolution of early childhood policy as a much more sophisticated, integrated, comprehensive, and family-oriented level of program and policy operation than the United States had experienced prior to the 1980s.

EFFECTIVE ADVOCACY STRATEGIES IN EARLY CHILDHOOD SETTINGS

F rom the preceding discussion, it is apparent that advocacy efforts and policy initiatives, even those developed informally by parents in school settings, can be creative, imaginative, purposeful, and effective. This section focuses on several types and strategies of advocacy for children and families within school settings or child-care arrangements.

Dye (1992) describes several models of politics in *Understanding Public Policy*. His understanding of the policy process is clear, and he suggests ways to determine whether a strategy or process is effective for its given purpose. Dye suggests that a policy strategy should clarify reality and identify what is significant. In addition, the strategy should facilitate problem solving and extend meaningful inquiry and research.

Organizing the Policy Process

Advocacy efforts on behalf of young children and their families that occur within the school setting can take many forms. These informal but organized efforts may, for example, take a simple but effective direction, described as **policy process**. Dye (1992) suggests the policy process should include such steps as identifying the problem, formulating policy proposals and possibilities, establishing an agenda to encourage public discourse, deciding on a strategy, and then building political support for the strategy. Dye elaborates on more formal processes for government and bureaucracies. Teachers will find Dye's suggestions helpful, but the ideas need to be adapted to the less formal advocacy processes of the school setting.

The effective ECE advocacy strategies discussed next are less formal than organized political action groups, but they may evolve from grassroots advocacy initiatives to more systematically organized political processes. Figure 3.2 describes advocacy strategies for classroom teachers.

Parent Interest Groups

A **parent interest group** may formulate its own policy proposals, perhaps in association with key decision makers within the school setting or the surrounding community. These key individuals might include a school administrator, superintendent, local political representative, respected community leader, Congressional representative, and other appropriate individuals. Interest group staff often brings valuable technical knowledge to the formation of a policy process. An interest group forms when a sufficient number of individuals, usually parents and teachers, desire to address a specific issue or concern.

FIGURE 3.2   Advocacy Strategies for Classroom Teachers

1. Serve as a contact person for a key issue or concern, and let parents, other teachers, and community members know of your special interest. Provide organizational leadership to bring advocates together to address this special issue.

2. Become a volunteer in an organization or group that supports children's rights; provide support for parent and community activists who are engaged in advocacy efforts in this organization.

3. Create a Parent Wall or Parent Space in your classroom where you can post important information about child advocacy efforts, organizations that focus on children with special needs, parenting support, and other information relevant to child and family advocacy.

4. Invite administrators, community leaders, and legislators into your classroom to observe, visit with the parents, and interact with the children. Make these decision makers aware of the pressing issues in your classroom, such as resource needs for parents and children, specialized services for children with special needs, the challenges of linguistic and cultural diversity, and other needs defined by the child and family population in your classroom.

5. Engage the children in your classroom in a project that models advocacy. For example, adopt a senior center, orphanage, children's hospital, or a school in another country. Become pen pals with these individuals and incorporate this advocacy initiative into your classroom curriculum.

6. Join other teachers and professionals in your school or center to advocate for a particular cause, and let the parents, children, and community know of your involvement. For example, you and five of your coteachers and administrators could participate in a Walk for Muscular Dystrophy project. You could include this information in your classroom or Web-based newsletter, post it on flyers in your room and throughout the school, and publicize it through the local media.

7. Encourage the children in your classroom to study, understand, and apply key concepts of advocacy. Engage them in letter writing, video presentations, and other effective means of advocacy to boost their own confidence in expressing their concerns about the welfare of others.

Examples of interest groups that might form within the school setting for younger students and children are:

- Attention deficit disorder
- Sex education
- Down syndrome
- Child management and discipline
- Learning disability
- Drug awareness and prevention
- After-school care
- Technology in the school and home

- Nutrition and health issues
- Curriculum integration
- School transportation
- Testing and assessment
- HIV/AIDS
- Developmentally appropriate learning settings
- Mixed-age classroom
- Inclusion in the classroom

Purposes of Parent Interest Groups. Interest groups can vary widely in terms of size, frequency of meeting, diversity of parent makeup, resources available, and amount of school personnel support. Interest groups can serve multiple purposes:

- Provide an informal forum for parents, teachers, and other individuals to discuss a focused issue or concern.
- Serve as a springboard for a formal advocacy or policy initiative.
- Serve as a means of bringing diverse families together.
- Become a community source of information and serve in a collaborative role with other community agencies.
- Provide current information through the sharing of books, journals, magazines, videos, and other educational means in an inexpensive, timely way.
- Provide a forum for constructive dialogue between parents and teachers or other school representatives.
- Become part of the systematic parent education and family involvement component of the school setting.

Parent-Organized Advocacy or Activist Groups

Parents can be tremendously effective in forming their own power-based groups, especially if (a) a central and committed core group of parents serve as leaders, (b) the level of commitment to the project is high, (c) parents understand the

THEME 4   *in practice . . .*

The Reggio Emilia schools of Italy are influencing the role of schools in child advocacy. Supporting the rights of children is considered to be an important role of the schools in Reggio Emilia. Discuss whether it is appropriate to use international approaches as advocacy models for schools in the United States. What issues should be considered when adopting international models or approaches?

give-and-take of the policy process, (d) parents understand the time that will be required, and (e) parents are able to solicit and recruit effective individuals to help them with their cause.

For example, Anderson (1992) described her efforts as a parent involved with a **parent activist group** advocating for a developmentally appropriate curriculum and classroom for kindergarten children in their Baltimore school district. Issues effectively addressed by this parent activist group included overcrowding of classrooms, lack of teacher aides, inadequate child–teacher ratios, and lack of administrative personnel and support to implement developmentally appropriate classrooms. The steps to forming an effective parent activist group are as follows:

1. Become organized, with adequate parent representation.
2. Write a proposal for change or to address specific issues.
3. Focus the parent group's efforts and develop a strategy.
4. Write letters of support to key decision makers.
5. Conduct follow-up and monitoring of desired change.
6. Evaluate and reinforce positive changes made by key decision makers and practitioners.

Anderson's (1992) poignant and realistic story of this Baltimore kindergarten parent group gives insight into the power of parents when they are organized and committed to change. Their story documents firsthand the struggle that they experienced as they changed traditional kindergarten classrooms to more developmentally appropriate classrooms for their daughters and sons. Perhaps most salient in Anderson's account is the commitment to time, struggle, negotiation, and perseverance that is required for successful parent advocacy groups. Anderson vividly describes lessons learned from this experience:

■ Form a strong core group of three to five very committed people who share responsibility for leadership. They need to talk with each other often and to give each other personal support when things look bleak.
■ Learn to call people "in the know" and ask their advice. Make contacts with "friendly" people in power. Start with one or two names and go from there. Pave the way for each request or demand.
■ Be willing to stick your neck out and demand that something be done even when you are told that it is impossible. Although this does not always work, parents become recognized as a force to be contended with.
■ Have teachers with energy, commitment, and the ability to adapt and learn; this is absolutely key. No amount of parent effort can make up for unwilling or unskilled teachers.
■ Have a coordinator who is in a position to mediate change and communication related to the school's curriculum, learning environment, teacher training, and other salient issues.

Figure 3.3 gives suggestions for selecting a site for an advocacy meeting.

FIGURE 3.3	Selecting a Site for an Advocacy Meeting: Questions for Teachers to Ask

- Are parents and other individuals familiar with the meeting site?
- Does the site reinforce the message of your advocacy event?
- Is the site comfortable and accessible for a diverse group of parents?
- Is there adequate parking, including for people with disabilities?
- Is the site large enough to accommodate the size of the group you anticipate?
- Will you be able to fill the space, or should you consider a smaller space?
- Can child care be provided appropriately?
- Does the site already have necessary equipment, chairs, tables, platforms, and outlets?
- Are there three-prong outlets for sound equipment?
- Are there microphones available? What kind and how many?
- Is the site conducive to verbal exchange, conversations, and oral presentations?
- Are conditions adequate: accessible restrooms, air conditioning and heating, insured?
- Do you need volunteers to help set up the event? How many and what types of volunteers?
- Can you provide refreshments and visual aids for participants?

Note. Adapted form *NAEYC Affiliate Public Policy Toolkit*, NAEYC, 2004, p. 42.

Reggio Emilia–Inspired Project Groups

The early childhood programs of Reggio Emilia, Italy, are influencing American preschool settings in an increasingly systematic manner. The view of the young child is perhaps the most crucial concept that has affected American efforts to understand and adapt this highly regarded early childhood approach. Central to the view of the child is the critical role of the parent in the life of the child and the school:

> Parents are considered to be an essential component of the program, and many among them are part of the advisory committee running each school. The parents' participation is expected and supported and takes many forms: day-to-day interaction, work in the schools, discussions of educational and psychological issues, special events, excursions, and celebrations. Parents are an active part of their children's learning experience and, at the same time, help ensure the welfare of all children in the school. (Gandini, 1997, p. 17)

Reggio Emilia's philosophy of schooling as a system of relationships (Malaguzzi, 1993) is put into practice in such a way that high-quality and enduring relationships are an integral part of children's lives. These relationships are reinforced and encouraged through the physical environments of the early childhood center, documentation of children's growth and progress, systematic involvement of parents in the curriculum planning and implementation, close ties between the (Reggio Emilia) schools and the surrounding community, and highly personalized exchanges between teachers and parents (New, 1998).

Parent involvement via Reggio Emilia preschools is redefining parent involvement in many American preschools. "I am the teacher; you are the parent; I'll explain education to you" is no longer valid for many preschool teachers in the United States (Geiger, 1997, p. 143). Indeed, the parent is seen as an important partner in the learning process. Parent involvement in Reggio Emilia schools includes participating in the daily routine; being involved in teacher–parent conferences throughout the year; planning for special events and projects; and facilitating fund-raising events, picnics, and other school-wide activities. Parents become partners with their children and the teachers both in the classroom and on the playground.

Parents can become involved in long-term projects, typified by the project approach of Reggio Emilia.

Examples of this high level of parent involvement can be seen in special projects that are representative of the **project approach**. The project approach, an integral part of the **Reggio Emilia approach**, involves children, teachers, parents, community representatives, and other supportive individuals in the planning, implementing, and evaluating of longer term learning projects. The project approach is influencing early childhood curriculum in the United States and is a key way that parents are becoming more involved in their children's learning experiences.

Projects may last several days, several weeks, or even many months. The project approach encourages children to plan an activity, project, or special event around a special interest of a small group of students. Documentation of projects is extensive throughout the Reggio Emilia schools, and examples can be found on the playground as well as in the classroom. Through the project approach, parents become advocates for their children's learning by helping to plan the curriculum; securing materials and needed resources; spending time building or developing the project; assisting the teacher with documentation through photographs, portfolios, or other means; and giving valuable feedback to the teacher and children about the experience.

School-Based Parent–Teacher Groups

On a national level, a system of parent groups—PTAs and Parent Teacher Organizations (PTOs)—has been established at schools. The level of organization of these groups varies widely from school district to school district. The advantage of these types of parent advocacy groups is that they have potential political power because of the large numbers of parents who are members. Many states hold local, regional, and state conventions of PTA or PTO groups, and in some states, these parent groups are courted by national educational associations or teacher lobbying groups. Usually, parents join these groups at the beginning of the school year, officers are elected, and an agenda for fund-raising and special school events is established. These groups are also effective in strengthening the relationships between parents and teachers, and teacher appreciation and teacher recognition days are an important part of these parent group agendas. For parents seeking an already established group with potential political power, the existing **PTA/PTO** may be a good choice. Parents who are advocates for curriculum changes, transportation improvements, enhanced after-school programs, developmentally appropriate primary classrooms, and reduced teacher–child ratios may wish to assume a leadership role in one of these school-based groups and provide needed direction for these causes.

EXAMPLES OF RECENT ADVOCACY INITIATIVES SUPPORTED BY SCHOOLS

The history of child and family policy has been described briefly, and it reflects an ongoing process of change and growth. Conflict between child-centered and instructional approaches, for example, has a history extending back to the first public-school kindergarten (Goffin, 1992). In 1908, Gregory stated:

> In passing from the kindergarten to the primary school, there is a break. Do what you will to soften the change, to modify the break, it still remains a break. Three general methods of dealing with the difficulty have been employed: (1) To provide a connecting class to take the child out of his kindergarten habits and introduce him to those of the primary school; in the words of some teachers, "to make him over." (2) To modify the kindergarten and make it more nearly resemble the primary schools. (3) To modify the primary school to make it more nearly resemble the kindergarten. (cited in Goffin, 1992, p. 22)

THEME 5   *in practice . . .*

Parkview Elementary School utilizes 14 modular classrooms to accommodate explosive growth in the school district. Parents have formed an advocacy group to seek financial and political support from local businesses and government agencies. Discuss whether this is an acceptable role for a school-supported parent-teacher advocacy group.

When we consider this description of the needs of kindergarten children in 1908, we readily recognize the more contemporary efforts to establish transitional first grades, to make first- through third-grade classrooms more developmentally appropriate, and to make kindergarten classrooms more like primary classrooms. History seems to repeat itself in this case.

Advocacy on behalf of children and families is an important part of American educational and social history. Issues that have received the most attention from child advocates include child-care accessibility and quality, developmentally appropriate learning environments, services for special needs and at-risk children, child poverty, child health concerns, and child violence. Recent examples of successful advocacy efforts on behalf of young children are provided in the following sources:

National Association for the Education of Young Children. **(NAEYC).** (1984). *Accreditation criteria and procedures of the National Academy of Early Childhood Programs.* Washington, DC: Author.

    These guidelines have provided a framework for the systematic improvement of child-care and early childhood learning environments and the provision of developmentally appropriate care and education in the United States.

National Association of State Boards of Education (NASBE). (1988). *Right from the start: Report of the NASBE task force on early childhood education.* Alexandria, VA: Author.

    This report, resulting from a task force study of the needs of young children in school settings, has helped standardize developmentally appropriate philosophy and programs for young children in public school settings. Advocates included parents, teachers, and administrators of schools serving preschool children, as well as national leaders of educational and advocacy organizations.

P.L. 99-457, the Education of the Handicapped Act Amendments of 1986.

    This public law provides for the services of young children with special needs, beginning at age 3, by the respective school district. Parents of special needs children, as well as early intervention researchers, practitioners, and policy makers, were responsible for a large part of the successful lobbying that resulted in this legislation in 1986.

P.L. 101-476, IDEA.

    Regulations governing IDEA require that children with disabilities be placed in the least restrictive environment (LRE) in which the individual child will learn.

P.L. 102-119, or Part H of the IDEA legislation of 1991.

    This public law requires that early intervention services be provided in regular settings with typically developing children, as appropriate for each child. The term *natural environments* is used to refer to regular settings for typically developing age peers.

Americans with Disabilities Act (ADA) of 1990.

    This act sets into place a broad range of services for individuals with disabilities. It requires businesses and publicly sponsored agencies to adapt to and provide services for individuals with special equipment and developmental needs. Included in this act are specifications for accessibility to public buildings and rest rooms, design of doorways and curbs, and other dimensions of the physical environment.

Bredekamp, S., & Rosegrant, T. (Eds.). (1992). *Reaching potentials: Appropriate curriculum and assessment for young children* (Vol. 1). Washington, DC: National Association for the Education of Young Children.

    This book is a compilation of guidelines by experts in the fields of ECE and early childhood special education that facilitates decision-making about assessment strategies for young children in various learning settings. Child advocates, including parents, teachers, teacher preparation professionals, educational leaders, and testing/assessment experts, all contributed to the advocacy effort that led to this important publication, which now influences decision making of individuals responsible for screening and assessing preschool children in educational settings.

SCHOOL, COMMUNITY, AND FAMILY COLLABORATION IN SUPPORTING THE NEEDS OF CHILDREN AND FAMILIES

> Today's schools are expected to do many things: resolve racial conflict and build an integrated society; inspire patriotism and good citizenship; provide values, aspirations, and a sense of identity to disadvantaged children; . . . reduce conflict in society by teaching children to get along with others and to adjust to group living; . . . fight disease and poor health through physical education, health training, and even medical treatment; . . . end malnutrition and hunger through school lunch and milk programs; fight drug abuse and educate children about sex; . . . In other words, nearly all the nation's problems are reflected in demands placed on the nation's schools. (Dye, 1992, p. 162)

Family–school involvement is a two-way street (Edwards & Young, 1992), and school professionals are having to rethink what they want for children and what they expect from families and communities. Where should schools draw the line? Are schools the new and primary place where the interwoven needs of children are to be met (Edwards & Young, 1992)? Schools must do more than encourage parent and family involvement within the classroom, which is frequently isolated from the broader context of the family itself. Schools must do more than become referral sources for other community agencies and service providers. Schools, in fact, are becoming the hub of multiple-service brokerage for children and their families.

Several efforts currently under way are redefining the relationships of school, family, and community. School professionals are forging new alliances and partnerships with community organizations and agencies. Schools are expanding their definitions of *family* to include single parents, working parents, foster parents, grandparents, and others who have significant responsibilities for children. They are challenging the separateness of systems designed to support children and their families (Edwards & Young, 1992).

Once again, we call on the ecosystem model (Bronfenbrenner, 1979) to help in understanding the need for interrelationships for children and their families. School professionals are becoming more creative at developing styles and strategies that acknowledge this important interrelationship of the social context and the individual. Moving to broader notions of community alliances means moving beyond incremental thinking for assessing the needs of parents, teachers, schools, and communities. Edwards and Young (1992) make recommendations regarding the role of the school in establishing an environment conducive to child and family advocacy. These recommendations suggest that family strengths should be the foundation of home/school strategies and that efforts should be focused on preventive strategies. They also emphasize the importance of school personnel making an effort to know and understand the children and families whom they serve, including families' social and economic stressors. Because of the complexity of contemporary families, both schools and teachers must utilize multiple strategies and approaches for reaching out to families and for identifying needed resources for them.

Borrowing from the Reggio Emilia early childhood programs of northern Italy, we can draw important parallels about the role of the school in advocating for young children and their families. New (1998) implored U.S. educators to view the child and the rights of the child in a much more committed and impassioned way.

> Thus, the gift of Reggio Emilia's illustrious example comes in the form of a challenge to American educators—a challenge not only to improve our practices and to align them more closely with our beliefs, but also to learn how to draw public attention to our work and to the children for whom we are working. It behooves us, if we truly wish to take advantage of what Reggio Emilia has to offer, to turn to the mirror our Italian friends hold up so that we might better know ourselves, discover children's capabilities, and acknowledge our responsibilities. Surely these are the most critical "next steps" that we can take on behalf of young children in our society. Reggio Emilia can point the way. But we must decide if we wish to follow. (New, 1998, p. 233)

The marginal status of American children is reflected in the paradox of the United States' having both the highest standard of living and the highest rate of child poverty among all industrialized nations (New, 1998).

Essential Components of Quality ECE Programs

Today, the debate over the role of the school in ECE is ready to move beyond the question of *whether* to the question of *how*. Necessary conditions for quality early childhood programs in school settings should include placing children in small groups, employing formally trained teachers who are caring and well prepared and administrative leadership that is knowledgeable about child development, demonstrating a clear underpinning of child development and theory, implementing a defined and cohesive curriculum, and fostering a partnership between parents and teachers (Molnar, 1991).

Schools play a crucial role in the continuous improvement of programs for young children. Perhaps in no other arena is the need for leadership for young children greater than in the school environment. The school setting should become a place where parents can gather, exchange ideas and concerns, seek advice and assistance, and know that the goals for their children are shared by the school's teachers and administrators.

School and community leadership must be committed to appropriate practice throughout child care, prekindergarten, kindergarten, and the early primary grades. The school's leadership role also includes a commitment to providing financial support, developing the staff, retraining teachers and administrators so that sound ECE can be accomplished, and providing space and time to support the advocacy efforts of parents.

Role of Collaboration in Child and Family Policy

The Task Force believes that when collaboration among early childhood programs does not occur, programs often compete for limited resources and staff, as well as for children and families. On the other hand, collaborative efforts can facilitate joint planning for staff development, and provide community for children and families. . . . [C]ollaborative networks can provide a strong voice for increasing needed resources for early childhood programs. (NASBE, 1988, p. 6)

Collaboration and *team effort* are terms that have become commonplace in early childhood education. Kagan (1991) stated that, "whether motivated by democratic ideals to assure involvement of all or by the latent skepticism that elicited our elaborate system of checks and balances, creating associations, organizations, and complex bureaucracies seems to be an inherent characteristic of our national psyche" (p. ix). Kagan goes on to define collaboration as "organizational and interorganizational structures where resources, power, and authority are shared and where people are brought together to achieve common goals that could not be accomplished by a single individual or organization independently" (p. 3).

Beginning in the 1960s and continuing through the next 3 decades, as reflected in the growing visibility of programs for young children and their families, the need for collaboration among service providers, practitioners, administrators, and parents has also increased. Collaborative efforts have been both informal and formal. Examples of more formal collaboration efforts include the use of interagency agreements to ensure role definition of service providers, defined goals and outcomes for children and their families, specified means of evaluating the success of the collaborative effort, and a way of documenting the actual process and progress of collaboration.

According to Kagan (1991), several mediating variables can affect the nature and outcomes of collaborative efforts. The most common variables are (a) goals, (b) resources, (c) the power and authority structure, and (d) flexibility afforded the participants of the collaborative effort.

Within the field of ECE are examples of effective collaborative initiatives:

- *The Community Coordinated Child Care* (**four Cs**) *Effort.* This was the first recognized federally initiated effort to coordinate early care and education.
- *The Child and Family Services Act of 1975.* This legislation was an attempt to coordinate the planning, development, establishment, maintenance, and operation of a variety of child and family service programs (Mitchell, 1989).
- *Child Care and the Schools.* This program was designed to assist families by providing child-care services on-site at the schools.
- *Head Start and the Schools.* Several federal initiatives linked Head Start and the schools, including Project Developmental Continuity, designed to ensure continuity of children's experience as they completed Head Start and continued on through the primary years.
- *Special Education and the Schools.* The field of special education may be one of the strongest examples of collaboration in ECE. Inherent in special education is the belief that children need coordinated services, LREs, family and community involvement and support, and inclusion of the parents in the planning process (Kagan, 1991).

- *Interagency Coordinating Councils.* These councils were mandated through P.L. 99-457, which legislated that schools would provide services for special needs children from age 3 onward.

- *Vertical Collaborations of the 1990s.* These are collaborative efforts, born in the 1990s and the new era of collaboration that is initiated directly by schools, families, and teachers, as opposed to the federal government, that encourage the use of local, state, and federal agencies and programs to construct unique service programs.

The political and economic climate of the 1990s has affected the nature of educational collaborations. Kagan (1991) describes this phenomenon as a new **zeitgeist**, or way of viewing and conceptualizing the meaning of collaboration. Grassroots efforts are now more responsible for the development of collaborative efforts. As states assume more responsibilities through block grants, there will be ample opportunity for school professionals and parents to develop their own unique collaborations.

Traits of Successful Collaborative Efforts

- The context is fertile, especially the political and social climate.
- The goals are clear.
- The structure matches the mission.
- The mandate is facilitative, not restrictive.
- People are truly invested.
- Resources are available.
- The process and policies are clear.

In short, the school serves as a fertile ground for collaborative efforts among parents, teachers, administrators, community and agency representatives, policy makers, and other interested constituents. The school, because of its location and commitment to serve the public's young children, can become the hub of the community's successful collaborative efforts.

SUGGESTIONS FOR COLLABORATING WITH PARENTS

According to Gargiulo and Graves (1991), early childhood teachers will be more successful in communicating and collaborating with parents about advocacy issues if they keep certain strategies in mind. Teachers should keep terminology simple, relevant, and sensitive to cultural differences. Teachers should listen to and validate parents' feelings and needs. In addition, teachers should demonstrate consistency and accountability in their communication with parents about advocacy concerns. Parents should be involved in all aspects of the planning process and given important roles. Documenting the collaborative process with parents will provide a written history for the school and for future advocacy efforts.

Collaboration in the school setting requires patience, planning, and a positive attitude. As teachers become involved in working with parents on advocacy issues and concerns, knowing how to collaborate successfully is essential.

Advocacy Organizations for Children and Families

American Federation of Teachers **www.aft.org**

Annie E. Casey Foundation **www.aecf.org/kidscount/kc2000**

Children's Defense Fund **www.childrensdefensefund.org**

Coalition for Asian American Children and Families **www.cacf.org**

Division of Early Childhood, Council for Exceptional Children **www.dec-sped.org**

Easter Seals **www.easterseals.com**

Families First: Kennebec Child Abuse and Neglect Council **www.familiesfirstcan.org**

Federal Interagency Forum on Child and Family Statistics **www.childstats.gov**

Federation for Children with Special Needs **www.fcsn.org**

Fight Crime: Invest in Kids **www.fightcrime.org**

National Association of Bilingual Education **www.nabe.org**

National Association for the Education of Young Children **www.naeyc.org**

National Association of Elementary School Principals **www.naesp.org**

National Association of State Boards of Education **www.nasbe.org**

National Black Child Development Institute **www.nbcdi.org**

National Center for Education Statistics **nces.ed.gov**

National Council of Jewish Women **www.ncjw.org**

National Education Association **www.nea.org**

National PTA **www.pta.org**

Parent Advocacy Coalition for Educational Rights **www.pacer.org**

Stand for Children **www.stand.org**

United Way of America **www.unitedway.org**

Critical Concepts

1. Social forces contribute to the growing complexity of families and classrooms, thus the role of advocacy continues to grow in importance. Teachers can assume several levels of advocacy within their role as a classroom teacher and parent liaison.

2. Child advocacy has evolved over the past 200 years and has become increasingly visible since the 1960s. Classroom teachers and students should become aware of the history of child advocacy in the United States to understand and appreciate the forces that contribute to its growing importance in national- and state-level policy.

3. Teachers can play a critical role in modeling child advocacy to parents, teachers, and members of the community. The integration of advocacy into the curriculum demonstrates to young students how they,

too, can become advocates for important causes.

4. The advocacy process should be well organized and implemented; many resources exist to support child advocacy, and teachers can make these resources available to parents and the community.

5. Collaborating with parents to support a cause is an important role for the classroom teacher, and parents will respond to well-organized and inclusive efforts to include them in various advocacy roles within the educational setting.

6. Many organizations in the United States provide leadership and resources for child and family advocacy. Informing parents and the community about these advocacy organizations will strengthen the advocacy efforts within a community.

Summary Statements

✓ Schools are called on to provide more services to children and families than ever before; one of these services is the support of child and family advocacy.

✓ Family and child policy has a more than 100-year history in the United States, but not until the 1980s did family policy gain the level of recognition and political power that it enjoys today.

✓ Advocacy is the act of pleading a cause and defending, endorsing, or promoting particular ideas, principles, or individuals.

✓ Public choice theory was conceptualized by economist James Buchanan and argues that individuals come together in the political process for their own mutual benefit.

✓ Common barriers to citizen involvement in advocacy include feelings of powerlessness

to change, lack of knowledge about governmental process, fear of the political process, lack of confidence in their own expertise, and lack of time.

✓ The integration of DAP into school settings in preschool through primary grades is an example of successful advocacy efforts in ECE.

✓ Parents today are more consumer oriented, well educated, and activist minded in their interactions with teachers and other school personnel.

✓ Child and family policy in the earlier years arose from national crises such as war. An example is the establishment of child-care centers for mothers who worked during the war.

✓ The era after World War II was a transitional period for child and family policy. After World War II, the momentum of efforts toward improved child and family policy rapidly escalated.

✓ Lyndon Johnson's Great Society and the early intervention movement, which targeted at-risk children, combined to make the 1960s a significant decade for child and family policy.

✓ The Child Development Associate program, developed in the 1970s, was evidence of a growing commitment to formal training of teachers who teach young children.

✓ The 1980s marked an escalation in policy efforts for young children, including initiatives by the NASBE, NAEYC, and the National Governors Association.

✓ During the 1990s, child and family policy in the United States came full circle as political candidates placed issues related to child care, early education, and family work issues high on their campaign priority list.

✓ Preschool children are viewed in a more holistic, integrated way than were children in the 1960s. Integrated services for children and families are seen as a real need for most families.

✓ Parents are involved directly in advocacy efforts and are sophisticated in their knowledge level about the policy process; parents are also consumer oriented.

✓ Parent interest groups, parent activist groups, PTOs/PTAs, and Reggio Emilia–inspired parent project groups are examples of current parent advocacy efforts in school settings.

✓ Early advocacy efforts on behalf of young children include the kindergarten movement in the early 1900s, which attempted to keep the kindergarten curriculum play based.

✓ Significant advocacy initiatives that have influenced child and family policy and programs include P.L. 99-457; P.L. 101-476; the ADA; DAP and assessment guidelines by the NAEYC; and *Right From the Start*, published by the NASBE.

✓ Schools have become brokers of services for young children and their families and the major source of information coordination and advocacy initiatives.

✓ School and community partnerships are becoming common ways of strengthening programs and opportunities for young children and their families within the school setting; businesses recognize the importance of investing in the young child as a future productive worker and citizen.

✓ Collaboration in services for young children and their families is essential and considerably more sophisticated than in the past, according to Kagan, 1992. Collaboration requires time, patience, commitment to excellence, and a child-centered focus.

✓ Vertical collaborations became more commonplace in the 1990s as federal programs were dismantled and more power was given to the states. Vertical collaboration requires cooperation and teamwork among local, state, and federal agencies and service providers.

✓ Because collaboration is an essential component of successful child and family advocacy and policy development, the early childhood professional needs to learn and practice the steps to collaboration and be aware of the barriers and limitations of collaboration.

Research to Practice:
Classroom Applications and Activities

1. Select child and family policy topics of interest, do an extensive review of the literature, and then write a summary paper to share with the class. Examples of appropriate topics include: (a) the history of child-care regulation, (b) maternity leave policies, (c) corporate child care, (d) school involvement in early intervention, (e) child-care programs for teenage mothers, (f) the Family Leave Act, (g) child poverty, and (h) the ADA. Students should interview individuals with knowledge and expertise, as well as study the research and policy literature.

2. Invite a local or state politician to class. Develop an itinerary of questions to ask this person about the current status of child and family policy as compared with 20, 15, and 10 years ago. Discuss with this person her or his own beliefs about the role of the school in advocating for children and families.

3. Select and interview a political figure, child advocate, or community leader about what she or he sees as the most salient child and family issues today. Summarize the content of this interview and present it in class. You may videotape or audiotape the interviewee.

4. Invite a panel of parents of preschool and primary children to class. Develop a set of questions and issues to discuss with these parents. Ask the panelists what the most important child and family issues are, what their role is in child advocacy, where they believe child and family advocacy should occur, and what role the school should play in encouraging and facilitating the discussion of issues relevant to parents.

5. Take a field trip to the state capitol and schedule a meeting with a political representative in her or his official office. Ask to see pieces of legislation that are currently being considered that affect the lives of children and families.

6. View a video by the Children's Defense Fund. Discuss how this video benefits children and families, in which settings it would be appropriate to show, and how the Children's Defense Fund serves as a silent legislator in the decision-making process.

7. Invite an administrator and several key staff of a federally or state-funded program for young children and families to your class. Ask these individuals to respond to a set of questions developed by the class, such as (a) What is the funding source for this program? (b) What are the specific goals and desired outcomes for children and families? (c) What evidence is there that collaboration is occurring in this program? (d) How is accountability addressed? Program and staff evaluation? (e) What child or family populations are targeted? (f) What is most challenging and rewarding about administering or implementing this program? and (g) How would they change this program to make it stronger?

8. Select a key piece of legislation of interest to you. Track this legislation from the point of inception to the point of legislation. Develop a calendar of significant events and a schedule that denotes when benchmark decisions were made regarding this legislation. Identify the barriers or opponents to this legislation, the strongest and most effective advocates, the key political figures involved in the process, and how you believe this legislation is currently affecting children and families.

9. During the Week of the Young Child, sponsored annually in the spring by the NAEYC, ask to participate with a local elementary school to promote the idea of child and family advocacy. You, along with other students, can hang posters of children and families, set

up a booth to interview parents and teachers about issues of concern, and cosponsor a key speaker at the school to address a prominent child issue in the local area.

10. Select an early childhood classroom and serve as a "partner" to strengthen the advocacy efforts within that classroom. Identify an early childhood teacher who will work with you to implement parent–teacher–child events. Meet with parents about important issues. Develop an understanding of how the school serves as a source of advocacy support for children and families. Document your advocacy partnership experience through a portfolio.

11. Review the newly published *NAEYC Affiliate Public Policy Toolkit* (NAEYC, 2004) as a class. Discuss this document in terms of its usefulness for child advocacy groups. Identify at least three advocacy strategies recommended in this toolkit that may be appropriate for your local community. What are the strengths of this document? How would you use it? How might you change it?

Resources for Parents and Teachers on Advocacy and Public Policy

Suggested Reading for Parents

Ashton-Warner, S. (1963). *Teacher.* New York: Simon & Schuster.

Bredekamp, S. (Ed.). (1987). *Developmentally appropriate practice in early childhood programs serving children from birth through age 8* (Exp. Ed.). Washington, DC: National Association for the Education of Young Children.

Elkind, D. (1987). *Miseducation: Preschoolers at risk.* New York: Knopf.

Goffin, S. G., & Stegelin, D. A. (Eds.). (1992). *Changing kindergartens: Four success stories.* Washington, DC: National Association for the Education of Young Children.

Kamii, C. (Ed.). (1989). *Achievement testing in the early grades: The games grown-ups play.* Washington, DC: National Association for the Education of Young Children.

Meisels, S. J. (1985). *Developmental screening in early childhood: A guide* (Rev. ed.). Washington, DC: National Association for the Education of Young Children.

National Association for Elementary School Principals. (1990). *Early childhood education and the elementary school principal: Standards for quality programs for young children.* Alexandria, VA: Author.

National Association of State Boards of Education. (1988). *Right from the start.* Alexandria, VA: Author.

Schultz, T. (1992). Developmentally appropriate practice and the challenge of public school reform. In D. Stegelin (Ed.), *Early childhood education: Policy issues for the 1990s* (pp. 137–154). Norwood, NJ: Ablex.

Stegelin, D. A. (1992). *Early childhood education: Policy issues for the 1990s.* Norwood, NJ: Ablex.

General Advocacy Issues and Strategies: Suggested Readings for Teachers and Administrators

Almy, M. (1985). New challenges for teacher education: Facing political and economic realities. *Young Children, 40*(6), 10–11.

Bennis, W., & Nanus, B. (1985). *Leaders: The strategies for taking charge.* New York: Harper & Row.

Bird, L. B. (1989). *Becoming a whole language school: The Fair Oaks story.* Katonah, NY: Richard C. Owen.

Davis, M. (1989). Preparing teachers for developmentally appropriate classrooms. *Dimensions, 17* (3), 4–7.

DeClark, G. (1985). From skepticism to conviction. In C. K. Kamii (Ed.), *Young children reinvent arithmetic: Implications of Piaget's theory* (pp. 195–202). New York: Teachers College Press.

Duckworth, E. (1987). *The having of wonderful ideas and other essays.* New York: Teachers College Press.

Freeman, E. B. (1990). Issues in kindergarten policy and practice. *Young Children, 55*(4), 29–34.

Fullan, M. (1982). *The meaning of educational change.* New York: Teachers College Press.

Goffin, S. G. (1991). Supporting change in a school district's early childhood programs: A story of growth. *Early Child Development and Care, 70,* 5–16.

Goffin, S. G. (1992). Creating change with public schools: Reflections of an early childhood teacher educator. In D. Stegelin (Ed.), *Early childhood education: Policy issues for the 1990s* (pp. 155–174). Norwood, NJ: Ablex.

Hitz, R., &Wright, D. (1988). Kindergarten issues: A practitioner's survey. *Principal, 67,* 28–30.

Hord, S. M., Rutherford, W. L., Huling-Austin, L., & Hall, G. E. (1987). *Taking charge of change.* Alexandria, VA: Association for Supervision and Curriculum Development.

Humphrey, S. (1989). Becoming a better kindergarten teacher: The case of myself. *Young Children, 45*(1), 17–22.

Kagan, S. (1989). Early care and education: Tackling the tough issues. *Phi Delta Kappan, 70,* 433–439.

Katz, L. G., & Chard, S. C. (1988). *Engaging children's minds: The project approach.* Norwood, NJ: Ablex.

Lieberman, A. (1990). Navigating the four C's: Building a bridge over troubled waters. *Phi Delta Kappan, 71*(7), 531–533.

McDonald, J. P. (1989). When outsiders try to change schools from the inside. *Phi Delta Kappan, 7*(3), 206–212.

Murphy, C. U. (1991). Lesson from a journey into change. *Educational Leadership, 48*(8), 63–67.

National Association for the Education of Young Children. (1990). NAEYC position statement on school readiness. *Young Children, 46*(1), 21–23.

National Association of Elementary School Principals. (1990). *Early childhood education and the elementary school principal.* Alexandria, VA: Author.

National Association of State Boards of Education. (1988). *Right from the start.* Alexandria, VA: Author.

Sarason, S. B. (1987). Policy, implementation, and the problem of change. In S. L. Kagan & E. F Zigler (Eds.), *Early schooling: The national debate* (pp. 116–128). New Haven, CT: Yale University Press.

Schlechty, P. C. (1990). *Schools for the 21st century.* San Francisco: Jossey-Bass.

Schultz, T. (1992). Developmentally appropriate practice and the challenge of public school reform. In D. Stegelin (Ed.), *Early childhood education: Policy issues for the 1990s* (pp. 137–154). Norwood, NJ: Ablex.

Walsh, D., Baturka, N., Colter, N., & Sith, M. E. (1991). Changing one's mind—Maintaining one's identity: A first-grade teacher's story. *Teachers College Record, 93,* 73–86.

Advocacy Related to ECE

Bredekamp, S., &Sheppard, L. (1989). How best to protect children from inappropriate school expectations, practices, and policies. *Young Children, 43*(3), 14–24.

Elkind, D. (1987). Early childhood education on its own terms. In S. L. Kagan & E. F. Zigler (Eds.), *Early schooling: The national debate* (pp. 98–115). New Haven, CT: Yale University Press.

Goffin, S. G., & Lombardi, J. (1988). *Speaking out: Early childhood advocacy.* Washington, DC: National Association for the Education of Young Children.

Mitchell, A., & Modigliani, K. (1989). Public policy report: Young children in the public schools? The "only ifs" reconsidered. *Young Children, 44*(6), 56–61.

National Association for Elementary School Principals. (1990). *Early childhood and the elementary school principal: Standards for quality programs for young children.* Alexandria, VA: Author.

National Association of State Boards of Education. (1988). *Right from the start: Report of the NASBE task force on early childhood education.* Alexandria, VA: Author.

Educational Organizations That Support Advocacy for Young Children

Division for Early Childhood of the Council for Exceptional Children (DEC/CEC), 1920 Association Drive, Reston, VA 22091

Innovations in Early Education: The International Reggio Exchange, Wayne State University, Merrill-Palmer Institute, 71-A E. Ferry Avenue, Detroit, MI 48202

National Association for Elementary School Principals, 1615 Duke Street, Alexandria, VA 22314

National Association for the Education of Young Children, 1834 Connecticut Avenue, N.W., Washington, DC 20009–5786

National Association of State Boards of Education (NASBE), 1012 Cameron Street, Alexandria, VA 22314

National Childhood Technical Assistance System (NEC*TAS), 500 Nations Bank Plaza, 137 East Franklin Street, Chapel Hill, NC 27514

National Head Start Association, 1220 King Street, Alexandria, VA 22314

Office of Special Education Services (OSERS), U.S. Department of Education, 400 Maryland Avenue, S.W., Washington, DC 20202

CHAPTER 4

Cross-Cultural Issues Involving Families and the Community

Respect generates respect; a modest loaf becomes many.

LAWRENCE-LIGHTFOOT, 2000, P. 10

acculturated	discrimination	interdependence	sociocultural
antibias	ecological approach	minority	stereotypes
biases	emergent curriculum	morality	values
care	enculturation	multicultural	webbing
character	ethnocentrism	prejudice	
culture	independence	social cognition	

GUIDING QUESTIONS

1. What are the facets of culture that impact individuals' participation in society?
2. Why don't many of the young people in the United States recognize themselves as part of a specific cultural heritage with traditions and distinct cultural events?
3. How do education and families support transmission of Culture?
4. What are some principles of cultural pluralism?
5. What are some of the goals for teaching from a multicultural perspective?
6. What are considerations parents and teachers have when helping children acquire antibias attitudes and beliefs?
7. Why is it important that teachers see individuals within the context of their sociocultural settings?
8. How can some of the distinct values and assumptions of families of various descents be considered in programs for young children?
9. How can children's questions serve as prompts for culturally sensitive curriculum adventures through webbing?

cross cultures, a young child's journey to adulthood is accomplished within the context of the family and surrounding communities. The child's unique spirit, personality, interests, abilities, ways of knowing, and ways of seeing himself or herself in the context of the immediate world result from the meshing of genetic predispositions and the cultural and environmental influences of both near and far environments. Exploring cultures is vital to understanding ourselves and others in our quest to build relationships with families and communities. Common themes include:

Theme 1. Across cultures, a young child's journey to adulthood is accomplished within the context of the family and surrounding community. The beliefs, values, attitudes, languages, and ideologies experienced in childhood will play a part in whatever path the child takes as she or he moves toward adulthood.

Theme 2. As our world expands, we experience our personal cultures and those of others. Before we understand the cultures of others, we must be able to recognize and reflect on our own and the significance of cultural practices in our growth and development.

Theme 3. As individuals whose cultures interact, we must develop ways of learning about beliefs and practices in our efforts to understand and respect the individuality of those with whom we live, learn, and work. Language is a powerful tool representing the common goal to communicate.

Theme 4. A multicultural approach reflects a concern for assisting children and adults in understanding individuals from other "worlds." This goal includes a realistic versus "tourist" approach to learning about other cultures and honoring the diversity of children and families.

Theme 5. Classrooms should reflect concern for diversity addressed through developmentally appropriate practices.

Theme 6. Children and adults are unique individuals and should be viewed accordingly. There are, however, some general characteristics that reflect family interactions within cultures. Becoming aware of these characteristics can help us foster communication rather than build stereotypes.

THE JOURNEY OF GROWTH AND DEVELOPMENT IN THE CONTEXT OF CULTURES IN OUR NEAR AND FAR ENVIRONMENTS

As children grow, their near environment extends beyond that of immediate family, close friends of the family, and other primary caregivers. It encompasses the "community of the neighborhood" as children become involved with other children and families through informal play situations, holiday celebrations, sports activities, special-interest activities, and the building of lasting friendships. It also includes those influences found in more formal settings, including child care, schools, and places of worship.

As children become young adults, many will move from the home of their childhood to experience new homes at college; in new cities where jobs are found; with husbands or wives; across the globe in the service of their country, their faith, or their jobs; or simply in another part of the neighborhood where their lives continue to intertwine with those of their families and childhood friends. Wherever the journey, their "humanness" urges them to seek the places where they feel a sense of connectedness with others and of "belonging." In these settings is a reciprocity as individuals influence, and are influenced by, others. The beliefs, **values**,

Supportive environments at home and school provide safe spaces for children to learn and play.

attitudes, languages, and ideologies experienced in childhood will play a part in whatever path a child takes as she or he moves toward adulthood. Some childhood practices will be cherished; others will be discarded as not in keeping with a new way of living. Added will be the beliefs, values, and practices adopted from experiences with individuals and institutions on the road to adulthood.

In his **ecological approach** to explaining human development and behavior, Bronfenbrenner (1988) noted that development occurs in the context of daily lives. In its complexity, "the developmental processes taking place in the immediate settings in which human beings live, such as family, peer group, and workplace, are profoundly affected by conditions and events in the broader contexts in which these settings are embedded" (p. x). The conditions and events include:

> the material circumstances in which the person and his or her family live, the actual behaviors of other parties toward the person in question in face-to-face situations, and the actions and decisions taken in external, structurally-defined contexts, such as businesses, government agencies, social organizations, and other institutions in the public and the private sector. (p. xiv)

How does this discussion relate to the topic of culture? York (1991) noted that culture includes "[t]he behavior, values, beliefs, language, traits, artifacts, and products shared by and associated with a group of people" (p. 22). **Culture** helps determine who we are; the roles we take; the ways we seek to communicate with, and respond to, the world about us; and the values and attitudes we bring to our families, our work, our schools, and our communities. Our lives are also determined by the responses of others to our cultural practices and beliefs and to our presence. The willingness and ability to respond to the cultural aspects of the lives of the children and families whom we as teachers serve help build a spirit of partnership with families within and across communities.

THEME 1   *in practice. . .*

A team of teachers has been asked to prepare a list of holidays that might be celebrated in the classroom and that are representative of various cultures. The team will also be researching and providing background materials to the teachers. Should this be done? Why or why not?

RECOGNIZING AND VALUING THE CULTURES OF OUR FAMILIES AND COMMUNITIES

S tated very simply, culture is about the roles we play in the context of our near environment and in response to the events of the outside world. It is about the things we surround ourselves with and the ways in which we express ourselves. It is about how we care for others. It is about how we express our humanness and the goals we set for ourselves and our families. It is about what we value and hold dear.

Discussions of culture are found in a variety of settings, including classes that prepare teachers to care for and teach young children. The ultimate goal is to assist teachers in creating classroom climates that support and value the culture of each child (Bruns & Corso, 2001). When asked to share something of their culture, however, many class participants may look surprised. It seems that culture is something only "those of color" or those from places foreign to us possess.

Unique and Shared Family Cultural Events

As teachers and caregivers, we must examine our attitudes and values regarding our own heritage before we can value the diversity of the children within our care. We must begin with our near environment and work to the far. We must ask, What is my culture? We must be willing to share the experiences of our kin before we can effectively elicit the sharing of cultural experiences from others—children, families, and members of the community. Perhaps we might consider the categories listed in Table 4.1 as we relate Theme 2 to practice.

TABLE 4.1	Categories of Cultural Events in the Lives of Families			
Communication	**Families**	**Dress**	**Holidays**	**Foods**
Body language	Roles	Gender	Types	Who prepares
Personal space	Size	Purpose	Celebrations	Types
Eye contact	Extended or nuclear	Textiles	Practices	Meals
Gestures		Style	Dates	Religious issues
Dialect		Who makes or	Religious affiliations	
Roles		purchases		
Religion	**Leisure/Recreation**	**Work**	**Politics**	**Education**
Formal rituals	Time spent	Job roles	Liberal	Gender issues
Belief in God or	Games or events	Training required	Conservative	Who educates
other spiritual	Gender roles	Gender issues	Power issues	Requirements
entities		Role in life	Gender issues	Types
Gender roles		Status issues	Role of government	Responsibility for cost
Written documents		Pay	Practices	Who determines
that guide practices				career path
Language				
Selection of leaders				

At Eastern Kentucky University, many students have roots deep in Appalachia, an area rich with heritage begun with the 18th-century settlers who came from Scotland, Northern Ireland, and northern England: "While Appalachians are not immigrants and are not necessarily racial minorities, they do share a cultural heritage with distinct childrearing patterns, attitudes, and expectations" (Klein, 1995, p. 10).

Fathers, grandfathers, great-grandfathers, and some women worked the coal mines, spending hours deep underground and emerging exhausted and blackened with coal dust. For many, the time spent breathing dust from coal resulted in black lung disease and disability. Declining jobs and fear for health and safety sent many families away from the mountains. They moved north to the factories of large cities such as Detroit, Cleveland, Cincinnati, and Indianapolis but never lost contact with their Appalachian roots, making frequent trips home for holidays and family celebrations. They took with them the values and practices of their culture and became different in the world of the big city. Although many of these families stayed in the big cities, others eventually returned to the mountains or to cities nearer their mountain homes, including Cincinnati and smaller towns nearby. Why do individuals descending from a culture so rich in a spirit of connectedness and resolve seem puzzled when they are asked to discuss their culture? This same concept seems to apply to other individuals with roots in many parts of the United States, including both urban and rural environments.

Many explanations have been offered for why many of the nation's young people do not recognize themselves as part of a specific cultural heritage. This nation's history details the coming together of people from many countries, resulting in a "melting pot," or meshing of cultures and individuals to form families that may not represent any one geographic or religious heritage (Derman-Sparks & Ramsey, 1993, p. 276). Also, it may not have been acceptable to differentiate oneself as unique or set apart by one's origins. Being an "American" may have superseded one's heritage from another country. This has been particularly true during times of war. Many of us have heard stories from grandparents who did not discuss their German roots with anyone during World War II. After the September 11, 2001, terrorist attacks on the World Trade Center, Middle Eastern people living in the United States—who had no connections to terrorism or the Taliban—maintained a low profile for months. Many feared that Americans might wrongly connect them to terrorism by nature of their skin color or religion and take retribution.

It is also important to consider the shifting patterns in geographic "connectedness" of families. Historically, members of one's extended family were close by, with grandparents, aunts, uncles, and cousins available for family dinners and celebrations and for helping one another. Several generations may have shared one household; it was common for families to care for their elderly parents and grandparents. Parents often looked to grandparents and other older relatives for parenting advice, rather than asking "experts" external to the family. Family businesses were common. Individuals experienced the "culture" of their families through time spent together, shared stories of the past, languages passed from one generation to the next, and the setting of common goals.

Today, people still search for a sense of community with others. Families, often fragmented by divorce, still struggle to provide for their children and to nurture their growth and development in healthy ways. As noted by Margie Carter (1995), however, in her discussion of building community cultures, "A real experience of being raised and acculturated in community has been missing from most of our lives for several decades now" (p. 52). Today, people may have fewer opportunities to share the "culture" of their families or communities.

Families become more separated as their members pursue jobs and educational opportunities in various parts of the country and world. Children and elderly relatives are cared for outside the home as daughters, sons, mothers, and fathers pursue careers and support their families. Many individuals view their families as dysfunctional and look to those outside the family for "familylike" support.

Families are perpetually bombarded with external information about how they should act, how they should look, and what they should have. "We are primarily shaped by the media and commercialism" (Carter, 1995, p. 52). Furthermore, many families live in "homes without walls" as the media bring into living rooms violence and adult material from which families once protected their children. Through the media and the advertising that permeates the environment, children are educated to believe that products are what matter (Pipher, 1996).

Finally, we as Americans seem to be on a perpetual quest to have more, know more, and be more—to go beyond the world of our parents. This quest (a) indicates a healthy desire for growth and (b) attempts to exist and compete in the global marketplace. We must recognize, however, that our own growth is rooted in the cultures of our families and that culture is still an inherent part of who we are and what we bring to our worlds.

Enculturation of Our Children

Carol Brunson Phillips (1994) stated, "The task of a society to prepare its children to take their place in the world of adults involves, in its broadest sense, the transmission of culture" (p. 137). Phillips further notes that, in U.S. society, the family and the educational system take primary responsibility for this transmission. Families do so through **enculturation**—"the things families do to enable children to know and understand society's shared ideas about values, attitudes, beliefs, and behaviors" (p. 137). Schools do this through *education*. Optimistically, the school and the family support one another in the complex task of bringing children to adulthood. At times, however, conflict arises between these two "giants" in the child's life because of differences in beliefs, values, and practices (Bruns & Corso, 2001).

Perhaps of greatest interest to early childhood professionals are the views of children held by varying societies; for example, how children develop, what roles they take in the family, how they are nurtured. Many of these practices take root in broader political, social, economic, and religious beliefs viewed as necessary for the survival of that group.

Having time in school to share stories about special times with grandparents helps children realize the value of the extended family, too.

Marian Zeitlin (1996), a nutritionist and adoptive mother of a Yoruban son, provides a provocative example in her account of the child-rearing practices of Yoruban (Nigerian) families. The Yoruba believe that the soul survives eternally in three states: the living, the ancestors, and the unborn waiting to be reincarnated with an ancestor from its own lineage. Before birth, a child is assigned by God or chooses her or his *ori*, or destiny. The family awaits the appearance of characteristics that will resemble the reincarnated ancestor. Motor development is a priority, with children being encouraged to support their own weight from birth. By age 7, children are "expected to obey and respect their elders, care for themselves and younger siblings, assist in the home, and contribute to the family economy by providing assistance either on the farm or with trading activities" (p. 413). The most valued skill possessed by the Yoruban child is the ability to complete errands for the family. Training begins with such tasks before age 1, and by age 2, children are sent on errands and given money to buy items for the family. Males are polygamous; women become heads of subunits of the family. In her role as head, the mother's nutritional status becomes more important than that of the child, with mothers given preference in food distribution. "Feeding more than remnants of these prestige foods (fish and meat) was feared to spoil the child's moral **character**" (p. 419). In this agrarian society, economic flow is from child to parent, not parent to child.

As you can see, "The behaviors that parents exhibit toward their children and expect from them in daily interaction are complexly determined" (Gaskins, 1996, p. 345). Their notions about child rearing are embedded in cultural expectations and experiences.

Acculturation of Our Children

Families are given the task of enculturation, but children also become **acculturated** as they encounter groups outside their ethnic group ("the commonality among people because of their ancestors; it includes race, religion, national origin, physical traits, values, beliefs, customs, language and lifestyle" [York, 1991, p. 19]). Acculturation involves the transfer of culture from one ethnic group to another.

Among the earliest of these experiences within a formal setting comes with child care, schooling, or both, where children are often expected to be and act like the majority of the population within the setting. This type of **ethnocentrism**—expecting others to think and act in the same way as a particular group—makes it difficult for children to ground their sense of self in who they are as they strive to be something desired by others. As explained by Saracho and Spodek (1983),

> [T]hey are expected to make major changes in what they do and how they speak, they may be forced to use a language that is foreign to them, and the social patterns and interactions expected of them may be equally foreign. These children must not only learn their own family language and culture but they must also learn to be competent in an alien language and culture. Often, they are made to feel that they have to reject their own language and culture and adopt those of the school. This can result in a sense of bewilderment, in rejection, and a loss of ethnic identity for the child. (p. viii)

One suggestion to facilitate communication and enhance staff awareness of culturally sensitive language is to enlist the assistance of community leaders as "cultural guides." Clergy and business leaders who speak families' primary language and understand the customs may be able to provide assistance as teachers enlist families as partners in their children's education (Lynch & Hanson, 1998; Tabors, 1998). If, instead, teachers learned important cultural communication styles of families, children and families would feel more welcome as participants in the learning community (Quintero, 1999).

THE POWER OF LANGUAGE IN COMMUNICATING WITHIN AND ACROSS CULTURES

Perhaps one of our best windows to cultural variations in family life is shared in the language used across and within cultures. In her discussion of Appalachian families living in northern cities, Helen Klein (1995) shared interesting anecdotes about the role of language in acclimating to a new environment. One of the most poignant is that of the school principal who attempts to elicit the help of families in providing cupcakes for a holiday party. The typical response was "I wouldn't care to do that" (p. 11). Thinking that the parents were declining, the principal continued to call more parents. On the day of the party, the school was flooded with cupcakes. The principal realized that this statement by the parents was an indication that they would not mind bringing cupcakes. (A recent discussion among college teachers at Eastern Kentucky University revealed that several teachers from other parts of the country did not understand what was happening when their students replied "I don't care to" to a request for participation in the classroom.)

Language, whether oral or written, verbal or nonverbal, is used universally to communicate thoughts, ideas, desires, feelings, needs, and rules among individuals and across generations. Because this desire to communicate is common to all cultures, the use of language within and across cultural settings is of great interest to study. Case studies of preprimary children have shown that children acquire information about language and its forms and functions through their observations of language and how it is used in their near environments (Teale & Sulzby, 1989). The importance of written language within the context of use by the specific culture determines the extent that young children acquire information about the written word (Ferreiro & Teberosky, 1992). However, "[b]ecause the markings four year old children produce prior to formal schooling reflect the written language of their culture, we can no longer assume that children come to school without some knowledge of written language" (Harste & Woodward, 1989, p. 148).

Not only may children bring some knowledge of the forms and functions of the written language of their culture to the formal classroom setting, but they also bring their home-rooted language with words and phrases used in culturally specific ways. As noted by Klein (1995), an understanding of the meanings and uses of phrases and words within cultural contexts is necessary for meaningful communication across cultures.

To make the concept of *home-rooted language* relevant to our experiences, it is helpful to begin with a discussion of language and the unique ways in which it is or was used within our home and community settings. An interesting place to begin is with words used to represent common objects. For example, the simple question, Where do you keep your clothes? elicits responses as diverse as the closet, the cupboard, the press, the chifforobe, the wardrobe, the chest, the bureau, the armoire, the highboy, the lowboy, the dresser, and more. One can also play with words for a couch—*sofa, davenport, divan, daybed,* and *loveseat.* Today, one might even say *futon.* You could add to these terms words from your personal experiences in "sitting."

Language provokes discussions that allow us to begin identifying other cultural aspects of our lives, be they practices in child rearing, the culture of our schools and churches, the ways people greet each other or avoid greeting each other, or what is seen as appropriate dress. In these discussions, the comments and love of a cherished grandmother may be revealed. It becomes okay, for example, to talk about helping with the planting of tobacco on a nearby farm or the way a family killed hogs every autumn for meat for the family. We talk about what we have learned from the experiences of our families and how our lives are affected today. Who we are and where our roots lie are accepted.

THEME 3   *in practice . . .*

One teacher in the preschool program you direct is of Asian descent. She is loved by the children as she works with them in her quiet, shy way. You are a bit more outgoing and want her to "express herself" in a more assertive manner. You suggest that she take some classes that focus on assertiveness in dealing with others. As a director, is this an appropriate recommendation? Why? Why not?

MULTICULTURAL PERSPECTIVE ON TEACHING AND CARING FOR YOUNG CHILDREN AND THEIR FAMILIES

The Role of Schools in Bridging Schools and Homes

Schools and other early childhood programs are vehicles for helping children build bridges between the cultures of their families and the cultures of broader communities where they may someday live and work. Through practices that respect and respond to diversity, teachers can take children from near to far experiences and assist them in building the type of cultural reciprocity that is needed to make sense of, and fully participate in, a changing world.

Teachers, administrators, child-care providers, families, and communities must work together to build a climate for children that encourages knowledge of, and respect for, the diversity of families. The early childhood profession has historically been the strongest nurturer of relationships with families regardless of the diversity represented. The idea of the parent as the most important teacher in a child's life has long been held by early childhood advocates. One clear example of this is found in the Head Start program, which began as a part of the war on poverty in 1965 and continues to grow today. The involvement of the parents and the community in the program is fundamental to the success of Head Start in making a difference in the lives of children.

"A central part of the professional early childhood community's ethos is that continuity should exist between family and program" (Powell, 1994, p. 167). U.S. society holds the fundamental belief that the family is the child's first and most important teacher and has the right to determine what is in the best interest of that child, given that families do not abuse that right. Quality programs require continuity between home and school. "Program–family discontinuities, which are of the greatest magnitude for children from low-income and ethnic minority families, are thought to have negative effects on children's academic outcomes and socialization experiences" (p. 167). "When children are in early childhood programs that are not culturally sensitive to and consistent with their home cultures, they are at risk" (Derman-Sparks & Ramsey, 1993, p. 285).

Building an Inclusionary Classroom

We participate in many communities, including those where we work, where we live, where we or our children go to school, where we worship, and where we experience fellowship with a group of friends. Everyone, regardless of race or color, gender or ability, religion or education, brings a rich heritage to that community or group. These heritages blend to form the culture of that group and the culture of the families. "Cultural pluralism is the notion that groups in the United States should be allowed, even encouraged, to hold on to what gives them their unique identities while maintaining their membership in the larger social framework" (Gonzalez–Mena, 1993, p. 2). Our role as teachers, caregivers, and administrators is to build a community within our classrooms that values language, culture, and life experiences as meaningful resources for learning environments that are culturally responsive (Ladson–Billings, 1995). This requires teachers to:

- Recognize and value the uniqueness of the life experience of each child and her or his family.
- Assist each child in recognizing and valuing her or his heritage.
- Assist each child in valuing and respecting the uniqueness of each individual even though that individual may not be just like that child.
- Recognize the need to use active teaching methods for children to acquire those skills needed to live in a diverse world.
- Communicate high expectations.

THEME 4   *in practice . . .*

The teacher has been told by a family that their child is not allowed by the rules of his religion to celebrate holidays or his birthday. Halloween comes soon after he enrolls, and the children are busy preparing for a Halloween party. The room is being decorated, snacks are being prepared, and costumes are being collected. The teacher feels bad about excluding this child and, in fact, has no one to watch him outside the classroom. What ideas or suggestions do you have for this teacher?

This class shared words from different languages, such as *uno.*

The Multicultural Classroom Environment

One avenue for accomplishing the tasks of building a culture within the classroom is to engage in educational and caring practices that are multicultural in nature. "Multicultural education is neither a unique phenomenon nor a recent innovation. . . . The socialization of young children into the larger society has long been considered an appropriate goal of early childhood education" (Saracho & Spodek, 1983, p. viii). **Multicultural** education is more than teaching children about the artifacts of various cultures (e.g., dress, customs, holidays, foods). It also means exposing children to other cultures and helping them to be comfortable with and respect all the ways people are different from each other. It is teaching children how to relate to one another and how to play fair (York, 1991, p. 22).

In her book *Teaching and Learning in a Diverse World: Multicultural Education for Young Children,* Patricia Ramsey (1987) concluded that multicultural education involves a way of thinking. This way of thinking is characterized by respect for oneself as well as for others regardless of the ways that they are different from oneself (e.g., gender, race, religion, wealth). It also reflects a concern for helping children acquire those skills that will help them build and maintain healthy relationships in the context of communities near or far. Ramsey set broad goals for teaching from a multicultural perspective.

1. To help children develop positive gender, racial, cultural class, and individual identities and to recognize and accept their membership in many different groups.
2. To enable children to see themselves as part of the larger society; to identify, empathize, and relate with individuals from other groups.

3. To foster respect and appreciation for the diverse ways in which other people live.

4. To encourage in young children's earliest social relationships an openness and interest in others, a willingness to include others, and a desire to cooperate.

5. To promote the development of realistic awareness of contemporary society, a sense of social responsibility, and an active concern that extend beyond one's immediate family or group.

6. To empower children to become autonomous and critical analysts and activists in their social environment.

7. To support the development of educational and social skills that are needed for children to become full participants in the larger society in ways that are most appropriate to individual styles, cultural orientations, and linguistic backgrounds.

8. To promote effective and reciprocal relationships between schools and families. (p. 5)

Avoiding Bias and Dispelling Myths

Ramsey's goals reflect a concern for assisting children in the development of attitudes and values that demonstrate concern for humanity. They also reflect a concern for promoting a perspective on living with other people, which is **antibias**, defined by Louise Derman-Sparks (1989) as "an active/ist approach to challenging **prejudice**, stereotyping, bias, and the 'isms'" (p. 3). These **biases** or **stereotypes** refer to gender, race, religion, disability, or any other aspect of one's life that is used to set one apart from and by others.

The actions that teachers take to meet these goals should also be designed to eliminate some accepted myths and misconceptions that tend to influence attitudes toward individuals who are in some way different from what is familiar (Battle, Black, Guddemi, & O'Bar, 1992). Such misconceptions include: (a) all children of the same ethnic background have the same abilities and interests (e.g., physical and intellectual), (b) all children who do not speak standard English are intellectually inferior, (c) all ethnic minorities receive government assistance and are content to be "on welfare", (d) all Asian children are academically gifted, (e) all children growing up in rural environments are "rednecks," and (f) all children growing up in mountainous areas are "hillbillies."

In her book *Black Children: Their Roots, Culture, and Learning Styles*, Janice Hale (1982) argued that American social scientists view African American families as pathological and incapable of preparing their children for school. Denny Taylor and Catherine Dorsey-Gaines (1988) are among the ethnographers whose work has dispelled this myth. Their fieldwork involved the study of the contexts in which African American families living in the inner city of a major metropolitan area in the Northeast accomplished literacy. From their ethnographic research, they concluded that gender, race, economic status, and setting cannot be used to determine literacy (p. 194). In fact, "a person who is poor must certainly be 'bright' as well as determined in order to survive in the face of potentially overpowering odds" (Bishop, 1988, p. ix).

These families spent time with their children, encouraging them to write by providing writing and drawing materials, space, time, and themselves as participants. The children spontaneously engaged in writing notes containing many *I love yous* and labeled the pictures of the family members that they drew with care. Interestingly, their budding knowledge of the functional uses of print was diminished in formal schooling when rote exercises in writing letters of the alphabet and in copying work from the chalkboard were shown to be of significant importance (Taylor & Dorsey-Gaines, 1988, p. 91).

Perhaps the most poignant of these stories is of a young mother living in a building with no heat or running water. Driven from the building by the cold, this mother, ill and in search of a home for her children, was very concerned about their education. She described how she helped her young daughter learn to read:

> I have some cue cards with sentences and words that I thought she should know in kindergarten . . . I bought them at the store. And, um, we go over them. I try maybe a half hour a day to spend some time with her going over them . . . That was more so in kindergarten or first grade. Now she's starting to read. (Taylor & Dorsey-Gaines, 1988, p. 6)

In summary, Taylor and Dorsey-Gaines's (1988) conclusions about the characteristics of these families included (a) a sense of conviction about their own abilities as parents and a determination to raise healthy children; (b) loving environments in which children were cared for with affection; (c) structured home environments with expectations for cooperation and a framework of rules understood by children and reinforced by parents; (d) concern for the safety and well-being of the children at home, in the neighborhood, and to and from school; and (e) the value that parents and family members placed on the growing sense of competence and independence demonstrated by the children as they participated in the events of the family and the neighborhood (p. 194).

Klein (1995) worked to dispel similar myths about children from Appalachia whose families had migrated to northern cities, looking for work. When Klein asked professionals working with these children, "Who are these people?" responses included the following: (a) "They're poor Whites from the South," (b) "Hillbillies," (c) "I think they beat their kids," (d) "Briars," and (e) "They live in shacks and make moonshine" (p. 10).

These individuals who spoke with a different dialect, had different mannerisms, and had different customs were labeled as ignorant, lazy, unclean, and immoral (Klein, 1995, p. 10). In her efforts to make sense of and remove the stereotypes associated with these children and their families, Klein (1995) turned to their history and wrote about the strong and proud heritage these families brought from their Appalachian homes. "Deeply rooted in the history of the Appalachians was a sense of individualism and self-reliance" (p. 13). This sense of self-reliance served these families well as they journeyed to new homes with new ways.

Appalachian culture is rooted in a sense of traditionalism and kinship. Children benefited from being raised in, and cared for by, the extended family. "The Appalachian family was multigenerational, and it was not unusual for children to be cared for by grandparents, elders to be cared for by teens, and so on" (Klein, 1995, p. 14). Given this strong sense of kinship, it was not surprising that families traveled home to visit relatives and the cemetery for Memorial Day regardless of the number of days remaining in the school year.

Appalachian families brought a history of hard labor as they worked their land and the mines. Strength and stamina were also of crucial importance as they entered the factories of the North. Honesty was very important in their interactions with people. "Appalachians were not impressed with status and degrees but rather looked to inner characteristics" (Klein, 1995, p. 14).

Both the African American families studied by Taylor and Dorsey-Gaines and the Appalachian families whose history was chronicled by Klein may have easily been stereotyped as not willing or able to care for and educate their children. In fact, determination and resolve were pervasive in both situations.

GROUNDING CHILDREN IN ANTIBIAS PRACTICES: DEVELOPING SOCIAL AND MORAL KNOWLEDGE

As educators and caregivers, we can create climates that address multicultural education and discourage the development of ideas that are biased. As parents, teachers, and caregivers, it is imperative that we understand how young children acquire social knowledge because such knowledge "provides a basis for all communication and interaction, for all learning and problem solving, at home and school" (Edwards, 1986, p. 5). "In all cultural communities worldwide, the years from two to six are a time of rapid changes in the development of social and moral knowledge" (p. 3). Indeed, this is a time when children begin to develop their ideas and beliefs about the equality or inequality of individuals with regard to differences, including gender, race, and disability. "[D]espite legal and educational efforts to diminish racial **discrimination**, the cycle of prejudice is still strong and easily takes root in the minds and feelings of young children" (Ramsey, 1986, p. 1). "Our children add up, imitate, file away what they've observed and so very often later fall in line with the particular moral counsel we wittingly or quite unself-consciously have offered them" (Coles, 1997, p. 7).

This is also a time when children begin to act out some of their beliefs about what is fair and what is appealing in other individuals. In your work with young children in classroom settings, you have no doubt experienced the cliques that can so easily form, leaving individual children isolated, lonely, and often angry at the exclusion. The sound of "You can't play" is brutal to the ears of the young child and to the caring adult who overhears. In her provocative book *You Can't Say You Can't Play*, Vivian Gussin Paley (1992) noted:

> By kindergarten. . . a structure begins to be revealed and will soon be carved in stone. Certain children will have the right to limit the social experiences of their classmates. Henceforth, a ruling class will notify others of their acceptability, and the outsiders learn to anticipate the sting of rejection. Long after hitting and name-calling have been outlawed by the teachers, a more damaging phenomenon is allowed to take root, spreading like a weed from grade to grade. (p. 3)

How does one get to be in the "in-group"? Is it gender, skin color, the color of a child's hair, the child's personality, or some other personal feature? Is it the occupation of the parent or the types of clothes the child wears? Is it the toys the child brings for show-and-tell? Is it the ability of the child to read or draw or paint or run fast? How do we know the rules?

Families with grandparents and parents from other countries can not only learn both languages, but can also bring to school rich stories about these countries that they can share with others.

We have already discussed examples of myths and misconceptions that may be held about cultural groups. Many misconceptions may also be held about what one needs to "fit." Consider the encounters that many children experience in the "culture of America" that suggest rules for stereotypes and about what is desirable to "belong."

Thin is beautiful. Commercial weight-loss programs find their way into homes through the media, and parents whose busy schedules seem to afford little time for healthful eating and exercise often resort to these programs. The "lean look" graces magazines and billboards with young girls and boys who model the latest lean fashions.

Busy is best. The child who is involved in several after-school activities such as dance or gymnastics, choir, and service activities is seen as achieving, popular, talented, and bright.

More is better. Religious celebrations that involve the giving and receiving of gifts, including Hanukkah and Christmas, have become more and more commercial, with children's expectations for more and bigger gifts increasing.

You'd better go into debt to be on the Net! Technology has brought many wonderful opportunities to children in helping broaden their knowledge of the world. Many parents, however, feel as though they must have the latest computer technology at home for their children to "succeed."

It's in the name. Children are convinced by the media that they will jump higher, run faster, and "be cool" if they just have a particular insignia on their shoes. In the United States, children have murdered other children for their athletic shoes! The labels of popular brands of jeans are prominently displayed on rear pockets, and even socks carry the appropriate "sign."

It's time to circle the wagons. In schools, we attempt to help children acquire accurate information about Native Americans and to avoid the stereotypes that have prevailed for years. Yet, the commercial aspects of U.S. society continue to characterize Native Americans in very stereotypical ways. This is particularly true during Thanksgiving, when posters and displays are made available for purchase and to accompany holiday sales promotions.

"Career days" are for doctors, lawyers, veterinarians, and basketball players. Asking parents to be visitors to our classrooms to share their careers has been a part of school programs for years. However, do we truly represent the broad spectrum of employment possibilities, or do we simply focus on such professions as law, medicine, and sports? How many children have parents whose jobs represent these careers? Are we shutting out parents and children

when we exclude the auto mechanic, the appliance-repair technician, the child-care worker, the workers who pave roads and build homes, and the mother or father who makes a life choice to spend time caring for her or his child at home?

These scenarios represent the subtle and not-so-subtle ways we as adults have responsibility for the biases that children exhibit in their behaviors. Perhaps, as parents and teachers, we have three considerations in helping our children acquire antibias attitudes and beliefs:

1. To examine together what is in our hearts and minds and, ultimately, our actions
2. To become more cognizant of how young children acquire social information and moral knowledge
3. To provide guided experiences for children to engage in moral reasoning and to practice antibias behaviors

Adults as Moral Figures in the Lives of Children

The topic of adults as moral figures in the lives of children has been addressed through our discussion of myths and stereotypes. As psychiatrist Robert Coles stated in his book *How to Raise a Moral Child: The Moral Intelligence of Children* (1997):

> The child is a witness; the child is an ever-attentive witness of grown-up **morality**— or lack thereof; the child looks and looks for cues as to how one ought to behave, and finds them galore as we parents and teachers go about our lives, making choices, addressing people, showing in action our rock-bottom assumptions, desires, and values, and thereby telling those young observers much more than we may realize. (p. 5)

The following are real-life examples collected through informal conversations with friends and parents:

- A young child accompanies his father to the grocery store. The father pays for the groceries and receives change from the clerk. The father and child leave the store, and the father, counting his change, comments that he has been given too much. The child also hears, "This is my lucky day!" from the father, and they begin their trip home. What did the child learn?
- A child is playing with her friend one evening while their mothers talk over coffee in the kitchen. The children overhear one mother complaining that the little boy in her daughter's classroom takes too much of the teacher's time and distracts the teacher from paying attention to her daughter. The mother thinks that children with "those kinds" of disabilities should be removed from the classroom. What did the children learn?
- A little girl whose family is Jewish discovers that other girls in her class have been invited to a friend's party. After investigating, the mother and the teacher discover that the only girls not invited to the party were her daughter and two African American girls in the class. What did these little girls learn?
- A young boy is repeatedly taunted because he is not thin. Finally, the boy's mother, who becomes exasperated at seeing her child hurt and in tears, confronts

the offender. The offender quickly denies the taunt and says he feels sorry for the boy because the boy is "fat." What has the offender learned?

■ A little girl comes crying to her father; she has been teased by other girls because her clothes don't match. She tells her father that she just wants to be "herself" but that others don't like her that way. How does the girl maintain her spirit of individualism?

■ Hurrying to get into the car and take the children to their activities, a mother becomes frustrated. In her frustration, she uses profane language, which her two young sons overhear. Later, one son uses the same language in front of the mother's friend. The mother, embarrassed, criticizes the child in front of the other adult, saying, "I don't know where you hear such language!" How will this child deal with the confusion created by this mother?

Constructing Knowledge About Moral Dilemmas

The situations just discussed serve as examples of the ways children witness moral dilemmas in their lives. We must, however, remember that children respond to these situations in varying ways across developmental ages. Young children construct knowledge about what is right and wrong from what they see, hear, and experience. Their perceptions of what is right and wrong reflect their development in terms of moral reasoning skills. Their **social cognition**—"an ability to read social situations and to interpret the feelings, motives, and intentions of others" (Trawick-Smith, 1997, p. G-9)—requires "systems for identifying and classifying self and others; for making inferences about people's thoughts, feelings, and intentions; for understanding institutions such as the family and the government; and about learning about rules and values that define right and wrong" (Edwards, 1986, p. 4). Let us explore the work of Jean Piaget and Lawrence Kohlberg, two theorists who worked to develop models depicting the growth or moral reasoning across the ages, experiences, and developmental levels of young children.

A "constructivist," Piaget (1983) believed that young children construct their knowledge about people, places, and events through their interactions with individuals, objects, and situations. Children bring their unique ways of thinking to encounters with the social aspects of their environments. For the young child, this way of thinking follows a process of development that proceeds in an orderly and predictable sequence, with children moving from thinking based on the concrete to thinking based on the more abstract. This concrete way of thinking also relates to the child's growing sense of "right" and "wrong."

Piaget (1932) used techniques in observation and play to understand the development of moral thinking in children. He asked children, during their sessions of play, a series of questions that posed moral dilemmas. Studying their answers, Piaget concluded that most preschool (preoperational) children are *premoral*, meaning that they would change the rules of the game in their favor. Similar experiences may be found with young children in sorting objects by various attributes when the rules being followed in sorting change periodically.

This way of thinking is also in keeping with what is known about the egocentric nature of the young child, who believes that all actions are centered around her or his being. The child who believes that a parent died because the child was "naughty" or that a parent left the family because the child did not eat her vegetables exhibits such egocentrism. This behavior does not indicate that something is "wrong" with the child; it is simply a reflection of that child's level of thinking at this particular stage of development.

A sense of moral realism appears during the primary years (concrete), with children exhibiting behaviors that are very rule bound. Authority figures such as parents, teachers, and God, or the child's higher power, become very important. Rules are unchangeable, regardless of the situation. Think about the exclamations of "You're not supposed to do that!" that you have heard from children when they see another child break a rule.

Individuals may not reach the final stage of moral development—*moral relativism*—until adolescence or adulthood (formal thought). Although rules are respected, it seems to be understood that exceptions can be made. The intent of the action may be taken into account. For example, the driver of a car does not usually intend to back into another car in the parking lot. This act, though unfortunate and costly, does not generally indicate an immoral act, as understood by someone in the stage of moral relativism.

Kohlberg (1984) continued to explore the work of Piaget, arriving at three levels of moral development. Each level contains two stages and depicts a developmental shift in the child's perspective of the "moral" situation. The stages are presented in abbreviated form:

Level 1: Preconventional (Egocentric Perspective)
- Stage 1: Obey rules to avoid punishment.
- Stage 2: Personal rewards determine actions.

Level 2: Conventional (Rule-bound Perspective)
- Stage 3: Obey rules to please others.
- Stage 4: Laws are absolute.

Level 3: Postconventional (Principle Perspective)
- Stage 5: Good is determined by agreeing on a social contract.
- Stage 6: Good is determined by ethical principles that are universal.

According to Kohlberg, most young children are at the preconventional level (Trawick-Smith, 1997). Note that, because Kohlberg's work reflected a limited population of children, a number of theorists have worked to expand Kohlberg's work to consider issues such as gender, culture, and experience. For example, Carol Gilligan (1982), a student of Kohlberg, has written extensively about gender and moral development, noting that girls are more likely to consider the aspect of **care** in moral reasoning and to look for solutions that will be of benefit to all.

We should take caution in making assumptions about young children and their levels of moral reasoning at specific ages. For example, some primary children are, in fact, capable of making exceptions to the rules of games to accommodate their classmates who have disabilities. Observations of individual children in given situations should be used to determine each child's ability to engage in moral reasoning. Consideration should also be given to the types of activities that serve to foster the child's development of moral reasoning. These activities are discussed in a later section of this chapter.

Children also experience developmental shifts in their understanding of issues regarding diversity (e.g., gender, race, social class) by using physical characteristics to make their judgments. Although children label people as girls or boys by such features as length of hair and gender-specific clothing, they generally do not understand that gender will not change (e.g., boys cannot become mommies) until the end of the preschool period.

Children appear to notice racial cues during infancy (Katz, 1976). By age 3 or 4, children can label people by racial group (Goodman, 1952). By age 5, children begin to relate to, and identify with, people of their own culture and race (Aboud, 1988). Until somewhere around age 7, however, children may think that race can be changed by washing the skin or by changing clothing (Ramsey, 1987).

Even though preschoolers do not understand the concept of *social class*, they do understand that there are differences in what people have in terms of material goods. They are also beginning to be able to discuss what is fair and unfair in terms of distribution of those goods (Ramsey, 1986).

DEVELOPMENTALLY APPROPRIATE PRACTICE AND ISSUES OF DIVERSITY

Even though young children may not yet have acquired the cognitive capacity for engaging in complex mental actions with regard to issues of diversity, they are capable of participating in concrete events and experiences that will assist them in acquiring social knowledge. As noted by Edwards (1986) in her discussion of facilitating social and moral knowledge of young children:

> Any early childhood setting presents many opportunities for adults and children to talk together about social and moral issues. Conversation can help children to organize their thinking about questions that are interesting to them. It gives teachers the kind of concrete information that they need in order to understand children's developmental needs and communicate effectively in guidance and disciplinary situations. (p. 21)

Much conversation results from the spontaneous play of children. Teachers, however, can provide activities about various social issues that will further stimulate and focus discussion. Edwards (1986) called such activities "thinking games." An example is a stereotype expressed by a child that all Chinese people eat in restaurants (this was the child's experience in seeing Chinese people). This type of overgeneralization is common in young children. Ramsey (1986, p. 97) suggests the following ideas for helping children broaden their ideas about the Chinese culture through specific activities: (a) Provide photographs of Chinese Americans in their home settings and (b) set up role-play areas of eating at restaurants and eating at home (chopsticks, bowls, and rice can be used in both settings).

Developing and implementing such activities provide many opportunities for teachers and parents to collaborate. In doing so, the adults engage in their own developmental growth as they share information and ideas and implement strategies for assisting children in their thinking about various topics. New (1994) noted that this type of work provides many opportunities for teachers to be engaged as researchers as they "not only seek out opportunities to learn from the diverse children in their classrooms, but incorporate parents into a partnership affiliation that is denied by such concepts as 'parent education' "(p. 79).

BUILDING "WORLD KNOWLEDGE": UNDERSTANDING CHARACTERISTICS OF DIVERSE GROUPS

The child walking through a classroom door must first be viewed as an individual whose life is embedded "in a family, a community, a culture, and a society" (Mallory & New, 1994, p. 8). The child and the family bring specific competencies, viewpoints, and practices that will become a part of the classroom's culture. The teacher who regards children and families with inquiry rather than with predetermined attitudes will be better able to understand each child's learning characteristics; styles of interacting with children, adults, and materials; and social, physical, and cognitive competencies. In doing so, the teacher will be better prepared to support each child's development within the context of the family and the community.

Teachers must see children as individuals within the context of their **sociocultural** settings. Noted African American author Janice Hale encourages teachers to broaden their awareness of the characteristics and competencies of specific groups so that children's development can be nurtured in the classroom setting. Teachers and caregivers are also encouraged to become aware of cultural differences in the way children's needs are met—"in how teachers and caregivers interact and relate to children, in the nitty-gritty of body language and nonverbal communication" (Gonzalez-Mena, 1993, p. 4).

Learning about the world helps children learn more about their neighbors.

One can learn about other cultures in many ways, but five strategies seem most effective:

1. Studying and reading about the culture
2. Working with individuals from the culture who can serve as guides
3. Participating in daily living experiences of the culture
4. Learning the language of the culture (Lynch & Hanson, 1998)
5. Developing culturally respectful and responsive dialogue skills (Barrera, Corso, & McPherson, 2003; Ontake, Santos, & Fowler, 2000)

Creating Persona Dolls in Kindergarten

Patrick McDonald had been teaching kindergarten for 15 years. Teaching has changed over the years for Mr. McDonald. The district mandates for academics have increased, and the focus on academics over social and emotional development have slowly infiltrated his once completely play-based curriculum in which sociodramatic play was the main vehicle for learning literacy and mathematics. But every year, he still did an "all about me" project with the children for one week at the beginning of the year. This project gave him the opportunity to learn about the families of the children in his class since children brought in family photos and they made stories of their lives. Children made full-size silhouettes of themselves and hung them around the room. There were many other activities that also provided opportunities for each child to feel good about him- or herself. At end of the week, each family brought in a dish of their favorite recipe to share.

But Mr. McDonald and his class were in Wyoming, where many families felt they were all of the same culture. Mr. McDonald saw some of the same recipes brought in every year—three-bean casserole, beef jerky, and great oatmeal cookies. He was also concerned that the "all about me" theme directed each child to focus on him- or herself. He really wanted to develop more of a community where the children learned how to work collaboratively with persons both alike and different from themselves. He felt he was doing more individual and whole group academic work with these 5- and 6-year-olds. He realized he was drifting from his personal teaching style that was so successful in building the foundation for kindergarten children to be highly successful in school and in life.

In his search on the Internet before the start of school this year, Mr. McDonald found a Web site in Great Britain (www.persona-doll-training.org/pd/about-us.php) where teachers were continuing the use of persona dolls based on Louise Derman-Sparks's (1989) book, *Antibias Curriculum: Tools for Empowering Young Children*. He quickly found his copy of the book to begin building a new theme this year—the friends project. This would be a simple name for a theme that would continue throughout the year as children built lasting friendships with other children, learning more about each other and how to get along with others while still developing a great academic learning base.

He built the "friends" theme with his students. As children entered the classroom on the first day, he asked each child what he liked to play at home. He wrote down favorite play-time activities, and together the children categorized and graphed these onto a large chart that hung on the wall for several weeks. At circle time each morning for the first week, Mr. McDonald and the children shared other likes and dislikes of each child. They often graphed or wrote and drew stories about other people they knew who liked the same ice cream or didn't like the same colors. In small groups, children counted out the same number of beans as the number of children in the room who ate cereal for breakfast.

Mr. McDonald read stories about children in other places in the United States who had friends with similar and different favorite foods or had unusual pets. Through their discussions, Mr. McDonald found that many children were familiar with using the computer, so he set up a computer center with some Internet sites bookmarked, such as Class Brain (www.classbrain.com), so that children could learn about the lifestyles of children in other parts of the country.

At the end of the second week, instead of doing the usual silhouettes, Mr. McDonald asked the children to create a two-dimensional paper figure of themselves. He asked them to think about how this doll would show others who came in the room how the children in this room are friends and learn to work and play together. Each wrote or drew a story about him- or herself as Mr. McDonald had done in the past years, but this time, he asked each student to think about how to be a good friend to others. He hung the paper figures with students' stories around the room. Through a district grant, Mr. McDonald was also able to purchase some persona dolls with stories of problems they encountered and how they worked through the problems, or how their special needs didn't stop them from participating in activities. Each day he told a different story.

This year, when Mr. McDonald organized parent night with food sharing, he asked each family to prepare a food that a friend of their child liked and bring in the recipe. Mr. McDonald shared the persona dolls with families. He also showed families how the children would be engaging in the friends theme all year to learn through cooperative activities, some of which could also be done at home. The children helped their teacher show this theme during center time activities they had prepared with academic games and projects in which children worked together. Picture cards on each table illustrated the ways children could accomplish the tasks. For those families who were unable to attend the family night, Mr. McDonald had a friend come in to videotape the event and make DVDs to send home with the children. This family night was a big hit with families and the next week, parents sent Mr. McDonald e-mails to let him know how much they enjoyed the night, and also to provide some other suggestions for the friends theme.

Each of these strategies, particularly learning the language of the culture, is helpful in increasing one's ability to communicate effectively with children and families of differing cultures. Further, communication effectiveness is significantly improved when the teacher:

- Respects individuals from other cultures
- Makes continued and sincere attempts to understand the world from others' points of view
- Is open to new learning
- Is flexible
- Has a sense of humor
- Tolerates ambiguity well
- Approaches others with a desire to learn (Lynch & Hanson, 1998, p. 51)

Let us begin our discussion of cultural variations with the Anglo European culture, keeping in mind that we are speaking in generalizations and that families will have their specific idiosyncrasies and characteristics. Time and space do not permit complete discussion of any one group, nor will descriptions alone take the place of actual experiences with people of cultures different from your own. These can be used, however, to aid you as you take your journey into teaching with culturally and linguistically diverse children and families. Characteristics will primarily relate to views of child rearing and communication strategies. For further information about lifestyles, beliefs, and practices of

FIGURE 4.1   Strategies for Classroom Teachers to Encourage Involvement of Diverse Families

1. One custom from the Montessori curriculum is that on each child's birthday, the teacher sets up a lit candle in the middle of the room while children sit around it in a circle. The birthday child walks around the lit candle with a globe of the world in his or her hands. The child navigates around the "sun" as many times as he or she is years old to signify the number of times the earth has gone around the sun since the child was born. The child's family is also asked to send in photos or mementos of the child's life to that point. This stimulates some lively discussion about the diversity and similarities of children's customs.

2. Instead of having families send in cupcakes for their child's birthday, ask families if they might send in some great ethnic snack they make at home so children can learn about other children's traditions and customs.

3. Schedule a morning meeting every day so children have this wonderful opportunity to bond and demonstrate how they are individuals with ideas and thoughts but also part of a learning community that supports diversity.

4. During circle and music times, include songs from children's heritage by inviting families to send in songs they sing. Families can be welcomed to come to the class and teach the song to the children.

5. Many schools have a family photo gallery of significant events such as the birth of a sibling or family reunions. Change the photos often to encourage frequent visits and conversations by the children.

6. Family-centered children's literature representing diverse cultures, especially those of children in the class, should be available in the book corner, but can also have a place in the dramatic play and block areas to help children feel at home in these areas.

7. Children can be invited to bring in a Family Treasure, some valued memento. Family members can explain the treasure and children can engage in labeling or writing short stories to go next to a display of this treasure (Brinson, 2005).

specific groups, we suggest that you read such texts as *Developing Cross-Cultural Competence: A Guide for Working With Young Children and Their Families* (Lynch & Hanson, 1998), *Knowing and Serving Diverse Families* (Hildebrand, Phenice, Gray, & Hines, 2000), and *Bridging Cultures Between Home and School: A Guide for Teachers* (Trumbull, Rothstein-Fisch, Greenfield, & Quiroz, 2001). Some specific strategies teachers can use to help children understand their own culture and others can be found in Figure 4.1. Most activities center on community building among diverse families.

Families of Anglo European Descent

Families of European descent are dominant in the United States. Their ancestors were among those who explored and settled in this country during the 19th and early 20th centuries. The first group was composed mainly of individuals from England, Ireland,

and Germany. The second group, in the 1860s to 1890s, included many Scandinavians. A third major group of immigrants, after the 1890s, came from Italy, Russia, and the Austro-Hungarian Empire (Hanson, 1992). Values and assumptions that have evolved from the Anglo European background are as follows:

- A high regard for individualism and privacy
- A belief in equality of all individuals
- A preference for informality in interactions
- A focus toward future, change, and progress
- A belief in the goodness of humanity
- A focus on time
- A focus on achievement and a strong work ethic
- A focus on materialism
- A directness and assertiveness in interactions (Althen, 1988)

Although these values speak to a general population from Europe, families may bring more specific practices from their own countries and communities.

Families appear more concerned with developing autonomy and **independence** in young children than in the **interdependence** of the family. One example is in the sleeping patterns and customs of families. Young children are generally expected to go to bed before adults, to comfort themselves in going to sleep, and to sleep by themselves from infancy. This is in contrast with today's Italian and Japanese families, who believe that parents should respond to their young children's needs to remain close to family members (New, 1994; Wolf, Lozoff, Latz, & Paludetto, 1996). Education and achievement are highly regarded among families of Anglo European descent, with parents expecting to be involved in their child's education and to be kept informed by teachers of the child's progress. Families also expect to be involved in decision making within the schools through boards, councils, and parent–teacher groups.

Families of African Descent

More than 4 million Africans—Mandingo, Ibos, Efiks, Hausas, Krus, Yorubas, Ashantis, and Senegalese (Bennett, 1966)—were brought against their will to North America. As slaves and later in freedom, they played a critical role in the development and building of America. Both plantation economies and the mercantile systems depended on slave labor. "Their contribution to trade, industry, and agriculture was significant and immeasurable, and they distinguished themselves in the major wars of their new land as well" (Willis, 1992, p. 123).

Through the years, many African Americans have been able to move beyond the legacy of slavery. A history of slavery, oppression, and abandonment by a society that enslaved them, however, has had overwhelming long-term effects for many families. In 2002, 36 million African Americans (13 percent of the total population) lived in the United States—now the second largest ethnic **minority**—and 23 percent of their families had incomes below the poverty level. In addition, 43 percent of children in African American families live in homes where the father is absent (McKinnon, 2003).

According to Hildebrand et al. (2000), "Endurance of suffering while moving ahead is a major theme found in Black families" (p. 59). How have African American families been able to survive and move forward under such economic and social constraints? They have persevered through:

- Strong kinship bonds among a variety of family households
- Strong work, education, and achievement orientation
- A high level of flexibility in family roles
- A strong commitment to religious values and church participation
- A humanistic orientation for perceiving the world and relationships (p. 59)

Teachers can build on family strengths by respecting the strong sense of kinship experienced by children. Within this system, children are expected to show respect for their elders and to obey their parents and older members of the family and community. Appropriate titles are preferred. The parents' style of interacting may be more authoritative, and showing an individual that you care about her or him through your actions may be more important than the verbal expression of love (Willis, 1992).

Teachers will also note a strong oral tradition in families of African descent, characterized by proverbs, songs, stories, and fables (Hale, 1991). As slaves, traditional ways of communicating (e.g., drumming) were often prohibited. Slaves used other ways to communicate the rich traditions of their African cultures and to transmit wisdom necessary for dealing with adversity across generations. Stories, proverbs, spirituals, and folktales were all sources of teaching for African families in bondage to their owners. Today, this oral tradition continues among African American families. In encouraging teachers to make use of this tradition, Hale (1991) noted:

> These stories transmit the message to African American children that quicksand and landmines characterize the road to becoming an African American achiever in America; however, they also transmit the message that it is possible to overcome obstacles. (p. 13)

Families of Asian Descent

Asian Americans represent more than 29 distinct subgroups that differ in language, religions, and cultural practices (Feng, 1994). This population, characterized by great diversity, originates from three major geographic areas: (a) east Asia (China, Japan, and Korea), (b) Southeast Asia (Cambodia, Laos, Vietnam, Burma, Thailand, Malaysia, Singapore, Indonesia, and the Philippines), and (c) south Asia (India, Pakistan, and Sri Lanka) (Chan, 1992).

Asian Americans are one of the fastest growing minority groups in the United States, representing about 4.4 percent of the population (Reeves & Bennett, 2003). Despite the many variations in practices and beliefs because of the great diversity of the origins, languages, and sociocultural experiences of these families, some practices, values, and beliefs are shared (Feng, 1994).

Many Asian cultures have been influenced by "the three teachings," or the philosophies of Confucianism, Taoism, and Buddhism. In his philosophy of humanity,

Confucius (551–479 B.C.) prescribed a way of living that reflected virtue and wisdom. Being moral, trustworthy, and benevolent to one's fellow human beings was highly valued. Loyalty and obedience to one's parents and reverence for one's ancestors were also taught.

Taoism focused on the value of meditation and transcending that which is worldly. Its legendary patriarch, Lao-tzu (born in 604 B.C.), advocated inner strength, selflessness, spontaneity, and harmony with nature and humanity.

Buddhism, founded by Prince Siddhartha Gautama (ca. 563–ca. 483 B.C.), entered China from India following the establishment of Confucianism and Taoism. This religion also focused on self-discipline, meditation, and the renouncing of that which is worldly (Chan, 1992). "The traditional collectivist values of Chinese, Koreans, Cambodians, Laotians, and Vietnamese in particular are rooted in the 'three teachings' " (p. 212).

The concern for maintaining the interdependence of the family and the individual's loyalty to the family is seen in child-rearing practices. Behaviors of the individual are seen as reflecting on one's ancestors and one's race. "While striving to defend the family's honor and enhance its reputation, one must properly observe historical events and maintain family traditions" (Chan, 1992, p. 212).

Whereas American schools emphasize individualism and competition, Asian children have generally been taught to think first of the group. "Most Asian-American parents teach their children to value education, respect authority, feel responsible for relatives, and show self-control" (Feng, 1994, p. 1). Consequently, informality among teachers and students may be confusing, and a quiet, structured environment with a good deal of teacher reinforcement is valued (Feng, 1994).

This Advent wreath, made by a parent, shares the culture of the family with the school.

Families of Hispanic Descent

During the 15th century, explorers from Spain conquered and exploited many parts of the New World, including what is now the southern part of the United States, Mexico, and Central and South America. Three Hispanic groups now compose the majority of Hispanics in the United States: Mexicans, Puerto Ricans, and Cuban Hispanics. The remainder are from Central and South America and the Caribbean. Composing the largest minority group within the United States (13.3 percent of the population), Hispanics living in this country are expected to undergo a rapid increase in number into the 21st century (Ramirez & de la Cruz, 2002) as individuals seek freedom from economic and political oppression.

Even though their geographic origins are varied, as with other groups, Hispanics share numerous cultural values, practices, and beliefs. Many of these are related to Catholicism as the dominant religion. In Hispanic or Latino cultures, marriage is for the purpose of having children, with the relationship between parent and child of more importance than the relationship between husband and wife. The attitude toward children is nurturing, and parents may be indulgent and permissive with young children. Children are taught to interact with others with respect and dignity and are expected to undertake work roles within the family. Children are reared within the context of the extended family, and respect for their elders is an important aspect of their teaching (Zuniga, 1992). Although education is valued, its goal is for the benefit of the family and not simply for the individual. Should education come between the individual and the family, it may receive a low priority. Consequently, the message that people are valued should be a high priority for the teacher working with these children (Hildebrand et al., 2000).

Families of Middle Eastern Descent

On September 11, 2001, the World Trade Center in New York was destroyed by terrorists in hijacked commercial planes. Thousands of citizens of the United States and countries around the world were lost in this mass destruction. Waves of disbelief and terror spread across the country and the world. At the time of this writing, the United States is engaged in war with members of the Taliban, an Islamic fundamentalist, extremist group, staging its battle in Afghanistan. The terrorists were from the Middle East, and suddenly, families of Middle Eastern descent living in the United States found themselves the target of prejudicial attacks based on fear and lack of information. Even second-generation families were suspect.

While some people reacted with physical and verbal taunts, others sought to find more information about the culture and practices in efforts to separate the extremist activities of terrorists from the daily lives of their neighbors. Mosques, churches, and schools became places to exchange information and focus on dampening prejudicial acts. The following information is provided in this spirit. It has been gleaned from the work of Virginia-Shirin Sharifzadeh (1992, pp. 441–478).

It is not easy to categorize cultural practices and family life of "Middle Easterners" because there are so many countries, groups, languages, traditions, histories, and religious practices within the broad geographic area known as the Middle East. Perhaps it is best to offer what is most common in our discussion of families of the Middle East, noting that care must always be taken to recognize differences among individuals and families.

Religion is a pivotal point in our discussion because it shapes much of the Middle Eastern cultural practices, social customs, and political activity. The most widespread religion in the Middle East is Islam in its Sunni form. This represents the main body of Muslims who believe that God gave his final revelation to the Prophet Mohammed. Sunnis believe that the Prophet Mohammed transmitted his temporal authority to a line of caliphs, or religious heads.

Language is a primary way that people from the Middle East define themselves. Arabic is most widely spoken and ranks sixth in the world's most common languages.

Immigration to the United States has been a common practice among individuals of Middle Eastern descent since the late 19th century. Individuals distinguish themselves by identifying their political allegiances. Political instability and oppression by fundamentalist groups have been driving forces behind immigration. The current Taliban in Afghanistan serves as one example, with rigid and extremist practices toward women.

Family is of utmost consideration in many families from the Middle East. The extended family has historically been used to care for children and the elderly. This contrasts with the Western style of going outside the family for more formal care for one's children. Loyalty to the family comes first. Life within the family is shaped by religious practices and a patriarchal family structure. Great pride is taken in the accomplishments of the family as opposed to a focus on individualism.

Children are important, and traditions may set a precedent for having a certain number of children and desiring boys. As with many groups, having many children meant that families could continue to care for each other and survive. Care of the elderly in the family is seen as a particularly important task of the children. It is seen as important that families care for their children, with caregiving roles assigned to women and providing for the family and dealing with external concerns assigned to the men. Mothers may be more permissive as they bond with their child.

Individuation is not seen as important as it is in Western cultures. Interdependence is more important than independence. This is reflected in the inclusion of children in family events and gatherings and responsibilities given to children.

As noted, fathers are seen as head of the household, and caregivers and teachers may interact with the father in discussions about the child. Because of the importance of the extended family, parents may have difficulty sharing their "power" with teachers and caregivers.

The interdependence of the family is apparent in the behavioral expectations of children. Children are expected to learn by watching their parents and family members, who serve as role models. Discipline revolves around respect and obedience of the parents and elders in the family. Children should be cooperative and reveal their friends to family members. Girls must be supervised when away from their home.

Those working with families of Middle Eastern descent should consider:

- The family's history of immigration
- The observed patterns of interaction within the family
- The family's support system
- Communication with the mother while never discounting the father
- Communication that is informal and personalized rather than direct and assertive (Sharifzadeh, 1992, pp. 466–467)

Families of Native American Descent

In 2002, approximately 1.5 million people in the United States identified themselves as American Indians, Eskimos, or Aleuts (Ogunwole, 2002). They make up only approximately 0.75 percent of the total U.S. population (Joe & Malach, 1992), and the numbers of those who report themselves to be of Native American descent on the U.S. Census seem to be dropping. These individuals, descendants of people indigenous to North America, represent many tribes and many languages. "European immigrants, explorers, traders, missionaries, soldiers, colonists, and trappers changed forever the culture and world of the native peoples and most of these changes were negative" (Joe & Malach, 1992, p. 93).

As noted, there are many tribes and, therefore, many different practices. Beliefs about the need for interdependence of the group and a focus on the collective are shared, however. Native Americans also hold a desire for attaining harmony with nature. Hildebrand et al. (2000, p. 143) concluded that four traits characterize the cultural expression of values:

- Self-reliance
- Noninterference
- Nonconfrontation
- Respect for elders

Children are viewed as gifts with unique characteristics that will help determine their place in the tribe. A period of time will pass to observe a child before a name is chosen that represents these characteristics. Elders are given the task of sharing the oral traditions of the tribe with the younger members by passing on stories and songs. Child-rearing responsibilities may be spread to extended family members, and parents may ask advice from older family members in matters relating to child rearing.

Given a history of oppression, Native Americans may have concerns relative to dealing with governmental agencies. Individuals are observed for their behaviors and what they do, rather than what people say.

The diversity of this group makes it particularly important that teachers carefully research the cultural practices of the family with regard to child rearing, participation in the child's education, and style of communication. The rich cultural heritage of this group also provides wonderful opportunities for shared experiences within the classroom setting.

THEME 5   *in practice. . .*

A father has enrolled his child in your center. You notice on the enrollment application that the mother's name is not mentioned. On further investigation, you discover that, in this particular culture, the mother will remain in the background, with the males and the father interacting with school personnel. What might your feelings be in this situation, and how might you best address involving the family in the child's school experience?

Families of Children with Dual Heritage

In the preceding discussions, the cultures of specific groups were addressed. A growing number of children in this country, however, are born into families that are biracial or multiracial. In coming years, these children may be regarded as "children," not as belonging to a representative ethnic group (e.g., Black, White). Parents may identify their child with one ethnic group, with both groups, or with little regard for cultural origins.

FIGURE 4.2	Advocacy Ideas for Teachers to Develop Modern Structures for Family–School Collaboration

1. Collaborate with a valued community leader who shares the language and heritage of families in your class—a "cultural guide"—to develop a survey that you give families to determine their interests in which training they would like the school to provide.

2. Explore the words and phrases that are a part of your life experiences and cultural origins. You can make a list and share it with friends and colleagues. Discuss how these words and phrases impact your beliefs about child rearing, the culture of your school and church, how you greet certain people or avoid greeting others, what you consider to be appropriate dress.

3. Create a list of questions you would ask someone who is interviewing for a position in your school as an aide or teacher and must be sensitive to differences in families and teachers:

   ■ Regarding roles and expectations
   ■ Regarding personality characteristics (e.g., comfortable in new situations, able to give input in decisions)
   ■ Regarding worldview associated with cultural beliefs and acculturation
   ■ Regarding family and professional background

4. Using Building Support for Better Schools: Seven Steps to Engaging Hard-to-Reach Communities (2000; available online at www.sedl.org/pubs/family27/building support.pdf), a guide for involving hard-to-reach families, create an outline of the seven steps suggested. Work with families, other teachers, and an administrator to fill in specific strategies that would work in your community.

Teachers should work with parents to determine the wishes of the family in acknowledging the heritage(s) of the child. In this way, the teacher can be more responsive to the child and the family in planning daily classroom experiences (Morrison & Rodgers, 1996). Some teachers at your center or school may inquire about various culturally sensitive family practices. Other teachers may not realize that there are more appropriate ways of helping families of diverse cultural backgrounds feel welcome. The suggestions in Figure 4.2 can be used as you advocate for more modern structures of family collaboration.

SUMMARY OF PRACTICES FOR INCLUSION OF ALL FAMILIES

T his chapter has taken us many places in our search for understanding how to build partnerships with families and within communities by regarding, respecting, and building on people's differences. We have attempted to define culture by beginning with that which is unique to our near environment and moving to "worlds" that are "foreign" to us. We have explored the role that culture plays in shaping our lives as we move into diverse worlds. We have tapped the roots of multicultural education—its meaning, value, and applications. We have given thought to the moral implications of valuing the diversity of our neighbors and looked into ways we can foster such responsibility in our children. We have wandered through various cultures, exploring their uniqueness and sense of family. This brings us to what we need as teachers and caregivers: practical ideas for implementing this perspective with families and within communities.

Before we begin to explore these ideas as shared in printed materials and through an interview with a respected teacher, keep in mind that our focus is always on the strength of the family. We should move away from a needs-assessment viewpoint, which in particular sees native language as a problem, to the "asset inventory" that focuses on native language as a resource (Garcia, 1997, p. 12). Garcia (p. 13) lists five practical applications that teachers can use in regarding the roots and wings of children:

1. Take the role of the ethnographer in learning about the linguistic and cultural diversity of children. Learn to pronounce the child's name as it is pronounced at home. Keep written notes about this information.

2. Demonstrate your willingness to learn about the language by learning some of the language that you will find useful in working with the child and the family.

3. Be up to date on new information about cultural inclusion. Incorporate songs, games, and poems from various cultures into the curriculum.

4. Share the knowledge you acquire with both the educational and noneducational community.

5. Be an advocate for the children "by nurturing, celebrating, and challenging them."

Designing the Learning Environment: Possibilities for the Inclusion of Families and the Community

Some controversy always surrounds bringing materials and information from other cultures into the preschool classroom because those cultures and ethnic groups might not be represented in the classroom. Children who are a part of homogeneous groups, however, need this type of experience even more than those who have opportunities to experience other cultures in the course of their daily living experiences as they move into a diverse world.

Ramsey (1987) suggested that the physical setting should be designed to foster children's (a) positive views of others from different races, cultures, and classes; (b) ability to empathize and to identify with children from other groups; (c) respect and appreciation for other ways of life; and (d) awareness of a larger social environment (p. 59).

Perhaps one of the most interesting ways for children and adults to participate in experiences designed to meet such goals is found in an approach to curriculum development known as **webbing**. In this approach, children's questions and ideas serve as prompts for possible curriculum adventures. As active participants in the learning experiences of the classroom, children engage in activities that are relevant to their interests and experiences. Teachers listen to the children, plan experiences, and watch learning events emerge from the children's active explorations with materials and individuals.

Some teachers have become interested in this type of **emergent curriculum**, including those teachers at the Burrier Child Development Center at Eastern Kentucky University. In helping the teachers take on the roles of researcher and developer of curricula, course instructors and preschool administrators introduced the work of teachers in Reggio Emilia, Italy. Information from *The Hundred Languages of Children: The Reggio Emilia Approach to Early Childhood Education* (Edwards, Gandini, & Forman, 1993) was shared along with videos depicting the project work of the Italian children (*To Make a Portrait of a Lion* [Comune di Reggio Emilia, Centro Documentazione Ricerca ducativa Nidi e Scuole dell'Infanzi, 1987]; *The Long Jump* [Forman & Gandini, 1991], and *An Amusement Park for Birds* [Forman et al., 1993]). Provocative work on emergent curriculum via webbing as shared by Elizabeth Jones and John Nimmo (1994) was also introduced.

Of course, the incredible graphic representations created by the children are of primary interest, as is the research these youngsters do as they create and re-create images. The role of the adult, both parent and teacher, however, is very significant in these schools of northern Italy. Teachers stay with the same group of children across the three years of their participation in the program, building strong bonds with the children and their families. Families participate in the children's projects, lending their opinions to selected school projects and participating in the projects by providing both human and material resources.

One of the most community based of these projects comes with the harvesting of grapes each year. The farmers come to the school to visit with the children and to discuss the process of the harvest. This gives the children an opportunity to build relationships with the farm "family" and to ask questions, predict, and begin investigations into the process of the harvest—a tradition of this Italian countryside.

The children are then taken to a farm, where they pick, sort, mash, and in every way become active participants of the process of the harvest. After the tasks are completed, the children return to their classrooms, where they are again visited by the farmers to share in the celebration of harvest—to drink the grape juice and to share food and memories. All events are documented in photographs and in the children's graphic depictions of the days of work and the time shared together (Department of Early Education, City of Reggio Emilia, Region of Emilia Romagna, 1987).

As a team of teachers, we watched these videos, shared our readings and impressions, and began the work of implementing a project approach in our classrooms, always watchful of ways to keep the families involved. Not yet ready to give up completely the control of selecting a topic, we decided to work on the topic of "homes" because this seemed to be a common denominator to our group of children (none were homeless). The topic also seemed to provide many ways to go with cultural activities—different locations, types, arrangements, and so on. Our original web of homes looked something like that shown in Figure 4.3.

Teachers and children took walks around our campus to see what the buildings were made of and how they were constructed. These walks served as provocations for creating homes. The children experimented with ways to build homes by using cardboard boxes and other trashables. We placed materials in our dramatic play center that might be used for taking care of homes. We invited parents in to talk about construction and took a field trip to a building center to explore building materials. Even after all that, much more was still to be done as we explored books with pictures of homes from other parts of the world (Maya Angelou's *My Painted House, My Friendly Chicken, and Me* [1994] is a wonderful resource), built homes with blocks and other manipulatives, and discussed the types of homes that our families shared.

We, as teachers, learned from this experience and made plans to work with the children again on this topic, which had caught and kept their interest for weeks. We also made plans to learn more about homes in cultures across the world and to explore possibilities

FIGURE 4.3   A Web of Subtopics Related to Homes

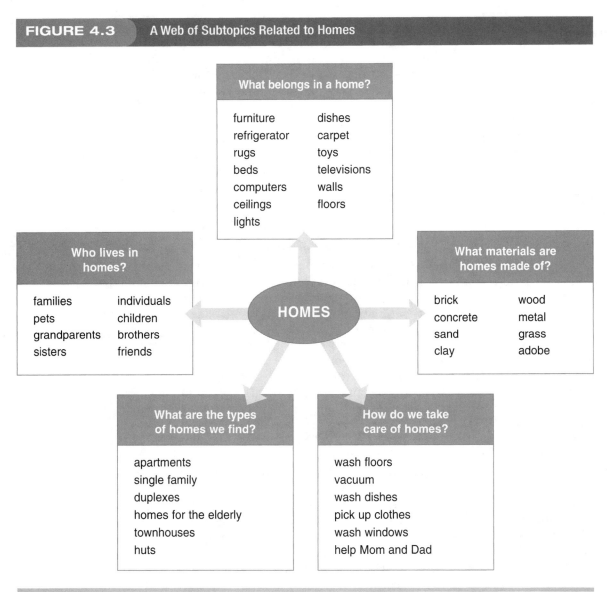

What belongs in a home?

furniture	dishes
refrigerator	carpet
rugs	toys
beds	televisions
computers	walls
ceilings	floors
lights	

Who lives in homes?

families	individuals
pets	children
grandparents	brothers
sisters	friends

HOMES

What materials are homes made of?

brick	wood
concrete	metal
sand	grass
clay	adobe

What are the types of homes we find?

apartments
single family
duplexes
homes for the elderly
townhouses
huts

How do we take care of homes?

wash floors
vacuum
wash dishes
pick up clothes
wash windows
help Mom and Dad

for extending this project. Figuring the cost of homes would be a possibility for older children, as would more sophisticated forms of measuring and construction.

Topics such as the home can be a wonderful focal point for discussions among teachers and families and children. Wellhousen (1996) and Harris and Fuqua (1996) presented many possibilities for exploring diversity through a study of homes across the preschool and primary years. Still, some teachers are concerned that children will feel uncomfortable that their homes are too small, too unkempt, or too "something" to share with others or that comparison will make children feel "less than" in some way. Such a case is a rich opportunity for teachers to put into practice the valuing of diversity and respect for each other. Even though we know that young children are aware of these differences, perhaps the prejudices created are those projected by well-meaning adults.

Edwards and Springate (1995) provided suggestions on how teachers can support the work of children in their emergent interests and creativity. These suggestions can also be related to the ways that teachers can include families and the community in their work with young children.

Time. Children need time to explore, investigate, and reflect on the topic being studied. Our work on homes took place over several weeks, and still many avenues were left untraveled. If teachers take time to present for study those relevant topics of interest to children, more time will be available for parents and community members to become involved. For example, our study of homes presented opportunities for bricklayers, carpenters, roofers, concrete suppliers, and so on to become involved. Opportunities for community field trips to relevant locations would be more viable as well. Word-of-mouth experiences also bring more ideas for input from families when time is given to share.

Space. Children need space to work where materials and projects under construction will not be disrupted. Similarly, adults may need space in the classroom to leave materials they are sharing for further discussion and exploration. A table or other space to house the T square and blueprints shared by the architect or the photographs of homes in other lands shared by a parent or community member lends continuity, allowing children to revisit the resource person's information.

Materials. Children need materials with which to work. In our exploration of homes, we found trashables to be wonderful resources for building. It was also helpful when community members and parents could share brick, mortar, stones, and so on so that the children could see and feel actual textures of materials. Even more interesting would have been some assistance in making adobe and exploring thatch and other forms of materials alternative to our area.

Climate for Learning. A climate that supports open-ended investigations is desirable, if not essential, to the success of project work. For example, in Reggio Emilia, parents meet together with teachers to discuss the work of projects. Perhaps communication with families about possible projects for the year and suggested meetings for those who are interested in collaborating on these projects would be helpful. It is also helpful to "interview" the families in an informal way during home visits and conferences to discover the interests and skills of the parents and whether they would like to share in the school setting. In this environment, the ways of knowing and contributions of all participants are valuable.

Occasions. Which occasions provoke a desire to learn about something unexplored—for children and for adults? Perhaps a new building is going up in town or some child is moving to a different home. Perhaps the school is being renovated or a barn is being raised. Whatever the topic, events and occasions about it will excite and attract the attention of both children and adults. Whether it is the harvest of the grapes in Italy or the harvest of a different crop in the United States, many real-life experiences can be used for learning and for bringing communities together.

THEME 6   *in practice. . .*

You have been working with several other teachers to plan tentative project activities for the year for kindergarten children. You are aware that the children may have taken short or long trips during their summers away from school. These trips may have involved camping, going to a family reunion, visiting a relative in a nearby community, or going to the beach. You decide to build a curriculum unit based on a travel theme and will introduce prompts for the children, including luggage, maps, and camping equipment. Subsequent activities will depend on the emergent interests of the children. How can families and members of the community be involved in this type of thematic experience?

An Interview with a Teacher

Several years ago, one of the authors of this book was searching for a preschool for her children that exemplified respect for, and appreciation of, the diversity of families and their children. None seemed to be in place, and she, along with several other mothers, decided to open her own preschool. Dr. Anne Brautigam, a longtime advocate and supporter of programs for children from diverse populations, served as the director. Today, the program continues and serves as a model to the community of how families of diverse cultures and languages come together for the purpose of loving and nurturing their children. Accredited by the NAEYC and highlighted in news articles and a national news show, Ecumenical Preschool is truly multicultural. It is also multiage, so children experience a sense of family as they share experiences with younger and older, brothers and sisters, and, yes, grandmas and grandpas. The school is housed in the same church facility as the Helping Hands program, a local program for individuals with Alzheimer's disease.

Kathy Healey served as the head teacher of Ecumenical Preschool for several years. She now also serves as director. Her work, as that of many other teachers, is worthy of discussion in a text for those preparing to work with diverse families.

QUESTION: Tell me about the children enrolled at Ecumenical.
ANSWER: This year, we had children from Zaire [Congo], Liberia, and Korea. We had children from the United States who were White and African American. We also had one child whose mother was from the Philippines and father from the United States. All children had some, if limited, English.
QUESTION: How do you find out about the cultural practices and, perhaps, expectations of the families with regard to their children?
ANSWER: We [Ms. Healey and assistant teacher Mary Anne Jolly] talk to the family at the time of enrollment and ask them to share information about their culture which would be helpful to us. We ask about special holidays which they celebrate and tell them about holidays which we celebrate, such as Thanksgiving. We also ask them if

they would like for their children to learn about and participate in such events. Many of these families are in the United States for a short period of time and want their children to know as much about our culture as possible before they return home.

We learn about the families when they include us in their lives at home. Recently, a mother of one of the children from Korea called Mary Anne to invite her to dinner. As is our custom, Mary Anne asked what she could bring. The mother was surprised and shared that, in her country, it would be unacceptable to make such an offer as it is the responsibility of the host to provide all food. Nevertheless, she was interested in participating in an American custom and suggested something for Mary Anne to bring. When she called me, I made the same offer, and we agreed upon something for me to bring.

QUESTION: How do you include cultural events in the classroom?

ANSWER: We ask the families to share information about special foods, recipes for foods, photos, special clothing, and to come to school and share.

QUESTION: How do you involve families in school activities?

ANSWER: As I said, we ask families to come to school and share. This year, the father of the child from Zaire came to school and shared with the children what it was like for him to go to school as a child in Zaire. The children were fascinated by his story. We also hold programs with potlucks where many ethnic foods are shared, a spring art show of the children's creations, parent conferences, and an end-of-year celebration.

QUESTION: What do you find most difficult about working with families of so many different cultures?

ANSWER: The expectations of parents about what teachers can do are often unrealistic. Parents seem to expect teachers to have all the answers. Often, there are unrealistic expectations of what children should be able to accomplish.

QUESTION: What do you find most valuable in being in this environment as a teacher? for the children? for the families?

ANSWER: This type of environment opens up the world to children and families. It is a learning experience for adults and for the children. The American children benefit because of their exposure to different languages and customs. One little boy was thrilled to be teaching his dog to "sit" in Korean, which he had learned from the Korean children at school. All children feel they are teachers as they share their language with other children. Each child makes a personal contribution. The children in the school give the observer a sense of the United Nations "look." I hope that when these children return to their own countries, they will have positive memories and that all children will remember those experiences in times of controversy. It is our contribution to world peace.

Critical Concepts

1. For teachers to create climates that support and value the culture of each child, they must first examine their own culture and values.

2. The real experience of being raised and acculturated in a community-type atmosphere has been missing for several decades now because people have been separated from the "culture" of their family through work or education that takes them elsewhere.

3. While families are given the task of enculturation, children also become acculturated in their encounters with groups outside their ethnic group (i.e., race, religion, national origin, values, customs, language).

4. Young children come to school with some knowledge of forms and functions of the written language in their culture and they also bring words and phrases used in culturally specific ways—home-rooted language.

5. Continuity between home and school is important for children's academic success and socialization experiences, but there still exist some program–family discontinuities for low-income and ethnic-minority families.

6. Between 2 and 6 years of age is a time when children begin to develop their ideas and beliefs about the equality or inequality of individuals with regard to differences in race, gender, and disability. Children begin to act out their beliefs about what is fair and what is appealing, including limiting access to play of those children who are "different."

7. Children "read" and respond to situations according to their developing moral reasoning skills. Their social cognition or the ability to read and interpret the feelings, intentions, and motives of others requires higher level thinking, such as being able to identify and classify self from others and making inferences about people's thoughts and feelings. Children also construct knowledge about what is right and wrong from what they experience.

8. When teachers listen to children and families to plan experiences and take children's learning into consideration as other activities are developed, this is known as emergent curriculum. Emergent curriculum that is afforded time, space, and appropriate materials for investigations holds the potential for individualizing learning for children from diverse cultures. Teachers must also create a climate for families to participate in the planning, and recognize occasions for learning that are relevant and meaningful to children.

Summary Statements

✓ Children first learn about the immediate worlds that include their parents, siblings, caregivers, extended family, and friends.

✓ We carry what we learn from our families and friends on our journey into new worlds characterized by growth in age and development.

✓ As teachers and caregivers, we must examine our attitudes and values regarding our own heritage before we can value the diversity of the children within our care. We must ask, What is my culture?

✓ Everyone, regardless of race or color, gender or ability, religion or education, brings a rich heritage to the community or group.

✓ Many individuals in this country do not recognize the characteristics of their own cultures; they believe instead that one has to be from another country or race to have a culture.

✓ The world is in a constant state of change. Children will need to be prepared to meet the challenges of change, which include meeting, working, and coping with individuals who have different beliefs, values, and practices in living. Helping children learn about and understand that people are different assists them in making choices appropriate for themselves and in dealing with the world in the context of an ever-changing society.

✓ The willingness and ability of teachers to respond to the cultural aspects of the lives of the children and families whom they serve open many doors to building the spirit of partnership with families.

✓ Teachers and caregivers must work with families to understand the caregiving beliefs of the family with regard to sleep patterns, feeding patterns, and comforting patterns.

✓ Teachers, administrators, child-care providers, families, and communities must work together to build a climate for children that encourages knowledge of, and respect for, the diversity of families.

✓ American families generally strive for the independence of the child. Families from some other cultures, including those of Hispanic and Asian descent, generally strive for interdependence, with less focus on autonomy. This is one way that families from different cultures may be different, although some differences among families are representative of the same cultures.

✓ Although we believe that certain developmental milestones are reached by children at certain ages, attainment of these milestones and the ages at which they are reached are dependent, in part, on the cultural practices and beliefs of families and the societies in which people live.

✓ Children are aware of, and talk about, differences in race, gender, and economic status prior to entering kindergarten.

✓ Adults pass along the stereotypes that exist across time about various cultural and ethnic groups both knowingly and unwittingly to their children.

✓ Children can engage in thinking games that are designed to foster an awareness of diversity and an appreciation for that which is different.

✓ Families can become involved in collaborative efforts with schools and community members by engaging in projects with children that emerge from the children's interests and community events.

Research to Practice: Classroom Applications and Activities

1. One family in your nursery school has a 4-year-old child whom they adopted as an infant. Both parents are White, and the child is of African American descent. The mother asks a young African American teacher to express her ideas about caring for the little girl's hair. The teacher shares this during a staff meeting and expresses her discomfort with the situation. As a director, how might you address this situation for the benefit of the teacher, the child, and the family?

2. You are teaching primary school in a Midwestern community. In recent years, some migrant workers of Hispanic descent

have spent a portion of the school year in the community. Several children of these families have been enrolled in your class for as long as 4 months. You have little experience in working with children who are Hispanic and are frustrated by the brief amount of time that the children spend with you. It almost seems pointless to attempt to involve these families. What suggestions might you have for dealing with your feelings and in working with the children and their families?

3. You notice that one girl in your primary class continues to shy away from children not of her race. She asks to be moved to other groups of children during group assignments and seeks other places to sit at lunch and during school activities. You finally ask her if she has a problem, and she divulges that she is acting on the advice of her parents.

4. A local church has "adopted" a family fleeing political strife in another country. The family will rely on contributions for all their needs until they can find employment. Both parents held prestigious jobs in their homeland but, because of differing credentials, practices, and language, will be forced to work in low-paying jobs. Their two young children are enrolled in your program and often seem sad. You do not speak the family's language but do wish to build a relationship with them in working with the children. What steps might you take to deal with this situation and to assist the children and the family in this dramatic change in their lives?

5. Two boys in your class are arguing over who has the next turn at the computer. One boy calls the other a "redneck," and the argument continues. How might you handle this situation?

Resources

Beaty, J. J. (1997). *Building bridges with multicultural picture books for children 3–5.* Upper Saddle River, NJ: Merrill/Prentice Hall.

Bete, T. (1997). Finding cultural information on the Internet. *Early Childhood News, 9,* 31.

Cech, M. (1991). *Global child: Multicultural resources for young children.* Menlo Park, CA: Addison-Wesley.

Chang, H. (Nov./Dec. 1996). Many languages, many cultures: Ideas and inspiration for helping young children thrive in a diverse society. *Scholastic Early Childhood Today,* 61–70.

Leister, C. (1993). Working with parents of different cultures. *Dimensions of Early Childhood, 21,* 13–14.

Levin, D. E. (1995, January). Getting to know us: Building classroom culture through our diversity and history. *Child Care Information Exchange Beginnings, 101,* pp. 39–42.

Levy, A. (1997). Culture in the classroom. *Early Childhood News, 9,* 28–30, 32–33.

Mesa-Bains, A., &Shulman, J. H. (Eds.). (1994). *Diversity in the classroom: A casebook for teachers and teacher educators.* Mahwah, NJ: Erlbaum.

Mesa-Bains, A., &Shulman, J. H. (1994). *Diversity in the classroom: Facilitator's guide.* Mahwah, NJ: Erlbaum.

National Association for the Education of Young Children. (1996). NAEYC position statement: Responding to linguistic and cultural diversity— Recommendations for effective early childhood education. *Young Children, 51,* 4–12.

Neugebauer, B. (1997). Parents' perspectives on mealtimes: Based on interviews by Cecelia Alvarado, Cam Do Wong, Robin Gadsen-Dupree, and Karen Kelly. *Child Care Information Exchange, 117,* 56–58.

CHAPTER 5

Creating Community and School Linkages for Parents of Children with Special Needs

All parents expect their children to be brighter, prettier, happier, and more successful than themselves. In fact, we want our children to be perfect in every way. We conceived them, love them, and feel responsible for them; we see them as extensions of ourselves. When something goes wrong and our hopes are dashed, we have to deal with a wide range of emotions, including depression, anger, confusion, anxiety, and embarrassment.

BATSHAW, 1991, PREFACE

KEY TERMS

at-risk children

developmental disability

family support
    programs

formal community
    resources

inclusion movement

individualized education
    program (IEP)

individualized family
    service plan (IFSP)

interagency collaboration

LREs

multifactored assessment

normalization

parent advocacy groups

parent education
    programs

parent empowerment

P.L. 94-142

superbaby

GUIDING QUESTIONS

1. What is the incidence rate for children with developmental delays and disabilities in the typical American classroom?
2. What are common transitional and adjustment needs for children with disabilities and developmental delays and their families?
3. What is the primary role of the early childhood teacher in planning, implementing, and evaluating individualized plans for children with disabilities and developmental delays?
4. What are traits and characteristics of children with common disabilities and developmental delays?
5. What are key pieces of legislation that have created the most recent changes in classrooms for families and children with disabilities and developmental delays?

erhaps no other area of need in today's schools are greater than that of inclusion and the important relationship between the parents and families of children with special needs and their teachers. Meeting the unique and individual needs of families of children with special needs requires special planning and teamwork between parents and professionals (Dunst, Johanson, Trivette, & Hamby, 1991; Mallory & New, 1994; Safford, 1989). The collaborative services of teachers and caregivers, along with those of such specialists as special education teachers; curriculum specialists; social workers; and physical, occupational, or speech and language therapists, are often required.

The emerging movement toward educational inclusion in the United States, evidenced through P.L. 99-457 (the Education of the Handicapped Act Amendments of 1986; see Figure 5.1), has brought together law and logic to ensure that children with special needs will receive the greatest possible normality in their educational experiences. Thus, the goal of services for families of children with special needs should be providing intervention appropriate to the needs of each exceptional child while promoting normalization (Dunst et al., 1991; Mallory & New, 1994; Rose & Smith, 1993).

This chapter addresses the unique needs of families of children with special needs as they interface with early childhood teachers in school and child-care settings. Included in this chapter are the following themes:

Theme 1. Children with special needs represent an important part of our society; knowing the incidence rates of specific developmental delays and disabilities facilitates serving these children in our schools.

Theme 2. Families of children with disabilities and special needs go through difficult adjustments and transitions. Being aware of the typical psychological, emotional, and social adaptations of these families of children with special needs will assist us in better meeting their intervention needs.

Theme 3. The early childhood teacher serves a critical role in assessing, planning, implementing, and evaluating educational and developmental individualized plans and

FIGURE 5.1	Definitions of P.L. 99-457, the ADA, and IDEA

P.L. 99-457: A public law passed in 1986 by Congress that extended all the rights and protections of P.L. 94-142, the Education for All Handicapped Children Act of 1975, to all handicapped 3- to 5-year-olds by 1990 and that made services available to all children 2 years old or younger on a discretionary basis.

ADA: The Americans with Disabilities Act of 1990 (P.L. 101-336) addresses accessibility issues for individuals with special needs and includes such factors as walks, curbs, ramps, public restrooms, telephones, water fountains, restaurants, emergency procedures and hazards, width of hallways and doors, and other related needs.

IDEA: The Individuals with Disabilities Education Act (IDEA), passed as P.L. 101-476 in 1990, shapes what educators and parents can expect and demand for their children who are differently abled. Part H is a grant program for infants and toddlers to assist states in developing early intervention programs; Part B states that, to the extent possible, children with disabilities should receive their special education service in LRE. The Individuals with Disabilities Education Improvement Act of 2004 aligns IDEA closely to the No Child Left Behind Act (NCLB).

Note. Summarized from *Issues and Practices in Special Education*, by D. S. Marozas and D. C. May, 1988, New York: Longman.

programs for families and children with special needs. Teachers should be able to identify the most helpful community resources for parents and families.

Theme 4. Children with designated disabilities, special needs conditions, and giftedness have common characteristics and descriptors. Being familiar with these characteristics strengthens the teacher's role in identifying and serving these children.

Theme 5. Many laws have mandated changes in the provision of services for parents and children with special needs. Becoming familiar with these laws and the current advocacy agencies for families of children with special needs and disabilities strengthens the role of the school and the teacher in meeting their needs.

We turn now to these themes to better understand the important role of the parent–school–community relationship related to serving parents of children with disabilities and special needs.

DEFINITIONS AND INCIDENCE RATES OF SPECIAL NEEDS CONDITIONS FOR CHILDREN IN THE UNITED STATES

 pecial needs are often defined through societal consensus: A person considered "normal" in one culture might be considered "special needs" in another (Mallory & New, 1994; Rose & Smith, 1993; Safford, 1989). Even specialists cannot agree on specific criteria for diagnoses and classification, and the definition of *special needs* or *at-risk* is confounded for younger children because some diagnoses or definitions do not apply until children reach school age (Marozas & May, 1988). In addition, early childhood development occurs rapidly and unevenly and is not clearly defined in terms of "typical" versus "atypical."

In general, children with special needs are those whose mental, communicative, social–emotional, or physical characteristics require some adaptations in the educational program for them to learn optimally (Mallory & New, 1994; Safford, 1989). Approximately 10 percent of all children are assumed to have special needs significant enough to qualify them as exceptional, whereas another 2 percent to 3 percent constitute gifted and talented children. Children with special needs display characteristics that involve disabilities or delays in one or more areas of functioning.

An estimated 1 million special needs children of preschool age live in the United States. **P.L. 94-142** (the Education for All Handicapped Children Act [EHA] of 1975) defines children with special needs in the following way:

> [Special needs] children are those children evaluated as being mentally retarded, hard-of-hearing, deaf, speech impaired, visually handicapped, seriously emotionally disturbed, orthopedically impaired, other health impaired, deaf-blind, multi-handicapped, or having specific learning disabilities, who because of these impairments need special education and related services. (Sec. 121a.5 [42 Fed. Reg.], p. 12478)

The ADA addresses accessibility issues for individuals with special needs.

Politically Correct Terminology

Being aware of current politically correct terminology related to special needs children is very important for the early childhood professional. The professional who focuses on meeting the needs of these children and their families should be aware that such terms as *handicapped*, *exceptional*, and *mainstreamed* have given way to *children with special needs*, *children at risk*, and *inclusive environments*. Without a doubt, the ADA (P.L. 101-336) and the early intervention movement of the 1990s have created heightened sensitivity and awareness of the importance of using appropriate terms when working with children with special needs and their families.

Dangers of Labeling

Educators and parents alike are concerned about the possible harmful and lasting effects of labeling young children with special needs. This concern is reflected in the recent policy initiatives for children with special needs; these do not require categorical labels for the following reasons:

- Young children develop rapidly; thus, their needs also change rapidly.
- Early labeling of young children can lead to long-term restrictions and limits that may not even be relevant.
- Least restrictive services for children encourage inclusion and integration of typically and atypically developing children, and labeling is counterproductive to this policy.

State-level educational reform has focused on families and children at risk. **At-risk children** have been defined as those "with a higher than average probability of problems in development and negative developmental outcomes as viewed as ranging from life threatening or handicapping conditions to school failure" (Safford, 1989, p. 25). The term *at risk* is seen throughout the educational literature. The term is frequently associated with income level, however, and children living in conditions characterized by poverty are considered to be more developmentally at risk too.

School–Parent Partnerships: The Law and Special Needs

Children with special needs can be defined from various perspectives: medical, legal, sociological, psychological, and educational. The law defines special needs from the educational perspective, and that is the focus of this chapter. Public laws in the United States determine that *all* children will be educated, special needs or not. These laws determine where, by whom, and with whom special needs children will be educated.

A **developmental disability** is defined as a chronic disability that:

- Is attributable to a mental or physical impairment or combination of mental and physical impairments
- Is manifested before the child reaches age 22
- Is likely to continue indefinitely
- Results in substantial limitations in function related to self-care, language (receptive and expressive), learning, mobility, self-direction, capacity for independent living, and economic self-sufficiency
- Reflects the child's need for a combination and sequence of special interdisciplinary or generic care, treatment, or other services that are individually planned and coordinated (Safford, 1989; Wiegerink & Pelosi, 1979).

One of the most exciting pieces of legislation on behalf of children and families with special needs, P.L. 99-457 (1986), clearly identifies a more basic role for parents of children with special needs. This law not only recognizes and emphasizes the concept of a partnership between parents and professionals but also reinforces the notion that the family shapes the child's life experiences. Thus, the role of schools and professionals is to *support the needs* of families of children with special needs, rather than supplant them.

As noted in the literature and from our life experiences, parents of exceptional children are impassioned with love and concern for their children's well-being.

Ethically and legally, the early childhood professional must work toward provision of least restrictive educational placements; thus, parents should not have to fight for this appropriate educational placement: *It is the right of the family and the child.*

The passage of P.L. 99-457 tremendously boosted the concepts of *early childhood special education* and *early intervention*. Because the law mandated public schools to provide comprehensive educational and developmental services for preschool children with special needs, the need for formal teacher-training programs in the areas of early childhood special education and early intervention proliferated. As a result of both legislative and fiscal support, the number of community- and school-based professionals trained to work with young children with special needs increased dramatically.

Each year nearly half a million infants are born prematurely.

Incidence of Special Needs for At-Risk Infants

The following descriptive statements provide insight into the rate and incidence of disability and special needs among America's infant population:

- Each year, nearly 500,000 infants are born who will manifest a disability within the first 4 years of life. At the end of 1990, approximately 600,000 children with special needs, from birth through age 5, were receiving intervention services.
- Some 350,000 to 375,000 newborns each year have been prenatally exposed to drugs, including alcohol. Fetal alcohol syndrome (FAS) is now recognized as the leading known cause of mental retardation in the Western world.
- Each year, almost 500,000 infants are born prematurely.
- HIV (human immunodeficiency virus) has become the greatest infectious cause of pediatric mental retardation in the United States (Sexton, Snyder, Sharpton, & Stricklin, 1993).

The range of variations in early development is considerable, even in a group of children of the same chronological age, gender, and ethnic group. In some children, the variation is so extreme that identification of a problem is relatively easy. In such cases, a child may clearly fit into a category defined by P.L. 94-142. Younger children, however, require a more flexible definition, which should include those children who, prior to their third birthday, have a high probability of manifesting a sensory motor deficit or a mental handicap in later childhood that was actually the result of a birth defect, disease process, trauma, or environmental conditions present during the prenatal or postnatal period (Dunst et al., 1991; Solit, 1993).

TYPICAL PSYCHOLOGICAL, EMOTIONAL, AND SOCIAL ADAPTATIONS OF FAMILIES OF CHILDREN WITH SPECIAL NEEDS

All parents, whether their children have special needs or not, have expectations for their children. Thus, it is difficult to comprehend fully the dynamics of families with young children with special needs unless one is, in fact, the parent of an exceptional child (Baker, 1991). Prospective parents who have waited so many months for the birth of their baby may suddenly learn that the newborn does not even approximate their idealized expectations. The amount of stress imposed on the family may depend on how radically the parents' expectations are violated.

> When you first learn that your child has a disability, you may experience profound grief, mixed with anger, denial, and guilt. In addition to coping with the loss of the normal child you expected, you must deal with the feelings of your family and friends. (Batshaw, 1991, p. 3)

The Family as Primary Socialization Agent

In the United States, most young children with special needs live at home with their families; thus, the role of the family in providing a strong, supportive environment for the child is crucial. Recognition of the family's role has only recently been realized and acknowledged formally in legislation based on the convergence of several societal trends: (a) the awareness that the family is actually the first and primary teacher for the young child, (b) the family system's perspective that acknowledges the family unit as a system of interdependent relationships, (c) the philosophy and belief in normalization as a goal for the young child and family, (d) the outcomes of numerous research studies that document the effectiveness of early intervention and ECE for long-term societal outcomes, and (e) the legal impact of P.L. 94-142 (the EHA) and P.L. 99-457 (the Education of All Handicapped Children Act Amendments of 1986).

The Family as Teacher

Through daily interactions with parents and extended family members, young children learn language, cognitive, and social skills, as documented in the developmental literature. The family is the primary agent in inducting the child into the complex, rule-based family system that reflects the larger society. Although teaching at home by parents is not as structured and planned as that in the school, the fact is that most language, cognitive, and social skills learned at home by the child are obtained through the daily routines of family life: doing chores and helping with other household tasks, playing, viewing television, and participating in other family activities, both at home and within the community. Children also learn important concepts from their families, and these concepts are transferred into larger learning settings as the children mature. Thus, the family should be included in the planning for children with special needs because the family plays such a primary role in teaching and socializing young children.

Bronfenbrenner (1974) described the crucial role of the family unit in support of the developing child with special needs:

> The evidence indicates that the family is the most effective and economical system for fostering and sustaining the development of the child. . . . Without family involvement any effects of intervention, at least in the cognitive sphere, appear to erode rapidly once the program ends. In contrast, the involvement of the parents as partners in the enterprise provides an ongoing system which reinforces the effects of the program while it is in operation and helps to sustain them after the program ends. (p. 55)

THEMES 2 AND 3   *in practice . . .*

Joan Snyder, a second-grade teacher in a suburban school district, learns that parents of Sarah, a child in her classroom, are expecting a baby with Down syndrome. The parents seem withdrawn from classroom activities, and Sarah seems distracted and agitated. Ms. Snyder is concerned about these parents and wants to offer support to them. What are appropriate strategies for Ms. Snyder to use in providing helpful information and intervention for Sarah and her parents?

Every parent imagines the new child as a "superbaby"— a future scholar, athlete, etc.

Emotional Reactions and Issues for Parents

The impact a child with a disability has on the family is usually a major one. As most people know, the arrival of even a nondisabled child into a family is a stressful, emotional event. Again, the parents' expectations play an important role in the explanation of this stress (Batshaw, 1991). Perske (1973) used the term **superbaby** to describe parents' images of the expected child. Every parent imagines the new child as a future scholar, athlete, beauty queen, and so on. For most families, whose children are typical, these initial dreams change slowly as the reality of the children's development unfolds. These families have time to adjust to their children and the emerging differences between their children and their initial expectations.

For families of infants who are identified at birth as having a developmental disability, dreams die quickly and painfully (Baker, 1991; Fallen & Umansky, 1985;

Rose & Smith, 1993; Sexton et al., 1993). The parents must deal with deep emotions that include shock, fear, and disappointment. These emotional reactions have been listed by Wolfensberger (1967) and elaborated on by Sexton et al. (1993) and Solit (1993), who described more than 40 reactions, including anger, ambivalence, avoidance, bitterness, disbelief, denial, envy, guilt, helplessness, mourning, sorrow, and shock.

Sarah Anne: A Case Study of an Infant with Down Syndrome

Sarah Anne Cagle is now 5 months old. She is Randy and Amy's third and much-anticipated child. Their other two children are Matthew, 6, and Susan, 4. When Sarah Anne was born at full term, her parents had anticipated the possibility of Down syndrome, although the prenatal testing had not been conclusive. Even with the strong possibility of Down syndrome, Randy and Amy chose to continue the pregnancy and never really considered any other option. Their personal values and their Catholic faith supported the continuance of the baby's life. When Sarah Anne was born, her parents experienced a range of emotions: elation, love, joy, pride, as well as fear, disappointment, and some anger. Amy is 36 and Randy is 38, and both are in good health. It was hard for them to understand and accept that their child had Down syndrome. Why, they asked, did this have to happen to Sarah Anne and to them?

According to Batshaw (1991), there are typical questions for parents of a new baby born with a disability. Professionals can assist these parents by giving them the words to explain the disability to friends, family, and siblings. Following are typical questions and suggested responses, according to Batshaw.

I'm afraid of my baby. What should I do?

Having a child with major medical problems can be very frightening. It is natural for you as the parent to worry about whether you are feeding him enough or if you are hurting him. You should make sure you understand instructions about caring for your child before you take him home from the hospital. All states have early intervention programs that start in infancy and are provided at no cost. Usually, a physical or occupational therapist will work with your child and train you. If there are severe medical problems, a public health nurse may be able to visit you regularly at home. The more you learn, the more confident you will feel in caring for your child. By the time he is a year old, you will probably feel quite safe and secure.

What do I tell our family, friends, and neighbors?

It can be painful to try to explain your child's condition to loved ones, but it is better to take the mystery out of the situation. Tell them briefly what is wrong and what is being done about it. Concealing your child's diagnosis only leads to rumors and future embarrassment and discomfort. Your family

(Continued)

and friends can be an enormous source of support to you, but not if you keep them at a distance. If they seem remote or uncomfortable at first, remember that you, too, may have felt uncomfortable around a person with a disability before you had your child. Give them time to understand and accept your situation, and then count on them for much-needed support and assistance. Although you may be fortunate in having supportive relatives and friends, you may find yourself extra-sensitive and easily offended by remarks from strangers, friends, and family members. With time, you will learn to respond appropriately to such awkward situations. You do not have to give an explanation to everyone who makes a well-intentioned but insensitive remark. If someone is genuinely interested and helpful, you may want to give a short explanation, but if he or she is simply prying, give him or her a dirty look!

What do I tell her sister and brother?

This depends on the ages of your other children. Young children require only simple explanations; be sure to be clear and specific. For example, if your child is mentally retarded, you might say, "Your sister cannot learn things as quickly as most children can, and we will all need to help her." If a young child wants more information, he or she will ask. Older children will need a fuller and more accurate description of their brother's or sister's disability.

Note. Based on *Your Child Has a Disability: A Complete Sourcebook of Daily Medical Care* (pp. 9–10), by M. L. Batshaw, 1991, Baltimore: Brookes.

The Grieving Process for the Family

The birth of an atypically developing infant or the diagnosis of a disability or special need in a child sets off a series of emotional reactions for the parents and other family members (Baker, 1991). The psychological process that parents experience is often compared with the grieving process that results at the loss of a loved one. Drotar, Baskiewica, Irwin, Kennell, and Klaus (1975) identified what they believed to be five stages of dealing with the birth of an atypical infant (see Figure 5.2).

These stages of grieving are predictable and are observed in today's parent population. Research indicates that the duration and intensity of each stage vary widely among individuals, and that rather than pass through these stages in a once-and-for-all sequence, the grieving person usually revisits the stages and reexperiences intense emotions from the initial emotional stage.

It is important to recognize that each family presents a unique profile for coping with this stressor event. For most families, progression through these stages is not an orderly, precise process. Initial feelings of denial and sadness may recur. If new crises occur, new demands for coping also occur. Some families adjust quickly; others require much more time. A family's response to a crisis depends on (a) the stressor event itself,

FIGURE 5.2	Stages of Grief: Adjusting to a Child with Special Needs

Stage 1: *Shock.* During this stage, the family experiences feelings of numbness, with an abrupt disruption in their normal thought and feeling patterns. Irrational thoughts and patterns are common at this time.

Stage 2: *Denial.* This stage is characterized by feelings and thoughts of "This can't be happening to me," "It isn't true," and "There must be a mistake." This stage provides an emotional buffer to the crisis and even provides a temporary escape.

Stage 3: *Sadness and anger.* Many negative emotions flood the parents at this point. The anger may be channeled toward themselves, toward the child, toward the doctor, and toward others. Families may feel such a profound sense of sadness that they may isolate themselves from family and friends. Some families share these intense feelings.

Stage 4: *Adaptation.* This fourth stage finds a lessening of emotions and anxiety, with a growing acceptance of the child.

Stage 5: *Reorganization.* The final stage finds a renewed sense of equilibrium for the family. The family redefines and restructures itself to accept and include the exceptional child. During this stage, the family finally achieves successful coping, when problems are addressed and solved.

(b) the resources that the family has for coping with the stressor, and (c) the specific meaning that the family gives to the event.

Normalization as a Goal

The concept of **normalization** centers around the notion that all children are more alike than different and that all children should be educated and served in similar ways. "Normalization" leads to such social policy initiatives as deinstitutionalization, **LREs**, inclusive classrooms, and fully integrated learning settings (Fallen & Umansky, 1985; Rose & Smith, 1993; Solit, 1993). As a result of normalization, infants and young children are rarely placed in institutionalized settings, and efforts to support the family are increased so that it can remain the primary agent of education. The notion of normalcy and normalization also plays out in legislation requiring that parents be the primary and first teachers of the child with special needs, so it is indeed a powerful notion.

Parent Advocacy

Parents of children with special needs have become vocal advocates for the rights of their children. Perhaps no other group of parents portrays a higher level of commitment and energy to effective and visible child advocacy. Examples of parent advocacy include the formation of **parent advocacy groups** such as the Association for Retarded Citizens. Parents' involvement in the legislative process at both federal and state levels has resulted in increased legislative initiatives and mandates, such as the successful passage of P.L. 99-457 in 1986.

In addition, funding avenues at the federal and state levels now must address specifically the role of the family and the need for family support as part of program implementation and evaluation. Professionals who write grants to obtain funds to serve young children with special needs and maintain these grants successfully now realize that one of the most crucial components of their successful grantsmanship is the inclusion of clearly defined mechanisms of parental involvement. Examples of these mechanisms are (a) assessment of family and parent needs as well as child needs; (b) ongoing monitoring of family support needs; (c) documentation of provision of collaborative support services for families; and (d) evaluation research that documents successful program outcomes for the child, the parent, and the family.

Goals for Family Involvement

Programs and organizations for families of young exceptional children may have multiple purposes. Some of the more common are (a) emotional, physical, and financial support for the family; (b) parent education; (c) participation in individualized education programs; and (d) child advocacy (Solit, 1993). The main goal of emotional, physical, and financial support programs is to provide emotional support to individual family members as well as to the family as a whole. As already described, the family of a child with special needs goes through stages of adjustment. Family resources are necessary to facilitate adaptation to a child born with special needs or in whom special needs have been diagnosed. Researchers in individual and family coping suggest that interpersonal networks are crucial as a source of social and emotional support in times of stress and crisis. Such support is often provided by members of the extended family, friends, coworkers, and clergy. Schools have become important resources for these families as well because they can aid in bringing together extended family members and decrease the burden for single-parent households.

Physical and financial resources are also called into action when crisis besets a family. Children with disabilities frequently require increased physical exertion for care through lifting, carrying, and pushing. Other family needs are financial in nature. Medical care, adaptive equipment, transportation, speech therapists, occupational therapists, psychologists, and other related services for a child with a disability can be very expensive. These demands can drain a family's financial resources. The amount of financial resources available to the family depends on the amount and type of insurance coverage, the income level of the family, the quantity and quality of free community services, and the capacity of the local school system to meet the needs of the child with the disability. Obviously, when financial resources are lacking, additional stress is placed on the family. Thus, when ample emotional, physical, and financial resources are present, family coping is made much easier.

Family support programs are available in varying degrees throughout the United States. Parents of children with disabilities frequently seek out parents and families of other children who have similar disabilities. Such families may serve as models, demonstrating the positive strengths that families can obtain and use in coping with the specific situation. Formal family support programs involve parent training in listening skills, discussion of the types and causes of childhood disabilities, and other relevant topics, so that they can provide needed support and information as families adjust to the knowledge that their children have disabilities. Another important role of the family support group is to assist parents in dealing with feelings such as grief and to provide an opportunity to vent and clarify their feelings and receive support that such feelings are legitimate.

Importance of Siblings

Siblings are sometimes overlooked when family support programs are planned. Sibling support groups, however, are becoming common. Siblings can actually serve as teachers for their brother or sister with a disability. The research literature documents that siblings of children with disabilities frequently reflect feelings of helplessness or empowerment similar to those of their parents.

Baker (1991) and Stoneman and Brody (1982) made suggestions for families with a child with a disability and siblings who are nondisabled, including the following:

- Children with disabilities should not be institutionalized for the sake of the sibling. Indeed, siblings may actually benefit from the relationship and life experiences with the child with the disability.
- Siblings should not be given extended caretaking responsibilities for a child with a disability that exceed their own level of maturity. This is particularly true for younger siblings who help care for an older child.
- Parents should make a special effort to spend time with the children without disabilities and to show a special interest in their needs.
- The child without disability should not be expected to compensate for parents' frustrated expectations for the child with a disability. This places an undue burden on the child without disability.
- Counseling programs can help siblings of children with disabilities share feelings and fears.
- "In-home mainstreaming" can be accomplished by encouraging the child with the disability to model behaviors of the sibling and by encouraging the sibling to involve the child with the disability in the everyday routines and chores of the home.
- Parents' ability to adapt to the child with the disability is reflected in the coping skills of the siblings. Thus, parents having difficulty in their adjustment should seek professional assistance, to alleviate these same maladaptive behaviors and feelings in the siblings.

Parent education is a second major goal of family involvement. Parent education can take many forms: strengthening general abilities to parent; modeling teaching efforts with the child with a disability; providing needed information for parents on a variety of topics such as health and medical issues and community resources; strengthening the parent–parent, parent–child, and sibling–sibling relationships; and teaching communication skills.

THEMES 3, 4, AND 5   *in practice . . .*

Sammy, a kindergarten student, moves into a rural community. He has moderate cerebral palsy and related motor delays. What are possible community resources for Sammy and his parents in this rural community? Who should assist Sammy's parents in seeking out these community resources? What is the role of Sammy's new kindergarten teacher?

Parent education programs exist in public and private school systems, in churches and other community institutions, in public agencies related to social services and welfare, and in private initiatives to provide quality parent education. Parent education programs can focus on nondisabling conditions and parent issues too, but these programs are particularly important for the parent of a child with special needs because of the level of stress and anticipated financial, educational, and emotional resources needed.

Individualized education program (IEP) and **individualized family service plan (IFSP)** participation is the third goal of family involvement. An IEP is now required for many educational programs that serve children with special needs; an IFSP serves the needs of infants and toddlers. Parents have the right to be active participants in the development of their child's IEP; to read all educational records related to the identification and placement of their child; and to pursue legal process, if needed, to obtain services to which they are entitled.

Parents can be encouraged to participate in the IEP and the IFSP process in various ways. Parents' work schedules should be considered when IEP meetings are being scheduled. Transportation may also have to be provided for parents in need. Parents should be encouraged to keep a log of important events and happenings at home that provide valuable insight and information about their child. Having this log at the IEP and IFSP meeting will facilitate planning for the child, validate the parents' role with the child, and actively involve the parents in the planning process. At no time should parents be patronized or "talked down to" during the IEP meeting. Indeed, parents of exceptional children have the right to speak up and assert their concerns, issues, needs, and requests, and should be encouraged to do so.

Child advocacy, the fourth goal of family involvement, grew dramatically in the United States during the 1980s and 1990s (Baker, 1991; Sexton et al., 1993; Vincent, 1992). Examples of the growing awareness of children's issues are seen in the publications and legislative work of the CDF, the NAEYC, the Division for Early Childhood (DEC), and other national and state organizations. Parents can be very effective and convincing advocates for their own child and for the rights of other children. Caring and committed parents who clearly understand the needs of their child and who are able to articulate these needs to decision makers are making

FIGURE 5.3	Suggestions for Working with Parents of Children with Special Needs

- Explain terminology, because this may be the parent's first experience with exceptionality.
- Acknowledge and accept the parent's negative feelings.
- Listen effectively and attentively.
- Use a two-step approach in informing parents about their child's special needs and planning for intervention; this allows time for parents to comprehend and deal with their own emotional reactions.
- Keep parents informed and demonstrate respect, concern, and a sincere desire to cooperate.
- Be accountable and follow through.
- Respect the parent's level of involvement.

Note. Based on "Parental Feelings: The Forgotten Component When Working with Parents of Handicapped Preschool Children," by R. M. Gargiulo and S. B. Graves, 1991, *Childhood Education, 67,* pp. 176–178.

profound changes in the legislative process on a regular basis. State advocacy offices and advocacy-oriented parents often receive assertiveness training, training in strategies to help make institutional change, and training related to the legal process. Figure 5.3 lists other suggestions for professionals working with parents of children with special needs.

THE TEACHER'S ROLE IN DEVELOPING INDIVIDUALIZED PLANS FOR FAMILIES AND CHILDREN WITH SPECIAL NEEDS

With the passage of P.L. 94-142 and P.L. 99-457, the role of the public school in the lives of children with special needs and their families increased dramatically. The passage of P.L. 99-457 in 1986 signaled the crossing of an important threshold for young children with special needs: The public school is legally responsible for the provision of comprehensive services to these children and their families, beginning at age 36 months, and for infants and toddlers as defined by each state's capacity.

Defining the role of the school and its professional staff is the goal of this section. Included are issues related to creating linkages with the school, identification, assessment, IEP development, program development and delivery, and ongoing evaluation of child progress and the program.

Creating the School–Family Link

Following is an example of the crucial link among the child with special needs, his or her parents, and the local public school system.

Caleb Smith: A Case Study of Early Intervention

Caleb Smith, age 3, had been slow to talk and to communicate with his parents and 7-year-old sister, Cory. Caleb's mother, Heather, read about the new legislation in a school brochure distributed by the PTA. She read about its impact on the public school's role in serving children with special needs beginning at age 36 months. With this in mind, Heather called her nearby elementary school, Springdale Elementary School, where her daughter, Cory, was in the second grade. She asked to speak with the special education coordinator, Ron Simmons. Heather described Caleb's speech patterns, his apparent delay in verbalizing his needs, and her own concern about possible language delay. Caleb's language development was clearly behind that of his older sister when she was 3, but Heather really did not know whether there was a delay: "What should I do?" asked Heather. Mr. Simmons made an appointment for Heather to bring Caleb to school for an assessment by the school district's speech therapist. This is an example of PL 99–457 at work and demonstrates why it is important for schools to inform families of available services.

Defining the School's Role

Even with the force of P.L. 99-457, which defines the public school's role in the provision of services for children with developmental delay or disability, or both, the actual availability of services for children and parents varies remarkably, in quantity as well as in quality. The school is legally responsible for providing services for these children, but how this process evolves for each child and family is dependent on many variables. This section addresses the role of the school from an *ideal* perspective; that is, the processes of identification, assessment, program development, IEP procedures, and child progress and evaluation are described because they constitute a complete set of services for a child with special needs and his or her family.

The ability of a school district to carry out these various services is dependent on the following factors:

- Size of the school and comprehensiveness of programs offered
- Availability of school psychologists, counselors, special education teachers, social workers, and other support personnel
- Financial status of the school
- Availability of community agencies, organizations, and other resources to provide collaborative services with the school district
- Philosophy of inclusion of children with special needs in classrooms for typically developing children
- Parent education, parent support, and child advocacy groups within the school system

Even in school systems that lack some of these variables, parents of children with special needs can exert tremendous political and legal pressure on the school to carry through on its responsibilities as mandated through P.L. 99-457.

Identification, Assessment, IEPs, and IFSPs

During the past several decades, educators have become increasingly aware that optimal learning can best be fostered by recognition of, and attention to, individual differences. Individualization of instruction, the development of individual programs for all children in Head Start, and the development of IEPs for children with special needs can contribute a great deal to meeting individual child needs. Individualization of instruction does not necessarily imply one-to-one instruction, except for possible short periods of time, but rather planning and providing activities and programs appropriate for meeting each child's individual needs.

In many children, a special developmental delay or condition is present and potentially diagnosable at birth. In other children, conditions present at birth may potentially lead to a disabling condition. In still others, no necessarily predisposing factors are present at birth; whether a child acquires a special condition in many instances depends on the circumstances of his or her early care (Safford, 1989). P.L. 94-142 specifically charges the public schools with the responsibility of identifying all children who may have special needs and, therefore, potentially are eligible for preschool special education services. This responsibility includes children not only of school age but also of preschool age. The major means of identifying children in need of special services include the following:

- *Screening procedures* conducted at predetermined and specific times each year by the school district
- *Referral procedures* initiated by anyone, including the child's parent (or other close relative), teacher, pediatrician or family physician, health or other social service agency representative, or concerned other who suspects a problem
- For children who are in school, a *systematic review* of their records, particularly if referred by a school psychologist, social worker, or teacher

Screening

Screening is a gross means of economically scoring possible "cases" from the general population (Safford, 1989). Screening is not equivalent to diagnosis. Screening procedures vary in their levels of effectiveness, and one major criticism of the screening process is that children with serious problems can fall through the cracks. Safford (1989) stated that familiar screening procedures are those used in public schools, community clinics, and doctors' offices for hearing and vision. Meisels (1986), who studied the screening strategies used by public schools, stated that instruments are frequently used for screening even though that is not their intended purpose. Meisels also cited the Early and Periodic Screening and Developmental Testing (EPSDT) as an example of a screening procedure that frequently fails to identify children in need.

Referral

Most schools have clearly defined procedures for making referrals. Referrals can be made informally, such as when a teacher mentions to a supervisor that a particular child seems to be having great difficulty. Written procedures must be followed, however, to state the reasons for referral. It is important to remember that referral is not the same thing as diagnosis and should be conducted with great caution. An appropriate referral is a descriptive one: a factual statement that describes a child's behavior. Therefore, a classroom teacher simply refers a child for a determination of whether comprehensive assessment is indicated, not for special education. According to Safford (1989), teacher referral is the primary means for in-school identification of students who may be eligible for, and able to benefit from, special education services.

Classroom Teacher Referral Skills. To make appropriate referrals, the classroom teacher needs certain skills. These include the following:

- Knowledge of the school system's or community-based program's referral policies and procedures
- Some understanding of typical child development
- Awareness of important symptoms or indicators that might be associated with certain problems
- Ability to make objective and documented observations of a child's behavior or development that may be causing concern
- Familiarity with the school's recommended procedures for communication with the child's immediate family or extended family members
- Willingness to follow through and provide support to the child and family as the referral and assessment process unfolds

Making a Written Referral. A written referral should include a description of what attempts have been made to provide for the student's needs through such means as (a) conferences with parents; (b) conferences with the child (if appropriate); (c) individual tutorial assistance and effort; (d) attempts to adapt the daily schedule, environment, assignments, and so on for the child; and (e) any special motivational or management procedures that have been used (Safford, 1989, p. 31).

In short, the teacher's role is to initiate a proper referral procedure for a particular child. The referral itself should be viewed as a facilitative and linked effort to obtain possible needed intervention. The purpose of the referral is not diagnosis, and the teacher should refrain from making diagnostic remarks or conclusions, especially to the parents. Self-referrals by children to school personnel are more common in intermediate and secondary schools than in elementary schools. Children below the age of 10 usually need assistance in interpreting personal needs. Thus, the school social worker or guidance counselor is another excellent source of child referral.

Multifactored Assessment

The passage of P.L. 94-142 (the EHA) ensured that the following crucial reforms were mandated in the assessment process:

- No single test can be used as the only basis for placement.
- Each child's needs must be analyzed on an individual basis and described in an IEP, along with specifications of how those needs will be met and how stated goals will be evaluated.
- Annual review (at least) of the IEP is required and must be completed by a team of professionals, including the parents, who are working to meet the needs of the child.
- Fully informed parental consent must be obtained before any procedures can be carried out.
- Assessment must be interdisciplinary.
- The major purpose of the assessment procedure is to link instructional strategies with assessment.
- Instruments used for screening, assessment, and diagnosis must be valid and reliable.

The local school offers affordable services for children beginning at age 3.

The IEP and the IFSP

The IEP (or the IFSP, for infants and toddlers) becomes the ongoing tool for providing, monitoring, and evaluating services for a child. Although each school district establishes its own format for the IEP, the law does set forth basic parameters:

> The term "individualized education program" means a written statement for each handi-capped child in any meeting by a representative of the local education agency (LEA) or an intermediate educational unit who shall be qualified to provide, or supervise the provision of, specially designed instruction to meet the unique needs of handicapped children, the teacher, the parents or guardian of such child, and, whenever appropriate, such child, which statement shall include (A) a statement of the present levels of educational perfor-mance of such child, (B) a statement of annual goals, including short-term instructional objectives, (C) a statement of the specific educational services to be provided to such child, and the extent to which such child will be able to participate in regular educational programs, (D) the projected date for initiation and anticipated duration of such services, and appropriate objective criteria and evaluation procedures and schedules for determin-ing, on at least an annual basis, whether instructional objectives are being achieved. (P.L. 94-142, Section 4 [19])

The school system represents the best hope of the child with special needs and his or her family for obtaining affordable, accessible, and reliable identification, assessment, and program planning. Because of legislation, the family of a child who is believed to have a developmental delay, disabling condition, emotional need, or some other form of special need is ensured free and ongoing services. The school personnel most involved in this process are the classroom teacher, school psychologist, social worker, school counselor, special education teacher, and immediate administrator.

SPECIFIC DISABILITIES AND SPECIAL NEEDS CONDITIONS OF YOUNG CHILDREN

This textbook addresses children from a developmental perspective; therefore, descriptions of children who vary from the typical pattern of development are described within the parameters of typically developing children. Table 5.1 provides a brief description of common special needs conditions and implications for classroom teachers in designing and implementing effective classroom intervention strategies.

TABLE 5.1	Disabilities and Special Conditions of Young Children

Disability or Special Needs Condition	Description of Disability or Special Needs Condition	Implications for Classroom Teachers
Mental retardation	The definition of mental retardation has three components: (a) The IQ score of a child with mental retardation is below 70; (b) mental retardation is a nonprogressive disorder evident during childhood; and (c) an individual who is mentally retarded has an impaired ability to adapt to his or her environment (Batshaw, 1991, p. 62). Grossman (1972) describes mental retardation as a generally significant subaverage intellectual functioning, along with deficits in adaptive behavior.	There are levels of mental retardation that include the following: Mild/educable, with IQ of 55–69 Moderate/trainable with IQ of 40–54 Severe mental retardation, with IQ 25–39 Profound mental retardation, with IQ below 25. Teachers will utilize special education resources in the school and community to meet the needs of the child and to make referrals for parent support.

TABLE 5.1	Continued	
Disability or Special Needs Condition	**Description of Disability or Special Needs Condition**	**Implications for Classroom Teachers**
Cerebral palsy (CP)	*Cerebral palsy* is the term used to describe a number of disorders of movement and posture that result from brain damage that occurred prior to birth or during childhood (Batshaw, 1991). CP is a nonprogressive condition in which voluntary control of involved muscles is impaired as a result of brain injury incurred during the fetal period (prenatally), at the time of birth (perinatally), or during the developmental phase (postnatally). However, although the brain damage itself will not worsen as the child grows older, the physical disabilities often change. The term *cerebral palsy* encompasses a broad range of causes, functional levels, and degrees of intellectual, sensory, motor, and communicative involvement (Baker, 1991; Safford, 1989).	Use of, or control over, arms and legs is most commonly affected. Some children may find it difficult to sit in an upright position, turn their heads from side to side, chew and swallow, or even speak normally. The classroom teacher or caregiver usually works with an occupational or physical therapist to determine specific child needs, to develop activities for intervention, and to evaluate the child's progress. Children with CP need to participate in an interdisciplinary program so that appropriate therapies can be altered as needed. Most children with CP have at least one other disability such as visual problems, communication problems, hearing loss, seizures, or mental retardation. Thus, the teacher will need to work with an interdisciplinary IEP team to design and implement an effective classroom and home-based plan.
Down syndrome (Trisomy 21)	Approximately 4,000 children are born with Down syndrome each year in the United States, making it the most common genetic cause of mental retardation. Most of these children are moderately retarded, with IQs in the range of 40–54. In the United States, 10 percent of all people who are moderately to severely retarded have Down syndrome. The overall incidence of Down syndrome is	All children with Down syndrome are mentally retarded, and most fall into the category of moderate mental retardation. In the classroom setting, these children will display a range of special needs, including need for physical support because of lessened muscle tone and more limited mobility. These children will usually function at a higher level socially than academically, and

(Continued)

TABLE 5.1   Continued

Disability or Special Needs Condition	Description of Disability or Special Needs Condition	Implications for Classroom Teachers
	1 affected child in every 700 births. Women over age 35 have a greater chance of having a child with Down syndrome. An extra chromosome causes the syndrome, and children with Down syndrome have distinctive physical features such as a smaller head that is rather flattened and shorter than it is wide. The bridge of the nose is flat, the neck is shortened and broad, and the eyes slant upward. There is no correlation between the degree of physical abnormalities and the severity of mental retardation. Some children with subtle physical signs of Down syndrome are severely retarded, while others with many prominent physical abnormalities are only moderately retarded (Batshaw, 1991).	the early gross motor problems become less over time. Handwriting difficulty is common, as are other small-muscle activities and skills. Speech and memory may also be impacted. Consequently, the teacher will need to collaborate with other professionals and parents to plan, implement, and evaluate effective strategies for the child with Down syndrome. A therapist will usually work with the child once a week and provide suggestions for exercises that will encourage sitting, walking, and increased vocalizing. Depending on the severity of the mental retardation, the child with Down syndrome may be placed in a regular or special education classroom. Sports and other extracurricular activities should be encouraged.
Hearing impairments	Each year in the United States, about 22,000 infants are born with or acquire a permanent hearing loss, which can be an isolated disability or part of a multihandicapping condition (Batshaw, 1991). Hearing loss may be conductive, caused by interference with the sequence of sound vibrations reaching the auditory nerve; sensorineural, caused by defects in the inner ear or in the auditory nerve that transmits the electrical impulses to the brain for interpretation; or	A hearing loss that occurs before a child learns language requires greater environmental modifications than does a loss that occurs after a child masters language. The teachers will need to work with the special education resource person to adapt the classroom environment and curriculum to the child's needs. Referral of parents to helpful community and medical resources is another important teacher role. In addition, parents may need assistance in helping their child

TABLE 5.1	Continued	
Disability or Special Needs Condition	**Description of Disability or Special Needs Condition**	**Implications for Classroom Teachers**
	mixed. Conductive hearing loss accounts for about 95 percent of all acquired hearing loss in infants and young children and is usually caused by middle ear infections (Batshaw, 1991). Hearing impairments may result from early infections during prenatal or postnatal periods, from an accident, or from exposure to certain prescription drugs. The severity depends on the degree of loss and the age of onset.	adapt to a hearing aid and in learning how to verbalize effectively with their child who has a new hearing aid or assistive device. Teachers usually need to focus on language development and speech within the classroom setting. Psychosocial issues may arise for the child with hearing impairment, and the teacher can help other children to understand the special needs of the child with hearing impairment within the social setting.
Speech and language delays and disorders	Young children exhibit a wide range of typical development of speech and language; therefore, it is difficult to delineate clearly what is and what is not a disorder. Communication disorders range from relatively mild speech problems in the normal population, such as pronouncing the word *rabbit* as "wabbit," to severe problems with understanding language or expressing oneself in a child with a developmental disability (Batshaw, 1991). Clear indicators of speech and language disorder are a cleft palate, no use of words at 4 years of age, and language limited to replicating the language of others. Care must be taken in identifying a child within this category, especially when cultural diversity and environment play such a crucial role in forming a child's speech and language patterns.	Teachers will need to work with speech and language specialists to develop appropriate interventions. A speech and language evaluation is the first step to developing a therapy plan. The person performing the evaluation should be a licensed speech–language pathologist, have graduate-level training in speech pathology, and be certified by the American Speech-Language-Hearing Association (ASHA). Parents may need referrals for community resources and assistance. Speech and language intervention may be needed on a regular basis, and teachers may need to learn sign language. Special sensitivity should be given to children with cultural and linguistic diversity, and these parents may need special support to deal with their child's speech and language delays and disorders.

(Continued)

TABLE 5.1	Continued

Disability or Special Needs Condition	Description of Disability or Special Needs Condition	Implications for Classroom Teachers
Autism	Autism is a syndrome: that is, it is a group of clinical symptoms that leads to a diagnosis (Batshaw, 1991). It has been diagnosed in children suffering from many different conditions, ranging from Fragile X syndrome to phenylketonuria. The diagnosis is often an educated guess. The major symptoms of autism are delayed and abnormal language; an inability to relate to people; and stereotyped, repetitive behaviors. Childhood autism is now classified as a chronic health problem rather than an emotional disorder. Language and communication are the major foci of concern and intervention. Children with autism often do not use language as effectively and appropriately as typical children of the same age do (Safford, 1989, p. 217). A child labeled as autistic is essentially a child who has a mixture of characteristics typical and atypical of most children of comparable age.	The most appropriate approach to treatment of autism is multifaceted, involving education, speech and language therapy, behavior-modification techniques, and possibly medication (Batshaw, 1991). Effective teachers of autistic children are those who are also effective with other populations of young children. Flexibility in teaching style is crucial, as are teaching characteristics such as nonthreatening manner, good observational skills, use of physical contact and physical prompts, the use of modified language, the initial use of a one-to-one teaching relationship, and a very positive attitude and approach (Grant, 1982). Children with autism need educational environments in which activities are kept interesting and varied, and in which tasks are broken down into simple subunits, with each task taking less than 30 minutes to accomplish (Batshaw, 1991). Preschool education that encourages communication skills and social interactions is very important for the child with autism. Inclusion is very important for this child population because teaching children with autism within naturalistic learning settings and classroom environments is recommended. The role of the parents and family is very important for the child with autism; what is learned at school should be practiced at home.

TABLE 5.1	Continued	
Disability or Special Needs Condition	**Description of Disability or Special Needs Condition**	**Implications for Classroom Teachers**
Fragile X-syndrome	Fragile X syndrome is caused by an abnormality of the X chromosome; it is carried by females but affects males. Recent evidence suggests that as many as 10 percent of males with moderate to severe mental retardation of undiagnosed origin may have fragile X syndrome (Batshaw, 1991). Fragile X syndrome is the most common form of inherited mental retardation, affecting about 1 in 2,000 girls and 1 in 1,250 boys. It is caused by a mutated gene on the X chromosome, and affected individuals have developmental delays, variable levels of mental retardation, and behavioral and emotional problems. Physical manifestations include large ears, a prominent jaw, and autistic-like behavior.	Teachers working with children with fragile X syndrome may apply instructional strategies that are similar to those for children with autism. Teachers may assist parents with appropriate referrals such as genetic tests that are definitive for the mutation. Also, children with fragile X syndrome may have frequent ear and sinus infections, nearsightedness, and lazy eye. These conditions may also require referrals for parent assistance, and teachers may need to adapt learning materials and environments to these special conditions.
Emotional disturbance	The origins of emotional disturbance in very young children are still not well understood. Environmental factors may be the cause, in combination with neurological and chemical factors also. Emotional disturbance among younger children is believed to encompass many types of problems and include withdrawal, depression, anxiety, aggression, and extreme phobias.	Teachers will have the opportunity to observe these children on a systematic basis, and this is important because the diagnosis of emotional disturbance is based on the frequency, duration, and intensity of these behaviors. Strategies used to remediate emotional disturbance reflect differing theoretical orientations of the respective programs that serve children and families. Intervention strategies include adjusting the diet and other environmental variables, restructuring the physical environment, and examining relationship dynamics between the child and significant others.

(Continued)

TABLE 5.1   Continued

Disability or Special Needs Condition	Description of Disability or Special Needs Condition	Implications for Classroom Teachers
Orthopedic impairments	This is a very broad category and includes any condition that interferes with the health or normal functioning of bones, joints, or muscles. Defects such as spina bifida, clubfoot, or cerebral palsy may be present at birth. Other problems, such as muscular dystrophy, may develop later as the child matures. Causes of orthopedic impairments include hereditary factors, the influence of infection or toxic substances on the mother during very early pregnancy, birth injuries, or diseases or accidents that occur after birth.	Many children in this category do not require special education services, and adaptive equipment for some children may help them to function more independently in typical settings. Teachers may need to adapt the learning environment to accommodate the need for more physical space for adaptive equipment, and teachers should be prepared to assist parents in referrals to community resources for financial, medical, and emotional support.
Visual impairments	Vision impairment comes in various degrees, the most severe of which is blindness. For young children, visual impairments are more likely to be caused by prenatal factors, serious infections such as rubella, and specific hereditary factors that may manifest themselves in blindness at birth or create the likelihood that the child will require special education services. A child is considered blind when visual acuity is poorer than 20/200 in the better eye after correction or when the field of vision is limited to an angle of less than 20 degrees. A child with partial sight has an acuity of less than 20/70 but greater than 20/200. An acuity of 20/200 indicates that the child can see at 20 feet what an individual with normal vision can see at 200 feet.	Preschool children whose vision is too poor for them to benefit from printed materials should begin a program that sensitizes them to tactile learning materials. This provides an introduction to prebraille and braille reading skills. Teachers should be familiar with community resources for families with children with visual impairments. The special education resource person in the school setting should be consulted for additional services and classroom adaptations. Many toys and playthings exist for the visually impaired child. These include mobiles, rattles, noisemakers, riding toys, bean bags, talking toys, small radios, CD players, and a variety of paints and art materials (Batshaw, 1991).

TABLE 5.1	Continued	
Disability or Special Needs Condition	**Description of Disability or Special Needs Condition**	**Implications for Classroom Teachers**
Giftedness	This child demonstrates some exceptional quality or potential for accomplishment. Determining or assessing giftedness has been the source of debate and educational reform. Young children who are very bright are also very heterogeneous. Gifted children vary widely in their talents and abilities.	Children who are young and gifted are still young children who need hands-on, developmentally appropriate learning activities. The fact that they are intellectually advanced does not make them more able to complete paper-and-pencil assessments. Teachers may need to work with parents to temper their expectations of the gifted child, and teachers should be familiar with community resources that will help parents meet the special needs of their gifted child.
	Individual traits that may be correlated with giftedness include excellent memory, curiosity, sense of humor, perfectionism, rapid learning ability, unusual alertness, long attention span, high activity level, keen sense of observation, and advanced ability to play with manipulatives such as puzzles and mazes. Creativity may be another measure of giftedness, although the highly creative child may not reflect the same level of intellectual advancement in terms of IQ testing. Creativity has to do with a child's ability to solve problems in multiple dimensions, capacity for organization, use of fantasy for problem solving, and ability to produce new combinations through manipulation (Safford, 1989; Torrance, 1983).	
	Of special interest is the child who has both giftedness and a disability. This child, because of	

(Continued)

| TABLE 5.1 | Continued | |

Disability or Special Needs Condition	Description of Disability or Special Needs Condition	Implications for Classroom Teachers
	his or her handicapping condition, may be overlooked for giftedness. According to Safford (1989), "the full range of intellectual potential is represented among children with impaired mobility, vision, or hearing or with chronic health problems" (p. 244).	
HIV and AIDS	The number of pediatric HIV/AIDS cases is expected to rise significantly (Savage, Mayfield, & Cook, 1993). With advances in treatment, more infected children are expected to live longer. These children function well within the regular classroom, and legislation requires that they be included in the typical classroom setting. The degree and nature of special needs will differ from child to child, and assessment is important to determine specific learning needs and adaptations. Generalized developmental delays are common in children who have pediatric AIDS, including motor and speech delays or regressions as well as delay or regression in social development. If the mother has passed the virus directly to the child, then there may also be both psychological and social negative outcomes (Bowe, 2000).	Legislation mandates that children with HIV/AIDS not be excluded from educational programs in which typical children participate (ADA of 1990). Most children with HIV/AIDS function well within the regular classroom, and they are eligible for special education services if they are evaluated and meet the stated criteria for specific disabilities. They may also qualify for other services, such as Other Health Impaired category, which means limited strength, vitality, or alertness due to chronic or acute health problems that adversely affect performance (Savage et al., 1993, p. 11). Teachers in early childhood settings should read about HIV/AIDS and attend in-service workshops to stay up to date on the latest medical information as well as on related teacher–child–parent needs and issues.
Crack, cocaine, and heroin effects	The use of crack, cocaine, and heroin by pregnant women and the general adult population in the United States has increased dramatically over the past decade, and teachers are reporting	Defining what is developmentally appropriate for this population is challenging, but educators have developed strategies that usually involve higher levels of structure, repetition, and teacher-directed

TABLE 5.1   Continued

Disability or Special Needs Condition	Description of Disability or Special Needs Condition	Implications for Classroom Teachers
	increased numbers of young children in their settings who demonstrate the effects of these drugs. Children with this background frequently display attachment disorders, asocial behaviors, aggressive or inappropriate peer interactions, and more social difficulties in general (Griffith, 1992).	activities. Because these children can display difficult interactional patterns from birth, it is important for teachers to be informed about the latest developments in this child population. Although these children may not automatically be categorized as "special needs," they clearly are at risk and should be monitored for assessment and screening and referral. In addition, dealing with parents of crack/cocaine/heroin-affected children is essential to maintaining consistency between the classroom and home environments.
Fetal alcohol syndrome (FAS)	FAS manifests itself in the form of specific growth, mental, and physical birth defects associated with the mother's high levels of alcohol use during pregnancy. Timing of alcohol use during pregnancy is also important; alcohol use during the first trimester is more damaging than use during the second trimester, which is, in turn, more damaging than use in the third trimester. There is a linear relationship between the amount of alcohol consumed during pregnancy and the degree of FAS. For the young child with FAS, there may be delayed development and evidence of mild to moderate mental retardation (IQ range from 50 to 85, with a reported average in the mid-60s); facial abnormalities (small head; small	FAS is seen throughout school settings in the United States, and the outcome for infants with FAS is considered poor. A diagnosis of FAS is required by a physician, and teachers suspecting the syndrome should refer children, as soon as possible, for examination and diagnosis. Teachers will need to consult with special education resource persons to develop individual intervention programs for children with FAS, depending on the features of their particular situation. The child with FAS may present a particularly challenging teaching profile and the needs of each child should be determined through an interdisciplinary team and the IEP process.

(Continued)

TABLE 5.1	Continued

Disability or Special Needs Condition	Description of Disability or Special Needs Condition	Implications for Classroom Teachers
	upper jaw; short, upturned nose; underdeveloped groove between nose and upper lip; and narrow, small, and unusual-appearing eyes with prominent epicanthic folds); skeletal abnormalities of the joints, hands, feet, fingers, and toes; and heart defects. In addition, neonatal growth may have been slower.	
Seizure disorders	Seizures occur as a result of brief periods of uncontrolled and abnormal electrical activity in the brain. Most people with seizure disorders are not otherwise handicapped and lead normal lives; however, seizure disorders occur more frequently in children with a disability than in the general population (Batshaw, 1991). About 1 in 10 children with a disability wil develop a seizure disorder, compared with only 1 in 200 for the general population. The exact cause of the seizures may not be known, but possible causes include a head injury, a brain tumor, or a separate medical condition such as meningitis (Batshaw, 1991, p. 96). Fortunately, seizure disorders can usually be controlled with the proper medication. However, if left untreated, they can interfere with the full expression of the child's abilities.	Teachers may be frightened by the seizures and inclined to overprotect the child. However, both teachers and parents need to avoid unnecessary restrictions on the child. Seizure medications usually maintain good control and permit the child to participate in most activities. The child with seizures should be observed closely without being overprotected (Batshaw, 1991). Despite medications, some children will still have occasional seizures. Teachers should learn the techniques for responding to a seizure and encourage the child to wear a protective helmet or headgear during very physical activities. Give the child as much freedom as possible and work with special education and community resource professionals to become comfortable in working with this child.
Attention deficit/hyperactivity disorder (ADHD)	ADHD is controversial in early childhood, and diagnosis is largely a matter of testing the child for other conditions or	Despite its current popularity as an explanation for socially unacceptable behavior, experts caution that very little is known

TABLE 5.1	Continued	
Disability or Special Needs Condition	**Description of Disability or Special Needs Condition**	**Implications for Classroom Teachers**
	problems and settling on ADHD only after other labels have been rejected (Bowe, 2000). Attention deficits may occur with other conditions, and children with ADHD or ADD may also have conduct disorders. Children who take medications for other conditions may exhibit attention deficit, and children may have learning disabilities in addition to attention deficits. For these reasons, diagnosis of ADHD is challenging for most experts.	about ADHD. Aggressive behavior, in particular, is more common among boys than among girls. Withdrawal, however, may be more common in girls (Bowe, 2000). Teachers will need to work closely with parents and school psychologists or other school personnel to determine an appropriate assessment, realizing that diagnosis is often tentative. Major challenges for the teacher include dealing with aggressive or withdrawn behaviors.

SCHOOLS, COMMUNITY RESOURCES, AND COLLABORATION STRATEGIES

One of the school's major responsibilities is to connect the family with appropriate community resources. Referring again to Bronfenbrenner's (1975) ecological model, we turn now to the interrelationships between the family of a child with special needs and the immediate community and its resources. The family with a child with special needs depends greatly on the resources of the school and the community to provide support for a variety of needs: financial, emotional, social services, and general family support. We have discussed the specific roles of the school professional in addressing the needs of the child with a disability. Now we turn to the use of community resources and **interagency collaboration** to address family financial and social support needs and resources.

Parents who are involved in child advocacy efforts often feel empowered to deal with their own personal situations.

Families Under Stress: A Community-Based Model

The conceptual scaffolding of families under stress depends on three variables: (a) the family, (b) a crisis-provoking event, and (c) the meaning attached to the event. Viewed externally, the family often appears to be a closed corporation, particularly in urban areas where the nuclear group of father, mother, and their children is clearly differentiated from the kinship extensions of maternal and paternal grandparents and other relatives.

FIGURE 5.4	Classroom Strategies for Teachers Working with Children with Disabilities and Developmental Delays

1. Make a special effort at the beginning of the school year to connect with the parents and siblings of a child with special needs in your classroom. Consider making a home visit to better understand the child's home environment and the parents' resources and to establish a sense of trust and rapport with the family.

2. Listen to the parents' concerns and establish a regular pattern and routine for communicating their child's progress. With their input, decide which communication strategies are best for them and then be consistent with your communication.

3. Invite parents of a child with special needs to be a regular part of your classroom. Determine what unique contributions they can make and then ask them to participate routinely. This can include reading to the children, working in a classroom center, assisting with project work or field trips, and other activities. Having them in the classroom on a regular basis will reassure them of your commitment to their child's well-being, allow them to experience their child's progress on a firsthand basis, and provide the other children with the opportunity to know these parents.

4. Actively involve parents of children with special needs in the parent leadership for your classroom. Developing relationships with other parents can provide important socialization and support for the parent of the child with special needs.

5. Partner with the parents of a child with special needs to be an advocate for materials, equipment, and other resources for your classroom. Learn together with these parents how to utilize community resources and to advocate for services that will enhance your classroom and their child's education.

6. Encourage conversations among all of the children in your classroom about their perceptions, concerns, and questions about special needs conditions. Children can learn valuable life skills and attitudes in your classroom about working with individuals who have some differences, and they can become more prosocial, nonjudgmental, and accepting of individuals with disabilities.

7. Include good literature in your classroom on developmental diversity, special needs, and disabilities. Post classroom posters and other visual aids that reflect inclusive practice and attitudes.

8. Invite community resource people into your classroom to talk about special needs conditions, and invite the children to have conversations with these resource people. This can include pediatricians; occupational, speech, and physical therapists; and other health-care professionals.

The closed nature of the family is nevertheless selectively opened for transacting business with other agencies, including kin and professionals. These agencies can be ranked according to their accessibility to the interior of the family: immediate kin highest, family friends and neighbors next, the family physician, the family pastor, the family lawyer, and so on.

Other agencies enter the family with greater difficulty and often through the inter-mediation of individual family members who act as liaisons for the family: the school, the employer, the health clinic, the casework agency, and other such formal agencies. Viewed historically, the family today is much more dependent on other agencies in society than were families in the past. Figure 5.4 describes classroom strategies for teacher to use when working with children with disabilities and developmental delays.

Seeking Help from Formal Resources

Families of children with special needs frequently need to turn to formal community resources to obtain information, help them cope, and make decisions. **Formal community resources** include agencies, institutions, governmental programs, local services, and so on, ranging from those using a wide variety of trained professionals to those using few or none at all (Rose & Smith, 1993; Solit, 1993).

The most common types of formal community resources include the following:

Social Security offices	Resource and referral agencies
Health departments	Social services offices (financial resources)
Mental-health clinics	School district main office and neighborhood sites
Crisis centers and hotlines	Parent support groups for designated disabilities
Social workers	Family physicians and pediatricians
Libraries	Human resource offices and departments
Community bulletin boards	Hospital social service departments
Churches	Local politicians

These formal community resources can be located in the Yellow Pages or a special city/county/state governmental listing in the local telephone book, as well as through interagency and network telephone lists and communication systems.

THEMES 2, 3, AND 4 *in practice...*

In Kevin Martin's new 4K classroom are several children with special needs. One girl has a visual impairment and a boy is autistic. What are developmentally appropriate ways for Mr. Martin to teach the other children about their peers' characteristics and needs? What are resources that Mr. Martin could use to teach the children and their parents about children with specific developmental delays and special needs?

Suggestions for Seeking Resources

When families need to refer to community resources for assistance, they may feel overwhelmed and intimidated by their lack of understanding of the roles of different agencies, the systems and procedures for gaining access to these community resources, and the organizational structure or hierarchy of the agency. Suggestions for families seeking community resources include the following:

- Use informal resources as much as possible and then turn to formal resources as the next step.
- Remember that no one kind of resource is the best. The best resource is one that works for that family, and this will depend on the quality of a particular resource, the individuals within each family, their needs, and what is available in the local area.
- Be aware that the mystique surrounding professionalism contributes to a self-perpetuating cycle in which professional help is seen as the only kind of help with any value, and the professional's view of a situation the only valid one.
- Understand that agencies and institutions have a varying degree of social responsibility. As professionals, we all must work to educate ourselves to understand the nature of our society and the problems facing it, and we must work to improve the ways that society relates to and supports its members. Hence, some agencies will leave parents feeling more overwhelmed, inadequate, and isolated, whereas others will contribute to a sense of strength and self-sufficiency on the part of the family.
- Understand that some agencies have deficiencies and biases that affect the accessibility and quality of services provided. Fathers, for example, are sometimes made to feel distinctly out of place when they try to function as parents to their children with disabilities. Lower income families and minority-group members often feel the sting of scorn or outright exclusion in contacts with institutions. Also, some agencies believe more in treating problems after they occur than in contributing to prevention or early intervention.

Most parents have not been instructed on how to interface effectively with formal resources such as agencies. Parents of children with special needs can be empowered to obtain services effectively by following these suggestions:

- Identify and state the problem. Parents may want to write out a description of the problem or need to more clearly articulate their needs before going to the agency. Asking for help is the crucial first step and can be very empowering.
- Start with what you already have. Informal networks often provide families with individuals who can gather or provide information related to child care, health care, employment, Social Security, and other governmental programs and benefits.

- Look for allies. Several parents with similar needs may get more action than just one parent alone. *Parent power* should not be overlooked.

- Write it down. Often when parents need help, they also feel confused and overwhelmed. Families should be encouraged to maintain a log or journal in which they identify resources, assistance provided, dates, names of resource persons and agencies, and general comments about services provided.

- Make contact. Some agencies are aware of how important the first contact is, and they make sure it is a welcoming one. At other times, families must deal with agency personnel who themselves are overworked and overwhelmed. Parents should keep trying and not assume that there is nothing for them behind that wall or that no one else in the agency has a genuine commitment to help.

- Be persistent. Unfortunately, when families seek formal assistance from community agencies, they are already feeling tired and demoralized. Breaking through the barriers of some agencies is challenging. Families should be encouraged to be persistent and *not give up*.

- Be open to new sources of information. Help can come from places families do not expect. Good sources of information on available local community resources are social workers, newspapers, libraries, community bulletin boards, hospital social service departments, churches, schools, mental-health centers, hotlines, politicians, and resource and referral centers.

- Let friends help. A good tip for families is to ask a friend or relative to help when they are feeling stuck. A relative or friend can sit with the parents while they make phone calls, visit a doctor's office, go to a mental-health clinic or welfare office, or attend a parent–teacher conference.

- Ask for referrals. If the community resource cannot provide needed help, families should ask for the names of two or three other community agencies that can.

- Keep the proper perspective. Sometimes parents may feel a power imbalance between them and the professionals, or they may run up against personal or institutional biases. Encourage parents to keep their perspective: People run agencies, and all people have their own personal needs and conflicts.

- Do not be intimidated. Remember that it can be a sign of strength to reach out for help, just as it is a sign of strength to give help.

Financial Assistance and Funding Mechanisms

Financial resources are available for most families of children with special needs. Knowing where these resources are located is a challenge for each professional because resources vary widely from one community to another. To begin with, the family should rely on the school system for this information. The special education director, school counselor, or other authority responsible for implementing services for children with special needs will have a list of community resources. These resources usually consist of the following:

- Financial assistance for medical care (federal and state programs)
- Food stamps; Women, Infants, and Children program: and other food-related programs
- Federal and state programs that cover all or partial payments for medical equipment, braces, and other developmental needs
- Community programs that provide care and educational support in addition to the school's for the child with special needs
- Insurance for children with special needs, and special programs that provide for outpatient services

Parent empowerment is a goal of home-school partnerships.

PARENT EMPOWERMENT AND SELF-CARE

As discussed in this chapter, parenting a child with special needs is a challenging life task. Regardless of the nature or severity of the problem, parents may at first feel overwhelmed with shock at seeing their image of an ordered and ordinary life so abruptly shattered. It is important to remember that as overwhelming a problem as it may seem, as deeply committed as a parent may always be to caring for his or her child, the parent's need for self-care and to separate from the problem should be a goal from the outset. Thus, in supporting parents of children with special needs, encouraging the parents to take good care of themselves is crucial so that feelings of isolation, fear, and loneliness do not surround them. Parents need to learn to take care of themselves so that they are able to problem solve and meet the needs of their child.

THEME 5   *in practice . . .*

The local Kiwanis organization offers to collaborate with the health department and the local school district to present informational workshops on child advocacy and the legal rights of parents of children with special needs. Is this an appropriate collaboration? Why or why not?

LEGISLATION IMPACTING SERVICES FOR PARENTS AND CHILDREN WITH SPECIAL NEEDS

I n recent years, families of children with special needs have gained advocacy successes and made tremendous legislative gains. This section identifies important pieces of legislation that are contributing to the expanded educational program and service options now available to these families. Also included is information on child and parent advocacy initiatives on behalf of children with disabilities.

Appropriate Education for All Children: P.L. 94-142

The key word regarding teaching exceptional children is not *mainstreaming*, but rather *appropriate* (Mallory & New, 1994; Safford, 1989; Sexton et al., 1993). The major policy document in this area, P.L. 94-142 (the EHA of 1975), is often referred to as "the mainstreaming law." In fact, the word *mainstreaming* never appears in this law, whereas the word *appropriate* appears repeatedly. The central purpose of P.L. 94-142 is to ensure that all children with disabilities are provided a *free appropriate public education* (FAPE). P.L. 94-142 also requires the use of an IEP as the tool to design and implement each child's appropriate education. Another important feature of this law is the requirement of an LRE for each student's school placement. As part of the IEP, the planning team, including parents, teachers, and other appropriate individuals, must indicate and define the extent to which the child will participate in regular educational programs.

One of the most important pieces of legislation for young children with special needs and their families, P.L. 94-142 mandates that parents be provided the opportunity to become involved in decisions concerning the education of their exceptional child. Thus, parental involvement in education programs is now a right guaranteed by law.

P.L. 99-457

In 1986, President Reagan signed into law P.L. 99-457, which mandates further and more specific criteria for identifying and serving children from birth to age 5 with disabilities and developmental delay. The goal of these identification procedures is not to screen out or otherwise segregate young children with special needs, as was done in the past, but to locate children to provide appropriate services for each child's unique needs. P.L. 99-457 has had a major impact on public schools and other institutions in the United States because it legislates that services for all children with disabilities be provided beginning at age 3. Thus, school districts are now responsible for serving families of children with disabilities in the preschool years.

P.L. 99-457 does not require or emphasize categorical labels for the following reasons:

- Young children's needs are difficult, if not impossible, to categorize with traditional labels.
- Especially during the early years, these needs change rapidly.
- Categorical labels have no utility for young children because categorical programs may not be appropriate.
- Early labeling of children may limit and restrict them because others may respond to these labels in limiting and restricting ways.

- Labels tend to follow children, even after they are no longer applicable or appropriate.
- Least restrictive services for young children, required by P.L. 99-457, are intended to foster interaction between children with and without disabilities. Labels tend to impede that interaction (Safford, 1989; Sexton et al., 1993; Solit, 1993).

P.L. 99-457 identifies a more basic role for parents of young children with disabilities than that stipulated in P.L. 94-142. This legislation (a) de-emphasizes disability labeling and categorical placement of children with disabilities, (b) encourages creative partnerships and collaboration between the public schools and other agencies, and (c) requires involvement with children without disabilities. Agencies involved may include both public and private programs, provided that services are appropriate and of high quality and integration is present. Such partnerships may increasingly involve programs that in the past have served mainly children without disabilities, including proprietary, cooperative, and other community nursery schools.

Other Important Legislation

Other examples of important legislation on behalf of children with special needs are the following:

- Handicapped Children's Early Education Act (P.L. 91-230)
- Head Start Handicapped Mandate (P.L. 92-424)
- Developmental Disabilities Act (P.L. 95-602)
- IDEA Legislation (P.L. 101-476, the Individuals with Disabilities Education Act of 1990)

Developmentally Appropriate Practice: NAEYC

Leaders in ECE have responded to the need for DAP in the education of young children (Bredekamp, 1988). The NAEYC has adopted position statements based on key dimensions of developmental appropriateness, including the following (Bredekamp, 1987; Mallory & New, 1994):

- Children learn best through self-initiated, self-directed, and self-chosen activity.
- The teacher facilitates learning by providing a variety of activities and materials and by reflecting with children about their play.
- Different types of activities and materials are appropriate for children of different ages.
- Children learn through play; transformational materials (sand, water, clay, blocks), puzzles, manipulatives, dramatic play props, science equipment, books, CDs, paper, paint and markers, and so on are all appropriate for early-education classrooms.
- All children should be exposed to multicultural activities, materials, and equipment.

As Mallory and New (1994) pointed out, DAP continues to be redefined and reconstructed, particularly in the areas of inclusion and multiculturalism.

ADVOCACY GROUPS AND INITIATIVES IN EARLY INTERVENTION

M ounting evidence indicates that, at least for some infants and preschoolers with special needs, early intervention can have a markedly positive effect on their development. Partly because of the influence of advocacy organizations such as the National Association for Retarded Citizens, the United Cerebral Palsy Association, the Society for Autistic Children, and the Epilepsy Foundation of America, decision makers have become more responsive to the needs of children with disabilities. In addition, the experiences of agencies offering early intervention programs have contributed to an atmosphere of urgency. They have also revealed such benefits as signficant long-term savings in program costs as children's needs for complex and expensive services decrease with time.

Advocacy and Parent Empowerment

Parents involved in child and family advocacy efforts often feel empowered to deal with their own personal situations. There is strength and comfort in numbers; people working together for a common cause can provide a much-needed outlet for parents of children with disabilities. The success of the described legislation is a result of the ongoing, effective, and persistent efforts of parents advocating for the educational, health, and social programs that their children need. In no other area of education is the need for parent involvement in advocacy groups so great or so well documented. Figure 5.5 describes advocacy strategies for teachers working with parents of children with special needs.

FIGURE 5.5	Advocacy Strategies for Teachers Working with Parents of Children with Special Needs

1. Invite the school principal, center director, or other administrator into your classroom on a regular basis to be a part of the educational experience. For example, invite the principal to read to the children in your classroom the first Tuesday of each month. Having the administrator in your classroom will increase his or her understanding of your classroom, including children with special needs.

2. Keep administrators informed about the ongoing progress and needs of children with disabilities in your classroom. If they feel vested in these children's progress, they are more likely to respond to requests for special resources for your classroom.

3. Consider taking a leadership role in an advocacy group in your community that serves the needs of children with disabilities and special needs. For example, you could provide a leadership role in an advocacy group for families with Down syndrome children.

4. Offer your classroom as a site for regular meetings for parents of children with special needs. Keep the door open to parents whose children require special education services, and offer your classroom as a safe place to meet and advocate for their children's needs within the school or center setting.

5. Invite a community resource person to speak to the school PTA or other parent group about a special needs condition or situation such as cerebral palsy, Down syndrome, autism, or FAS. This informs the entire parent population about the needs of both children with disabilities and their parents and reflects an inclusive attitude and approach on the part of the school.

Information Sources: Advocacy Groups and Agencies

Federal

Administration on Developmental Disabilities
U.S. Department of Health and Human Services
200 Independence Avenue SW
Washington, DC 20201
www.hhs.gov

The federal agency coordinating state-run programs for children with severe and multiple needs.

Department of Education
400 Maryland Avenue SW
Washington, DC 20202
www.ed.gov

The federal agency responsible for administering the IDEA and other laws providing services to people with disabilities.

National Council on Disability
1331 F. Street NW, #1050
Washington, DC 20004
www.ncd.gov

A small, independent federal agency that advocates for laws on behalf of people with disabilities.

National Institutes of Health
Bethesda, MD 20892
www.nih.gov

The NIH sponsors research on hearing (National Institute on Deafness), aging and age-related disabilities (National Institute on Aging), and so on.

General

Division for Early Childhood
Council for Exceptional Children

1920 Association Drive
Reston, VA 22091–1589
www.dec-sped.org

DEC is the division of CEC that focuses on early childhood social education (ECSE). An association of special educators and related services personnel, CEC is a long-standing advocate for special education and early intervention.

National Early Childhood Technical
Assistance Center
Suite 500, Nations Bank Plaza
137 East Franklin Street
Chapel Hill, NC 27514
www.nectas.unc.edu

NECTA is a federally funded center on ECSE. Each year, it issues numerous reports on issues important to the field. It also maintains current and comprehensive contact information about Part C and preschool Part B programs in all states, for which reason it is an excellent source of names, addresses, telephone and fax numbers, and so on for parents and professionals alike.

National Easter Seals Society
230 West Monroe Street, #1800
Chicago, IL 60606–4802
www.easterseals.com

Legal Advocacy

Disability Rights Education and Defense Fund (DREDF)
2212 Sixth Street
Berkeley, CA 94702

A private advocacy organization of and for people with disabilities, DREDF has been active in advocating for human and civil rights for Americans with disabilities. It offers legal representation and cocounsel in selected cases.

ADHD

Attention Deficit Disorder Association
P. O. Box 9972
Mentor, OH 44061

A national organization providing information on ADHD and related disorders.

Attention Deficit Information Network, Inc.
58 Prince St.
Needham, MA 02492
adin@gis.net
www.addinfonetwork.com

Children and Adults with Attention-Deficit/Hyperactivity Disorder
8181 Professional Place, Suite 150
Landover, MD 20785
www.chadd.org

AIDS

AIDS Action Council
1875 Connecticut Avenue NW #700
Washington, DC 20009

Representing some 900 community groups, the council promotes legislation protecting people with AIDS and advocates for more research and better care.

National AIDS Clearinghouse
P.O. Box 6003
Rockville, MD 20849–6003

This information service offers materials in Spanish as well as English and operates a hotline. The clearinghouse is sponsored by Atlanta-based Centers for Disease Control and Prevention.

Autism

Autism Society of America
7910 Woodmont Avenue, Suite 650
Bethesda, MD 20814–3015

With more than 185 chapters nationwide, the ASA offers factual information about autism and urges research and treatment advances.

Blindness and Visual Impairment

American Council of the Blind
1155 15th street NW, #720
Washington, DC 20005
www.acb.org

A consumer organization of blind and low-vision adults, ACB has 52 state or regional chapters and about two dozen affiliates. An excellent source of information about the consumer perspective.

Cerebral Palsy

United Cerebral Palsy
1660 L Street NW, #700
Washington, DC 20036
www.ucp.org

A private organization with 183 affiliates nationwide.

Deafness and Hearing Impairment

National Association of the Deaf
814 Thayer Avenue
Silver Spring, MD 20910
www.nad.org

A consumer organization with state chapters nationwide.

(Continued)

(Continued)

Families

Beach Center on Families and Disability
Bureau of Child Research
University of Kansas
Haworth Hall
1200 Sunnyside Ave., Room 3136
Lawrence, KS 66045-7534
beachcenter@ku.edu

A federally funded research and training center, Beach focuses on childhood disability. Its directors, H. R. and Ann Turnbull, are experts on special education law.

Children's Defense Fund
25 E Street NW
Washington, DC 20001

An outstanding public-interest advocacy group, CDF has a long-standing interest in lobbying for children with disabilities. It publishes low-cost (most under $6) publications on how to be an advocate, how to use the mass media, and how to lobby and raise funds for programs.

National Dissemination Center
for Children with Disabilities
P.O. Box 1492
Washington, DC 20013
www.nichcy.org

A federally funded center that offers readable information and referral services especially for families. Many of its publications are free.

Fragile X Syndrome

National Fragile X Foundation
1441 York Street #215
Denver, CO 80206
www.fragilex.org

An information resource on genetic testing, family needs, and family counseling support groups and experts, the foundation is a good source of information about this disorder.

Mental Illness

National Alliance for the Mentally Ill
200 N. Glebe Road #1015
Arlington, VA 22203

The alliance is a self-help, consumer organization run principally by individuals who themselves are mentally ill or mentally restored. It advocates for better treatment and greater rights.

Retardation

The Arc of the United States
500 East Border Street #300
Arlington, TX 76010
www.thearc.org

A private, nonprofit association of affiliates providing services, information, research, and advocacy on behalf of people with retardation. The Arc (formerly Association for Retarded Citizens/United States) has 1,200 chapters or affiliates.

National Down Syndrome Society
666 Broadway
New York, NY 10012
www.ndss.org

Sponsors research, information, and outreach on behalf of children and adults with Down syndrome.

Speech and Language

American Speech-Language-Hearing
Association
10801 Rockville Pike
Rockville, MD 20852

A professional organization for speech, language, and hearing pathologists and for audiologists.

Critical Concepts

1. Children with special needs represent an important part of our society, and early childhood classrooms reflect this incidence level, which is usually at least 10 percent of the total child population.

2. Early identification and intervention provide optimal outcomes for children with disabilities and special needs and facilitate their success as future citizens.

3. Parents and siblings of children with special needs and disabilities go through difficult stages of adjustment; there is a grieving process and phases of adjustment that are beneficial for teachers to know and understand.

4. Teachers should become familiar with the common characteristics of the most frequently observed conditions of special needs and developmental delays to provide classroom support and parent assistance.

5. Giftedness is a special condition that should be recognized and addressed by classroom teachers, and gifted children with disabilities are often overlooked in the identification process.

6. Several key pieces of legislation have been passed that provide comprehensive services and support for families and children with special needs and disabilities; teachers play a pivotal role in the development and implementation of effective IEPs and IFSPs for children with special needs.

7. Community resources are a critical component for children with special needs and disabilities; teachers should become familiar with the unique school and community resources available to parents and children with disabilities and special needs.

8. Advocating for children with disabilities and special needs is a key role of the classroom teacher; becoming an activist for these children and their parents will increase the quality of their services.

Summary Statements

✓ The emerging **inclusion movement** in the United States has brought law and logic together to ensure that families of children with special needs will receive the greatest possible normality in the educational experiences of the children.

✓ Exceptionality is generally defined through societal consensus and from various perspectives: medical, legal, sociological, psychological, and educational.

✓ Children with special needs are typically those with mental, communicative, social–emotional, or physical characteristics requiring some adaptations in the educational program for optimal learning to occur. An estimated 1 million children of preschool age with disabilities live in the United States.

✓ Children from less advantaged environments are overrepresented in special education classes in the public schools, relative to their numbers in the total population.

✓ The amount of stress imposed on the family with a special needs child may

✓ depend on how radically parental expectations are violated; the impact of a child with a disability on a family is major.

✓ The identification of a child with a disability sets off a process of adjustment for the parents that includes shock, denial, sadness and anger, adaptation, and reorganization.

✓ Recent legislation on behalf of children with disabilities recognizes the family as the first and primary teacher and emphasizes the role of the family in the support of the child's growth and development.

✓ The philosophy of normalization has made a major impact on services delivered to exceptional children and their families, and schools serving children with disabilities must now comply with legislative mandates for the least restrictive learning environments for these children.

✓ Parents' involvement in the legislative process at both the federal and state levels has resulted in increased legislative initiatives and mandates, such as the successful passage of P.L. 99-457 in 1986.

✓ Family support programs can serve multiple needs: emotional, physical, financial. Advocacy groups also provide many of these support mechanisms.

✓ The decline of neighborhood networks, the increased mobility of the population, the increase in single-parent families, and the increased distance between members of the extended family have combined to create a situation in which many families with children with disabilities feel isolated and alone.

✓ All members of a family of a child with a disability are in need of support, including siblings and extended family members.

✓ An IEP or IFSP is now required for many educational programs that serve children with special needs, and parents have the right to be active participants in the development of their child's IEP.

✓ The school professional provides a crucial link among the family of a child with a disability, the school system, and relevant community resources and agencies.

✓ Public schools are legally responsible for providing education-related services for all children beginning at age 3, as mandated through P.L. 99-457.

✓ Screening is a gross means of economically scoring possible cases of disability from the general population and is a first step in the identification process.

✓ **Multifactored assessment** is required through P.L. 94-142 and P.L. 99-457 and includes individual assessment, annual review, fully informed parental consent, and multidisciplinary assessment.

✓ The family under stress must somehow adapt to the stressor event, and the resources located in the immediate community provide the next available rung of assistance to families, after immediate and extended family members, friends and neighbors, and pastors and family lawyers.

✓ Accessing formal community resources can be an intimidating and confusing process for families of children with disabilities; families need support in negotiating the referral process.

✓ Public laws and advocacy initiatives for children with disabilities increased dramatically during the 1980s and 1990s. Parents who become involved in advocacy efforts frequently feel empowered to deal more effectively with their particular situation.

Research to Practice: Classroom Applications and Activities

1. What evidence indicates that early intervention for children with special needs really makes a long-term difference?

2. P.L. 94-142 is referred to as the All Handicapped Children's Act. Explain your interpretation of this statement.

3. P.L. 99-457 was passed in 1986 and opened the door for younger children with disabilities. Explain what doors were opened and how this legislation has affected public school systems.

4. Define *early labeling* and explain why recent legislation discourages the use of labeling, especially for preschool children.

5. To what does *least restrictive environment (LRE)* refer, and how is this policy implemented in current school systems in the United States?

6. Accepting a child's disability is a major challenge for a parent. Describe the five stages involved in reaching adaptation.

7. Explain Bronfenbrenner's ecological model as a frame for the successful coping of families of children with disabilities. Give two examples.

8. Explain the concept of *normalization* and describe its impact on services delivered to exceptional children and their families.

9. Name at least three advocacy groups related to disability and explain ways that these groups could assist or support parents and families of children with disabilities.

10. Explain how parents can most effectively access and use formal community resources such as agencies, organizations, and advocacy groups. Name at least five community resources.

11. Explain how the family system, including siblings, is affected by the presence of a child with a disability.

12. Describe the IEP and IFSP processes in a typical school setting.

13. Explain multifactored assessment and its importance in current school policies and practices for children with disabilities.

14. Why are **parent empowerment** and self-care so important? Give examples of how parents can nurture and take care of their own health, emotional, and other needs.

15. Relate NAEYC's DAP to the inclusion movement and the philosophy of LRE.

Additional Activities

1. **Peer visitor.** Children learn about disabilities by interacting with other children who have disabling conditions, retardation, developmental delays, and other types of disabilities. Because attitudes toward disability are formed at a young age, inviting

a peer to the classroom to talk about his or her disability can be a very meaningful experience. The child should be included in the classroom routine, taking part in lunch, recess, or other activities, so that the class learns positive attitudes toward inclusion.

2. **Integrated curriculum activities.** Involving children in language arts, science, art, and other curricular activities related to disability can be an effective way to increase their knowledge about disability, as well as affect their attitudes. Children can share their written reports through small groups, oral reports, posters, videotapes, and other strategies.

3. **Role-playing.** Children learn best through hands-on activities. Engaging young children in dramatic play and role-playing that includes the challenges and rewards of a child with a disability can be an effective way of integrating the curriculum and increasing their understanding of what it is like to have a disability. Children can use wheelchairs, crutches, seeing-eye dogs, and other means to act out the real-life encounters of a child with a disability.

4. **Resource persons.** Many people in the local community have connections to children and families with disabilities. Invite a mother of a special needs child, a physical therapist, an occupational therapist, a pediatrician, a surgeon, or an animal trainer to class to discuss support for persons who are blind or visually impaired. Involve the class members in discussion and then assign a follow-up activity for the class. As much as possible, document students' work through photographs, audiotapes, videotapes, and so on.

Resources for Further Information

Council for Administration in Special Education (CASE) of the Council for Exceptional Children, 615 16th Street NW, Albuquerque, NM 87104, (505) 243–7622

Division for Early Childhood (DEC) of the Council for Exceptional Children, 1920 Association Drive, Reston, VA 22091, (703) 620–3660

National Association of State Directors of Special Education (NASDSE), 1800 Diagonal Road, Suite 320, King Street Station 1, Alexandria, VA 22314, (703) 519–3800

Sibling Information Network, Department of Educational Psychology, Box U-64, University of Connecticut, Storrs, CT 06268

Special Olympics, 1350 New York Avenue NW, Suite 500, Washington, DC 2005

U.S. Office of Special Education Programs, Early Childhood Branch, 400 Maryland Avenue SW, Washington, DC 20202, (202) 708–5366

Suggested Readings and Resources for Teachers and Parents

Ahanin, S. (1987). *Songs for language learning.* Tucson, AZ: Communication Skill Builders.

Becker, W. C. (1990). *Parents are teachers: A child management program.* Champaign, IL: Research Press.

Berg, F. S. (1987). *Facilitating classroom listening: A handbook for teachers of normal and hard of hearing students.* Boston: College Hill Press.

Bess, F. (1988). *Hearing impairment in children.* York, PA: York Press.

Buscaglia, L. (1983). *The disabled and their parents* (Rev. ed.). New York: Henry Holt.

Carson, M. A. (1991). *Guide for friends, neighbors and relatives of retarded children.* Chicago: Claretian.

Cohen, D. J., Donnellan, A. M., &Paul, R. (1987). *Handbook of autism and pervasive developmental disorders.* New York: Wiley.

Cunningham, C. (1982). *Down's syndrome: An introduction for parents.* Cambridge, MA: Brookline Books.

Ferry, P. C., Banner, W., & Wolf, R. A. (1985). *Seizure disorders in children.* Philadelphia: J.B. Lippincott.

Fraiberg, S. H. (1984). *Magic years: Understanding and handling the problems of early childhood.* New York: Scribner's.

Hanson, M. J. (1986). *Teaching your Down syndrome infant: A guide for parents* (2nd ed.). Austin, TX: PRO-ED.

Jablow, M. M. (1982). *Cara: Growing with a retarded child.* Philadelphia: Temple University Press.

Milunsky, A. (1989). *Choices, not chances: An essential guide to your heredity and health.* Boston: Little, Brown.

Pueschel, S. M. (1990). *Down syndrome: Towards a better future.* Baltimore: Brookes.

Thain, W. S. (1980). *Normal and handicapped children: A growth and development primer for parents and professionals.* Littleton, MA: PSG.

Thompson, G. H., Rubin, I. L., & Bilenket, R. M. (1983). *Comprehensive management of cerebral palsy.* Orlando, FL: Grune & Stratton.

Sing, L. (1985). *Autistic children, a guide for parents.* New York: Brunner-Mazel.

CHAPTER 6

Children of Divorced and Blended Families

Meeting the Needs of "New" Families

For all parents, creating and raising a family consist of one adjustment after another. . . . All families worry about making mistakes. Not only are mistakes unavoidable, . . . but parents learn their job through mistakes.

BRAZELTON, 1989, P. 1

KEY TERMS

anger inhibition
bibliotherapy
blended family
disruption of attachment
divorced family
instant love

logical consequences
myths about stepfamilies
nonresidential home
permeable boundaries
Phoenix concept
pileup

rates of divorce
reconstituted family
stages of divorce
  adjustment
stepchild
stepfather

stepmother
superdad
teacher self-assessment
wicked stepmother

GUIDING QUESTIONS

1. What is the current divorce rate in the United States and what percentage of children under 18 can expect to be impacted by divorce?
2. What are typical stages of adjustment to divorce for children of different ages?
3. Why do most children want their teacher to know about a divorce or remarriage, and what are the implications for teachers and professionals?
4. What are blended families, and what should teachers know about working with children from blended families?
5. What are effective classroom strategies for teachers to use when working with children from divorced and blended families?
6. Why must teachers rely on multiple strategies in working with children of divorced and blended families?
7. Why is cultural sensitivity necessary in contemporary classrooms when addressing issues related to divorce and remarriage?

The idealized model of an ever-married couple with children, with the father as the economic provider and the mother as the homemaker, is no longer a good fit for today's families. Only a minority of contemporary U.S. families fit this description, and U.S. schools and child-care settings provide educational and support services for a changing population of children who are a part of this marital revolution. Projections indicate that more than one third of children in the United States can expect that before their 18th birthdays, their parents will divorce (Strangeland, Pellegreno, & Lundholm, 1989).

Significantly, recent research indicates that divorce can have a major and disruptive effect on the long-term development of an individual's attitudinal and emotional development (Axinn, 1996; Wallerstein & Blakeslee, 1995).

Indeed, numerous research studies suggest that the trauma of divorce remains with children throughout their entire lives. Because of the powerful emotional effect of divorce on children (Keith & Finlay, 1988), it is important that teachers be aware of related issues that affect children and their families. Further, research indicates that children in preschool and early elementary settings want their teachers to know about and understand their parents' divorce (Frieman, 1993). Helping children at an early age to express and deal with their feelings will enable them to enjoy healthy and mature relationships in the future.

Two family forms that continue to increase in number are *divorced* and *blended* (remarriage) families, and U.S. schoolchildren reflect this growing trend. Although **rates of divorce** leveled off somewhat during the 1990s, the divorce rate for first marriages is still approximately 50 percent (Darden & Zimmerman, 1992;

Single-headed households are a growing norm in the United States.

Walsh, 1992). The divorce rate for remarriages is even higher. This means that at any given time, approximately half of all youths are destined to become stepdaughters or stepsons (Glick, 1989; Walsh, 1992). Thus, divorced and blended families have become increasingly normative in U.S. society (Darden & Zimmerman, 1992).

Because research indicates that teachers frequently have negative perceptions of children who are a part of divorced families (Ganong, Coleman, & Maples, 1990), it is important to include information on the impact of divorce and remarriage on children's development. In addition, teachers benefit from understanding the legal differences between, and the rights of, stepparents and biological parents (Fine & Fine, 1992).

This chapter focuses on children from divorced and blended families and makes suggestions for appropriate teacher and caregiver decisions, as well as school and community services and interventions. This chapter explores the following themes:

Theme 1. Divorce in the new millennium in the United States includes many definitions and demographic descriptors.

Theme 2. Children and parents who are experiencing the divorce process have special needs and issues, and teachers who work with these families in the classroom setting benefit by knowing about these special concerns.

Theme 3. Blended families are complex entities and they face special problems and issues. Teachers need to better understand the stages of adjustment for children and parents in blended families to meet their needs in classroom settings.

Theme 4. Teachers and schools must rely on multiple intervention strategies when working with divorced and blended families. A number of effective communication and program strategies are available to deal with the special issues and needs of these families.

Theme 5. Contemporary classrooms reflect increasingly diverse child and family populations. Teachers must be sensitive to these cultural and linguistic differences as they plan effective classroom activities for children affected by divorce and remarriage.

Figure 6.1 shows the change of the family system from predivorced state, through the divorce process, and to the establishment of the remarriage system. Note the relative complexity of the **divorced family** subsystem (ex-spouse subsystem, single-parent subsystem, visiting parent–child subsystem, and sibling subsystem) and the remarriage (**blended family**: couple subsystem, parent–child subsystem, and sibling subsystem).

DEFINITIONS AND DEMOGRAPHICS OF DIVORCE IN THE UNITED STATES

Divorce is the legal process of two individuals dissolving a marriage relationship or the dissolution of a marriage bond by legal process or by accepted custom (*American Heritage Dictionary*, 1996). A *blended family* is defined as a family in which one or both spouses in a remarriage have a child or children by

FIGURE 6.1   Process of Transition to the Blended Family

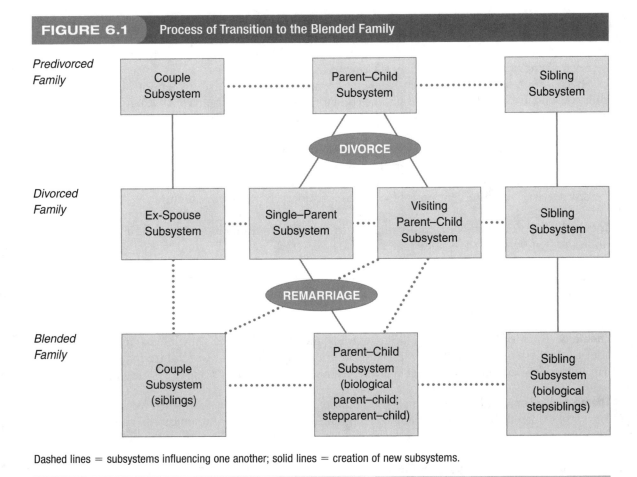

Dashed lines = subsystems influencing one another; solid lines = creation of new subsystems.

Note. Based on "Transition to the Blended Family," by W. Poppen and P. White, 1984, *Elementary School Guidance & Counseling,* *14*, pp. 50–61

a former marriage (Walsh, 1992). Other terms used to describe blended families are *reconstituted families, stepfamilies,* and *reorganized, combined,* or *remarried families.* Historically, most terms associated with blended families seem to be surrounded by guilt or some other negative quality (Lindner, Hagan, & Brown, 1992; Smith, 1992; Walsh, 1992).

Divorce in the United States is so common that teachers often report that a majority of the children in their classrooms are from homes where divorce is either occurring or has already taken place (Brazelton, 1989; Walsh, 1992). This text is written to assist school-based personnel and child-care professionals in addressing the changing needs of children in their care. In an effort to bring professionals up to date on divorce and remarriage in the United States, it is important to provide current data on the frequency of divorce and some demographic variables related to divorce.

The following list of demographic descriptors will help the professional in understanding the frequency of divorce in the United States and why the divorce process can be potentially very stressful for the child in a school or child-care setting (Anderson & White, 1986; Diamond, 1985; Galston, 1996; Smith, 1992; Walsh, 1992):

- Slightly more than half of all couples have children at the time of a divorce, accounting for more than 2 million children whose parents divorce each year.

- More than 1.5 million children under the age of 18 are affected each year by family breakups.

- Seventy-seven percent of children not living with both biological parents are from families with incomes of less than $5,000; only 16 percent of children not living with both parents are from families with incomes greater than $25,000.

- Divorce rates differ dramatically according to race, age, and socioeconomic status: Blacks are more likely than Whites to divorce, but particularly they are more likely to separate and live apart without a legal divorce; younger couples are more likely to divorce than those who marry at a later age; and divorce is much more prevalent among families at the lower end of the economic ladder.

- Divorce is likely to be followed by remarriage, and statistics indicate that five of six divorced men and three of four divorced women remarry.

- Remarriage rates among Whites are higher than among Blacks, and 1 child in 10 will undergo two or more family disruptions before the age of 16.

- Today's couples are less likely to remain married for the children's sake.

- Children's ages may affect the parents' decision to divorce, with divorce rates of couples with preschool children about half that of couples with children of school age; for couples with school-age children, divorce rates are about equal to the rates for childless couples.

- The number of children in a family is related to the divorce rate: Families with one or two children have considerably lower divorce rates than families with three or more children.

- Divorce rates are higher when a marriage is preceded by a premarital pregnancy or out-of-wedlock birth and when stepchildren are a part of a remarriage.

- About 40 percent of children living in mother-only households have not seen their fathers in the past year.

- Despite popular views that the rate of paternal custody cases is increasing, about 10 times as many children reside with a single mother as with a single father.

- Older children, particularly older boys, are more likely to live with their fathers than are younger children.

- The divorce rate is higher for remarriages than for first marriages, about 60 percent.

- In first marriages with biological children, there appears to be a disincentive to divorce, whereas in remarriages with stepchildren, there is an increased likelihood of divorce.

SPECIAL PROBLEMS FACED BY CHILDREN AND PARENTS EXPERIENCING THE DIVORCE PROCESS

The increasing rate of divorce and remarriage helps to explain why teachers report how complex their classrooms are, especially when compared with a decade ago. This complexity is the result of several factors, but the changing family structure is one of the most significant variables. For schools, the issues related to divorce are many. They include the simple, technical aspects such as keeping track of the child's last name, living arrangements, and who has primary custody. More serious concerns are related to such issues as *entry and exit*, the moving back and forth between custodial and noncustodial parents and possible custodial disagreements, which can result in intense parental disputes on the school grounds or even in kidnapping situations (Walsh, 1992). Typically, Mondays and Fridays are most difficult for children of divorce because of the emotional stress of leaving one parent and going to another (Francke, 1983). Custody arrangements are correlated with academic achievement, with children in shared-custody arrangements reflecting better adjustment and higher academic achievement levels (Livingston, 1983; Luepnitz, 1982).

Wallerstein and Blakeslee's (1995) research cautioned professionals not to take divorce too lightly. Longitudinal outcomes for adult children of divorce suggest that myths about quality versus quantity of time lack validity and that children between ages 8 and 10 at the time of their parents' divorce may have more negative long-term outcomes that affect their own personal relationships as adults.

Melissa and Meredith: A Case Study of Divorce and Remarriage

Melissa, age 10, and Meredith, age 14, are adjusting to a new lifestyle. Three years ago, when the girls were 7 and 11, their father told their mother that he had met someone else through his work and wanted a divorce. The news rocked the worlds of Melissa, Meredith, and their mother, Sandra, age 41. Married for 16 years, Sandra thought her marriage was sound. While the relationship had had its ups and downs, Sandra and her husband, Sean, seemed happy to their friends and family. Sean had met another woman through his work as a university professor, and the relationship had been kept a secret for nearly 2 years. When Sandra recovered from the shock of her husband's relationship with another woman, she began to do some serious reflection on the marriage, the stages of adjustment they had been through, and what signs or indicators there were that trouble might be developing. She was able to piece together some indicators that there were problems, and Sandra's mother and sisters shared some insights and perceptions also. It took a full year for Sandra to come to terms with her husband's new relationship and how it had developed.

After the initial separation, Melissa, Meredith, and Sandra went through a difficult period of adjustment. Everything seemed different now: Daddy was no longer in the house; they all had to adjust to another woman in their lives; Sandra's self-esteem was badly wounded; and all of them were angry at Sean. Some of the questions they asked were:

- What was so wrong with their family that Sean wanted to leave?
- Did he love them still?
- Why would he reject their mother for someone new (and much younger)?
- How were they going to survive financially?
- What would their close friends think?
- Could they still have friends over to the house and could they socialize?
- Could they afford to go to college?
- Could they afford to go shopping and out to eat?
- Would Sean continue to be their father or would he ignore them?

To deal with the anger and emotional distress, Sandra arranged for family counseling for each of the girls and herself. They had separate as well as shared sessions, and through this counseling, they came to terms with their anger and hurt.

It is now 3 years later, and Sean has married the younger woman. She has two very young children, so visitation for Melissa and Meredith has been difficult. A few times, Sean has asked Melissa and Meredith to babysit their two younger stepsiblings while he and his new wife went to a movie or out to eat. This has created resentment on the part of Melissa and Meredith, and Sandra has had to intervene to make sure that weekend visits are appropriate. Sean and his new wife have just accepted new positions at a university in a nearby state, which means that he will see Melissa and Meredith only one weekend a month. Sandra has regained her sense of self and is successfully employed in work that gives her great flexibility and adequate income. Money is still tight, and careful decisions have to be made before shopping or making large purchases. But, all in all, 3 years later, Melissa and Meredith have survived the breakup of their parents' marriage, learned to verbalize their feelings and emotions, moved on successfully in their lives at school and at home, and are adjusting to their father's remarriage and relocation.

The most difficult period was the first two years, which were characterized by shock, anger, hurt, and psychological reorganization. How did they make this difficult transition? Sandra has formal training in counseling, Melissa's and Meredith's teachers and schools have been very supportive, Sean maintained telephone contact on a regular basis over the 3 years, and time and maturity have given the girls a new sense of self and inner strength. Because of their ages, Melissa and Meredith will deal with the ramifications of their parents' divorce as they begin to date and explore their own relationships. They may be hesitant to trust and make long-term commitments. Sandra is still single and exploring her own life and future. Through counseling, teachers, family, and regular processing of their feelings, all have arrived "on the other side" of divorce and remarriage. Their story is a typical story of divorce, and their outcomes may be better than many because of the strengths that they brought to the situation.

Typical Child and Parent Emotions in Divorce

Parents' emotions at the time of separation or divorce range from relief that a bad relationship is over to severe depression (Diamond, 1985; Smith, 1992). Although some parents contact their children's teacher or other school personnel without hesitation, many are too emotionally overcome to make this contact. Many parents try to cover up their feelings and to project a strong image to their children's teachers. In fact, a study by Wallerstein and Blakeslee (1995) found that half of the children's teachers did not know about the divorces among the children in their classrooms.

Common emotions and respective verbal expressions of divorcing parents include the following:

- *Failure:* "I couldn't make my marriage work."
- *Shame:* "There's a stigma attached to being divorced; there's a strike against the children."
- *Guilt:* "I'm very sad that I've had to put my children through this. I feel guilty about not having given them the best I could give them."
- *Insecurity:* "I had no identity. When the 'Mrs.' came away, I collapsed."
- *Sensitivity:* "Unsolicited advice is awful." (Diamond, 1985; Walsh, 1992)

So, despite broader acceptance of divorce in U.S. society today, the fact is that divorce imposes tremendous emotional turmoil on families undergoing it. With experience, teachers become more sensitive to parents who are divorcing, and this sensitivity can be a major support mechanism for both children and parents (Walsh, 1992).

The nature of a child's reaction to divorce depends on many factors: strength of ego; age; gender; relationship with parents; extended family support; communication about and understanding of the divorce; and perceived support at school, at church, and within the community. Research reflects, however, that divorce is very painful for just about all children. Teachers should be alert to a variety of possible emotional reactions to divorce, including sadness, depression, denial, embarrassment, anger, guilt, concern about being cared for, regression, maturity, and physical symptoms (Diamond, 1985; Frieman, 1993; Hagan, Hollier, O'Connor, & Eisenberg, 1992; Hayes & Hayes, 1986; Smith, 1992). Table 6.1 lists characteristics of these various emotional states.

Children's Responses in the Classroom to Divorce

According to Frieman (1993), children explicitly state that they want their teacher to know about a separation or divorce so that the teacher will be more tolerant and understanding of their behavior. Examples cited by Frieman include Karen, a first grader, who says, "I'm thinking about the divorce sometimes in school and not doing my work. I don't want my teacher to think that I don't care about my work." Scott, another first grader, states, "I want her to know so that when I'm feeling sad, she will know the reason and not yell at me" (p. 86).

For the preoperational child, including infants, toddlers, and preschoolers, reactions can be intense. Separation distress can be observed in toddlers whose parents are separating or divorcing, even after showing no separation distress in the earlier months of life (Godwin, Groves, & Horm-Wingerd, 1993). Separation distress can be

TABLE 6.1   Emotional Descriptors of Children in Divorce

Emotional State	Description
Sadness or depression	Sadness or depression is a normal reaction that may last for months. Younger children may even say "I feel sad." Children may look fatigued, tired, or sad. Depression is serious and should be anticipated. Eating and sleeping habits may change. Children who are depressed may state that they feel very alone or that no one really cares about them.
Denial	Denial allows the children to shelter themselves from the pain at hand. Children are not aware of this process. Reasons for denial are to escape pain and to hope for some kind of reconciliation on the parents' part.
Embarrassment	Embarrassment is perhaps the most common emotion with which teachers will have to contend. Children do not like being different from their peers and feel that their parents' divorce makes them different, even though their peers are also experiencing divorce. Research indicates that embarrassment can last for years after a divorce and is very common as a childhood response.
Anger	Intense anger is common among children of divorce, especially for 9- to 12-year-olds. Anger results from a fundamental feeling of collapsing: Everything that they have known has now given way. Unless parents contribute to anger, it should subside in time.
Guilt	Guilt is really anger turned inward. Children experience feelings of guilt especially about parent loyalty. They want to show a commitment to both.
Fear of abandonment	A common reaction for children is to feel abandoned. Basic feelings of "Who will take care of me?" are typical and understandable. Even older children report these feelings. Younger children miss the noncustodial parent and fear that if one parent has left, maybe the other one will too.
Regression	Teachers especially see evidence of regression. Regression involves the child's freezing at the current point of maturity or moving back to earlier stages. Younger children may whine, cling, and seek attention from the teacher. Older children may try to befriend the teacher in excessive ways. Children who were once independent may display more dependent behaviors.
Physical symptoms	Wallerstein and Blakeslee's (1995) research on divorce reflected that elementary-age children may express more frequent somatic symptoms such as headaches and stomachaches. School nurses report that children of all ages seem more emotional, tearful, and needy. Mostly, they just need to interact with a caring adult.

observed in infants after 7 months of age and reappear in toddlers 18 to 24 months of age. These typical behaviors are intensified during parental separation or divorce because routines and relationships at home have been disrupted.

Recent research indicates that teachers should be particularly attentive to children who reside in homes where the father is the custodial parent. Findings show that both boys and girls who reside with their fathers do not perform as well academically as their matches from two-parent families or children who reside with only their mothers (Pike, 2000). In general, schools and child-care centers must deal with the more pervasive, day-to-day emotional struggles that are evident among many young children as they learn to cope with new living arrangements, estranged relationships with noncustodial parents, new financial limitations, and the lack of emotional support from parents who themselves are struggling to cope and redefine their lives (Walsh, 1992). Usually, teachers learn about a child's divorce experience by observing changes in the child's behavior and then questioning parents. Thus, teachers comment that their roles have taken on new dimensions, such as informally counseling and supporting children, referring parents and children to community agencies for formal intervention, and generally expending more emotional energy themselves on the classroom and teaching processes (Lindner et al., 1992; Walsh, 1992). Children are resilient, however, and 80 percent to 90 percent of children recover from the initial shock of divorce in about a year (Jellinek & Klavan, 1988).

THEME 2   *in practice . . .*

Mr. Todd is a single, first-year teacher who just graduated from college. He feels unprepared to deal with issues that he is confronting in his class related to divorce and stepparenting. He wants to better understand the school's role, and specifically the teacher's role, in providing support to these families and in carrying out custody arrangements for children in his classroom. What are possible avenues for Mr. Todd to pursue to further his understanding of divorce and stepparenting?

How Teachers Should Respond

Even if teachers and other school personnel have intense feelings about divorce or the specific dynamics of a child and her or his family (Lindner et al., 1992), they should make every effort not to project those feelings. In general, teachers should remain as neutral as possible. Their focus should continue to be on the child's well-being, not on making judgments about the parents. In the process of objectively listening to a divorcing parent, the teacher can provide emotional support and also collect much-needed information.

According to Diamond (1985), pieces of information that should be gathered from the divorcing family by the school or child-care setting include the following:

- When did the separation or divorce occur?
- When did the parents tell the child?
- Has the mother or father left? When? Where did she or he go? Should the school have her or his telephone number? Address?
- Does the mother or father visit regularly?
- Do both parents want to be informed of school events?
- What is the school's responsibility to the noncustodial parent if she or he contacts the school?

- Who should be contacted about emergencies?
- Have any other changes occurred in the home situation?

Other suggestions for teachers include the following:

- Hold separate conferences for estranged parents.
- Mail report cards, school calendars, and notices of major school events to parents who do not live with their children, especially upon request.
- Try to collect addresses for students' mothers and fathers, whether separated or not.
- Ask parents to provide school officials with the details of custody arrangements.

Individual families will handle the divorce situation differently. All parents, however, seem very sensitive at the outset of the separation and divorce process. Thus, the teacher or other professional should seek information that is comfortable for the parent to share, rather than attempt to elicit a great deal of factual information at one time.

The underlying reason for a parent to disclose anything about the divorce is usually for the well-being of the child. The teacher can take into account the child's stress level and adjust classroom expectations, such as by saying, "Chris, I know it's difficult to concentrate when you are concerned about your parents' separation. Instead of reading, why don't you write about how you're feeling in your journal?" (Frieman, 1993, p. 87). Encouraging the child to talk about her or his feelings also validates what the child is experiencing. "How did that make you feel?" "It's hard, isn't it?" "That must have made you feel bad" and "Tell me about how you're feeling" are examples of what teachers can say to children experiencing separation or divorce to help them open up and communicate.

Teacher–Parent Responses. Parents simply need support during this time. The teacher can convey this support and concern by asking for a separate meeting with each of the parents to discuss how the child is doing in class and any issues that seem relevant. Mostly, parents need someone to listen to them. They may take some comfort in knowing that the teacher has dealt with this issue before, because the most pressing emotion during the separation and divorce process is the tremendous feeling of "aloneness" (Diamond, 1985). The teacher can be supportive and empathetic by stating, for example, "Oh, we've dealt with this many times before," or "Several children in the class have experienced divorce; perhaps that will be helpful for [child's name]."

Teacher Self-Assessment of Divorce. Teachers need to consider their own feelings and attitudes about divorce. If they are strongly against divorce (Lindner et al., 1992) or if they have had very little direct experience with divorce, they especially need to reflect on their own possible reactions to parents undergoing divorce. Parents need an objective, professional response. If teachers are not in touch with their own feelings, they may react very emotionally themselves. Researchers cite situations in which teachers actually cried, took the side of one or the other parent, gave the parents personal advice, scolded parents and encouraged them not to divorce, or referred parents inappropriately (Diamond, 1985; Lindner et al., 1992). Usually, these reactions are attributable to lack of readiness on the teacher's part to deal with this information and with the emotional intensity expressed by the parents. Parents are extremely sensitive and insecure during this time, and they remember for a long time the teacher's reaction to their divorce situation. Thus, it is very important that **teacher self-assessment** be conducted.

During a self-assessment, teachers should ask themselves the following questions:

- How many times have I been involved in a divorce situation?
- Has anyone close to me gone through a divorce?
- How does my own marital situation affect my attitudes about divorce?
- What are my value judgments about divorce?
- Can I be truly objective with a parent who is divorcing?
- What can I say to parents to support them as they announce their divorce?
- Can I separate my own personal feelings about divorce from my actions and attitudes toward the children I teach?
- What appropriate community agencies can I refer parents to for assistance?
- Am I prepared to ask appropriate questions of, and offer emotional support to, the child who is experiencing divorce?
- What developmentally appropriate activities in the classroom (e.g., sensory experiences, open-ended expressions of art, puppets and language arts experiences, opportunities to help children verbalize their feelings) encourage children to express their feelings in a safe way?

The Need for Order and Consistency. Teachers and other professionals working with children whose parents are divorcing can offer a precious gift: consistency. Because the home situation seems so unstable and even frightening at this time, school can actually serve as a haven and constructive outlet for a child. The teacher should assess each child in the classroom for individual needs; the child experiencing divorce is especially in need of this assessment. The teacher's personal qualities can have a very positive impact on the child; this is especially crucial during the first year after the separation and divorce. According to Robert Weiss (in Diamond, 1985), parents experience disorganization, depression, unmanageable restlessness, and a chaotic search for escape from distress immediately after the separation (Lindner et al., 1992; Smith, 1992). Figure 6.2 describes strategies for teachers to use when working with children with families involved in divorce.

A Teacher's Limits. Although a teacher cannot solve the problems of children or families in divorce situations, she or he can help the children and parents cope. Giving the children a chance to feel in control in the classroom will help alleviate the out-of-control

FIGURE 6.2   Classroom Strategies for Teachers Working with Children Involved in Divorce and Remarriage Family Situations

Children undergoing divorce and remarriage experiences at home are more emotional and sensitive than other children. They are easily embarrassed, and feelings often seem out of proportion. To minimize embarrassment and to facilitate class process, teachers should follow these suggestions:

1. Assume that some of your students are not living with both natural parents, and then identify those students. Gather family information at the beginning of the school year or immediately after a child enters your classroom during the school year.

2. Get the names right. Learn which name is for biological parents and which is for stepparents.

3. Make it easy when written communications or gifts are to be sent home. Talk to parents to determine who would like to receive regular classroom communications from you.

4. Avoid embarrassing questions and model respect for all of the children to observe.

5. Respect confidentiality and keep family records in protected files.

6. Recognize that certain class projects may cause embarrassment; then take advantage of opportunities to legitimate differences.

7. At Open House and similar events, expect from one to four parents and be sensitive to the nature of their relationships.

8. Maintain an open mind regarding the worth of single-parent homes. Incorporate books and other learning materials in your classroom that represent the diversity of today's families.

9. Include books on divorce, stepparents and stepsiblings, and feelings about divorce and remarriage, and stories that allow the children in your classroom to share and verbalize their own experiences.

10. Invite a school or community counselor into your classroom to talk about major changes in families, and encourage children to ask questions, to represent their feelings through art, and to write about their own families.

11. Hang posters and other visuals that depict single-headed households as well as more traditional family forms.

12. When children seem disrupted by separation, divorce, or remarriage, provide as much consistency for them as possible in the classroom; assign the child a special and important role or task and praise the child for his or her efforts. This child needs validation during this difficult period.

feelings that they experience related to their families and parents. Relating to parents who are in a conflict is challenging, but the teacher should make an effort to communicate with both parents, rather than just the custodial parent (Frieman, 1993). Staying out of the parents' dispute will help the teacher remain neutral and constructive.

Children in blended families have unique emotional and academic needs.

There are limits to what a teacher can do during a child's divorce situation, but many valuable classroom interventions will increase the chances for the young child to cope with the transitions and changes until the family is redefined and more stable.

In this section, we have discussed the incidence of divorce for American families and the divorce issues that affect the school or child-care center and the teacher. Divorce is usually the beginning of a new and somewhat painful odyssey for children, frequently resulting in the reconstitution of a new family in subsequent months or years. The prevalence of divorce has given rise to another new family form: the blended or reconstituted family, which is discussed next.

THEMES 3 AND 4   *in practice . . .*

Sharon Johnson is an experienced primary teacher. In early August, she learns from school records that 12 of the 21 children in her upcoming class have stepparents. At the beginning of the school year, Ms. Johnson sends a letter to parents asking if they would be interested in a series of community workshops on blended families and adjusting to the stepfamily. Is this an appropriate strategy? What are other possible parenting strategies for Ms Johnson to use?

DEMOGRAPHICS AND DESCRIPTORS OF BLENDED FAMILIES IN THE UNITED STATES

Why should teachers, caregivers, and school personnel be concerned about the needs of children from blended families? Demographers now document the growing numbers of families and children who represent this emerging lifestyle and family form. As of 2000, the stepfamily outnumbered all other types of families in the United States (Darden & Zimmerman, 1992). Remarriage is becoming increasingly common, and the majority of remarriages include children. Of all marriages, 30 percent are a remarriage for at least one partner. Other demographic information on remarriage and blended families follows:

- Almost one in five married-couple families with children have a stepchild living in the household.
- In Black married-couple families, one in four children under age 18 is a stepchild.

- Most stepchildren live with their biological mothers and stepfathers, and prevailing data suggest little conscious effort on the part of divorced parents to collaborate on child care; parallel parenting prevails over coparenting.

- More than 6 million children, or 9 of 10 stepchildren in married-couple families, live with their biological mothers and stepfathers. Only 740,000 stepchildren live with their biological fathers and stepmothers.

- Most stepfamilies are at an economic disadvantage compared with families with biological children, but they are more economically secure than single-parent families.

- Parents in stepfamilies are less well educated than parents in first-marriage families, in general.

- Approximately 13 percent of American children under age 18 live in families in which one of the two adults is not the biological parent.

- The proportion of children in blended families will increase because 80 percent of all divorced persons remarry, and 60 percent of these remarriages involve an adult with physical custody of one or more children.

- Annually, 500,000 adults become stepparents in the United States. Both girls and boys in stepfamilies demonstrate more behavioral problems than children in families that have not undergone divorce (Darden & Zimmerman, 1992; Furstenberg, 1988; Lindner et al., 1992; Smith, 1992).

- Demographers anticipated that by 2000, nearly one of every six children under age 18 would be a stepchild, representing 13 percent of the child population in this age group (Kosinki, 1983; Smith, 1992).

Characteristics of Stepfamilies

Stepfamilies and nuclear families are dissimilar in terms of structure, roles, and boundaries. Stepfamilies are of three basic types: (a) a stepmother with no children and a father and his children; (b) a stepfather with no children and a mother and her children; and (c) a couple, each partner of which is both a parent and a stepparent. Visher and Visher (1983) insist that stepfamilies are structurally the most complex of all families and that the most structurally dissimilar families are stepfamilies and nuclear families.

According to Visher and Visher (1983), the major characteristics or traits of stepfamilies are as follows:

- A biological parent is elsewhere.
- Virtually all family members have sustained a primary relationship loss.
- An adult couple is in the household.
- The relationship between one adult (parent) and child(ren) predates the marriage.
- Children are members of more than one household.
- One adult (stepparent) is not legally related to a child (**stepchild**).
- The complexity of stepfamily structure tends to discourage cohesiveness.

The boundaries of blended families are more "permeable" than the boundaries of nuclear families, according to Walsh (1992), Lindner et al. (1992), and Smith (1992), who have analyzed families from the perspective of family boundaries and roles. Several factors promote this permeability. A **reconstituted family** lacks the common household residence of natural parents and the common household locus of parents' authority, and economic subsistence may be shared with the former spouse of one or both adult partners. Children in a blended family find their affection and loyalties divided between two parents' households. Roles are more clearly defined in nuclear, rather than blended, families.

We now turn to more specific information about the blended family, America's newest and fastest growing type of family. Included in the discussion are myths about the roles of stepfamily members, the special needs of children, families who have experienced blending, and suggested activities for these families that can be carried out by the child's lead teacher as well as by other child-care and school personnel.

Myths and Roles of Stepfamily Members

Teachers should be aware of how the stepfamily is viewed in order to better understand the child's role (Walsh, 1992). Assuming a new role in a blended family or stepfamily is a challenge, and several **myths about stepfamilies** exist regarding the roles of the stepfamily's members. In this section, we address the common problems, issues, and myths that surround the roles of stepchild, stepmother, and stepfather.

Stepchild's Role. A child who becomes a "step" child through remarriage of a parent experiences a wide range of emotions (Lindner et al., 1992; Walsh, 1992). Even in the most well-adjusted blended families, both boys and girls report feelings of loss for their original family and its unique characteristics. Emotional responses to remarriage depend significantly on how the new relationship has been explained and integrated into the child's living situation. Most stepchildren report feelings of anger, hostility, denial, loss, anxiety, fear, excitement, curiosity, hesitancy, happiness, jealousy, and unrealistic expectations. Because the child has already experienced one major loss (one parent from the original family), she or he may fear future abandonment by the remaining primary parent, the new stepparent, or both (Walsh, 1992). Adjustment to the new reconstituted family takes years. Teachers, caregivers, and other school personnel can facilitate this adjustment period by helping the child to recognize and accept the wide array of emotions experienced and to set realistic expectations for accepting and adjusting to a new life.

Stepmother's Role. The role of **stepmother** is a complex one. Many stepmothers may try to make up for the upset caused by the divorce or death in the original family (Hayes & Hayes, 1986; Walsh, 1992). A stepchild may resent the stepmother's warmth and love as an attempt to replace the child's biological mother, and her husband may feel left out because of the inordinate amount of attention paid to the children. Also, stepmothers may unrealistically attempt to keep all members of the family happy and content; expect that the stepfamily will be equal to an effective nuclear family in cohesiveness, stability, and interpersonal warmth; and rationalize that it is feasible to please everyone (Visher & Visher, 1983).

Common myths that stepmothers frequently must deal with are those of the **wicked stepmother** and of **instant love**. For example, a new stepmother may attempt to be a super-perfect stepparent to disprove the wicked stepmother myth, and she will likely become very frustrated. In addition, "instant love" between stepmother and stepchild is almost never achieved. Thus, if a new stepmother assumes her role with these two myths in mind, she is likely to feel that she has failed. In reality, her expectations are not realistic (Walsh, 1992).

The amount of adjustment required by the stepmother depends on many variables. A remarried mother with no stepchildren has fewer conflicts than other women in stepfamilies. Her husband can relate to her children more like natural children, and there is no competitiveness between her children and his. A remarried mother with no stepchildren may experience two problems, however. First, she may desire assistance from her new husband in disciplining her children but, at the same time, may become protective or defensive when her husband tries to implement discipline. Second, she may feel guilty because her husband does so much for her children but she

A stepfather may tend to overcompensate by playing superdad to his natural children when they visit.

has no stepchildren to do things for in return. Stepmothers with no children of their own may have a more difficult time. They are inexperienced, and they also have the more negative image of "stepmother" without enjoying the positive image of "mother." In addition, the husband who has children will have more need to stay in touch with his ex-spouse. This contact can lead to jealousy on the part of the stepmother.

Stepfather's Role. A **stepfather** is usually less involved than a stepmother in parenting and, therefore, is less likely to have problems (Lindner et al., 1992; Walsh, 1992). Visher and Visher (1982, 1983) outlined three important psychological tasks for a stepfather: (a) joining a functioning group and establishing a place for himself, (b) working out rules regarding family behavior, and (c) handling unrealistic expectations both on his part and on the part of the new family.

Most stepfathers experience resistance because they are trying to break into a unit of mother and child or children whose bonds predate the relationship between the adults. Furthermore, mothers tend to think that stepfathers discipline too harshly. Children may say, "I don't have to do what he says; he's not my real father." The stepfather is often caught in a bind of trying to become a disciplinarian too soon and of choosing not to become actively involved in discipline, thus isolating himself and appearing not to be interested in the children. In addition, the stepfather may feel guilty for having abandoned his own children. He may tend to overcompensate by playing **superdad** to his natural children when they visit. Because of this guilt, some stepfathers may withhold themselves from their stepchildren.

Stepfathers must join a functioning group and establish a place for himself.

Conflict may also surface over money and the use of surnames. Stepfamilies may have to cope with sexuality issues as well. Teenage stepchildren who have not grown up together may be attracted to each other, and stepfathers and stepmothers may be sexually attracted to stepchildren or vice versa (Kosinki, 1983).

SPECIAL ISSUES FOR CHILDREN IN BLENDED FAMILIES

Children in blended families have unique emotional and academic needs that can be addressed by teachers, caregivers, and school personnel. This section describes special issues of stepfamilies and appropriate school programs and interventions. Despite the increasing prevalence of stepsons and stepdaughters, few individuals have been socialized to live in a stepfamily environment. Consequently, many stepfamily members have unrealistic and inappropriate expectations. They have even been surprised at their own emotional reactions to daily stepfamily living, and they may feel alone in their attempts to cope (Coleman & Ganong, 1990). Unexpected feelings such as embarrassment, ambivalence, and guilt add to their stress (Lindner et al., 1992; Smith, 1992; Visher & Visher, 1983).

Unfortunately, in traditional teacher education programs, professionals such as educators and caregivers typically are not adequately trained to understand stepfamilies. This lack of professional training and preparation affects the effectiveness and appropriateness of teacher–child interactions, parent–teacher communication, curricular decisions, classroom environment and activities, and selection of books and other learning materials. Intervention strategies appropriate for other families are often not successful for stepfamilies. Counselors note that many conflicts and problems encountered by stepfamilies are not a result of individual psychopathology, but instead are attributable to potentially preventable situations (Stanton, 1986; Visher & Visher, 1988).

What the Teacher and the Caregiver Need to Know

Common issues for students who are members of stepfamilies include (a) embarrassment over divorce and remarriage (Visher & Visher, 1988; Walsh, 1992), (b) social stigma over "step" status that may inhibit the sharing of family experiences with others (Coleman & Ganong, 1990; Lindner et al., 1992), (c) unresolved mourning of the loss of a previous family member that interferes with the formation of a new family unit, and (d) feelings of confusion and the need to answer "Where do I belong?" that are common for children in the process of family reorganization. This confusion is compounded by the fact that children become members of two households, each with its own style and pattern, and one is not necessarily better or worse than the other. Adjusting to the **nonresidential home** is challenging.

Hostility problems are extremely common in stepfamilies (Gardner, 1984; Lindner et al., 1992), and **anger inhibition**, which is the turning inward and suppression of feelings of anger, is understandable for stepchildren. They have already been "abandoned" by a parent, often a father, and they fear that the other parent may also abandon them. Anger inhibition can be serious and may result in childhood depression, particularly for elementary-age children and young adolescents. These children are afraid to express their resentment because they fear that their father will reject them further. Children may be afraid of expressing anger toward their mother because she, too, might abandon them (Walsh, 1992).

Sibling rivalry between full siblings is fierce, and the rivalry between stepsiblings is even more virulent (Gardner, 1984). Adjustments to new stepbrothers and stepsisters are abrupt, in contrast with the gradual adjustment to a newborn full sibling.

Ambivalent feelings toward new stepparents are common. Development of a loving relationship between a child and a stepparent takes time, and the child often does not realize this. Parents and teachers tend to view girls in stepfamilies as better adjusted than boys in stepfamilies (Lindner et al., 1992).

Loyalty conflicts are almost inevitable in the stepfamily, as children wonder and question their natural parents, "Whom do you love more—your legal spouse or your natural-born children, your own flesh and blood?" (Walsh, 1992). Feelings of hope for a new and better family situation, known as a **Phoenix concept**, are typical. The hope is that the stepfamily can be a reborn family, reborn from the ashes of the old, dead marriage (Gardner, 1984). The Phoenix concept embraces the idea that the new marriage will be a stronger and better marriage than the previous one was.

Disruption of attachment is normal in the adjustment process, and recovering from this sense of loss may take 2 to 5 years (Lindner et al., 1992; Visher & Visher, 1988). Bringing past family histories with them is common for stepchildren. These histories affect the definition of roles, rights, and responsibilities. The lack of continuity is a source of stress. In a blended family, the spouses have no time to solidify their bond before they attempt to face the demands of parenting. Stepchildren feel this stress and yearn for the continuity and familiarity of their own original family.

The new stepparent's discipline and parenting techniques can be a source of major stress for the stepchild, particularly during the first $1\frac{1}{2}$ to 2 years (Gardner, 1984; Lindner et al., 1992). Limited financial resources cause additional stress for the stepchild because funds are being stretched now in more directions. Wallerstein and Kelly (1980) reported that the standard of living in a blended family is considerably lower than in the predivorce family.

Effects of Cumulative Stress

McCubbin and Patterson (1982) introduced the concept of **pileup**. This concept simply means that children in stepfamilies may experience the cumulative effects of major changes and stresses, rather than any one factor or situation in isolation. Pileup occurs mostly during the first 1 to 2 years, and the stressors previously described are concrete examples of why pileup is likely to occur.

Building Blocks and Assets of Blended Families

Thus far, our discussion has placed the new, blended family in a rather complex, somewhat negative context. Teachers and professionals should also realize that blended families can bring together many assets and strengths. Interventions with children will certainly be more effective if the positive outcomes and aspects of their new families are emphasized. Teachers can facilitate children's adjustment process by helping them to identify and build on specific and positive characteristics and traits of the newly formed family units. The following suggestions can help teachers accomplish this:

- Set realistic expectations about stepfamily life (Visher & Visher, 1983).
- Recognize cultural and ethnic differences among blended families.
- Identify special, positive personality traits of the new parent and how these traits and skills can benefit the child.
- Identify mutual interests of the child and the new stepparent and begin to schedule special times and events with that new parent.
- Describe ways that the new parent is making the biological parent happier and more content.
- Discuss how finances and shared resources may now be stretched because the new parents are sharing with the children in the stepfamily.

Teachers and caregivers can help members of a blended family to cope with the complexities of their situation in three ways: by consulting, by coordinating resources, and by informal support and referral to counseling (Poppen & White, 1984). Research on stepfamilies and the unique intervention needs of stepchildren has only recently emerged in the literature. Professionals in education, child development, psychology, sociology, counseling, and marriage and family therapy all are contributing to the growing understanding of stepfamilies and their adjustment tasks.

Community-based and elementary school counselors can work with teachers and caregivers to facilitate improvement in stepfamily relationships. Froiland and Hozman (1977) have developed a model based on Elisabeth Kübler-Ross's concept of loss, which is still applicable to today's families. They state that, for couples and children, a divorce signifies the death of a relationship. The divorce process is conceptualized as similar to the process of facing and coping with death. The model consists of these stages of adjustment: denial, anger, bargaining, depression, and acceptance. The Froiland-Hozman model is useful conceptually because an almost universal characteristic of stepfamilies is mourning the loss of a relationship.

The role of teachers and caregivers is to help children (a) come to terms with these normal feelings of loss, (b) acknowledge their existence and origins, (c) verbalize feelings, and (d) move toward acceptance of their new family situation. Because teachers, caregivers, and school support personnel consistently spend large periods of time with the child, they have ample opportunity to observe the children in social and academic settings in the school or center, to intervene on an individual basis with each child, and to become familiar with each child's family members and situation.

THEMES 4 AND 5 *in practice . . .*

Divorce is more common among Caucasian and African American families than Hispanic families. In an effort to understand these differences, Mr. Simpson, an elementary school principal, invites community agency representatives to do an in-service workshop for teachers. He includes local pastors who do family counseling and representatives from the health and social services agencies. Is this an appropriate strategy for Mr. Simpson to use? Why?

Actions that teachers can take to facilitate children's feelings of loss include the following:

- Acknowledge to the child her or his feelings of loss.
- Validate the child's feelings as being normal and acceptable.
- Engage the child in language arts and art activities that promote the expression of feelings.
- Share a book about a child who experiences divorce in her or his family.
- Talk about the advantages of having two homes.
- Encourage the child to talk regularly about new changes in her or his life.
- Provide the child with a special place in the classroom for conversations with you or to engage in special activities.
- Validate the child's identity and sense of self-worth.
- Involve the child in caring for a pet in the classroom.

Focusing on the child first and then gradually involving the parents can forge an effective intervention that merges the role of the teacher or caregiver with the role of family advocate. Helping a child acknowledge feelings of loss and then facilitating as she or he moves through each stage can result in positive outcomes for the child emotionally, academically, and socially.

The teacher should not attempt formal counseling intervention, but rather should learn from these models about the sense of loss experienced through remarriage. The teacher can effectively devise learning activities that encourage the children to express orally, through written work, or through art expression their feelings of loss. Teaming with a community-based counselor is a good strategy for a teacher dealing with postdivorce and remarriage issues involving students. The counselor will be able to suggest both general and specific strategies for the teacher to implement that will encourage the healthy expression of feelings by the children.

Children in a blended family seem to function more effectively when there is a strong, caring alliance between the couple, along with more **permeable boundaries** than is optimal in intact, nondivorced families (Visher & Visher, 1983). Stepfamilies seem to require boundaries that are more ambiguous and permeable. For example, children need the freedom and independence to move freely back and forth between two different living situations. Thus, stepfamilies may appear to be more disengaged and less cohesive than is considered optimal for intact or nuclear families.

Goals for Stepfamily Education

The main purpose of supporting children of divorce in educational settings, especially those in preschool and primary grades, should be to help them cope with the changes of transition until things stabilize. Teachers and caregivers have both advantages and disadvantages in their work with stepchildren. On the one hand, the children are a captive audience 5 to 7 hours (or more) a day, and they can benefit therapeutically without direct cost to parents. On the other hand, parents are often less available to a teacher or caregiver than to a private practitioner (Gardner, 1984). The goals for the teacher or caregiver should be in a supportive role rather than in a formal counseling role. By spending some time observing the child, identifying the child's needs, and communicating these needs to parents, the teacher or caregiver can facilitate the referral process to a community-based or private practitioner who specializes in family therapy and specific divorce and remarriage issues.

Research outcomes for remarried families are mixed, and recent case study research by Wallerstein and Blakeslee (1995) painted a discouraging picture for adult children of divorce. Remarriage generally improves things for younger children, but researchers have found that, for about one fourth of children in their study, remarriage was not seen as improving their lives, especially if the children were age 10 or older at the time of remarriage (Lindner et al., 1992; Wallerstein & Blakeslee, 1995; Wallerstein & Kelly, 1980). In either case, the children's problems were fewer if the original parents and remarried parents were not warring with one another. Thus, teachers and caregivers seem to need a stepfamily education program that attempts to accomplish the following goals:

- Helping stepchildren understand the complexity of stepfamily functioning
- Helping stepchildren and their parents develop positive relationships
- Teaching stepchildren and their parents how to communicate effectively with one another
- Teaching stepparents how to manage their emotions in stepparenting by learning to think rationally and to dispute their irrational beliefs
- Teaching stepparents and stepchildren how to use principles of social learning and logical or natural consequences to solve adult–child conflicts in stepfamilies

A school- or center-based program for stepfamily education should include two elements: (a) giving participants information about the cultural and structural characteristics of stepfamilies and the roles, expectations, and difficulties of individual stepfamily members and (b) teaching communication and parenting skills to all (Kosinki, 1983).

EFFECTIVE INTERVENTION APPROACHES FOR WORKING WITH CHILDREN OF DIVORCED AND BLENDED FAMILIES

This section describes several recognized models or approaches to effective intervention for children adjusting to a blended family situation, as well as for children experiencing change in their lives generally. These models are derived from the literature on family therapy, school counseling, child psychology, and child development. All the models presented include a theoretical basis involving parent involvement, family participation, the family systems approach, and child development. These models are now discussed, with suggestions for implementation in a school or child-care center learning environment.

Bibliotherapy

The use of shared and mutually selected or assigned readings, also known as **bibliotherapy**, may be especially useful in educational, preventive programs for stepfamilies (Coleman & Ganong, 1990). *Merriam-Webster's New Collegiate Dictionary* (2003) defined bibliotherapy as "the use of reading materials for help in solving personal problems or for psychiatric therapy" (p. 119). It has also been defined as "a family of techniques for structuring an interaction between a facilitator and a participant... based on their mutual sharing of literature" (Berry, 1978, p. 187). Through books, readers can escape into new roles and identities and sample lifestyles vicariously. Both fiction and nonfiction can provide children and adults with models to help them handle situations that they might encounter. Both types of books can be important aids to educators, caregivers, counselors, and other helping professionals working with stepfamilies.

The goals of bibliotherapy include the following:

- Teaching facts about particular life situations, such as stepfamilies, divorce, death, and remarriage, and the incidence of these situations in society as a whole
- Informing stepchildren and their parents about step relationships and the unique challenges that they may encounter
- Helping parents and children obtain insight or self-understanding as they read about a character who is facing a situation similar to their own
- Helping children and their parents better understand their own emotional reactions, conflicts, cognitions, motivations, feelings, and thoughts through identification with a central character in an assigned reading
- Stimulating discussion between children and their parents by allowing the family to react to the characters in the reading, thus providing the children and parents with a safe outlet and forum for discussing their own issues

Selecting reading materials for children and parents of stepfamilies is not necessarily an easy task. Several criteria have been identified to aid in this selection:

- The stepfamily issues should be the main focus.
- The book should be at an appropriate reading level.

- The stories should be about modern children and families or have universal appeal.
- Characters and the solutions to problems should be realistic.
- Materials should not offend the reader's religious beliefs or values.
- Problems should be dealt with in a manner consistent with research or prevailing clinical opinion about stepfamily functioning.
- Good coping strategies should be modeled in the reading. (McInnes, 1982)

Selecting Books for Bibliotheca. Books or other reading materials cannot be chosen until the specific stepfamily's situation is known. With cultural diversity becoming so much a part of contemporary classrooms, teachers should assess the family's cultural, language, and religious systems before providing books and other written materials. For example, the Latino child population is growing steadily in the United States. Because divorce and remarriage is less frequent among these families, teachers should provide written materials that are sensitive to these cultural differences. If the teacher is going to focus on divorce as a classroom topic, parents should be informed beforehand. This will facilitate parent–child conversations at home and prepare parents to discuss these topics with their children. It also informs parents who are less open to divorce that the topic will be covered in the classroom. Thus, the family's structural characteristics, such as the number of siblings, stepsiblings, and half siblings; the cause of the dissolution of the parents' marriage (death or divorce); and the extent of contact with the nonresidential parent, are considered part of the family situation. The presenting problem or central issue for child and parents should also be considered (Coleman & Ganong, 1990). Many appropriate books are now available for children of all ages related to divorce and blended families, and these books open the door to meaningful dicussions, classroom activities, and deeper understanding among children about issues facing themselves and their peers.

The counselor can help members of the blended family cope with the complexities of their situation.

Choosing self-help books designed for children, teachers, and parents is relatively easy compared with selecting fictional books. The main reason is that fewer books exist in this domain. Selecting a self-help book depends on the age of the child, the child's reading ability, the nature of the issues and problems being presented by the child, a positive perspective on stepfamilies, and the concreteness of advice and suggestions. Other important considerations include the use of appropriate illustrations, reference lists, appendixes, and the overall visual appeal of the book (Coleman & Ganong, 1990).

Using bibliotherapy with children and their parents from blended families involves three steps:

1. **Planning:** Includes identification of the individual's needs and selection of appropriate material. Planning demands that the helper have some knowledge about the family and the reading material.

2. **Motivating:** Involves introducing and presenting the reading materials to the child or parents or both in a way that immediately connects them to the reading. Comments such as, "You know, a boy in this book had a family situation pretty much like yours. It might be interesting for you to read this, just to see how he handled it. We could talk about it afterward and think of ways the story could have been different," might serve as motivation (Coleman & Ganong, 1990).

3. **Following up:** A critical step that can involve a discussion based on previously prepared questions, or it can take whatever format has been decided on. This is a time to clarify any information presented in the book, to review concepts, to evaluate the story or characters in the story, and to explore feelings. Some readers may need assistance in summarizing and evaluating reading materials; others may need help in exploring their own attitudes and feelings. *Whatever the follow-up activity entails, it is important that the teacher, caregiver, or school counselor respond in a nonjudgmental way to readers' comments.*

Individual and Family Intervention and Referral

The teacher or caregiver can provide and facilitate intervention for children who are experiencing divorce and remarriage by working with the school counselor or a community-based counselor. In this case, the teacher is a facilitator of intervention through the referral process. Classroom teachers typically do not have the time or expertise to provide direct intervention, and this would also create conflict of interest and ethical issues for the teacher. The teacher must remain as neutral and objective in the family dynamics arena as possible; providing direct intervention would violate this goal.

The counselor can help members of the blended family cope with the complexities of their situation in three ways: by consulting; by coordinating resources; and most important, by counseling. Providing effective counseling intervention with children or parents or both in a stepfamily situation can become quite complex. Nonetheless, joint counseling can prove to be the most effective and efficient way to provide intervention.

Important tasks of the counselor in either individual or group counseling are as follows:

- To help children assess how well and in what ways they are coping with the transition to remarriage; children often report feeling responsible for what happens in the family, feeling unworthy, and feeling helpless about what is happening to them.

- To recognize the fears that are common among client members of stepfamily situations; children experience a wide range of emotions.

- To assist in identifying the roots of those feelings, verbalizing existing fears and anxieties, and assisting in learning to communicate effectively with new stepparents.
- To alleviate parents' fears, because parents, too, may be afraid to become involved in a counseling situation; one primary fear of parents is that the counseling experience will reunite former partners.

Thus, the main purpose of counseling children, especially those in early childhood and early elementary settings, should be to help them cope with the changes of transition until things stabilize (Lindner et al., 1992; Visher & Visher, 1982).

The school counselor's role in this intervention process depends on several factors:

- The level of formal training of the school counselor
- Adequate time for direct intervention with schoolchildren and their parents
- The space and facilities available for counseling services
- The willingness of the administration to support this effort
- The willingness of the parents to become involved at this level in the educational setting
- The willingness of the parents to disclose details about their personal lives

Self-Help Parent Education Model

Sheehy (1980) proposed an educational model for working with stepfamilies and has helped to design a self-help parent education program for stepparents (Sheehy & Fisher, 1980). He emphasizes two critical mistakes that stepparents make. The first is the tendency for the stepparent to rush in and assume a disciplinarian role before a good parental subsystem has been established. The second is using the withdrawal of affection to punish children for misbehavior. In stepfamilies, punishment and withdrawal of love are counterproductive; stepchildren are likely to resent being punished by a stepparent who has not been integrated into the family and are not likely to be influenced positively by the withdrawal of love by that stepparent (Hagan et al., 1992; Walsh, 1992). Thus, Sheehy advocated the use of natural or **logical consequences** (Dreikurs & Grey, 1968) as a principal method of discipline. Stepparents need to be taught how to use natural or logical consequences, to support each other, and to differentiate between the age and characteristics of each child when administering discipline.

Role of the School or Center

Programs and interventions designed for stepfamily members are most effective if they are surrounded by administrators and organizations that understand the usefulness of these programs. Because many schools are becoming a hub of community resources, provision of resources and referrals for counseling for families engaged in the divorce or remarriage process is an appropriate role for the school. Schools and child-care centers play an important role in recognizing, assessing, addressing, and evaluating the educational and emotional needs of children in stepfamilies.

Institutional support for intervention initiatives and programs for stepchildren and their parents include encouraging teachers and other school professionals to view the needs of blended families and students as a unique part of their support roles. For example, administrators can provide adequate space for teachers, caregivers, and other collaborative professional personnel to meet on an individual basis with students and their parents. This space should be private and reflect sensitivity to the need for confidentiality. In addition, financial resources should be provided for purchasing current educational, self-help materials for parents and for reimbursing community resource professionals to assist the teacher, school counselor, school social worker, or other personnel in conducting workshops, parent education programs, and other types of informal educational initiatives in the school setting. Administrators can be more supportive of these efforts if they are well read themselves on issues related to child development; the impact of divorce on children, parents, and family systems; and the most current research literature on effective intervention programs for reconstituted families. Finally, encouraging school personnel to collaborate in their interventions for children of divorced and remarried families will result in the most comprehensive and effective services for these children. Teachers can advocate for children and parents of divorce; Figure 6.3 lists some strategies.

FIGURE 6.3   Advocacy Strategies for Teachers Working with Children of Divorced and Blended Families

1. *Parent Wall:* Create a Parent Wall in your classroom and include helpful items for single, divorced, and remarried parents. Examples are workshops on divorce, job training, employment opportunities, and community-sponsored events.

2. *Parent Peer Leader:* Ask a parent to serve as a Parent Peer Leader for your classroom. Encourage this parent leader to connect with all of the parents in the classroom and to help identify those parents who may have particular needs related to divorce or remarriage.

3. *Workshops on Divorce:* Offer to set up a series of workshops on topics related to divorce and remarriage. Use your classroom or other school-based site as a meeting place.

4. *Community Counselor as a Classroom Resource:* Identify a community- or faith-based counselor to serve as a family liaison to your classroom. Invite this professional to your classroom to get to know the children and to parent events for parent support. This professional can provide educational activities for both children and parents in your classroom.

5. *Family Events:* During the school year, sponsor three or four family events that encourage parents to come together for a potluck dinner with favorite family dishes; making family scrapbooks or photograph albums; developing family portfolios or journals; or other shared-interest events. Encourage all families to participate and be open to whom the child brings to the event.

(*Continued*)

FIGURE 6.3   Continued

6. *School Counselor:* Invite your school or school district counselor to become part of your classroom. This person can engage children in conversations, lead classroom art and curriculum activities designed to support family discussions, and encourage children to talk to one another about shared family experiences.

7. *Parent Meetings or Events Just on Divorce:* If you have a sizable number of divorced and remarried parents in your classroom, determine if they are interested in attending a workshop just on topics related to divorce or remarriage. If so, offer your classroom as a site for the workshop.

8. *Post Community Resources and Events Related to Divorce and Remarriage:* Make available to all parents, including divorced and remarried parents, community resources that are available at low cost or sliding-scale fees. This information can be sent to parents through newsletters, posted on a classroom Web site, or shared on the Parent Wall described above.

9. *Financial Workshops:* Many parents who are single or going through a divorce would benefit from a workshop on family finances. Locate a community resource person to provide helpful information on budgeting, economy shopping, taxes, and other financial concerns.

10. *Discipline and Family Communication Workshops:* Newly formed families are complex, and stepparents often can benefit from a workshop on disciplining and family communication with new family members, including stepchildren.

11. *Divorced Parent as a Classroom Resource:* Locate a divorced parent who has a good understanding of the adjustment process and issues that are common for children in your grade level. Invite this parent to be a resource person in your classroom and to provide support to other parents.

12. *Classroom Projects to Celebrate Family Events:* When special family events such as Mother's Day occur, be open to the child's unique way of celebrating. This child may have two mothers, a new stepmother, or a single mother. Be open and creative in helping all children celebrate as they want to celebrate.

13. *Offer Child Care for Parent Events:* Child care is a challenge for all families and especially those with more limited incomes. Offer child care during parent meetings and other parent events in your classroom. This will encourage the whole family to come to school and will increase the attendance rates for your parent events.

Critical Concepts

1. The current divorce rate in the United States has leveled off but remains at about 50 percent for first marriages and slightly higher for second marriages. Many children under the age of 18 are impacted by divorce in the United States.

2. Postdivorce adjustment consists of predictable stages that include shock, denial, anger, guilt, and gradual acceptance. The child's age is one predictor of adjustment to divorce, and teachers should understand this and other factors that contribute to good or poor adjustment to divorce.

3. Parents may be reluctant for teachers to know about a divorce or remarriage, but children usually want their classroom teacher to be

aware of changes in their family to better understand the child's classroom behavior and academic performance.

4. Marriage is a desired state in the United States and most divorced individuals remarry. Blended families are the most complex family form, and teachers should understand the makeup of each child's family. Blended families often include stepsiblings as well as stepparents, and there are a host of myths about stepfamilies.

5. There are many effective classroom strategies for teachers to utilize related to divorce and remarriage. One of the most successful is bibliotherapy, in which books and other written materials are used to address common feelings, emotions, adjustments, problems, and issues for children going through a divorce or adjusting to a blended family situation.

6. Because contemporary classrooms are becoming so culturally diverse, teachers should be sensitive to each child and family's religious, cultural, and language background. Books and other materials in the classroom should reflect the diversity of beliefs of the children and families in the classroom. Divorce and remarriage is not as readily accepted in some groups, such as Latinos, and the teacher should be aware of their sensitivity to classroom activities about divorce and remarriage.

7. There are a host of community and faith-based resources available to teachers and families related to divorce and remarriage. Teachers can provide valuable information to parents and children about counseling services and family support programs that will ease a difficult life transition.

Summary Statements

✓ Divorce among first marriages in the United States is around 50 percent; for remarriages, the divorce rate is higher.

✓ Divorce is related to the couple's age, socioeconomic status, educational level, and race, with Blacks having a slightly higher divorce and separation rate than other races.

✓ Teachers bring to the classroom their own values and attitudes toward divorce; self-assessment of these attitudes is necessary for teachers to meet constructively the needs of the children in their classrooms.

✓ Emotional reactions vary greatly, but distinct stages of emotional adjustment are reflected in the research. Teachers should become familiar with these stages and with the intense emotional states that are often displayed by young and elementary-age children.

✓ Effective strategies for communication between the teacher and the divorcing parent are available. These strategies allow the child to cope with the stress of divorce; ensure that school–family communications will be appropriate; and provide legal protection for the child, parent, and school or child-care center.

✓ Recovery from the divorce experience is long and sometimes very difficult. Research indicates that adult children of divorce are still recovering in various ways. Teachers should be aware of the depth of emotional distress and pain usually associated with divorce and divorce recovery.

✓ Most divorced adults remarry; thus, children of these adults usually experience several **stages of divorce adjustment**— from predivorce to postdivorce and the creation of a new, blended family.

✓ Well over half of today's youth will become stepsons or stepdaughters.

✓ Several terms are used interchangeably to describe stepfamilies: *blended, reconstituted, reorganized, combined*, and *remarried*.

✓ Stepfamilies are structurally the most complex of all families and the most unlike nuclear families.

✓ Assuming a new role in a blended family is very challenging, and several myths exist for stepmothers, stepfathers, and stepchildren.

✓ Stepchildren have unique emotional, social, and academic needs, yet most teachers, caregivers, and school professionals have very limited formal training in working with stepfamilies.

✓ Specific intervention approaches are very effective with stepchildren and stepfamilies. The goal of stepfamily education is to ease the transition and roles of the reconstituted family.

✓ Institutions such as schools and child-care centers can provide much-needed administrative and organizational support for teachers, caregivers, and other professionals.

Research to Practice: Classroom Applications and Activities

1. *Peer resource person:* Invite an older child, perhaps a teenager, who has experienced the divorce of parents to come to your classroom or school site to talk with a child or small group of children about this important transition. It is important that this peer resource person be sufficiently mature to verbalize and reflect on her or his personal experience in such a way that younger children can identify and relate in a positive way.

2. *Language arts activities:* Numerous books on divorce, remarriage, and blended and reconstituted families are appropriate to share with small groups of children. Group discussion and sharing can take place as a follow-up activity, which gives the child experiencing this life event a chance to listen to peers' ideas, relate personal experience, and perhaps verbalize needs that she or he is experiencing. Follow-up activities such as the writing of a narrative, personal diary, story, or play or an art activity that integrates the reading experience with the use of paint, chalk, sculpting, or some other art form are all appropriate.

3. *Video or television program:* The teacher, counselor, caregiver, or other school professional can show a video or television program, such as *The Brady Bunch* or *Step by Step*, that depicts routine life events in stepfamilies. Although these programs are often humorous, they also provide a good context for discussing unique issues and problems encountered by children growing up in blended families.

4. *Role-playing:* Children who are part of blended families can work collaboratively on projects that encourage and safely allow them a chance to talk about, face, and work through their personal issues. For example, a small group of children from blended families could be assigned to write a script for a television show, radio program, or play. At least some of the main characters should be involved in blended-family situations. These projects provide an integrated learning experience for the student participants that can include writing, editing, videotaping, audio-taping, musical production or recording, script writing, and publishing. In addition, these projects provide a constructive avenue for stepchildren to share their common

experiences, to find commonalities with their peers, and to experience feelings of success in an academic special assignment.

5. *Community resource person:* Invite a family therapist, counselor, pastor, or other community professional to talk with the class as a whole or with a smaller group of children about her or his experience in working with

stepfamilies. Encourage this resource person to bring a video to show and to relate to the children how common divorce and remarriage are within their own community. As a language arts activity, children can complete a follow-up assignment such as writing a review or description of the resource person's presentation.

Resources for Teachers, Caregivers, Parents, and Children

Classic Books for Children

Arnold, W. (1980). *When your parents divorce.* Philadelphia: Westminster.

Brown, M. (1986). *Dinosaur's divorce.* Boston: Little, Brown.

Danziger, P. (1982). *The divorce express.* New York: Delacorte.

Gardner, R. (1977). *The boys and girls book about divorce.* New York: Bantam Books.

Glass, S. M. (1980). *A divorce dictionary: A book for you and your children.* New York: Four Winds.

Helmering, D. (1981). *I have two families.* Nashville: Abingdon.

Jackson, M., & Jackson, M. (1981). *Your father's not coming home anymore.* New York: Richard Marek.

Lindsay, J. W. (1992). *Do I have a daddy?: A story for a single-parent child.* Buena Park, CA: Morning Glory Press. (Reading level for ages 4–8.)

Makris, K. (1995). *Crosstown.* New York: Avon.

Ricci, I. (1980). *Mom's house, Dad's house: Making shared custody work.* New York: Collier Books.

Rofes, E. (1981). *The kids' book of divorce: By, for, and about kids.* Lexington, MA: Vintage.

Sharmat, M. (1980). *Sometimes Mama and Papa fight.* New York: HarperCollins.

Simon, N. (1983). *I wish I had my father.* Niles, IL: Whitman.

Simon, N., & Rubin, C. (1987). *All kinds of families.* Warsaw, IN: Albert Whitman. (Reading level for ages 4–8.)

Wyeth, S. D. (1997). *Always my Dad.* Rexville, NY: Dragonfly. (Reading level for ages 4–8.)

Books for Parents

Barnes, R. (1997). *Winning the heart of your stepchild.* Grand Rapids, MI: Zondervan.

Berman, C. (1986). *Making it as a stepparent: New roles, new rules* (Updated ed.). New York: Perennial Library, Harper & Row.

Bienenfield, F. (1987). *Helping your child succeed after divorce.* Claremont, CA: Hunter House.

Chambers, D. (1997). *Solo parenting: Raising strong and happy families.* Minneapolis: Fairview Press.

Cohen, M. G. (1991). *The joint custody handbook.* Philadelphia: Running Press.

Enger, A., & Kluneness, L. (1995). *The complete single mother.* Holbrook, MA: Adams Media.

Fassel, D. (1991). *Growing up divorced: A road to healing for adult children of divorce.* New York: Pocket Books.

Ford, J., & Chase, A. (1999). *Wonderful ways to be a stepparent.* Berkeley, CA: Conari.

Francke, L. B. (1983). *Growing up divorced.* New York: Linden.

Friedman, J. (1982). *The divorce handbook.* New York: Random House.

Frydenger, T., & Frydenger, A. (1997). *Stepfamily problems: How to solve them.* Cambridge, UK: Baker Book House.

Hill, G. A. (1989). *Divorced father: Coping with problems, creating solutions.* White Hall, VA: Betterway.

Kalter, N. (1990). *Growing up with divorce.* New York: Free Press.

Lansky, V. (1989). *Divorce book for parents.* New York: Penguin.

Marta, S. Y. (1996). *When death or divorce occur: Helping children cope with loss.* (ERIC No. ED 402023)

Morgan, E. (1985). *Custody.* Boston: Little, Brown.

Reed, B. (1992). *Merging families: A step-by-step guide for blended families.* St. Louis: Concordia.

Salk, L. (1978). *What every child would like their parents to know about divorce.* New York: Harper & Row.

Wallerstein, J., & Blakesee, S. (1989). *Second chances: Men, women, and children after a decade after divorce.* New York: Ticknor & Fields.

Wallerstein, J. S., & Kelly, J. B. (1980). *Surviving the breakup.* New York: Basic Books.

Books and Articles for Teachers

Bernstein, J. E. (1983). *Books to help children cope with separation and loss* (2nd ed.). New York: Bowker.

Caughey, C. (1991). Becoming the child's ally: Observations in a classroom for children who have been abused. *Young Children, 46*(4), 22–28.

Dreyer, S. S. (1981). *The bookfinder* (vol. 2). Circle Pines, MN: American Guidance Service.

Ford, J., & Chase, A. (1999). *Wonderful ways to be a stepparent.* Berkeley, CA: Conari Press.

Francke, L. B. (1983). *Growing up divorced.* New York: Linden Press.

Frieman, B. B. (1997). Two parents—two homes. *Educational Leadership, 54*(7), 23–25.

Jewett, C. (1982). *Helping children cope with separation and loss.* Cambridge, MA: Harvard University Press.

Mack, C. (1991). *Separation and loss: A handbook for early childhood professionals.* Pittsburgh: Center for Social and Urban Research.

McCracken, J. B. (1986). *Reducing stress in young children's lives.* Washington, DC: National Association for the Education of Young Children.

Metcalf, L. (1995). *Counseling toward solutions: A practical solution-focused program for working with students, teachers, and parents.* West Nyack, NY: Center for Applied Research in Education.

Miller, K. (1996). *The crisis manual for early childhood teachers: How to handle the really difficult problems.* Beltsville, MD: Gryphon House.

Wallach, L. B. (1993). Helping children cope with violence. *Young Children, 48*(4), 4–11.

Videos and Films

Kimmons, L., & Gaston, J. A. (1986). Single parenting: A filmography. *Family Relations, 35,* 205–211.

Whitely, J. M. (1980). *Stepparenting* [Film]. Alexandria, VA: American Association for Counseling and Development. (This 20-minute film defines problems that occur in remarriage when children are involved. It is useful for the general public and for adults or children going through the experience.)

Professional Journals

Journal of Divorce. Haworth Press, 174 Fifth Avenue, New York, NY 10010.

The Single Parent. The Journal of Parents Without Partners, Inc., International Headquarters, 7910 Woodmont Avenue, Bethesda, MD 20814.

Agencies and Organizations Supporting Divorced and Blended Families

Sources for Help: Children

International Youth Council (IYC), a division of Parents Without Partners. Offers help for teens who have a single parent.

National Runaway Switchboard, (800) 621–4000; national runaway hotline; number for runaways to call free to contact relatives. Call to leave a message for friends or relatives.

Stepfamily Organizations

Remarried Parents, Inc., c/o Temple Beth Sholom, 1782 Second Street, Northern Boulevard, Flushing, NY 11358. Monthly meetings, lectures, weekly support groups, socials.

Remarrieds, Inc., Box 742, Santa Ana, CA 92701. Offers educational and social programs.

The Stepfamily Association of America, Inc., 900 Welch Road, Suite 400, Palo Alto, CA 94304. Offers educational material, stepfamily survival courses, referral services, newsletter.

Stepfamily Foundation, Inc., 333 West End Avenue, New York, NY 10023; Tel: (212) 877-3244.

Parents' Groups

Divorce Anonymous, P.O. Box 5313, Chicago, IL 60680. Regular meetings for the divorced.

Mothers Without Custody, Inc., P.O. Box 602, Greenbelt, MD 20770.

Parents Anonymous, 2810 Artesia Boulevard, Suite F, Redondo Beach, CA 90278. Help for parents of abused children.

Parents Without Partners, 7910 Woodmont Avenue, Washington, DC 20014.

Sisterhood of Single Black Mothers, 1360 Fulton Street, Brooklyn, NY 11216.

Special Web Sites for Divorce and Blended Families

www.parentingtoolbox.com (parenting toolbox)

www.parentsplace.com/family (family: single parenting)

www.stepfamilies.com (Stepping Stones Counseling Center, Ridgewood, New Jersey)

www.stepfamily.net (Stepfamily Network)

www.stepfamily.org (Stepfamily Foundation)

www.stepfamily.asn.au (Stepfamily Association of South Australia Inc. and Stepfamily Australia)

www.saafamilies.org (Stepfamily Association of America)

Local Agencies and Community Resources

Education, psychology, and human development departments and libraries in community college and university settings

Family counseling agencies

Health department

Marriage & Family Therapists Association

Mental health/mental retardation department

Pastoral counseling—individuals and associations

Private counseling centers and professionals

Regional and local public libraries

United Way agencies

University training centers for counseling, social work, and marriage and family therapy

Videos from educational catalogs, institutes, and video stores

CHAPTER 7

"Born in Our Hearts"— Families of Adoption

Partnerships Across Schools, Families, and Worlds

In our hopes and dreams, we made plans for you
In our minds and hearts, we loved you
In our arms, we longed to hold you
And then you came and we were whole.

K. WRIGHT, 2001

GUIDING QUESTIONS

1. What are the factors that have made adoption a more complex issue since the 1950s?
2. What are some of the strategies families can utilize to adopt children?
3. What are some of the issues families should consider when deciding whether to adopt a child from another country?
4. What is an agency that provides information and guidance for families who are considering adoption?
5. What are some of the reasons there are many children with special needs available for adoption?
6. What is the process of the "search for self" for adopted children?
7. How is the emotional journey of an adoptive parent different from and similar to that of a biological parent?

 growing number of people, both couples and single persons, are involved in the journey of adopting and rearing children. The process has changed across our history regarding the sources of children, the characteristics of the individuals seeking to adopt, and the legal issues that must be resolved. In this chapter, we explore the journeys of those who choose to adopt and the children who are adopted. The complexities and joys of adoption are discussed via the following themes:

Theme 1. The history of adoption reflects changes involving attitudes toward children and adoption, sources of children to adopt, and legal concerns.

Theme 2. Many paths lead adults to adoption and there are a number of strategies for adopting children.

Theme 3. There may be special considerations when children who are adopted are part of transracial adoptions, international adoptions, or both.

Theme 4. There may be special considerations when children who are adopted also have disabilities.

Theme 5. There are specific challenges to families who are foster parents to children.

Theme 6. Each child who is adopted goes through a series of stages depicting his or her adjustment across the life span.

Theme 7. Each adult who follows a quest to adopt a child experiences an emotional journey that begins on entering the experience and extends through the process of parenting the child who is adopted.

Theme 8. Teachers become better able to assist children in their journey through adoption when they are well informed and have strong relationships with family members.

A HISTORY OF ADOPTION

Wasson's (1977) classic *The Chosen Baby*, first published in 1939, depicts the warmth and love that adults and children can bring to each other as a family is created through adoption. It also represents the traditional form of adoption that people may have grown accustomed to expect. "In the first half of this century, adoption typically involved the placement of an infant with a childless, infertile couple of the same race (and often the same religious background)" (Brodzinsky & Schechter, 1990, p. xi). Today, adoption is a more complex issue as (a) family compositions and the lifestyles of individuals desiring to adopt children become more varied; (b) the number of children available for adoption in this country decreases with the greater availability and acceptance of abortion; (c) the geographic origins of the infants and children being adopted broaden as do the political complexities; (d) the number of individuals, including attorneys, physicians, and agencies, both public and private, involved in child procurement and placement increases; (e) the laws designed to protect birthparents, adoptive parents, and children become more restrictive; and (f) the strategies that prospective parents employ to locate and legally secure a child become more diverse and aggressive.

In the history of our children, the primary goal of the adoption process has not always been the building of loving families. Prior to the 20th century, adoption, rarely formalized, was characterized by matching children who were homeless or whose families could not financially support them with labor. Until the early part of the 20th century, children might be placed in situations in which they could be used as cheap labor, as indentured servants, or as apprentices to tradespeople in return for food, shelter, and perhaps a skill. This practice was particularly common in America during colonization. There was little reason to legalize adoptions during this time because inheritance was "determined solely by blood lineage" (Sokoloff, 1993, p. 17). One well-known example of matching family and labor in the United States is the "orphan trains." In 1853, Reverend Charles Loring Brace founded the Children's Aid Society in New York City so that children could be placed with families settling the rural sections of America. Between 1854 and 1929, some 100,000 children were placed on trains and transported to communities where they were shown for selection by local residents. In some cases, siblings and family groups were separated. Most of these adoptions were not formalized (Hollinger, 1993).

Understandably, the humaneness of this type of "adoption" has been debated. Some hailed Brace as a visionary in child welfare because he recognized the need to move children from institutions at the earliest age possible. Others thought that the Children's Aid Society did not screen prospective families or make certain that children placed did not, in fact, have living relatives (Sokoloff, 1993).

The 20th century was characterized by the onset and continued revision of laws designed to protect the rights of children and adults involved in the adoption process. **Adoption** severs the legal relationship between a child and the child's biological family and establishes the adoptive parents as the child's legal parents. Legal adoption was not generally recognized before the 1850s (Hollinger, 1993, p. 43). The 20th century was also characterized by a shift from the "taking in" of older children to a desire by prospective parents to adopt infants. This shift in attitudes has resulted from the decrease in infant mortality because of advances in prenatal and infant care, the development of successful formulas for feeding infants, research that has highlighted the child's environment as a major factor in growth and development, and a growing acceptance of "building families" with children who are not "our own" by virtue of blood.

THEME 1   *in practice . . .*

Historically, children were not told of their adoptive status. It was important to maintain the adoptive family as the biological family even though others in the community might know that the children were adopted. What might your feelings be toward yourself, your "family," and others in your community if you inadvertently discovered your adoption status at age 14? Consider your reactions first and then join with a group to share common concerns and ideas.

Listening to the needs of families is crucial in planning strategies that are supportive of families and children.

ADOPTIONS: TYPES AND STRATEGIES

Characteristics of Families with Adopted Children

In the 2000 U.S. Census, 1.6 million children in households, 2.5 percent of all children under 18 years of age, were reported as adopted. Twice as many children were reported as stepchildren (Kreider, 2003). This figure correlates with the increased rates of divorce and subsequent remarriages that characterize American families and the growing number of stepparents adopting or living with children of their spouses.

Today, an estimated 1 million individuals make up the growing list of potential parents (Harnack, 1995) who attempt to adopt children (primarily infants) in the United States each year. Who are these individuals? Many are men and women, married and unmarried, faced with fertility issues. Despite advances in modern medical technology, including fertility drugs, in vitro fertilization, and specialized surgeries, some individuals remain unable to become biological parents or choose not to seek treatment for economic or religious reasons. Some individuals do choose to seek and use surrogate mothers and sperm donors via artificial insemination.

The number of single men and single women who desire to have families as single parents is also increasing. These individuals may have had life experiences that prompt them to avoid traditional marriage, or they simply may not have found partners with whom they can parent. **Single-parent adoption**, artificial insemination, and surrogate mothers are options for these single prospective parents.

The number of gay and lesbian couples seeking to have families has increased as well. It is estimated that about 10 percent of the U.S. population is homosexual, with approximately 8 percent of the gay and lesbian population being parents (Ferrero, Freker, & Foster, 2005). It is also estimated that the number of children raised by them may be as high as 6 million (Collum, 1995; Ferrero, Freker, & Foster, 2005). Children in many of these families originated from marriages and relationships that occurred during a previous heterosexual lifestyle. Acceptance of the gay and lesbian lifestyle in the United States has increased. A study by Briggs (1994) reported that the percentage of Americans who preferred not to have homosexuals as friends declined from 54 percent to 41 percent between 1979 and 1993. Respondents who showed increased tolerance were generally female, more highly educated, or residents in urban areas, whereas blue-collar workers showed a decrease in tolerance. Resistance to same-sex marriages and other legal arrangements that recognize the couples as legal partners is still great. Consequently, gay and lesbian couples and individuals seeking to adopt children legally meet with resistance and may resort to alternative strategies to build families, include using sperm donors, artificial insemination, and surrogate mothers. Issues such as health insurance, rights of the coparent, and custody are still controversial and continue to be tested in the judicial arena (Ferrero, Freker, & Foster, 2005).

Although most adoptive parents continue to want a newborn (generally White), the number of prospective parents is far greater than the number of newborns available in the United States for adoption. Legalized abortion, improved and more accessible methods of birth control, and a heightened acceptance of unmarried mothers parenting their own children have all contributed to reduced numbers of healthy infants available for adoption. In the 1950s and 1960s, 90 percent of all adoptions were of children born to unmarried mothers (Solinger, 1992). These young women were sent to homes for unwed mothers or to live with relatives and friends in other communities. Today, young women in these circumstances have more options, and some choose to have an abortion or to raise their own children with the help of school-based child-care centers and family members.

Strategies for Adopting Children

Historically, couples registered with state government–affiliated adoption agencies or private agencies. In some cases, aunts, uncles, and others "adopted" the children of young unmarried relatives or friends. Many of these adoptions were secret, and adoptees might never be told of their true biological heritage. "During the first half of the twentieth century, secrecy, anonymity, and the sealing of records became statutorily required and standard adoption practice" (Sokoloff, 1993, p. 21). Proponents of laws such as the Minnesota Act of 1917 were concerned about keeping adoption proceedings from public scrutiny. Social workers were particularly concerned about protecting the adopted children from the stigma of illegitimacy (Sokoloff, 1993).

As the number of people attempting to adopt infants has increased and the number of healthy infants available for adoption has decreased, state adoption waiting lists have become longer, and years may pass before a waiting couple is called. Available figures indicate that the number of women who seek to adopt exceeds the number of unrelated adoptions formalized annually by a ratio of 3.3 to 1 and that the waiting period is 2 or more years to adopt healthy, White infants (Stolley, 1993, p. 37). Consequently, alternative strategies for matching children and families emerged. More than half of all adoptions are arranged through public and intercountry agencies. Public agencies account for 40 percent, up from 18 percent in 1992, of adoptions. Intercountry agencies account for 15 percent to 20 percent, up from 5 percent in 1992, of adoptions. The other 40 percent of adoptions are by kin or private agency (U.S. Department of Health and Human Services, 2004).

As the number of children available for adoption decreases and the complexity of locating and having a child placed in one's family increases, many prospective parents are looking for alternative opportunities, including international adoptions, adoptions of children with special needs and challenges, and transracial adoptions. These adoptions require that individuals be resourceful and prepared to deal with financial, political, and social issues that surround the adoption process.

There are some census data to illustrate trends in adoption and numbers of reported stepchildren by such categories as time, family groups, regions of the country, gender, and cultural background. According to the U.S. Department of Health and Human Services (2004), in 2000 and 2001, 127,000 million children were adopted annually. Since 1987, the rate of adoptions has remained relatively constant (118,000 in 1987). In the 2000 census, Kreider (2003) there was almost no reported variations of percentages of adopted children per all children within a region (Midwest 2.6 percent, Northeast 2.4 percent, South 2.4 percent, and West 2.4 percent). Yet, the percentage of stepchildren per all children within a region varied greatly (Northeast 3.3 percent, South 6.1 percent, Midwest 5.1 percent, and West 5.1 percent). More girls were adopted than boys, while only 9 percent of adopted girls and 15 percent of adopted boys were reported to have a special need or disability.

More than 2.4 million grandparents are the primary caregiver, and in some cases, the adoptive parent of more than 4.5 million children (Goyer, 2005). African American children are more likely to live with a grandparent than are Caucasion or Hispanic children (Rothenberg, 1996). Often the children are living with the grandparent because of parental substance abuse, incarceration, or military duty, adding to the family stresses.

Comparing the overall populations of each race of children under 18 living in households—biological children to adopted children and stepchildren—there were less Caucasian adopted children (58 percent) than biological (64 percent) children reported, but more stepchildren (69 percent). For African American children, those percentages were 16 percent adopted, 13 percent biological, 12 percent stepchildren. The comparisons for Asian children showed even higher percentages of adopted children living in households—7.4 percent adopted, 3.5 percent biological, 1.2 percent stepchildren—which may be due to the increases in foreign adoptions of Asian children. The adoption rate for Hispanic children was lower than for biological children: 14 percent adopted, 16 percent biological, 15 percent stepchildren.

THEME 2   *in practice . . .*

You are the director of a hospital-funded child-care center serving infants through school-age children. Most children enroll as infants or toddlers and remain in the program until they are old enough to care for themselves. You have a waiting list for infants and are frequently visited by prospective parents desiring to put newborns on the list. Recently, you were visited by a single mother-to-be who disclosed that she had become pregnant through artificial insemination using a sperm donor. What thoughts do you have about this method of building a family, and what issues do you think you might need to discuss with the parent?

Adopting Children from Other Countries and of Other Races

In her book *Family Bonds: Adoption and the Politics of Parenting* (1993), Elizabeth Bartholet provides the reader with important insights into the **international adoption** experience. The Harvard law professor details her experiences in separate journeys to Peru to adopt each of her two sons as a single mother. Her stays in Peru, where her care for each child was scrutinized and where she negotiated the legal and social systems, language, economics, and culture and customs, required both wisdom and tenacity. The fear that she would not be able to return to the United States with the child so precious to her was pervasive throughout the adoption process. She witnessed prospective parents being given a child only to have the child taken away, and birth mothers both reluctantly and obediently handing over their children for adoption. Her insights into the political nature of international adoptions reflect both joys and hardships.

Single parents often choose international adoptions, such as from Russia, to begin their families.

International adoptions become more prevalent following periods of war in countries where children are left without parents and homes. One such example followed the period of the Korean War (1950–1953), when Harry Holt, an American farmer, worked to place Korean children in homes. Today, the Holt agency represents the largest international adoption agency and places children throughout the developed world

(Silverman, 1993). During the 1980s, more than 40,000 children from Korea alone were adopted by North Americans.

> Over the years, I (author) have watched a number of families—friends and neighbors and families of children with whom I have worked—adopt children from Korea through the Holt agency. Perhaps the fondest memory is of the young couple living next door who had waited patiently for their baby to arrive. The call came during the Christmas holidays, and they drove to a city some 4 hours away to pick up their baby girl arriving on a plane from Korea. I recall feeling such anticipation as we waited for them to return. In our community, families adopting children from Korea through Holt gather on a regular basis to provide time for sharing their experiences and for the children to play and talk with other children who have had a similar experience. Families discuss the same issues that all parents of young children discuss, as well as ideas for helping children to acquire information about and to maintain aspects of their cultural heritage. The support that families bring to each other is invaluable.

In 2000, foreign-born children made up 13 percent of adoptions. Of those foreign adoptions, the 48 percent were Asian, 33 percent were from Latin America, and 16 percent were European (Kreider, 2003). More recently (1997–1999), the former Soviet Union led the way with the most children adopted by families within the United States (McGuinness & Pallansch, 2000, p. 457). These placements are complicated by the laws of various governments, changing political situations that affect the release of children from other countries, and cultural practices that often determine who will be allowed to adopt a child. (Note that children from other countries adopted by U.S. citizens become U.S. citizens on becoming a resident of this country.)

Adopting a child from a reputable foreign adoption agency may be more desirable since more foreign agencies assure the process in a year's time frame whereas American adoptions can take much longer. Proponents of international adoptions cite the blessings of taking a child from a situation of poverty and aloneness to a home where the child will be safe physically, economically, and emotionally. Those who oppose such adoptions view this as exploitation by

> the privileged classes in the industrialized nations of the children in the least privileged groups in the poorest nations, the adoption by whites of black- and brown-skinned children from various Third World nations, and the separation of children not only from their birthparents, but from their racial, cultural, and national communities as well. (Bartholet, 1993, p. 180)

Families of children adopted from other races and cultures, and teachers and caregivers who work with and love these children, are indeed faced with the challenges of building each child's awareness of cultural customs and traditions so that each child's heritage is preserved. "These are families whose members must learn to appreciate one another's differences, in terms of racial and cultural heritage, while at the same time experiencing their common humanity" (Bartholet, 1993, p. 180).

Americans have engaged in **transracial adoption**—adopting children of a race not one's own—for a long time, including Asian children from Korea and Hispanic children from South and Central America. Most transracial adoptions that have occurred in the United States have involved the placement of African American children with White parents. This practice became increasingly popular during the 1960s and continued into the 1970s. Such adoptions leveled off, however, following a resolution adopted by the National Association of Black Social Workers (NABSW) during its first annual conference in 1972 that vehemently opposed transracial adoption out of concern for maintaining the **cultural heritage** of the African American child (Silverman, 1993). The NABSW reaffirmed this position during the 1994 conference with a declaration that "it is the right of a child to be raised in a permanent, loving home which reflects the same ethnic or racial group" (Russell, 1995, p. 188). Proponents of transracial adoption stress that the positive effects of being placed in a loving environment outweigh the negative effects of not being placed with a same-race family. This position is supported by resolutions presented at the 1992 conference of the National Association for the Advancement of Colored People (Simon, Altstein, & Melli, 1995). The placement of African American children with non-Black families is, once again, becoming a more accepted practice in this country.

> Students in a practicum class shared their questions about an African American child adopted by White parents. One student, also African American, was somewhat uncomfortable that the mother had asked her questions about how best to care for the child's hair. It was a wonderful opportunity to address our self-consciousness about discussing our differences. It was also a wonderful opportunity to acknowledge the student's success in building a relationship with the parent that made the parent comfortable enough to be able to ask for help.

Similar concerns surround the adoption of Native American children by White families, and in 1978, the Indian Child Welfare Act placed responsibility for child custody matters, including adoption, under the jurisdiction of the tribe to which the child was born. Adoption of Native American children by families who are not Native American remains very low (Silverman, 1993).

THEME 3   *in practice . . .*

You and your staff have recently engaged in a self-study involving all aspects of your program, including curriculum, relationships with families, and child guidance. From your work, it appears that the multicultural component of the classroom needs enhancing. In staff meetings designed to plan resolution of this situation, one teacher notes that two of the children in her classroom are Korean and were adopted by a local family as infants. As a teacher, should you pursue building aspects of the Korean culture of these children into the curriculum? If so, what would be the considerations, and how might this be accomplished?

Parenting Adoptive and Foster Children with Special Needs and Challenges

Special Needs Adoptions. "Special needs adoption refers to the adoption of children who are particularly difficult to place in permanent homes" (McKenzie, 1993, p. 62). Generally, children with special needs are those who:

- Have physical or health problems
- Are older
- Are members of ethnic or racial minorities
- Have a history of abuse or neglect
- Have emotional problems
- Have siblings and need to be adopted as a group
- Test positive for HIV
- Have documented conditions that may lead to future problems
- Were prenatally exposed to drugs or alcohol (National Adoption Information Clearinghouse [NAIC], 2000)

The NAIC reports that more than 110,000 children with special needs in the United States are waiting for permanent homes. Those who are interested in exploring **special needs adoption** must decide whether they are emotionally, physically, mentally, and financially prepared to be successful as a parent in this situation. Such adoptions are successful when families seek and receive the support of a network consisting of appropriate agencies; schools; families and communities, or both.

Families are not always aware that they have adopted a special needs child. Some adoptive parents may think that they have adopted a typically developing child or a child with slight developmental delays. However, over time, it becomes apparent that the child has more serious and, perhaps, long-term needs. One example is found in adoptions of children from other countries. In a study of the families of 50 male and 55 female children adopted from the former Soviet Union, McGuinness and Pallansch (2000) found that these children often had mental or physical disabilities and serious health issues that may have resulted from periods of institutionalization (orphanages); poor health care during a period of social and economic change and uncertainty; abuse and neglect; and the effects of alcohol ingestion by the mother. They noted that length of time in the institution was the strongest predictive factor influencing the child's competence. The average age of entry into the institution was about 1.8 years, and the average age at the time of adoption was about 3.9 years. At the time of the study, the average age of the children was 7.7 years, and many still showed the effects of being institutionalized.

As mentioned, these and other families of special needs children need resources and respite to sustain the family. The Adoption and Safe Families Act of 1997 (P.L. 105–89) focuses on not only finding homes for children with special needs, but making sure that families receive postadoption services as needed (NAIC, 2000).

My Baby: From Russia with Love

Brenda's career as an ultrasound technician at a women's hospital in Las Vegas provided an important service to the community as well as a substantial salary, but it didn't provide a lot of opportunities to meet single men. She moved to Las Vegas from Pennsylvania for adventure, and because that area of the country pays Ultrasound technicians better than the national average (the growing area around Las Vegas has a shortage of persons in that profession). Brenda always felt she would have children, but once she reached the age of 36, she wasn't sure if she would marry. She met a woman in her office who had adopted a child from China and felt positive about the adoption experience from a respectable agency.

Brenda investigated adoption through that agency but she also looked into other agencies. There seemed to be hundreds of agencies, and to her delight, she found an agency with adoptions from hospitals or orphanages in Russia, which happened to be the nation of origin of her Great Grandmother. It took several months for Brenda to screen agencies and find the agency she felt she could trust. The rest of the process was also lengthy, with mounds of paperwork and background checks on Brenda. Brenda filled out all of the required paperwork and waited for the adoption agency to make the required home visit to assure Brenda was a suitable adoptive parent. Single mothers can adopt, but this agency also wanted to be sure that Brenda's income could support the baby. The cost of the adoption alone, over $20,000, would be out of the question for many couples who are both employed, let alone a person with a single income. If she had been older, beyond 45years of age, this agency would only provide children over 18 months old.

Brenda finally told her family back in Pennsylvania once she knew the agency had accepted her application. Brenda's dad's first reaction was not as accepting as she had thought. He said he couldn't see why a single woman would want to go to all that trouble and expense. Brenda's mother was delighted. She said she had raised Brenda to be a loving and giving person and could see why Brenda would want to share her love with a baby who might otherwise spend the rest of his or her life in an institution.

It took 10 months for the agency to let her know that they had selected a baby for her. Regulations did not allow any pictures or videos to be shared with Brenda so she was anxiously awaiting the next step—her first visit to Russia. The wait for the first visit was almost 10 months, and she knew she would have to take off with only a few days notice to her employer and stay a week. Fortunately, the women's hospital where she worked was very understanding.

Brenda's first trip to Russia went smoothly; she was filled with excitement and anticipation. All hotel and travel arrangements had been made by the agency. When she finally got to the orphanage just outside of Moscow, Brenda's arms were filled with toys for Christina, the name she chose for her new baby. Brenda had to refrain from running up the steps. The attendants placed Christina in her new mother's arms, and Brenda could not hold back the tears of joy as she looked into the baby's eyes. Brenda thought it was amazing how close she felt to this child, as if she had birthed the child herself. A week's stay seemed to pass like hours. It would be four months before Brenda would return to Russia for the court hearing and final adoption procedures.

(Continued)

Back in Las Vegas, Brenda's dad saw Brenda with Christina, and Brenda held out Christina for Grandpa to hold. He soon forgot his earlier doubts. Grandpa and Grandma decided on this first visit that they would move to Las Vegas to be with their first grandchild. The first year with Christina went very smoothly, as Christina spent some time in child care and some time with her grandparents. It went almost too smoothly, as Christina was very quiet and didn't make the usual babbling sounds or say any words by her first birthday. The pediatrician had suspected that Christina had a hearing loss. Further investigation by Brenda revealed that Christina had been given an antibiotic for an infection and that recent medical research in the United States banned this antibiotic because side effects were sometimes sensorineural hearing loss. The damage was severe and in both ears.

The good news to Brenda is that medical advances in cochlear implant surgery was available for Christina to fully recover her hearing and that her insurance would cover most of the cost of this expensive surgery. Because the doctors decided to wait until Christina was 2 years old to perform the surgery, Brenda and her parents learned sign language and taught Christina some simple signs which she easily learned to use. Brenda's best friend said to Brenda, "That baby just won the lottery. What would Christina's life had been if you had not adopted her?" Brenda said she was so strongly bonded with Christina that she couldn't even imagine Christina's life any other way than as her child.

THEME 4   *in practice . . .*

You are teaching kindergarten in a suburban public school. You often collaborate with a first-grade class to provide both groups with opportunities to engage in learning experiences in multiage groupings. Several children in your class have siblings in the first grade. One child, Bennett, has a sibling in the first grade who is adopted and has apparent disabilities. Several kindergartners have continued to ask, "Is that really your brother? What's wrong with him, anyway?" Bennett becomes frustrated and asks you, "Why did my parents have to adopt him, anyway?" What do you think would be an appropriate response on your part to this situation?

Children in Foster Families.   As reported by the Adoption and Foster Care Analysis Reporting System (AFCARS) data for 1999, 581,000 children were in **foster care**. The average age was 9.9 years. Four percent of the children were under age 1, and 25 percent were ages 1 through 5. Of those who exited foster care during this time, 59 percent were reunited with a parent or guardian, 10 percent went to live with another relative, and 16 percent were adopted. Almost one half (47 percent) of the children lived in a nonrelative, foster family home during their time spent in foster care; only 10 percent were in institutions. Of those who adopted children, 64 percent had been the child's foster parent prior to the adoption. Married couples accounted for 66 percent of these adoptions (*Adoption and Foster Care Analysis and Reporting System*, 2001).

Many foster families care for children who fall into the "special needs" category. "Almost all children who meet the special needs guidelines and who are available for adoption are currently in the public foster care system" (NAIC, 2000, p. 2). Although adoptive families of children with special needs are a diverse group, "the single most dominant feature of the special needs adoptive family is that the vast majority of them have been foster parents first" (McKenzie, 1993, p. 68). Extended family members; recruited, prepared special needs adoptive families, including single- and two-parent families; and infertile couples make up the remaining groups that typically adopt children in the special needs category. Encouraging statistics from the Evan B. Donaldson Adoption Institute (2004) illustrate a trend of increases of these foster care adoptions—50,000 children were adopted from foster care in 2001, 37,000 in 1998, and 28,000 in 1996.

Chapter 9 provides strategies such as home visits and parent conferences that are useful in communicating and building bridges with families. What situation specifics do teachers and caregivers need to consider when cooperating with adoptive families, foster families, and grandparents (or other individuals) caring for young children? The insights from parents in Figure 7.1 are quite useful to us in this discussion.

FIGURE 7.1	Insights for Teachers and Caregivers on Supporting Adopted Children and Families

Insight 1: The "Real" Child

I have two children. The older is adopted; the younger is not. Both are boys. The older is quite a bit smaller than the younger, and they really do not resemble each other. A recent experience in the grocery store represents a type of incident that happens frequently. At the checkout, the clerk asked, "Are both of these boys yours? Why don't they look alike? Why did you adopt him?" All of these questions were asked in the presence of my sons. Ever since they were small, people have asked, "Which one is yours?"

The comments described in this example are hurtful and will likely prompt families to close communication. In a warm environment, families will generally share information about the family composition. Get to know the family situation. This can be done through conferences, home visits, and informal conversations. Determine with whom you will be responsible for establishing a parent–teacher bond. Recognize that children who are adopted are "real" children and "real" sons and daughters even though they were not born to the adoptive parents. Find out what the children know about their adoptive or foster situations and what the legal guardians think should be shared in the classroom setting. Respect the privacy of each family. Trust is built between families and teachers when parents or legal guardians see that teachers and caregivers act in an ethical manner and protect the family's right to privacy.

(Continued)

FIGURE 7.1	Continued

Insight 2: Take This Home to Mommy

My sister was unable to care for her young daughter, Janie. Janie came to live with me, her aunt, for a year. One day, she came home from school crying because the teacher had asked her to bring home a note to "Mommy." All of my niece's feelings about not living with her mom and not "fitting in" were triggered. I had had several talks with the teacher, and she was well aware of Janie's family living arrangements.

Be aware of the language and activities you use in the classroom. When a child is being raised by a grandparent or a series of foster parents, it is discouraging to be directed repeatedly to take a note to "Mom" or to ask "Dad." Children often feel "less than" and "not a part of" the group. Similarly, teas for "moms" and "daddy" nights are also difficult for children who do not have moms and dads readily available. Building "family trees" can also foster a variety of emotions in children who may have been abandoned.

Insight 3: What Does *Adopted* Mean?

As I looked around my son's classroom, I saw several children who I knew had been adopted. Some were from other countries. I could not help but think what a wonderful opportunity it would be for children to learn about the different ways that families come together to love and care for each other. It seemed, however, that the subject of adoption made the adults uncomfortable, so I did not pursue the idea.

Include opportunities in your curriculum for adopted children to share the uniqueness of their situation. Adoptive parents of children from other countries may find this a wonderful opportunity to share something about the culture of that child's family of origin. Similarly, a grandparent or foster parent might become a special visitor to the classroom, sharing an experience or skill or reading books to the children. Use children's books to foster discussion about adoption and the many ways that families are formed. Appropriate books include the following:

Banish, R., & Jordan-Wong, J. (1992). *A forever family.* New York: HarperCollins.
An 8-year-old girl describes living in many foster families before she was adopted at age 8.

Caines, J. (1973). *Abby.* New York: HarperCollins.
Abby is adopted by an African American family living in a city apartment. She loves to hear how she was adopted and to be reassured by her older brother that he loves her.

Girard, L. W. (1986). *Adoption is for always.* Morton Grove, IL: Albert Whitman.
A little girl deals with her feelings of anger and frustration at being adopted, with the help of her adoptive family.

Girard, L. W. (1989). *We adopted you, Benjamin Koo.* Morton Grove, IL: Albert Whitman.
A 9-year-old Korean boy details what it is like to be adopted from another culture.

Livingston, C. (1978). *Why was I adopted? The facts of adoption with love and illustration.* New York: Carol.
Questions are answered in a fun manner through the use of cartoonlike characters and illustrations.

Stinson, K. (1992). *Steven's baseball mitt: A book about being adopted.* North York, Ontario: Firefly.
During a search for his baseball mitt, Steven wonders about his birth mother and what she might be like.

FIGURE 7.1   Continued

Turner, A. (1990). *Through the moon and stars and night skies*. New York: HarperCollins.
A little boy travels by plane to his new family in this story about an intercountry adoption. He
   shares his fears and his need for a momma and poppa of his own.

Insight 4: I Need Someone Like Me

*When my daughter reached third grade, she began to talk about her birth mother. We had always
been honest about her being adopted. She had really shown no interest, however, until she was
8 or 9 years old. I thought she was happy.*

Even the most secure parents can become disconcerted when their children wish to
find out more about their heritage. Parents need information and support from those who can
acknowledge their feelings and who understand the developmental shifts that children
experience. Offer workshops, reading materials, and parent–teacher discussions that will assist
the child's guardian in understanding the developmental shifts that children experience in their
growth and as they relate to an adoption experience. Build a resource file of community service
offerings for families and children. Provide opportunities for support groups for families and
children to form within the school setting. Understand the complex journey that many parents
and children have taken to become families. Be proactive in keeping open the line of
communication between the school and the families. Be responsive to parents' needs for
sharing and receiving information.

Insight 5: My Child Is Special

*I have a beautiful son adopted at birth. He is a loving and wonderful child whose life is challenged
by a hearing impairment, attention deficit, and learning disability. When I go to school, I am
overwhelmed by the number of people whom I have to deal with and the extent to which I have
to advocate to get services that are appropriate for my child.*

Parents with children who are adopted and who have special needs have unique challenges.
Assist these parents by collaborating with other teachers, guidance specialists, social workers,
and family members and building your knowledge about appropriate methods for introducing
and addressing the issues arising from adoption and foster parenting.

THEME 5   *in practice . . .*

You may work in a program for children and families represented by a significant
number of foster placements. Do you know the requirements for being a foster family
or parent in your state? If you do, make a list of those requirements to discuss during
class. If not, explore information available through The Administration for Children
and Families' Children's Bureau. Compare and contrast requirements of different
states. Do you think the requirements are sufficient to ensure quality child care?

THE PSYCHOSOCIAL JOURNEY OF CHILDREN WHO ARE ADOPTED

Thomas was 11 when he casually told his adoptive mother that he wanted to meet his birth mother. He had known since he was a very young child that he was adopted, but he had never expressed any interest in knowing more about his birthmother. Surprised by the fear that rose in her throat, Thomas's mother told him that she would help him find his birth mother when he reached 18. Later, when she reflected on the conversation, she realized that she was trying to delay the possibility that Thomas would somehow be "lost" to her and that she would need to deal with her fears in meeting the very natural desire of her son to know more about his heritage.

Simple routines such as cleaning up after an experience with finger paint assist children in feeling competent in their daily routines.

The Search for Self

Thomas's question is one indication that, even as young as 11 years old, he had begun the complicated psychological search for self. This concept of *self* evolves from birth through our experiences in relating to the people and events in our immediate worlds. It encompasses our awareness of our

Physical self: Perceptions and feelings about how we look in terms of our physical traits in relation to others

Psychological self: Perceptions and feelings about our own intelligence and personality traits

Social self: Perceptions and feelings about how others see us and whether they "like" us

The evaluative component of the self is "self-esteem." "Self-esteem is the value an individual places on himself or herself" (Barrett, Kallio, McBride, Moore, & Wilson, 1995, p. 391). This value or sense of self-worth derives from a blending of our reactions to experiences with those who serve as our "mirrors" in life—birth parents, adoptive parents, stepparents, grandparents, teachers, caregivers, siblings, friends, coworkers, and children—and the genetic predispositions that we have to behave in certain ways or to exhibit certain personality traits.

As with nonadopted individuals, children and adults who are adopted will engage in the lifelong search for self, that is, who they are. This journey of self-discovery "begins at birth and continues through old age, with many ups and downs along the way to resolution" (Brodzinsky, Schechter, & Henig, 1992, p. 3). As we will see, the issue is complicated by coping with the sense of loss and the process of grief that each adopted individual must face. As one would expect, although some patterns that guide the knowledge we have about adjustment to life as an adopted child are universal, each individual copes in unique ways dependent on his or her life experiences, genetic predispositions, and development with respect to cognitive and psychosocial skills.

In *Being Adopted: The Lifelong Search for Self* (1992), Brodzinsky and coauthors explored the developmental process that characterizes the adoptee's search for self. They noted, "The experience of adoption—like any other experience—is not static. It changes with time as the forces of development shape and reshape the way we think, feel, relate, and grow" (p. 2).

The focus on understanding the developmental changes that people experience should not be limited simply to the early childhood period, because we are, in early childhood, dealing with issues that lay the groundwork for the life span.

The Emotional Journey and Tasks of Adults Who Adopt Children

The parenting journey is an emotional one filled with love, joy, compassion, delight, fear, frustration, and many unknowns. Healthy parents want their child to be happy and secure in their love and will work very hard to ensure that the child's environment protects and nurtures those feelings. Nevertheless, parents cannot control every aspect of their child's life, be it a genetic predisposition or an environmental influence. An adoptive parent faces even more unknowns about a child: his or her genetic history, prior experiences, how he or she will make adjustments to being adopted throughout life, and the child's connection with his or her family of origin.

While providing a wonderful opportunity for sharing love with a child, the journey that begins for both child and adult as their lives become intertwined is a path marked by changes in the child's cognitive and emotional understanding of the adoption process and search for self, and the adult's emotional taking in and letting go of the child conceived by and born of another but seen as one's own.

To better understand the developmental changes that adoptees and others experience over time and with changing cognitive and psychosocial understanding, Brodzinsky and coauthors (1992) used Erik Erikson's (1950) model of psychosocial tasks. Erikson, a Danish-born psychoanalyst, developed an eight-stage model noting universal **psychosocial tasks** that individuals experience as they move through the life span. According to Erikson, each stage in life finds the individual experiencing a two-dimensional conflict (e.g., trust versus mistrust). As conflicts are resolved, individuals move to the next stage. Each stage's conflicts can be "revisited" throughout life, however. "We are forever struggling with the issues we seem to have resolved at an earlier period of life" (Brodzinsky et al., 1992, p. 15). Let's consider each of these stages and how the resolution of their respective conflicts relates specifically to the psychosocial development of the adoptee.

Infancy. The first of Erikson's (1950) stages involves the infant's acquisition of a sense of **trust versus mistrust**. During this time, the infant is forming important attachments to primary caregivers. As noted by Brodzinsky et al. (1992),

> a true attachment to a primary caregiver, the kind that lasts a lifetime, doesn't happen in utero or in the first moments after delivery. It is something that grows slowly, over weeks, months, and even years of loving interaction, and it can grow just as well between a parent and infant who are not biologically connected as between a parent and infant who are. (p. 32)

A sense of trust is acquired when the infant's primary needs (e.g., food, clothing, shelter) and needs for nurturing and love are consistently met by those with whom attachments are forming and when the infant knows that he or she can depend on the caregiver's personal behavior for comfort. Mistrust occurs when the infant comes to know that he or she cannot depend on primary caregivers or self for nurturing and comfort.

With mistrust comes a flawed sense of self-worth and limits on the individual's abilities to trust those encountered throughout life. These issues will be revisited at varying stages of the life span. This stage has added implications for the adopted child particularly with respect to the age at which the child is brought into the adoptive home, the frequency with which the child is moved from one caregiving situation to another, and the quality of the caregiving environments.

As noted earlier, the quality of attachment between adoptive mothers and children can be like that of biological mothers and children. Differences can be noted, however, when children are adopted after 6 months of age because "these babies have usually already formed an attachment with their biological or foster parents," and "they come to the adoptive parents following a sense of disruption of a previous relationship, which often leads to a sense of loss and emotional or behavior disorganization" (Brodzinsky et al., 1992, p. 36). During the first 6 months, the greatest amount of stress can be seen when children change placements during the period from 4 to 12 weeks. Distress takes the form of difficulty in eating and sleeping and irritability. At this age, infants can attune to all new stimuli but have difficulty closing it out when it becomes too much. When placement occurs during the second 6 months of life, babies grieve for the loss of their primary caregivers by exhibiting searching behaviors, withdrawing, engaging in uncontrollable crying, clinging, and experiencing frequent illnesses (Call, 1974).

This adjustment to new parents can also be affected by the child's personality and the match of that personality to the personalities of the adoptive parents. Each individual has a unique personality based on certain genetic predispositions, as well as features that result from life experiences. High-risk pregnancies involving such factors as drugs or alcohol, teenage mothers, and poor prenatal care may result in a child who is temperamental, quite active, and generally difficult for some adults to manage.

Regardless of the obstacles that adoptive families face in helping children transition from one home to another, children are quite resilient and will generally adjust to the new home situation. This is, of course, dependent on the quality and availability of the consistent nurturing that is required of adoptive families and on the infrequency of moves and adjustments that a child is expected to make.

Toddlerhood. Toddlerhood, or the period from 18 months to 3 years of age, encompasses the psychosocial task of **autonomy versus doubt and shame**. Those who spend time with toddlers will witness the growing sense of self as statements such as "mine," "me want," and "me go" punctuate their rapidly expanding language. As toddlers "set their boundaries" with adults, peers, and siblings, their independence and separateness, so necessary for growth, become mightily apparent. Adults foster this growth by providing opportunities for children to engage in developmentally appropriate self-care and play routines and by encouraging their competence while continuing to provide a loving "home base." This home base also includes a set of reasonable limits for behaviors that all children need in order to provide a sense of structure in their lives and some beginning understanding of right and wrong.

During this period, many adoptive families focus on telling the adoption story to their children. Young children love the warmth and affection that accompany reading stories about adoption and hearing their parents tell about their adoption. These events become particularly important when families engage in various forms of open adoption wherein the birth parents may remain involved in their children's lives. Adults must be aware, however, that during this age, children cannot cognitively comprehend the complexities of how they were born and adopted. In fact, they may be just at the beginnings of understanding something about birth, given the opportunity to witness people and other living creatures during pregnancy. Children brought from another country will not comprehend that Korea, for example, is another country in another part of the world. They are at the beginnings of their awareness of this abstract concept. (One of the authors is reminded of a preschool classroom where 3-year-old Daniel asks how Jipu, a child from China, travels to school each morning. The teacher, sharing the globe with the children, points out Jipu's homeland and tells Daniel that Jipu rides a bicycle with his mother each morning. Given his age, Daniel's response is not surprising: "Jipu sure has a long way to ride!")

At this age, adults are building stepping-stones in the child's growing awareness of the meaning of adoption. These stones must be laid with realistic expectations of the child's cognitive capabilities. As adoption researchers (Brodzinsky et al., 1992) explain:

> The advice of most adoption experts is to start talking to children about being adopted during toddlerhood, before they have a chance to develop their own ideas about adoption. Most parents dutifully follow this advice. But our research suggests that most children haven't the foggiest idea what Mom and Dad are talking about. (p. 50)

Preschool. The preschool years, from ages 3 through 5, are characterized as a period of egocentricity with respect to the child's thinking. According to cognitive theorist Jean Piaget (1929), this is a period of preoperational thinking in which children begin to understand cause-and-effect relations but as yet are unable to engage in the mental operations required for logical thought. Most children do not begin to understand the meaning of being adopted until 5 to 7 years of age, and even during this time their understanding is limited (Brodzinsky, Singer, & Braff, 1984). The preschool child may be able to describe the events leading to being adopted, but this is based on the repeated stories provided by the adoptive parents. The warm and loving shared storytellings and cognitive limitations characteristic of the preschool child provide assurance that the young child will view the adoption in a positive light (Brodzinsky & Schechter, 1990).

What psychosocial tasks are to be accomplished during the preschool years? According to Erikson (1950), preschool children are

Sensory experiences are soothing for children as they cope with the stresses found in their young lives.

engaged in establishing a sense of **initiative versus guilt**. During this period, children continue to build their competence and autonomy in all aspects of their development—social, emotional, physical, cognitive, and aesthetic. Adults nurture this aspect of growth by providing opportunities for children to engage in developmentally appropriate experiences in play with materials and other children. Guidance strategies that focus on reinforcing the positive behaviors that children exhibit and on helping children understand the logical consequences of their actions also foster the children's increasing sense of competence and initiative. Primary caregivers who have a positive sense of their own competence and self-worth are much more able to foster such growth in a healthy way than are adults who do not possess this characteristic.

With increasing cognitive capabilities and social experiences, preschool children become more aware of the physical and social differences in the individuals in their lives. Gender identity and racial identity appear, with the child recognizing that he or she is a boy or a girl and of a particular skin color. Not until the child is at the upper end of the preschool age group, however, does he or she begin to understand that gender and race do not change as one becomes older (Edwards, 1986). This awareness of physical differences is necessary for the child to define self and relationships with others.

During this time, children adopted across racial lines begin to feel that they look different from the other members of their families. Adults sometimes expect children to understand cognitively the nature of the adoption when they, again, have limited cognitive and social capabilities to do so.

Adoptive parents may rationalize their children's questions as evidence that they fully understand the meaning of being adopted. But generally this is not true. A preschooler may recognize that Mommy is White and he is Black, but this is a far cry from understanding how this difference came to be or what it means to have another mommy who is Black. As we shall see, the cognitive foundation for this type of understanding usually does not develop until the elementary school years (Brodzinsky et al., 1992, p. 60).

Preschoolers define family as people who live together. Families who adopt children during the preschool years will need to be prepared for the possibility of dealing with the children's **grief** at losing their previous caregiving placements, regardless of the nature of those situations. Children mourn the loss of their "families" and, in cases in which another language was spoken, their mother tongue. Children adopted during this time need adoptive parents to accept their need to talk about their prior families and to grieve. This grief can be eased when adoptive parents and caregivers are aware of the children's routines, schedules, and habits and the names of the children's previous caregivers. This type of loving acceptance and continuity is critical for easing children's grief and adjustment to their new families and surroundings (Brodzinsky et al., 1992).

Middle Childhood.   Erikson (1950) defined the psychosocial task of middle childhood, ages 6 to 12, as **industry versus inferiority**. Although there are great differences between the child at age 6 and the child at age 12, it is generally a time when children seek to broaden their relationships with peers and to be accepted. Also during this time, each child formulates a sense of self or self-image. Self-esteem is based on how children see themselves in relation to others. At a time when being different is not perceived as "good" by many children of this age, adopted children may be faced with being not only physically different from family members but also different from their peer group. Middle childhood is often the time when being adopted is seen by children as being a problem (Brodzinsky et al., 1992).

The response to physical differences and other adoption concerns occurs in accordance with an increasing level of social and cognitive sophistication. According to Piaget (1929), the elementary-age child's thinking is characterized as the period of concrete operations. Children are now capable of more logical and reflective thought processes. Not only do they recognize the physical differences among members of the family, but adopted children also understand that no biological relationship exists between them and their adoptive parents. "As children mature cognitively . . . their capacity for understanding logical reciprocity leads them to a profound insight—to be adopted, one must first be relinquished or surrendered" (Brodzinsky, 1990, p. 13). The sense of loss that comes with understanding that birth parents "gave them up" before they came into an adoptive family can take the form of emotional and behavioral changes. These changes are associated with the different ways that children deal with the grieving process as they move through and revisit shock, denial, despair, recovery, and reintegration. Adoption is a more pervasive loss than the death or divorce of parents because children may have little or no connection to the birth parents. Society does little to validate the adopted child's grief (Brodzinsky et al., 1992).

During middle childhood, we "begin to see a rise in psychological, behavioral, and academic problems that are more common in adoptees" (Brodzinsky et al., 1992, p. 69). As difficult as it may be, family members will need to be accepting of the child's feelings in discussions of the child's adoption. It is natural for adoptive parents to feel somewhat threatened when a child expresses grief over losing or a desire to find a birth parent. It is also natural for adoptive parents to feel threatened and angry when the child rejects them. Many of these expressions, however, are a part of the child's experience in dealing with feelings of grief as well as guilt in wishing to know more about the birth family at the emotional expense of the adoptive family. All of this occurs at a time of increased cognitive understanding and heightened social pressure.

As done historically, some parents wish to keep the adoption a secret. Although citing protection of the child, parents often keep this fact secret to protect themselves from the discomfort of sharing such information with the child, family members, and other adults. Such secrets are detrimental to the child's sense of trust in those who care for him or her. Denying the child's feelings and discouraging the child from expressing those feelings in open discussion also protects the adult from discomfort but denies the child the right to express the grief that may be a part of accepting the loss of a birth family and an identity with a biological family. Providing a supportive and nurturing environment is essential in helping a child move through and revisit stages of grief.

Adolescence. Although the focus of this text is the period of early childhood, it is important to reflect on the human way of coping with adoption throughout the life span. According to Erikson (1950), adolescents experience **ego identity versus identity confusion**. Teenagers often resist parental authority and become part of cliques as peer relationships and approval become increasingly important. As teenagers move toward independence, adoptive parents may become easy targets and biological parents idealized. Adoptive families may worry that the teenagers will become like the biological parents, and the teenagers may attempt to take on characteristics of the birth parents. It often becomes more and more important to acquire information about the birth parents. For many young people, acquisition of this information is a relief (Brodzinsky et al., 1992).

Young Adulthood. **Intimacy versus isolation** describes the period of young adulthood. This is often a time when couples date and marry and when children are born. Adoptees often worry about the genetic background that they bring to their offspring. They may also revisit feelings of grief because they are unable to share the joys of childbirth and grandchildren with their birth parents. Such concerns and feelings often increase an adoptee's interest in searching for birth parents.

Midlife. In midlife, adults experience a stage Erikson (1950) described as **generativity versus stagnation**. For many individuals, this is a busy time of life when aging adoptive parents may need care and when children may continue to need adult support. Adoptees recognize that the time to search is becoming limited as birth parents are also aging.

Late Adulthood. Finally, in late adulthood, individuals are sharing the wisdom gained through their life experiences with their children and grandchildren. During this period of **ego integrity versus despair**, those who remain in good physical and mental health may share the knowledge of their heritage and continue to pass on those values and beliefs that they have come to hold as important. Even though their birth parents may no longer be living, they may still search for knowledge about their birthright, siblings, and other family members as they resolve their personal conflicts about being adopted.

In addition to understanding the developmental changes that occur throughout the life of the adoptee, it is important to realize that some individuals are more resilient than others to stressful life events such as adoption or being raised in foster homes of varying quality. Wolin and Wolin (1993) identified seven characteristics that help people endure and overcome stressful life events: (a) a willingness to take initiative in engaging in appropriate experiences; (b) insight into the realities of the family situation; (c) healthy independence; (d) the ability to seek relationships with healthy people; (e) the ability to find outlets for creativity such as play, art, and writing; (f) humor; and (g) a sense of morality.

As teachers, caregivers, and administrators, it is important for us to see each child as an individual in the role that he or she plays in the adoption process. Although there are common challenges and joys, as well as reactions to those challenges and joys, each individual brings unique characteristics and needs to the building of families through adoption. Teachers will need some understanding of this as they select appropriate strategies for building bridges with families. While it is important for teachers to assure that children who are adopted feel like part of the classroom community, teachers should also play active roles in informing the community of contemporary adoption services. The resources in Figure 7.2 can be used to supplement a community-parent center or parent area at the center of the classroom.

FIGURE 7.2	Advocacy Strategies for Adoptive Families and Their Children

1. Create a handout for families about specific subsidies available for adoption, such as federal adoption tax credit, increasing employer assistance for adoption costs, low- to no-cost foster care adoptions, and ongoing government subsidies of foster care adoptions.

2. Search the database—*Connection Collection*—an online database of 270 abstracts of journal articles, books, reports, conference papers and proceedings, and literature reviews related to school–family–community connections (www.sedl.org/connections/resources/bibsearch.html)—To find articles and briefs about adoptions that you can use as handouts for your parent center at the entrance to your class.

3. Interview a family that has adopted a child from another country, to understand the process and adjustments for the family to prepare yourself for working with an international child that has been adopted by a U.S. family.

4. Create an area on your class Web site that provides a new case study of a nontraditional family each month (that you can access electronically) so families of children in your class can become more informed about other family structures. Start with a family who has adopted a child from another country.

THEMES 6, 7, AND 8   *in practice . . .*

The after-school program where you work serves children ages 5 to 12. Consequently, you have some brothers and sisters coming to the program from the local elementary school. Two of these children are brothers, the older adopted. The older child, Robert, is very small. The younger child, Adam, is very tall. These children are quite different, not only in size but also in facial characteristics and personalities. During a rainy afternoon, the brothers are building an indoor fort with several other boys. Ten-year-old Martin comments, "How can you be brothers? You don't even look alike! How can you be older? He's taller than you!" Later, Robert comes over and stands by you and says, "I wish I wasn't so different." What do you think would be the best way to assist Robert in dealing with his feelings? Remember the work of Brodzinsky.

As with the children to whom we give birth, the children we adopt as our own bring joy, love, and myriad other emotions. Added complexities, however, have to be considered at the time of adoption and throughout the life of the individual. This chapter has provided some insights into those complexities and some strategies that you can begin to employ as you create partnerships with these and other families.

Critical Concepts

1. Adoption laws came into effect in the 1800s, and since then, the shift has been away from adoption of older children into rural households who needed help with farmwork to adoption of infants.

2. Single-parent and gay- and lesbian-parent adoptions have been increasing as public sentiment about families has expanded to include more diverse systems.

3. The number of children available for adoption has decreased as birth control has become more accessible and more unwed mothers choose to keep their babies, so families are searching for alternative solutions such as international adoption.

4. While some Americans have been engaging in transracial adoption, some ethnic groups have protested this to preserve the cultural heritage of these children.

5. Many of the children available for adoption have one or more special need. These children are often placed with foster families and many foster families do adopt these children. It is important that families who adopt children with special needs receive follow-up support after the adoption process.

6. The adoption experience is not static. Adopted children will go through their search for self throughout their lifetime, with many influences on that development along the way.

Summary Statements

✓ Adoption is a complex issue because of the varied compositions of families seeking to adopt children, the declining number of children available for adoption, the varied geographic origins of children to be adopted, more comprehensive adoption laws, and more aggressive strategies employed by prospective parents to build families through adoption.

✓ Changes in adoption include telling the child that she or he is adopted.

✓ Historically, children were adopted to help families sustain their lives through labor.

✓ Stepparents constitute the highest percentage of adoptive parents.

✓ Increasing numbers of individuals and families are seeking adoption through international and transracial adoptions.

✓ Information is available about potential adoptions through Web sites such as that of the NAIC.

✓ It is important to assist children adopted from other races and cultures in maintaining their cultural heritage.

✓ International adoptions are governed by countries' specific rules and cultural customs.

✓ Families adopting children through international adoptions should be aware of the amount of time that children have spent in institutions and the quality of care that they have received to prepare for life at home.

✓ A majority of families who adopt children with special needs were foster families first.

✓ Parents who may wish to adopt children with special needs should consider many issues, including their emotional, physical, mental, and financial strengths.

✓ There are specific challenges to families who choose to become foster families.

✓ Most foster families who adopt are married couples.

✓ Each state has specific requirements for foster families.

✓ Each adult who follows a quest to adopt a child experiences an emotional journey alongside the child.

✓ Brodzinsky provides a model for understanding the adoptee's journey based on Erikson's eight stages of psychosocial development.

✓ Some people may be more resilient than others in dealing with issues such as adoption and placement in foster care. Characteristics of resilient people include initiative, insight, independence,

relationships, creativity, humor, and a sense of morality.

✓ Teachers and parents must respect the cognitive characteristics and the age of the individual in explaining the process of adoption to children who are adopted.

✓ Teachers and caregivers must be sensitive to the language and activities that they use in the classroom so that children with legal guardians other than birth parents are not excluded.

✓ Teachers must build partnerships with families to support children in their journey through adoption.

Research to Practice: Classroom Applications and Activities

1. You are observing the 3-year-olds in your classroom during an independent choice (free play) time of day. Three children are engaged in pretend play in the housekeeping area of the classroom. Soledad is rocking a baby doll, and Jason and Julia are putting on dress-up clothes. Julia tells Soledad and Jason, with some pride, that her mom will soon have a new baby. In response, Soledad announces, "I'm adopted." Jason asks what she means, to which she replies, "My mom and dad chose me!" Jason looks puzzled and again asks Soledad what she means. She responds, "I was so special, they adopted me." Rick and Jamal enter the area and distract Jason and Soledad from their conversation. You know that Soledad is adopted by the information sheet submitted by the family. After hearing the conversation among the children, what should your role in the situation be relative to the family, classroom activities, and Soledad?

2. Four-year-old Sara is African American. She was adopted at 6 months of age by

Mark and Patty. During a family conference, Mark and Patty (both are White) ask your advice on how to assist Sara in maintaining her African American heritage and how to prepare her for the issues that she will face as a member of a transracial family. What might your response be to Mark and Patty?

3. As a kindergarten teacher, you often experience the excitement of the birth of new siblings in the classroom. Children become excited and sometimes insecure, and sometimes they regress temporarily. This year, you have a somewhat different experience. Alli's mother and father are adopting a new baby. They are waiting for the birth mother to deliver the child and to make a final decision to give up the baby for adoption. The adoption is open, and the adoptive parents meet and talk with the birth mother. The adoptive mother plans to be present at the delivery. Alli has been told that she will have a new brother or sister whom her family will adopt from a mommy who will not be able to take care of her baby and will need help

from Alli and her mother and father. Alli's parents prepare for the new baby's arrival, including setting up the baby's room and purchasing clothing. Alli's mother attends the delivery. The baby's mother decides, after she sees her baby, that she will not give him up for adoption. As a teacher, what might you do to assist Alli in understanding the situation and in dealing with her disappointment?

4. You are a child-care provider working with school-age children. Each day, you supervise a homework period during a portion of your program. Josef is 8 years old and has a history of "losing" his homework and procrastinating until it is too late in the evening to complete his assignments at home. His parents ask that you supervise his homework after school, which you do. Josef becomes angry and tells you that he knows his real mother and father would not make him do homework after school. At this point, you realize that this is the first time Josef is indicating that he is adopted, and it may be a good time to discuss this with him. What do you do?

Learning materials that are self-correcting offer children opportunities to explore new concepts in ways that continue to build their sense of initiative.

Resources

Books

Gilman, L. (1992). *The adoption resource book.* New York: HarperCollins.

Keck, G. C., & Kupecky, R. M. (1995). *Adopting the hurt child: Hope for families with special needs.* Colorado Springs: Piñon.

Melina, L. R. (1986). *Raising adopted children: A manual for adoptive parents.* New York: HarperCollins.

Melina, L. R. (1989). *Making sense of adoption.* New York: HarperCollins.

Melina, L. R., & Rosia, S. K. (1993). *The open adoption experience.* New York: HarperCollins.

Sweet, O. R., & Bryan, P. (1996). *Adopt international: Everything you need to know to adopt a child from abroad.* New York: Farrar, Straus, & Giroux.

Wirth, E. M., & Worden, J. (1993). *How to adopt a child from another country.* Nashville: Abingdon.

Online Resource

National Adoption Information Clearinghouse, The Administration for Children and Families, 330 C Street SW, Washington, DC 20447 http://naic.acf.hhs.gov/

CHAPTER 8

The Care and Education of Children Living in Families with Alternative Lifestyles

A family is " . . . a group of persons who share common resources and a commitment to each other over time." . . . While understanding a family format requires objectivity, it does not require you to adopt it personally.

HILDEBRAND, PHENICE, GRAY, & HINES, 1996, P. 298

KEY TERMS

bisexual

donor insemination

gay

gay-headed families

heterosexism

heterosexuality

homophobia

homosexuality

identity

lesbian

lesbian-headed families

prejudices

self-concept

surrogate mother

two dads

two moms

1. Do adults choose a homosexual lifestyle, is this genetic, or is this a combination of biological and sociocultural?
2. What are the stages of identity for homosexual individuals?
3. What cultural themes effect gay and lesbian identities?
4. What factors influence the composition and makeup of a gay or lesbian family?
5. How are households headed by gay and lesbian parents challenged by societal, political, legal, and cultural beliefs?
6. How are the challenges facing lesbian parents different from and similar to those facing gay parents?
7. What is the impact on children who live in families with gay and lesbian parents?
8. What can teachers do to make the classroom welcoming to families headed by gay or lesbian parents?

 everal years ago, my sons were participating in a weeklong day camp. I had heard positive things about this camp and was surprised that neither child seemed to be enjoying this experience. Finally, my 8-year-old opened doors to a new world for me. "Mom, the camp counselor (who was about 14) asked me if I was gay." "Why?" was the best I could manage. "I don't know, Mom. He just said, 'What's the matter with you? Are you gay?'" Further talk revealed that this was the young counselor's way of chastising his wards when they did not listen to his directions. To say I was surprised is mild. This was, after all, a camp sponsored by a religious organization! Did they not monitor their adolescents' expressions of prejudice? Furthermore, I was not ready, as I should have been, for the question that came with this experience: "Mom, what does it mean to be gay?"

As my sons have moved through both elementary and middle grades, I have witnessed the use of such words as *stupid, retarded,* and, yes, *gay* among children and young adolescents. We have discussed the implications of these remarks in terms of their meaning, the feelings of others, and the prejudices that they express both wittingly and unwittingly. I am grateful that my sons no longer use these words. Perhaps it is a matter of maturity. I think, more likely, it has been the experiences that they have had in coming to know peers whose parents lead a gay or lesbian lifestyle and in witnessing the love that these young people have for their parents—the same type of love that they have for me.

Affirming the child's trust, love, and belongingness of family, regardless of our attitudes toward the family lifestyle, is the reason for inclusion of a discussion of family members who are gay, lesbian, or bisexual. We readily acknowledge families as the first and most important teachers of children. Knowledge about family lifestyle and individual growth and development is critical to supporting parents and family members in this role.

Pennington (1987) shared an anecdote of a situation in which a young girl accepts her mother's lesbian lifestyle until she encounters stereotypes at school:

When I was around five, my mom and Lois told me they were lesbians. I said good, and thought I want to be just like my mom. Well, when I reached about the fifth grade . . . I heard kids calling someone a faggot as a swear word, and I thought, "My God, they're talking about my mom." (p. 67)

Helping my sons to filter out the prejudicial remarks that they hear and to understand the meaning of these words for them and for others has, like many of my experiences in parenting, brought me to deal with my own ideas and knowledge about the alternative lifestyles of families. As an educator, this was critical. It brought me closer to understanding how I could support diverse families in caring for their children and how my feelings and attitudes might stand in the way of providing that support. Through self-reflection and discussion with others, the following themes emerged as topics for exploration:

Theme 1. We spend a great deal of time wondering why someone "chooses" a homosexual lifestyle. Is homosexuality the result of genetic predispositions or is it truly "chosen"?

Theme 2. There are stages that seem to characterize the unfolding process of coming to realize that one is homosexual. Understanding these stages assists us in understanding the experiences and decisions made by parents.

Theme 3. Culture influences the establishment of lesbian and gay identities. Some cultures are more accepting of individual lifestyles and offer more support to individuals with children.

Theme 4. Gay and lesbian families are formed in diverse ways. Some may form through the process of adoption. Others form through the merging of original families to become stepfamilies. Common to all is the decision about what roles adults will take with the children.

Theme 5. There are many challenges to families headed by gays and lesbians, including challenges for their children. These challenges relate not only to matters of choosing to lead an "authentic" life or to remain closeted, but also to common family concerns of finance, stress, communication, parenting, and conflict resolution.

Theme 6. There are many ways that teachers and caregivers can support children in their love for their families and support families in nurturing their children. This can occur regardless of whether the teacher or caregiver embraces the gay or lesbian lifestyle. Loving and caring for children in positive ways is the goal of the family as well as of the teacher and caregiver.

"CHOOSING" A HOMOSEXUAL LIFESTYLE

any family members spend a good deal of time searching for answers to why their child, grandchild, husband, or wife is homosexual and whether the family member was always homosexual or it was something that the person "chose." Seeking answers becomes a factor in the relationships among and between family members.

The question, of whether individuals are born as homosexuals or become homosexuals through the course of sociocultural experiences has been debated for decades. This question has become of extreme public interest as a result of (a) the political actions of the lesbian and gay liberation movement to obtain equal rights for gays and lesbians and (b) HIV and its association with homosexuality (DeCecco & Parker, 1995, p. 2).

In addition to the heightened awareness of issues facing gay and lesbian individuals is the ever-increasing effort to locate the biological roots of **homosexuality**. In a review of recent biological research conducted relative to the determinants of homosexuality, DeCecco and Parker (1995) noted that, thus far, investigation has occurred in three major areas: hormonal, genetic, and brain research (p. 5). They also note that in the late 1980s, the focus shifted from an emphasis on hormones to genetic research. Examples include the studies published by Pillard and Weinrich (1986) and, later, by Bailey and Pillard (1991) suggesting the inheritability of homosexuality.

The fascination with the variations in the brain, however, seems to have gained the greatest public attention during the 1990s. Simon LeVay's (1991) report in *Science* about the uniqueness of the hypothalamus of the brains of homosexual men compared with those of heterosexual men was followed by reports by Allen and Gorski (1992) that brain structures are, indeed, different.

Titles of articles in news magazines and newspapers, such as *Time*'s "Are Gay Men Born That Way?" (Gorman, 1991) and the *Wall Street Journal*'s "Study Raises Issue of Biological Basis of Homosexuality" (Winslow, 1991), highlight the importance being placed on finding a biological basis for homosexuality. Although the acquisition of such knowledge is important in the understanding of the various aspects of human growth and development, one should also wonder at the use of this knowledge to bring acceptance of homosexuality. We might ask ourselves and others some hard questions as we explore this aspect of humanness. Does homosexuality become more acceptable when it is something the person "cannot help"? Do family members become more comfortable with their homosexual child when they know that she or he did not "choose" this lifestyle? Can the course of one's life be biologically altered?

Perhaps we should address the human growth and development of those individuals who are homosexual using the same approach as we do with those individuals who are heterosexual. In doing so, we would take a broader perspective, looking at the intertwined relations between what is biological and what is sociocultural:

> This is not to deny a biological substratum to sexuality, but to emphasize the powerful role of social forces in shaping sexual conduct. *Time* in history, the requirements for *survival* at a specific time, the *geographic* location, and *sociocultural* expectations of a given period are also important factors. Because sexual learning occurs within specific historical eras and sociocultural settings, sexual conduct and its meanings vary across history and among cultures. (Troiden, 1993, p. 192)

THEMES 1 AND 2   *in practice . . .*

Reading about a given lifestyle is only one aspect of understanding someone's life. It is also important to hear viewpoints, experiences, and concerns of those living as homosexuals. You may have a friend or family member who is homosexual. Many universities have organizations that serve as support and advocacy groups for students who are homosexual. Read the following section about the journey toward self-identity to guide your questions. Work with your classmates to develop a list of questions addressing the journey of one or more individuals. Perhaps you might ask questions about parents' experiences or plans for parenting and what is needed to support parenting. Look for things that are in common with other individuals and things that are different. Edit questions for quality and evidence of respect for the individual. Depending on the class situation, conduct individual interviews or interview as a class. Discuss reactions to the interviews with class members. What did you find as common ground? What did you discover as challenges of the homosexual lifestyle?

STAGES OF SELF-IDENTITY

How do individuals view themselves in terms of **self-concept** and **identity**— that is, who they think and feel they are in relationship to others? Perhaps a clear understanding of the meaning of self-concept should be explored:

> Self-concept refers to people's mental images of themselves: what they think they are like as people. . . . Identity, on the other hand, refers to perceptions of self that are thought to represent the self definitively in specific social settings (such as the "doctor" identity at work, the "spouse" identity at home). (Troiden, 1993, p. 193)

According to Troiden (1993), the "homosexual identity is one of several identities incorporated into a person's self-concept" (p. 193). The homosexual identity may function as a self-identity, a perceived identity, a presented identity, or all three (Cass, 1983/1984). The homosexual identity is *self-identity* when people see themselves as homosexuals in terms of romance and sexuality. The homosexual identity is *perceived identity* when individuals think or know that other people view them as homosexuals. The homosexual identity is *presented identity* when people present themselves as homosexuals in social settings:

> Homosexual identities are most fully realized, that is, brought into concrete existence, in situations where self-identity, perceived identity, and presented identity coincide— where an agreement exists between who people think they are, who they claim they are, and how others view them. (Troiden, 1993, p. 194)

It is understandable that individuals who are gay or lesbian experience an increased desire to disclose their identity to other individuals who are gay or lesbian and to those with whom they work, live, and interact on a daily basis. Unlike overt physical characteristics such as gender or skin color, homosexuality is not something seen.

People with homosexual identities are therefore not only invisible to others, but also are actively misclassified by others as heterosexual. Homosexuals are thus required to negate explicitly this classification by disclosing their identities to prevent others from developing and acting on false expectations of their behavior (Strommen, 1993, p. 249). This explicit revealing of one's homosexuality to others, including family members, is known as *disclosure* (p. 249).

The realization that one is **gay** or **lesbian** is an unfolding process in which the individual comes to terms with her or his homosexuality. This "coming out," or self-realization of one's homosexuality (Strommen, 1993), may progress through a series of nonlinear stages such as those described by Vivenne Cass (1984). These broad developmental stages depict the use of coping strategies that are both cognitive and behavioral as one deals with one's identity. "In each stage, identity foreclosure in which individuals may choose not to proceed any further in the development of homosexual identity is possible" (p. 150). The stages proposed by Cass are as follows:

Stage 1: Identity confusion. During this time, individuals perceive that their thoughts, actions, and feelings may be seen as homosexual. Confusion occurs as the individual deals with previously held ideas about sexual orientation. A homosexual identity may be seen as positive or negative or be rejected entirely, precluding further development.

Stage 2: Identity comparison. "Having accepted the *potentiality* of a homosexual identity, the individual is then faced with feelings of alienation as the difference between self and nonhomosexual others becomes clearer" (Cass, 1984, p. 151). If the individual does not perceive the probability of a homosexual identity as negative, development will proceed and the individual may consider making contacts with other homosexuals as a means of lessening feelings of alienation.

Stage 3: Identity tolerance. The individual seeks out the company of other homosexuals to fulfill social, sexual, and emotional needs. These contacts may be seen as necessary, rather than desirable, and there is a selectiveness about choosing these contacts. The "quality of the contact with other homosexuals becomes an important factor that leads to different forms of behavior depending on whether the contact is perceived as positive or negative" (Cass, 1984, p. 151). Individuals maintain a public heterosexual image and a private homosexual image.

Stage 4: Identity acceptance. According to Cass (1984), this stage is a relatively peaceful time because the individual has come to terms with who she or he is and where she or he belongs. Friends and relatives may be told, but the heterosexual image is maintained at times when negative reactions would be forthcoming. If the individual accepts the idea of homosexuality as negative and can maintain a heterosexual image to avoid confrontation, development does not proceed.

Stage 5: Identity pride. The individual who has accepted homosexuality as a positive image expresses loyalty to homosexuals as a group and a sense of pride in one's homosexual identity. Anger may be expressed at the view of heterosexuals toward the gay community. Where confrontations are seen as consistently negative, identity fore-closure takes place.

Stage 6: Identity synthesis. "A homosexual identity is no longer seen as over-whelming the identity by which an individual can be characterized. Individuals come to see themselves as people having many sides to their character, only one part of which is related to homosexuality" (Cass, 1984, p. 152). The positive experiences that individuals have with some heterosexuals lead them to drop a good deal of their anger toward heterosexuals. A lifestyle in which one's homosexuality is no longer hidden is developed. One's view of self and the views believed to be held by others of self become integrated, and the public and private aspects of life are united. Again, according to Cass (1984), this process of integrated identity gives rise to a sense of peace and stability, and the process of identity formation is completed.

CULTURAL ISSUES AND EFFECTS ON GAY AND LESBIAN IDENTITIES

lthough the proposed continuum may seem rather straightforward, many issues affect an individual's progress in development toward identity formation as a homosexual:

> Prior to acquiring a gay or lesbian identity, one has a racial or ethnic identity, which is part of the core of childhood identity. Moreover, racial and ethnic groups experience prejudice and discrimination based on their minority status, which may place con-straints on various life options. (Garnets & Kimmel, 1993, p. 331)

Furthermore, the fact that individuals have sexual orientation in common does not mean that they have a great deal in common. Cohen (1991) saw a need for a model of sexual orientation based on multiplicity, not sameness, that examines overlapping identities and statuses of gender, race/ethnicity, and sexuality.

In their review of the literature relative to developing an understanding of cultural influences on the lesbian and gay male identity, Garnets and Kimmel (1993) noted several topics deserving of reflection and study:

1. *Religion* within the context of culture plays a significant role in the disclosure of a homosexual lifestyle. For example, African American gays and lesbians cannot be comfortable as a part of the religious community if their homosexuality is known. Also, Catholicism plays an important role in many Latino communities and purports homosexuality to be a sin (Garnets & Kimmel, 1993).

2. *Gender roles*, which may be made very specific in given cultures, "increase the difficulty for gay men and lesbians to carve out a nontraditional or androgynous role" (Garnets & Kimmel, 1993, p. 332). This appears to be true for Latino and Asian cultures, which see lesbianism as violating gender role expectations for women to be passive and to rely on and defer to men (Shon & Ja, 1982).

3. The *role of the family within the community* is another aspect that should be considered. The family may be seen as the primary vehicle for social support and an important tie to one's ethnic community. "The expectations of the group are often paramount over individual desires" (Garnets & Kimmel, 1993, p. 332). Furthermore, "a gay or lesbian identity may be perceived as a betrayal of one's own people, a loss of connection with one's own heritage, a public statement about something that reflects badly on one's culture or religion, a violation of gender role expectations of the culture, or a sign of assimilation into White mainstream culture" (p. 333). In some groups, including African Americans, a homosexual lifestyle is seen as negative in that individuals are not promoting survival of the group through propagation of the race (Icard, 1985/1986). Rates of disclosure to families appear to be relatively low among Asian, African American, and Latino gays and lesbians (Garnets & Kimmel, 1993).

4. "A fourth theme centers on the *process of reconciling one's ethnicity, gender, and sexual orientation* and has been referred to as forming a dual or triple identity (e.g., Latina, lesbian, and female)" (Garnets & Kimmel, 1993, p. 333). Multiple identity integration requires that individuals establish priorities among distinct communities, including racial/ethnic, gay/lesbian, and society at large. These groups may have conflicting value systems.

5. The *degree of the individual's interaction with, and integration into, the White majority culture*—in particular, the Anglo gay and lesbian culture and community—is an additional theme proposed for study by Garnets and Kimmel (1993). "If gay men and lesbians rely on groups and networks outside of their family and culture in which their sexual identity is more accepted, they may lose support for their racial or ethnic identity" (p. 334). Lesbians and gays of color may not receive the same types of psychological support from the gay community that their White counterparts receive and often are faced with racial issues in addition to sexual issues.

As with heterosexuals, the development of self-identity in homosexuals is affected not only by their biological origins but also by the sociocultural realities of their worlds. In addition to personal self-doubts relative to recognizing and accepting their sexual orientation, issues of prejudice, fear, and misunderstanding are still prevalent and vary across cultures and communities.

FORMATION OF GAY AND LESBIAN HOUSEHOLDS

I t is difficult to acquire exact estimates of the number of same-sex partners cohabiting in the United States today. This difficulty is attributable, in part, to the fear of reprisal in terms of loss of a job, loss of status as an individual within the community, or loss of custody of children sharing the household. Even though the increased acceptability of the gay and lesbian lifestyle and advocacy for rights for gays, lesbians, and their families have been accompanied by more information about the number of gays and lesbians cohabiting in the United States, numbers provided are still broad estimates. The *New York Times* ("The 21st Century Family," 1990) declared that 2 million fathers and mothers in this country were living a gay or lesbian lifestyle. In the 2000 U.S. Census, almost 600,000 households reported they were same-sex households (Simmons & O'Connell, 2003), but it may be a low estimate considering it does not count single gay or lesbians, and some homosexuals may not report their sexual identity for fear of reprisal. Of these households, 33 percent of same-sex female and 22 percent of same-sex male households reported having more than one child living with them. Other data report that gay and lesbian families live in 99.3 percent of counties in the United States (Smith & Gates, 2001), yet one in four gay or lesbian couples do not live near other gay couples (Gates & Ost, 2004).

A home is where we gather to love and care for one another.

For many individuals, the terms *parenthood* and *homosexuality* are seen as contradictory. "This contradiction, however, is of social not biological origin" (Sears, 1994, p. 140). **Gay-headed families** and **lesbian-headed families** are created in a variety of ways. Yet, same-sex couples and their children do not have the same legal rights to marriage, Social Security benefits, veteran's benefits and other benefits that heterosexual couples do (Oswald, Patterson, & Kuvalanka, 2004).

Women leading a lesbian lifestyle may have formerly been in heterosexual married or unmarried relationships in which children were conceived. They may also conceive through **donor insemination**, or they may adopt children. "The 'lesbian baby boom' and the increasing visibility of lesbians who become mothers through donor insemination or adoption constitute the most dramatic and provocative challenge to traditional notions both of the family and of the non-procreative nature of homosexuality" (Lewin, 1993, p. 19). Men leading a gay lifestyle may have been in married or unmarried heterosexual relationships through which children were born. Gays are also seeking to become parents after "coming out" (Bozett, 1989). They do this through adoption or foster care of biologically nonrelated children or through donor insemination or sexual intercourse with women who may be lesbian or heterosexual. In such a case, the woman may be seen as a coparent to the child, or a same-sex partner may be seen as the coparent (Patterson, 1992).

Whatever the source of children, in this situation the term *family* is used

> to denote a cohabitive living arrangement involving two same-sex adults and their children, biological, adopted or conceived through artificial insemination, from previous heterosexual relationships, marital or commonlaw. The relationship is characterized by mutual commitment, property sharing, and sexual intimacies similar to that found among cohabiting heterosexuals with children. (Baptiste, 1987, p. 224)

As with heterosexual single parents, it seems important to stress that the single parent who is gay or lesbian living alone with a child or children also constitutes a "family."

CHALLENGES TO ADULTS AND CHILDREN LIVING IN HOUSEHOLDS HEADED BY PARENTS WHO ARE GAY OR LESBIAN

This is an appropriate juncture to introduce the concept of homophobia. **Homophobia** refers to an irrational and distorted view of homosexuality or homosexual persons. Among heterosexual persons, homophobia is most commonly manifested as prejudice or general discomfort with homosexuality. The intensity of these feelings is modulated by several factors, including personal history, contact with homosexual individuals, and individual psychological makeup (Gonsiorek, 1993, p. 471). Homophobia and the discomfort of those who anticipate homophobic reactions of others has implications for the study of child development and families, the exploration of teaching practices that address inclusion of various family forms, and both private and public policy.

The lives of children and adults living within alternative lifestyles are clouded with myths, stereotypes, and prejudices about the individuals who head these families (i.e., lesbians, gays). These attitudes and stereotypes must be explored, as should the effects of such prejudices on the children who grow up amid them. We know that children suffer from the **prejudices** of adults and peers.

In addition, although there continues to be more openness in recognizing alternative family forms, there is still limited recognition of gay and lesbian partnerships by formal religions and in legal situations. Legislatures and judicial bodies are being called on to "define, redefine, and clarify the concept of family" (Wisensale & Heckart, 1993, p. 199). Churches are being challenged to sanctify the partnership as a marriage recognized by the church and its community.

The traditional family—that is, a family headed by a mother and a father living in the same household with their children—has had more rights than the nontraditional family has (Wisensale & Heckart, 1993). Examples include the rights to insurance and death benefits, to inherit, and to authorize emergency medical care. As definitions of who constitutes a family change, members of nontraditional family forms are challenging the withholding of rights for partners and children. Wisensale and Heckart (1993) cited several cases, including *Marvin v. Marvin* (1976), *Renshaw v. Heckler* (1986), and *Watts v. Watts* (1987), in which the rights of unmarried partners are supported. They also note cases that have been historic for the gay and lesbian community. The decisions in *Baker v. Nelson* (1971) and *Jones v. Hallahan* (1973) clearly denounced same-sex marriages, but the decision in *Braschi v. Stahl Associates Co.* (1989) found that a gay couple's relationship went beyond that of roommates and that the individual who survived his partner's death of AIDS was considered family under New York City's rent-control regulations. The surviving partner was, therefore, able to maintain the rent-controlled apartment that the couple had shared.

In response to the growing numbers of partnerships, local governments and some corporations are adopting domestic partnership laws and arrangements. These laws and arrangements allow unmarried partners benefits traditionally deemed for spouses. Wisensale and Heckart (1993) surveyed 14 cities with domestic partnership laws: the California cities of Los Angeles, Berkeley, West Hollywood, Santa Cruz, San Francisco, and Laguna Beach; Takoma Park, Maryland; Madison, Wisconsin; Seattle, Washington; New York and Ithaca, New York; Ann Arbor, Michigan; Minneapolis, Minnesota; and West Palm Beach, Florida. Thirteen of the 14 communities passed city ordinances that recognized domestic partnerships, 7 required the domestic partners to register, 5 included medical benefits, and 13 allowed for bereavement leave.

Wisensale and Heckart (1993) also surveyed corporations and found that of those surveyed in 1992, 14 corporations or nonprofits offered domestic partnership benefits to employees. Individuals were required to register their domestic partnerships with their employers.

It does seem reasonable that, as in heterosexual marriages, employers require employees to register or name their domestic partners for the purposes of accountability in providing benefit packages. For male–female partnerships, this may not pose a problem. It also may not pose a problem for same-gender partners. For partners who are gay or lesbian *and* parents, however, this disclosure could be problematic and bring discomfort. As stated by Sears (1994), two of the greatest challenges for families with gay, lesbian, or **bisexual** parents are securing and maintaining custody of children and disclosing the nature of their lifestyle to their children. These challenges are, in part, a result of heterosexism in our society. According to Sears, **heterosexism** refers to

> the presumption of superiority and exclusiveness of heterosexual relationships—(it) is evidenced in the assumption that parents of all children are heterosexual or that a heterosexual adult will *prima facie* be a better parent than one who is homosexual. (p. 148)

Baptiste (1987) addressed specific fears held by parents who are gay or homosexual that their children will be taken away from the family by grandparents, ex-spouses, or other forces. These fears force some families into secrecy about the sexual orientation of the adults and into isolation from those who might reveal their homosexuality.

Although both families headed by gays and by lesbians face disapproval of their lifestyle by those whom they encounter in the course of daily living, gays face even greater burdens in this area because two men living together raising children are seen by many as more suspect and unacceptable than two women in the same situation. Both types of families face societal concerns that children raised in these families will be gay, will be exposed to illicit sexual behaviors, and will be at risk for AIDS.

Many of these concerns are grounded in the myths and misconceptions that surround the gay and lesbian lifestyle. In an effort to explore and "bring light" to these notions, Garnets and Kimmel (1993) engaged in extensive reviews of the literature and provided the following summary statements that typify stereotypic attitudes:

> *Myth 1:* Homosexuals do not want enduring relationships—and cannot achieve them anyway . . .
> *Myth 2:* Gay relationships are unhappy, abnormal, dysfunctional, and deviant . . .

Myth 3: "Husband" and "wife" roles are universal in intimate relationships . . .
Myth 4: Gays and lesbians have impoverished social support networks. (pp. 397–403)

Although these concerns seem universal for both gay and lesbian individuals and their families, other concerns are specific to gays and to lesbians. These issues relate to coming out and to parenting.

Challenges to Men Who Are Both Gay and Fathers

As discussed, men who are gay may become fathers through adoption from a nonrelated source or through a **surrogate mother** using the gay father's sperm. The majority of gay fathers, however, are engaged in heterosexual relationships that generally include marriage prior to adopting a gay lifestyle. Many of these individuals remain in the heterosexual marriage even though they perceive themselves as gay, to maintain their relationships with their children. A major move in their lives involves divorcing their wives and a heterosexual way of life, risking a relationship with their children, and adopting a gay lifestyle.

Achieving an identity as a gay male and as a father follows a progression:

> By participating over time in both the father world and the gay world, the gay father progresses from being attached primarily to the heterosexual world to a primary connection with the gay world. This progression is achieved by means of disclosing his gay identity to nongays and his father identity to gays and receiving mostly positive sanctions, which have an integrative effect. (Bozett, 1993, p. 439)

This progression leads to *integration*, which Bozett (1993) defined as "a state in which the gay and father identities are congruent, and are appropriately overtly manifested; both identities are accepted by both the father himself and others in his proximate social worlds as nondichotomous" (p. 439).

In his studies of this transition, Miller (1978, 1979, 1983, 1986) organized data along a 4-point continuum: covert behavior, marginal involvement, transformed participation, and open endorsement. Although drawn to the gay world, men operating at a point of *covert behavior* do so on the periphery of the gay world, compartmentalizing their family lives and gay activities. At the point of *marginal involvement*, individuals engage in same-sex behavior. Although their self-identities are homosexual, their public identities remain heterosexual. At the point of *transformed participation*, the individual has a self-identity that is gay and, to some extent, has disclosed this aspect of his life to the public. His wife and parents have been told, but not his children and employer. He has moved beyond only the sexual aspects of being gay and has embraced those aspects that are both emotional and social. At the *open endorsement* point on the continuum, men are public about their lifestyle and have self-identities that are homosexual. Many have custody of their children and spend time away from work with their partners, children, and networks of friends.

In his studies of gay fathers and their move from a heterosexual to homosexual lifestyle, Miller (1978, 1979, 1983, 1986) drew some conclusions. In his review of Miller's work, Bozett (1993) summarized these conclusions in a succinct and helpful manner:

1. Falling in love with another man was the event most responsible for initiating the move.

2. The progression across lifestyles was hindered by concerns relative to economics, wives, family pressure, homophobia, and perceived lack of support. For other gays, poor health and religious and moral scruples were also concerns.

3. Gay relationships were found to be more harmonious than marital relationships.

4. Gayness was found to be compatible with fathering.

5. Men who came out found less discrimination than those closeted anticipate.

6. Daughters tend to be more accepting than sons, although both sons and daughters felt their father's honesty brought them closer.

7. Few families reported neighborhood homophobia directed at the father. However, children may have only told those they felt would be accepting.

8. Children of gay fathers showed no evidence of disproportionate homosexual lifestyles. Of the children who were homosexual, there were more lesbian daughters than gay sons.

9. As men moved across the continuum toward integration, their sense of well-being increased and occurrence of stress-related illnesses decreased. A supportive gay community was seen as responsible for much of this heightened sense of well-being. (pp. 441–442)

Gay fathers have more trouble coming out than do lesbian mothers. Gay fathers also have more trouble disclosing their homosexuality to their children than do lesbian mothers (Murray & McClintock, 2005). This is particularly true of gay men who are African American (Bozett, 1993). Fathers fear that they will damage their children, be rejected by their children, or upset their children; that their children will not understand; or that peers will reject their children. Some simply think that it is not their children's business. Although most children of lesbian mothers find out from their mothers, children of gay fathers are more likely to find out from their mothers, to be told by both parents, or to overhear conversations, or they simply figure out the situation themselves (Wyers, 1984).

The average age of children finding out about their mothers' sexual preference is 8, and for fathers, 11.1 (Wyers, 1984). Some studies indicate that children who learn that their parents are gay or lesbian at an earlier age have fewer difficulties than those who find out later (Harris & Turner, 1986; Turner, Scadden, & Harris, 1985). Another study found no significant difference in anxiety levels among different-age children of same-sex couples, although fathers did wait longer than mothers to disclose, perhaps due to the stronger social stigmatism for gay parents (Murray & McClintock, 2005). In studies (Harris & Turner, 1986; Turner et al., 1985) of gay fathers and lesbian mothers, researchers note that homosexual adults heading families may try harder to create stable home lives and positive relationships with their children than one would expect from traditional families. Attempts to engage children with role models of the opposite sex were made by both mothers and fathers. Roles within the home were more androgynous, with partners not taking specific gender-related roles. Gay fathers were seen as nurturing and reported positive relationships with their children. Typical parenting issues were held in common with heterosexual families.

My Two Daddies

I can't imagine two better parents than Robert and Michael. My two dads have great friends, two women—Clara and Grace, a couple who I also think of as family, because Grace agreed to be inseminated by Michael to have me, Alicia, 12 years ago. Clara was inseminated by Robert and their son, Brendan, is now 10 years old. I am growing up in San Francisco with this extended family and am around many other gay and lesbian couples who also have children. I have lots of grandparents, but none of them live in San Francisco.

My parents have always been open about their lifestyle, and there are plenty of other children in the San Francisco area who live in similar same-sex parent families, so I guess I just thought my family was normal. I do have some friends with heterogeneous parents, but they seem to be living the same family life as I am, with some parent arguments, great family dinners, chores, and challenges. Robert does a lot of the cooking and carpooling for soccer practice, while Michael does a lot of the cleaning. Both of my parents work—my dad Robert is an architect who can work at home sometimes, and my dad Michael is a landscape consultant, so he is always going somewhere with his truck full of plants. Robert is more strict than Michael. Michael is always the parent who stops to play with me—anything I want—swinging, card games, even swimming. I overheard Robert saying that he is surprised he is as strict as he is because his parents were very easy on him and gave him a lot of space.

Robert's parents live in the Los Angeles area and they come to visit often. They seem pretty accepting of Robert being gay, and they said how happy they are that Robert, their only child, has given them a grandchild. I don't know Michael's parents very well, because they live in Washington, DC. Michael's parents don't seem to accept that he is gay, though they do send Christmas cards and call us once a month. They tell us about spending time with their other grandchildren who live nearby in the Virginia area. This sort of bothers me, but I forget about it since I have other grandparents, too—Clara and Grace's parents.

Clara and Grace live about five blocks from us, and their families have accepted their relationship. Those grandparents visit us often. Clara's whole family lives in Portland, and Grace's family lives near Berkeley. Brendan, their son (I call him my brother), sometimes shares with me that the kids at school give him a hard time about having two mothers. My dads said that boys sometimes have a harder time accepting having a different family from the families with a mom and dad we see on TV. Brendan once hit a boy at school who said his moms are lesbians. I am glad I have a brother to play with and talk to, but we don't always agree, I guess like any brother and sister. I sometimes wonder what I will be like when I grow up. Dad says I can be anything I want to be and I know he means that.

Challenges to Women Who Are Both Lesbians and Mothers

"Lesbians and gay males typically define themselves as homosexual at different ages and in different contexts" (Troiden, 1993, p. 204). Whereas males usually begin the process of self-identification as homosexual during their teens, females generally define themselves as homosexual during their twenties (Calfia, 1979). Lesbians see themselves as homosexual in the context of meaningful, emotional relationships with other women; this is in keeping with sex-role socialization patterns of women (Troiden, 1993).

Lesbians appear more likely to have been involved in heterosexual marriages. This may be attributable to such factors as the later age at which they begin to define themselves as homosexual and family pressures to marry and have children and to conform to societal expectations (Strommen, 1993). Although some lesbian couples seek donor insemination as a means of having children, the majority of children in lesbian relationships are from heterosexual marriages of one or both partners.

How do women view their roles as mothers and lesbians? Scant research appears to have been conducted on this aspect of being lesbian, as compared with the same aspects of the lives of men who are gay. Strommen (1993) suggested that "lesbians view the mother role as an aspect of their identity as a woman, and therefore do not experience the role conflict that gay men do" (p. 257).

Regardless of their comfort in the roles of mother and lesbian, women face societal and judicial prejudices and concerns in their attempts to parent their children similar to those faced by fathers who are gay. Falk (1993) noted that, with respect to child custody issues, "Legal decision makers often focus on the mother's homosexuality without even attempting to establish a causal relationship between the mother's sexual orientation and the child's welfare" (p. 422). Concerns include the amount of time that the parent will spend with the child as compared with pursuing her relationship with another woman, the possibility that the child will become homosexual or be exposed to sexual behaviors considered deviant, or that the child will suffer the social stigma of having a lesbian parent.

While women who are lesbian are becoming more open about their lifestyle, issues about child custody often prompt many who are mothers to remain closeted. According to Coleman (1985), disclosure of a wife's homosexuality or bisexuality almost always leads to divorce. Male partners appear generally to react in an angry manner, and disclosure to a male spouse is often avoided. A husband may view his wife's homosexual feelings as a kind of infidelity and, in keeping with the double standard between men and women, view this as worse than a man's infidelity (Coleman, 1985). This may be a source of the husband's anger and the ongoing legal battles for child custody that often ensue (Hanscombe & Forster, 1982). Those lesbian mothers who were married when their children were born experience two kinds of transitions on leaving their heterosexual life: (a) They "came out" to themselves and perhaps to others, and (b) they left their husbands. In addition to these transitions, lesbian mothers experience similar issues as do single, heterosexual mothers—leaving a marriage; getting a divorce; and dealing with its legal, economic, and emotional ramifications (Lewin, 1993, p. 20). In her interviews with women who have gone through this experience, Lewin (1993) noted a common theme that seemed to emerge, in which women talked of finally feeling comfortable and "at home" with themselves. (As noted earlier, lesbian mothers are more likely to disclose their lifestyle to their children themselves and at an earlier time than gay fathers do.)

A woman's choice to disclose her homosexual identity is affected by many factors. We have already discussed fear of losing custody of children and reprisals by the spouse in custody matters. We must also be aware that given cultures may view this revelation with openness or with anger and denial. Oliva Espin's (1993) observation of the Latino community is an example:

> Although emotional and physical closeness among women is encouraged by Latin culture, overt acknowledgement of lesbianism is even more restricted than in mainstream American society. . . . Because of the importance placed on family and community by most Hispanics, the threat of possible rejection and stigmatization by the Latin community becomes more of a psychological burden for the Hispanic lesbian. (p. 353)

Loiacano (1993) detailed similar findings in the African American community and further noted that support groups for lesbians often do not provide the kind of affirmation that Anglo members receive. Such support is needed because "lesbianism is largely considered incompatible with the role expectations of the women in the Black community" (p. 365).

In a study of Asian American lesbians and gays, Chan (1993) found that these individuals identified more with their lesbian and gay organizations than with their Asian American identities. Their desire was to be accepted by both groups. In the Asian American community, however, being lesbian might be seen as a rejection of one's primary role and obligation to a family, particularly to one's responsibility to carry on the family through marriage and the bearing of children. Such behavior would be seen not only as the rejection of the mother–child role but also as an indication that the parents had failed in their role of raising their daughter. To make families of all compositions feel welcome in their classrooms, teachers may need to seek information from resources outside of their regular reading. The suggestions in Figure 8.1 include references and strategies for teachers' self-reflection on appropriate practices.

Children of Gay and Lesbian Parents

"Central to the problems faced by children of lesbian and gay parents is the heterosexism and homophobia rampant in today's society" (Sears, 1994, p. 148). Surrounding this problem is the reluctance of society to recognize households headed by gay and lesbian individuals as "families."

Studies have been conducted to determine the effects of being raised by gay or lesbian parents. Some of these studies have evolved from the homophobic viewpoint of proving that this type of lifestyle is detrimental to the children. Others are designed to disprove the homophobic view by determining that children raised by parents who are gay or lesbian are as healthy and happy as those raised in heterosexual families. Regardless of the acknowledged or unacknowledged viewpoint of the researcher, much remains to be studied about children raised in alternative family forms, particularly with respect to the diversity of the individuals and their strengths and needs within the family and to the response of the broader community, including schools and child-care providers.

Patterson (1992) conducted a comprehensive review of existing studies of children regarding their own sexual identities (gender identity, gender-role behavior, sexual orientation), aspects of personal development (separation–individuation, psychiatric

FIGURE 8.1	Advocacy Strategies That Support and Respect Alternative Lifestyles

1. Interview a lawyer who has defended a suit of a married parent with children who realized that he or she is homosexual and got a divorce, but wanted custody of the children. What are some issues the lawyer can share with you that you should consider if you were the teacher of the child? (Of course, the lawyer will protect the anonymity of the family.)

2. Read one of the family interview articles in the *Gay Parent* magazine (http://www. gayparentmag.com/11323.html). The story "Yellow Hawk and the Child of His Heart" is one example of a story about a family with a gay or lesbian parent(s). Make a list of issues that this family may be confronted with due to the parents' sexual preference that may not be an issue for a parent who is heterosexual.

3. Make a list of reading and resource materials for families with alternative lifestyles you would have in your parent resource area at the entrance to your classroom.

4. If you were a Head Start teacher, you would make home visits. Are there any ways you might prepare differently to do a home visit to a family with an alternative lifestyle than you would a family with male and female parents? Are there some questions or activities you might avoid or modify?

5. You are planning a parent night, and you know that some of the parents are opposed to families with alternative lifestyles for various reasons, some religious. Two families of children in your class that you know of have "two mommies." What preparations or themes for the parent night might you plan to allow for all families to feel welcome?

6. Enlist the help of a community person you know has experience with alternative lifestyles (personally or professionally) as a "cultural guide" (refer to the ACLU Web site [http://aclu.org] and search for "Lesbian and Gay rights; parenting" for up-to-date articles and legislation) to help you prepare to work with families with alternative lifestyles. Make a list of questions that you have, and make a list of goals you have for making your classroom environment welcoming for all families.

evaluations, assessments of behavior problems, self-concept, personality, locus of control, moral judgment, and intelligence), and social relationships. In her review of studies conducted on 300 children across 12 samples, Patterson concluded that no evidence has been found for "significant disturbances of any kind in the development of sexual identity among these individuals" (p. 1032). Patterson also concluded that existing work reveals no empirical support that children of gay and lesbian parents suffer in the area of personal development, including intellectual and moral development. Existing work also supports the notion that children of gay and lesbian parents are able to form and maintain positive social relationships with both peers and adults. In their meta-analysis of studies of the effects of gay and lesbian parents on child outcomes, Stacy and Biblarz (2001) suggested that sociological research has not addressed or factored in the social stigma of homosexuality that weighs heavily on polical matters such as same-sex marriage, adoption, and religious taboos that impact both the children and the families. Stacy and Biblarz suggested that both genetics and sociocultural factors should be considered. In addition, the levels of development of children and their parents during significant life events such as adoption or marriage factor into the overall family dynamics (see also Murray & McClintock, 2005; Patterson, 2000; Patterson & Chan, 1999; Tasker & Golombok, 1997).

These studies appear to indicate no differences in the psychological health of children growing up in families headed by heterosexuals or by homosexuals. "Common sense tells us, however, that growing up with two mothers or two fathers is different from growing up with a mother and a father, or with a single parent, for that matter" (Casper, Schultz, &Wickens, 1992, p. 113). Children may be learning to live in blended families, with adoptive parents, with **two moms**, between households headed by heterosexual parents and households headed by homosexual parents, and with children who are siblings and those who are not.

These are complex issues for both adults and children. We do know that "in an oppressive situation such as lesbian families face, redefining their lesbian family as a strong family model instead of a deficit model may lessen the impact of homophobia" (Wright, 1998, p. 12).

In his work with educators attempting to support families headed by individuals who may be gay, lesbian, or bisexual, Sears (1994) summarizes research into statements that may be helpful to teachers and child-care providers:

- Children are less accepting when a parent of the same gender as the child "comes out" than when a parent of the other gender discloses sexual identity.
- Children of a lesbian or gay parent are no more likely to define themselves as homosexual than children of heterosexual parents, nor are they any more likely to display atypical sex-role preferences.
- Lesbian, gay, and bisexual parents often seek to provide their children with a variety of gender role models.
- The earlier the disclosure to the child, the fewer problems in the parent–child relationship.
- Children of a lesbian or gay parent follow typical developmental patterns of acquiring sex-role concepts and sex-typed behaviors.
- Children of homosexual parents who have experienced marital turmoil face similar difficulties common to children of divorce of heterosexual parents.
- Gay fathers may have a more difficult time disclosing their sexuality to their children than lesbian mothers and the coming-out process is more difficult for men who are gay fathers with children at home.
- Children of gay fathers are less likely than those of lesbian mothers to know of their parent's sexual identities.
- Sons are less accepting than daughters when learning that a parent is gay.
- As children enter adolescence, the likelihood increases that they will experience peer harassment about their parents' sexual identities and engage in a variety of self-protective mechanisms.
- Gay fathers are more likely than lesbian mothers to report their children experiencing difficulty with peer harassment because of the parent's homosexuality. (pp. 151–152)

As we have discussed, it is difficult for many people to consider the household headed by one or more parents who are gay or lesbian a family. It is also difficult for many people to recognize that such families face many of the same dilemmas that stepfamilies or blended families do. Consider the mother who leaves a heterosexual marriage and forms a partnership with another lesbian as one example. Baptiste (1987) addressed issues that face children raised in stepfamilies. In addition to those issues that are common to children growing up in heterosexual stepfamilies, children growing up in gay and lesbian stepfamilies have unique concerns. "The primary complaint of children living in gay stepfamilies is feeling isolated from peers and their community" (p. 229). There is also a lack of identification with parents who, by and large, grew up in heterosexual families and cannot relate their own experiences as children to those of their offspring. Baptiste further notes that even though children know about their parents' homosexuality, the need to keep it quiet or secret from others wears on the children and, in a sense, creates a closeted effect. Additional problems may arise with the parent's desire to create stepsibling relationships with the partner's children. Because children may not know that the adults are partners and because the relationship has no legal sanctions, children may become confused as to the nature of these relationships and will not be heavily vested in building and maintaining such relationships.

Wright's (1998) *Lesbian Step Families: An Ethnography of Love* chronicles the lives of five lesbian stepfamilies. Issues of building relationships that are common in all stepfamilies appear in Wright's qualitative study. These generally involve (a) the role of the nonbiological mother regarding issues such as parenting and discipline, (b) maintenance of positive relationships with nonpresent biological parents, (c) the attitudes of the children toward the stepparent and characteristics of the children, (d) the impact of the personal histories of both adults, and (e) job stress.

Families need a great deal of family, community, and societal support to raise their children. This support is also needed by those in alternative families. Differences in support between families with different-sex parents and those with same-sex parents lie in how and from whom same-sex parents receive support. Same-sex parents can avoid isolation by having those with similar lifestyles and those who are accepting of the lesbian lifestyle available for support:

> Positive resources include a tolerant community, a significantly open lesbian/gay population, other lesbian families to socialize with, any legal status for lesbian/gay families and people, and a connection with supportive heterosexual friends, families, and acquaintances. (Wright, 1998, p. 192)

The quality of support provided to the adults within the family has a great deal to do with the quality of life for the children. Children are affected by the treatment that their parents receive. Children suffer when those whom they love and trust suffer. As stated, as teachers and caregivers, our responsibility is to provide experiences that are loving and appropriate for the young child. The relationships we build with families headed by gay or lesbian parents are a reflection of that responsibility. Figure 8.2 provides suggestions for teachers and caregivers to examine their beliefs and practices to build those relationships.

THEMES 3, 4, AND 5   *in practice . . .*

Read the article "The Attitudes of Undergraduate College Students Toward Gay Parenting" by Crawford and Solliday (see "Resources"). As a class, reach a consensus about your responses to the situation involving the adoption of a child. Do you and your peers feel the same way as the college students in the study, or do you vary in the attitudes expressed? Discuss reactions that you have in common and those that are different. How might those attitudes impact your role as a teacher or caregiver of young children?

THEMES 3, 4, AND 5   *in practice . . .*

Investigate the types of advocacy and support groups available in your community and state for individuals who are gay or lesbian and their families. Parents, Families and Friends of Lesbians and Gays (PFLAG; www.pflag.org) is an example that can be researched through the Internet. What is the specific objective of the organization? What issues are addressed? What type of support is provided to families?

Granted, some may have a difficult time dealing with "two moms" or **"two dads,"** not to mention a parent who is bisexual. Their concerns stem from religious beliefs, personal values, and fears. As professionals, we cannot disregard their feelings. We can, however, keep our focus on the children—their joys and triumphs, their smiles and personalities, their successes and challenges. We can remember that parents are parents first. This is our task.

FIGURE 8.2   Strategies for Teachers Working with Children Whose Parents Are Gay or Lesbian

Examining Our Own Beliefs and Attitudes

Although schools have given attention to addressing the needs of gay and lesbian students in a nondiscriminatory manner, little attention has been given to addressing the needs of children who come from alternative family structures. "If we are to truly serve all of our students, then educators must become more aware of the challenges facing lesbian, gay, and bisexual parents and their children" (Sears, 1994, p. 140).

The school serves as a social institution that represents the values of a dominant culture and socializes children into mainstream cultural norms:

FIGURE 8.2	Continued

Young children with gay parents who enter school for the first time, and who previously held an unquestioning acceptance of the naturalness of their family, are suddenly confronted with countless situations in which totally different family configurations are the norm. These children must contend with the frequent representation of *their* family configuration as deviant or, perhaps most common, with the fact that it is not represented at all. (Casper et al., 1992, p. 115)

A child-care director recently shared her concerns about several staff members who avoided greeting and talking with a child's lesbian parents. Our focus should always remain on providing a loving and developmentally appropriate environment for the child. Doing so requires that we first acknowledge the adult's role as the child's parent and show respect for the child's family in this context. We should regard this aspect of the adult's life before we regard her or his career, ethnic origin, economic situation, or **heterosexuality** or homosexuality.

Such acceptance may require that we examine out attitudes about alternative lifestyles and how those attitudes affect our work with children and their families. Many of these attitudes are present in the behaviors we exhibit. Consider the following questions:

- Do you avoid greeting a mother because you are uncomfortable with her arrangement with a female partner?
- Have you asked a child not to engage in play about two moms in the dramatic play area?
- Have you made efforts to find out about the lifestyle of a dad who you suspect is gay even though he has not disclosed this information to you?
- Do you continue to represent a family as composed of a mother and a father in daily activities with children?
- Have you labeled a child as emotionally traumatized because of her or his family situation even though the child seems happy and interacts well with other children?
- Have you adopted a "deficit" approach to viewing the family, "knowing" that the homosexuality of adults heading the family is destructive to the child's growth and development?

Many of these behaviors are based in our own fears about what is different and unknown and about what threatens who we are in some way. This may involve our religious beliefs, personal values, and cultural practices. "A generation ago, negative biases on the part of school personnel, neighbors, and often even relatives made it hard for heterosexual mothers who divorced. The problem of prejudice against nonstereotypic families is not new" (Clay, 1990, p. 33).

As teachers, administrators, and caregivers, we must be willing to look at, and deal with, our attitudes and teaching practices as they relate to the topic of homosexuality so that we can demonstrate to children and adults that we value their families and want to support them:

When the teacher is not gay but the parents are, the cultural values and meanings carried within a lesbian and gay identity have to be added to class, racial, ethnic, and other cultural differences that create rich contexts for one's life, but [may] not be easily understood by an outsider. (Casper et al., 1992, p. 121)

(Continued)

FIGURE 8.2   Continued

Educating Ourselves

We must also be willing to learn more about these aspects of homosexuality to alleviate the myths and misconceptions that may exist in our minds and the minds of our fellow teachers. This is not to say that we must forfeit personal values. It simply means that we must learn more about other lifestyles to support the children and their families.

Just as we consider the uniqueness of each child, we consider the uniqueness of the family. Guidelines for working with families headed by gays and lesbians must be considered and implemented in light of the particular needs of each family.

Guidelines for Interactions

Possible guidelines (Baptiste, 1987; Sears, 1994) that may be adapted for children during the early childhood years are as follows:

- Use language that shows you value and recognize the diversity of cultures and families within your classroom. Asking children to take something home to "mom" or "dad" can be detrimental to children of gay or lesbian parents. Assuming that fathers are heads of households is also misleading for both single and married parents.
- Avoid "quizzing" a child to determine the lifestyle of parents who have not chosen to disclose this to you. Trust is an important part of the young child's life. The child must be able to trust caregivers, just as the child trusts his or her family.
- View a parent as a child's father or mother, not as the child's gay father or lesbian mother. Children need to witness teachers and parents building relationships through the actions that they see, including talking, making eye contact, and exhibiting interest in discussing the child.
- Respect and honor the right of parents to maintain silence about their homosexuality. As we have learned, while parents need support in raising their children, they know best about the quality of support they will receive should they disclose their lifestyle in some communities.
- If a parent chooses to disclose her or his homosexuality to you, avoid prejudicial remarks or behaviors. This can lead to seeing the child in a different light—perhaps in terms of deficits.
- Realize that the parent is the most important person to the child and that this relationship should be nurtured by the child's teacher or caregiver. Avoid discriminating by excluding the parent from parent involvement activities.
- Be knowledgeable about homosexuality as a lifestyle. Understand how it affects children, including the issues that children have in common with all children and those issues that are different.
- Be alert to any situations in which a child might be teased because of a parent's lifestyle. Put an immediate halt to the teasing. Alert parents should such problems occur so that they may provide additional support for their child.
- Be aware of other issues that are a part of a child's life, including being adopted, being a part of a stepfamily, or experiencing the divorce of parents. Remember, being a member of a household with an alternative lifestyle is only one aspect of the child's world.

FIGURE 8.2   Continued

Preparing the Classroom to Support Children and Families

- Become familiar with organizations and support groups for families within your community.

- In written materials designed for adults (e.g., policy manuals, forms, newsletters, and handbooks), broaden terms to include *parent* rather than simply *mother* or *father*. This applies in many situations in which children do not share a home with a mother or father, for whatever reason.

- Provide visual representations of family/cultural diversity in classroom displays and children's books. This begins with photos of the children in the classroom and of the children and their families. Children are given the opportunity to share who is in the photo with other children.

Children's Book List

Combs, B. (2001). *1, 2, 3: A family counting book*. Ridley Park, PA: Two Lives.

Combs, B. (2001). *A, B, C: A family alphabet book*. Ridley Park, PA: Two Lives.

Newman, L. (2000). *Heather has two mommies* (D. Souza, Illus.). Los Angeles: Alyson Wonderland.

Vigna, J. (1995). *My two uncles*. Morton Grove, IL: Whitman.

Willhoite, M. (1990). *Daddy's roommate*. Los Angeles: Alyson Wonderland.

Willhoite, M. (1995). *Daddy's wedding*. Los Angeles: Alyson Wonderland.

For further children's books and ideas for using literature to develop partnerships with diverse families, see Lilly and Green (2004).

Involvement in Decision Making

Depending on the nature of the school organization, parents may also be involved in decision making relative to the inclusion of materials depicting gay/lesbian lifestyles within classrooms. For more information about this process, you may wish to read about Jennifer Lackey's (1997) experience in doing so in an Oregon preschool cooperative. As a board member and parent, she offers a unique and thorough look at this democratic process.

THEME 6   *in practice . . .*

A mother brings her 5-year-old son to school one morning and asks to speak with you, his teacher. She indicates she has "found out" that another child's father is gay and living with a man. She expresses concern for the gay father's son as well as concern that her son will get the "wrong idea." How might you handle this situation?

Critical Concepts

1. Taking a broad perspective of how individuals come to the conclusion they are gay or lesbian allows for the same respect for the biological and sociocultural factors that effect all people's development and lifestyles.

2. Homosexual identity is an identity hidden to others, unlike gender or skin color, yet it is one of several identities that are incorporated into a person's self-concept. It is important for teachers to realize that some people may not be ready for public disclosure of this identity and may be misidentified as heterosexual. Thus, as teachers, we should be aware that certain questions—such as asking a female parent, "What does the child's father do for a living?"—may not be appropriate to ask during an initial meeting, as they may force an awkward disclosure that the parent may not be ready to give. Asking more generic questions of parents allows them to disclose information as they feel comfortable doing so and on their own terms.

3. Many "cultural themes" affect an individual's progress in development toward identity formation as a homosexual, such as religious restrictions, traditional gender roles, and ethnicity. And the ways each individual processes the interaction of these themes is also personal. Don't assume that all persons with the same homosexual orientation have a lot in common any more than you would assume all persons with the same heterosexual orientation have a lot in common.

4. Gay and lesbian households are formed by unmarried adult relationships of same-sex partners, since marriage or civil union is not legal in most states. But a growing number of homosexual couples are made up of adults who were once married and have at least one child living with them from a previous marriage, adoption, or donor insemination.

5. Same-sex couples with children experience challenges by prejudice and unequal legislation. Adults and children in same-sex couple families are subject to prejudice by some heterosexual people who are uncomfortable about this alternative lifestyle or have been told by religious leaders that this lifestyle is not acceptable. Further, some of the same laws that support married heterosexual couples, such as those providing for veteran's and other benefits, don't apply to same-sex couples, who cannot legally marry.

6. Gay men who are fathers and lesbian women who are mothers experience both similar and unique challenges. For example, gay fathers have more trouble "coming out" than lesbian mothers do, and gay fathers have more trouble disclosing their homosexual lifestyle to their children than do lesbian mothers.

7. Research on children to determine effects of being raised by same-sex parents indicate these children are as happy and healthy as those raised by heterogeneous families. Further, a comprehensive review of studies on children raised by same-sex families indicated there were no significant disturbances in the development of children's sexual identity. Yet, growing up in families with alternative lifestyles does include experiences of outside ridicule that must impact family members with same-sex parents in some way.

8. There are several ways teachers of children from same-sex couple families can educate themselves on the impacts for children, children's views, and families' rights as well as learning important culturally sensitive classroom practices. For example, the classroom photos should include visual representations of not only other cultures, but all family styles. Also, the interactions teachers have

with children should include culturally sensitive language, such as *parent* rather than *mother* and *father*. Finally, teachers should be mindful of and take action against any teasing of a child with same-sex parents.

Working proactively with all children through stories and other methods can introduce and provide needed information for other young children who don't understand the concept of "two mommies."

Summary Statements

✓ We spend a great deal of time wondering why and how individuals choose nontraditional lifestyles.

✓ There appear to be biological as well as sociocultural components involved in lifestyle "choice."

✓ *Self-concept* refers to people's mental images of themselves: what they think they are like as people.

✓ *Identity* refers to perceptions of self that are thought to represent the self definitively in specific social settings.

✓ *Homosexual identity* is one of several identities incorporated into a person's self-concept. The homosexual identity may function as a self-identity, perceived identity, presented identity, or all three.

✓ *Coming out* refers to the developmental process that is characteristic of achieving a homosexual identity.

✓ *Disclosure* is the disclosing of one's homosexuality to others.

✓ The fact that individuals have sexual orientation in common does not mean that the individuals are alike.

✓ The development of self-identity in homosexuals is affected not only by their biological origins but also by the sociocultural realities of their worlds.

✓ Because of fears of losing children in custody battles, many gay and lesbian parents do not disclose their homosexual identities.

✓ The majority of children living in gay- or lesbian-headed households are children born to these individuals during prior heterosexual marriages.

✓ Lesbian couples seek to have children through donor insemination and through adoption.

✓ Gay couples opt to have children through surrogate mothers and through adoptions.

✓ *Heterosexism* refers to the presumption of superiority and exclusiveness of heterosexual relationships. It assumes that a heterosexual adult will be a better parent than one who is homosexual.

✓ A review of studies conducted by Miller (1978, 1979, 1983, 1986) found that it is easier for mothers to disclose their homosexuality to their children than it is for fathers to do so.

✓ Children raised in situations in which both parental partners have children must deal with the same issues as children in stepfamilies. The lack of legal recognition of these partnerships, however, makes the nature of these relationships unclear to the children.

✓ Children growing up in homes headed by gays and lesbians reveal no differences with respect to gender choices or sexual preferences, their intelligence, or their ability to make moral judgments.

✓ Children raised in households headed by gays and lesbians may experience a sense of isolation prompted by their inability to relate to children raised in a heterosexual household and by the family's choice to maintain the secrecy of the living arrangement of the adults.

✓ Teachers can exhibit respect for the diversity of families through classroom displays, materials, and books that depict different cultures and gender roles.

✓ In working with children of families headed by gays or lesbians, teachers will need to examine their personal attitudes, prejudices, and behaviors and to practice behaviors that show regard for the role of the adult as first being a parent.

Research to Practice: Classroom Applications and Activities

1. Interview an early childhood teacher about her or his experiences in serving the children of families who are headed by gays or lesbians. Without identifying those families, discuss issues that may have arisen specific to the family's lifestyle. How did the teacher respond to these issues?

2. Investigate the legal rights of partners of gay or lesbian individuals within your state and at the local level. Consider health benefits, death benefits, rights to inherit, and so on.

3. Consider the following situation. You are a preschool teacher with a mixed-age group of 3- and 4-year-old children. You are observing two girls playing with dolls in the dramatic play area. One child says, "I have two moms. You can be a mom, and I'll be a mom." The other child asks her to explain.

Seeming confused, she looks at you and asks you to explain. What is your response?

4. An 8-year-old child comes to you in tears because another child has teased her about her father, who is gay and living with his partner. How can you help this child? Should you discuss this incident with her father?

5. Organize a list of children's books that deal with the topic of children in families with gay or lesbian parents. (*Daddy's Roommate* by Michael Wilhoite is one example.) Discuss aspects of the book that should be considered with respect to what is developmentally appropriate for children ages 3 through 8. For additional children's books and ideas for using literature to develop partnerships with diverse families, see Lilly and Green (2004).

Resources

Alpert, H. (1988). *We are everywhere: Writings by and about lesbian parents.* Freedom, CA: Crossing Press.

Baringa, M. (1991). Is homosexuality biological? *Science, 253,* 956–957.

Belcastro, P. A., Gramlich, T., Nicholson, T., Price, J., & Wilson, R. (1993). A review of databased studies addressing the effects of homosexual parenting on children's sexual and social functioning. *Journal of Divorce and Remarriage, 20,* 105–122.

Benkov, L. (1994). *Reinventing the family.* New York: Crown.

Briggs, J. R. (1994). *A Yankelovich monitor perspective on gays/lesbians.* Norwalk, CT: Yankelovich Partners.

Card, C. (1992). Lesbianism and choice. *Journal of Homosexuality, 23*(3), 39–52.

Cramer, D. (1986). Gay parents and their children: A review of research and practical implications. *Journal of Counseling and Development, 64,* 504–507.

Crawford, I., & Solliday, E. (1996). The attitudes of undergraduate college students toward gay parenting. *Journal of Homosexuality, 30,* 63–77.

Gates, G. J., & Ost, J. (2004). *The Gay & Lesbian atlas.* Washington, DC: Urban Institute Press.

Gibbons, A. (1991). The brain as "sexual organ." *Science, 253,* 957–959.

Hare, J., & Richards, L. (1993). Children raised by lesbian couples: Does context of birth affect father and partner involvement? *Family Relations, 42,* 249–253.

Koepke, L., Hare, J., & Moran, P. (1992). Relationship quality in a sample of lesbian couples with children and childfree lesbian couples. *Family Relations, 42,* 224–229.

Oswald, R. F., Patterson, C. J., & Kuvalanka, K. A. (2004). *Same-sex marriages: Facts Sheet.* Minneapolis, MN: National Council on Family Relations. Retrieved August 20, 2005, from www.ncfr.org

Rafkin, L. (1990). *Different mothers: Sons and daughters of lesbians talk about their lives.* Pittsburgh: Cleis.

Schulenburg, J. (1985). *Gay parenting: A complete guide for gay men and lesbians with children.* Garden City, NY: Anchor.

Simmons, T., & O'Connell, M. (2003). *Married-couple and unmarried-partner households: 2000,* Census 2000 Special Reports, CENSR-5. Washington DC: U.S. Census Bureau.

Smith, D., & Gates, G. (2001). *Gay and lesbian families in the United States: Same-sex unmarried partner households.* Washington, DC: Human Rights Campaign Fund.

Weston, K. (1992). The politics of gay families. In B. Thorne (Ed.), *Rethinking the family: Some feminist questions* (pp. 119–139). Boston: Northeastern University Press.

Wickens, E. (1993). Penny's question: "I will have a child in my class with two moms—What do you know about this?" *Young Children, 48,* 25–28.

Support for Families and Friends

Colage: Children of Lesbians and Gays Everywhere
www.colage.org

Family Pride Coalition
www.familypride.org

Gay Family Options
www.gayfamilyoptions.org

Gay Parent magazine
www.gayparentmag.com

Parents, Families and Friends of Lesbians and Gays (PFLAG)
www.pflag.org

CHAPTER 9

Strategies for Building Partnerships

A school and school system exist in a community.

SARASON, 1999, P. 43

KEY TERMS

common goal	culture	diversity	multiple intelligences
communication	decision-making councils	learning styles	respect

GUIDING QUESTIONS

1. What is meant by "the parent is the first and most important teacher"?
2. Why is it important for each teacher to consider the multiple perspectives of families to build partnerships?
3. How can teachers attend to situations that challenge home–school–community partnerships?
4. What are some successful ways to communicate information from schools to families and for families to communicate information to schools?
5. What are two ways to utilize portfolios during family–school conferences?
6. What are some important guidelines to follow for setting up and conducting family–school meetings?
7. How can teachers involve parents as volunteers or assistants in class and outside the classroom setting?
8. In what ways can parents participate in educational decision making?
9. What are some safety issues impacting contemporary schools that teachers and families should be trained to handle?

 his quote is taken from a wonderful book by Seymour Sarason (1999) entitled *Teaching as a Performing Art*. The comment is made in a summary of John Dewey's position on teaching and continues with:

> The community contains the human and material resources about which school personnel *and* students should have working knowledge so that those resources can be tapped for educational purposes. The boundaries between school and society should be porous. The more schools are encapsulated places—the more the individual classroom is isolated from the rest of the school and community—the more completely potential resources remain just that: potential, unmined, unconnected to the education of children. (p. 43)

This poignant statement serves as an introduction to the main thrust of this chapter, which deals with building partnerships among teachers, administrators, families, and community members in which *all* support the growth and development of our young children. The following themes emerge as we explore building partnerships:

Theme 1. Parents are the first and most important teachers of young children. Children grow in the contexts of families.

Theme 2. Successful partnerships with families and communities occur when all individuals involved put aside their prejudices regarding culture, family lifestyle, income, perceived quality of parenting, authority figures, and past school experiences.

Theme 3. The best partnerships are those in which all participants emerge with a sense of equality and contribution.

Theme 4. There are many strategies for collaborating with parents and families. Some strategies are common across groups; others are chosen to fit the specific needs of the individual, family, community, or combination of these.

Theme 5. Safety of children is a factor that must be considered as we build partnerships in such a manner that families and communities are involved.

(Many children are cared for by grandparents, aunts, uncles, stepparents, adoptive parents, foster parents, older siblings, and other individuals. The terms *family* and *parent* are used to encompass those individuals who are providing primary care for the child.)

THE PARENT AS THE FIRST AND MOST IMPORTANT TEACHER

What is a "teacher"? "Teaching" describes the action of a teacher. Both *teaching* and *teacher* reflect choices in profession: "I am a teacher." However, uses for these terms do exist outside our profession. Parents teach their children. Coaches teach children. Dentists and doctors teach children. Grandparents teach their grandchildren. Religious leaders teach children. What do children learn? They learn right from wrong, how to tie a shoe, how to use a spoon, manners at the table, how to negotiate with a sibling, how to care for someone in need, how to share a storybook, and how to write their names, among numerous other things. While less formal than school, these "teachings" are the foundations of our learning as we first begin school. They go with us into our adult worlds along with what we learn in school.

Astute and caring teachers and caregivers of young children will recognize how much parents and families know about their children and build on that knowledge rather than assume the position of authority on the child's development. This form of respect is reflected by teachers in many programs. Head Start typifies this respect in its historic approach to inclusion of families of young children in the classroom as volunteers and in positions of authority on policy-making councils. It is of little wonder that many parents who serve as classroom volunteers later become Head Start classroom teachers.

While recognizing the irreplaceable role of the parenting adult as a "teacher," it is important that we do not see the parent as replacing the early childhood teacher. This seems to happen when programs for very

In planning parent inclusion activities, it is important to share and reflect upon various viewpoints of those involved.

young children focus heavily on "academics." Parents may be expected to assist children in completing complex work sheets, memorizing all letters and letter sounds, and supervising various handwriting tasks. In this sense, we are "misusing" and, perhaps, abusing the teaching role that is a natural part of parenting.

THEME 1   *in practice . . .*

As you are a teacher of 4-year-old children, parents often inquire of you how they can best help their children learn at home. Think about what you have been doing with the children in the classroom. Perhaps you have been singing a favorite song, acting out a puppet story, sharing books about neighborhoods, or helping the children understand friendship. How could you inform parents about this play and assist them in becoming a part of the child's school learning at home? Pay attention to what is developmentally and culturally appropriate for your children.

SEEKING "COMMON GROUND": MULTIPLE PERSPECTIVE TAKING

At some point during the discussion of parents as teachers, you were probably reminded of one or more family situations in which parents are unable, for a variety of reasons, to be positive teachers of their children. Chemical dependency, economic concerns, marital discord, illness of parents and family members, homelessness, limited human resources, and a variety of other issues may play roles in this scarcity of emotional and physical parenting. Yes, this does happen with far greater frequency than children deserve. However, with support, many parents do overcome such issues to return to parenting and to become better parents.

Our goal, whether we are parents, teachers, or other committed adults, is to nurture the growth and development of children. This is our "common ground." Each of us brings to this process multiple ideas and perspectives about how to nurture what we have experienced in our personal childhoods and what we have learned in our life's journey. For teachers to provide best practices for children, teachers must find ways to connect their experiences with diverse views of families. Early childhood teachers must be able to understand their roles by taking the multiple perspectives of the families and children in each class. Teachers develop rich explanations of how children learn through their observations of children beyond their products of academics and into the processes and lives children bring to academics.

In *Schooling Homeless Children: A Working Model for America's Public Schools* (Quint, 1994), Principal Carol Williams stresses the role of schools in helping parents and children. Homeless children, like many other children in America and across the globe, deal daily with issues of survival, including physical and emotional violence in their shelters, schools, and neighborhoods; parents who are emotionally or physically unavailable for parenting; and general lack of support systems. Teachers will serve families with diverse configurations as illustrated in Figure 9.1. This is important for teachers to realize as the numbers of young children experiencing homelessness are increasing, and the greatest number of homeless children (Pre-K–age 18) are preschool- and elementary-age children (U.S. Department of Education, 2000). Williams's answer to such problems was to recognize that professionals within the

FIGURE 9.1	Serving Diverse Families

The educational professional may serve:

- Families headed by one parent responsible for supporting the family, managing the home, and raising the children;
- Families with well-educated parents;
- Families of children with disabilities;
- Families headed by individuals who have been incarcerated;
- Families with hours committed to volunteer time at the local school;
- Families who distrust schools because of past personal experiences;
- Foster families; and
- Families who place their children's education above all else.

Note. Based on *Schooling Homeless Children: A Working Model for America's Public Schools* by S. Quint, 1994, New York: Teachers College Press.

schools must concern themselves with more than academics, which for many children and families were secondary to issues of survival.

Regardless of lifestyle and resources, both human and material, families are the first teachers of young children. Even when those resources are limited, families care deeply about their children (Dorfman & Fisher, 2002; Henderson & Mapp, 2002; Thorkildsen & Stein, 1998). Among the most poignant examples describing the work of families with their children is the ethnographic research of Denny Taylor and Catherine Dorsey-Gaines (1988). In *Growing Up Literate*, they document their fieldwork with families living in poverty in the inner city of a major metropolitan area in the Northeast. Irrespective of their financial situation, parents (a) were determined to raise healthy children, (b) provided loving environments, (c) created structured home environments with expectations for cooperation and participation, (d) were concerned about their children's safety and well-being, and (e) valued a growing sense of competence and independence.

As noted by Principal Williams, "If this school was going to change its course and assume more than academic responsibility for its students, it would require a collaboration of mind, hearts, and hands" (Quint, 1994, p. 5). This effort takes a partnership created by joining heads, hands, and hearts of loving adults—teachers, parents, grandparents, stepparents, administrators, caregivers, social workers, medical personnel, community members, and others. It also takes economic commitment and a willingness to advocate for family resources. If partnerships are to be successful, all of those involved must be encouraged to make contributions of their gifts, talents, and resources to the lives of the children and families.

In summary, Richard Clifford (1997), former president of the NAEYC, affirmed the position of early childhood professionals with respect to the family:

> We agree that we must recognize the child in the context of the family; appreciate and support the close ties between the child and the family; respect the dignity, worth and uniqueness of each family member; and help both children and adults reach their full potential. (p. 2)

As teachers and caregivers working to build partnerships with families, we must do the following:

- Examine our own prejudices and preconceived ideas about how interested and capable families are on the basis of such factors as income, education, or ethnic background.
- Ask parents what they need to assist them in nourishing the growth of their children, rather than make those decisions for them.
- Be creative in developing strategies for involving families with diverse life situations, including dual-career families, single-parent families, families in need of child care to attend meetings, families with limited transportation, and families who feel intimidated by the school environment.
- Advocate for the time and economic and human resources that are needed to implement programs involving families.
- Make declarations in print, spoken words, and actions that address the school's commitment to involving families in the lives of children at school.

THEME 2   *in practice . . .*

Individually or as a part of group discussion, answer the following questions:

1. How would you define *family?*
2. What was your family of origin like?
3. In what ways is your family like no other family?
4. What do you perceive as the strengths of your family regarding parenting skills, and how do you view those strengths as contributing to your personal goals for education, career, and personal growth?
5. In what ways were your parent(s) involved with the school and/or caregiving situations in which you participated?
6. How do you think parents should be involved in school and/or caregiver situations?
7. As a parent, how are you, or how would you like to be, involved in your child's school?

PARTNERSHIPS THAT FOSTER A SENSE OF EQUALITY AND CONTRIBUTION

One of the ways in which we learn to understand and value the work of families in our schools is to identify the capacities in which families serve their children's care and education. This also helps us to understand the focus of our work with families and communities. In chapter 2, we discussed a number of roles that parents play. The roles cited by Henderson and Berla (1994) serve as an example. We have already discussed parents as *teachers*, perhaps their primary role. However, parents are also *supporters* of their children's learning; they provide a *supportive* learning environment at home. They are *advocates* for their children; they negotiate for school practices and policies that support their children's learning. Finally, parents are *decision makers*; they make decisions about their children's care and education and engage in joint problem solving as members of councils, committees, and advisory boards.

As we recognize and label these roles, we become more aware of areas where we need to provide support for families. Unfortunately, many adults working with children are not prepared to support families in these roles (Wright, Daniel, & Heimelreich, 1999). We explore possible strategies in the next section.

THEME 3   *in practice . . .*

Recently, a family from Mexico moved into the rural Midwest town where you teach first grade. On enrollment of the children, it is obvious that language is a barrier for both the adults and children. What might you do to include the family in school activities and assist them in their roles as teachers, advocates, supporters, and decision makers?

STRATEGIES FOR PARTNERING WITH FAMILIES WITHIN THE CONTEXT OF COMMUNITIES

Assisting parents in their various roles reflects our concern for the child, the family, and a partnership with the family. The process of sharing information is one of the most important goals we have in building partnerships. Communication across schools, homes, and communities involves a commitment to be informed as well as to inform as we support families in their parenting roles. Schools typically share information about program aspects such as curriculum, schedules, routines, discipline/guidance strategies, rules, philosophy of teaching, and child progress. Families may share information about their perceptions of their child's personality, previous experiences, health, strengths and needs, and their personal goals for their child. Communities serve as a source of leadership on boards and committees; resources for "real-life" experiences in teaching children; services to assist families in fostering the growth and development of their children; and advocates for children, families, teachers, and schools. Families function in the context of these communities.

Cooperative activities foster the spirit of community within classrooms.

Potential Challenges to Partnerships

The journey for all involved is to find communication strategies that will reach everyone involved. First, let us review some of the potential challenges to partnership. Challenges to partnerships fall into three basic types: communication, resources, and beliefs and values. Figure 9.2 presents potential challenges to partnership.

FIGURE 9.2   Challenges to Partnerships

Communication

- Families' native language is not English, or families' dialect or colloquialisms differ from the teacher's.
- Families' literacy skills may be low, and family members may feel inadequate about that or unable to communicate with the teacher.

Resources

- Parents may be too busy, not always by choice, with their work lives to become involved in the lives of their children at school. Some may have to work two jobs to make ends meet, and others may have demanding jobs by choice.
- Teachers may lack knowledge of the need for, or the ability to provide, multiple ways of sharing information (such as auditorily, visually, in print, and experientially) with families.
- Both parents and teachers may have concerns for the safety of schools. The locked doors may inhibit parents from accessing the schools. Teachers may fear staying beyond school hours for conferences and special meetings.

Beliefs and Values

- Some parents may have had negative experiences when they were in school, so they might not want to participate in school events, thinking that some of the same experiences might occur again.
- Older community members or single adults may believe that because they don't have children in school, they don't need to participate in schools.
- Some parents may have unresolved issues with school policies, that is, dress code, attendance, and so forth, so they will avoid involvement in school activities.
- Some parents may not feel competent to work with teachers in the classroom or with schools on decision-making committees.
- Some schools don't ask for parental or community support.
- Some schools or teachers may not value families as resources in the educational process.
- Schools or teachers have put forth signals (i.e., behaviors, wording of notes home) that teachers are the authority figures and are not open to question.
- Both schools and families may not be knowledgeable or open to certain cultural practices that differ from their own.

Potential Resources for Partnership

Teachers and families must make decisions about the best ways to communicate in both individual and group situations. Many of the tools that we use are designed to meet such needs as those experienced by dual-career families and single-parent families. Contemporary tools for **communication** reflect increasing availability of technology in schools and in some homes. One idea that we have found very helpful is dissemination of an electronic newsletter by a school's PTA. A member of the PTA board compiles the e-mail addresses of as many families as possible. Each week, an electronic newsletter is sent with reminders of important dates, child and parent responsibilities, and new happenings within the school. Another good idea is for schools to leave mass voice-mail messages for brief reminders of evening events, school schedule changes, and so forth. School Web pages are also effective ways to communicate. Many post information about teacher e-mail addresses, schedules of school activities, philosophies and mission statements, and other items. Additionally, e-mail has become important as a means for parents, teachers, and administrators to converse about school events or a child's work or play at school.

Obviously, we cannot rely solely on technology to build partnerships with others. Many families do not have access to computers or even telephones. All schools and programs do not have access to technology. Finally, we sometimes experience electrical power failures, but we still need to be able to communicate with and about our children.

Selecting Appropriate Strategies

As we select strategies for building partnerships, we need to consider our purpose(s). Strategies can serve a variety of purposes, including, but not limited to:

- Providing information about policies and practices
- Sharing themes and concepts being addressed at school
- Seeking information from families that relates to concepts being taught at school
- Seeking actual classroom assistance
- Sharing child progress with families

Gaining knowledge and experience in collaborating with families and communities begins in early childhood teaching preparation programs.

It is important to remember that adult learning reflects various ways of learning and particular interests. *While children learn by building new assemblies and sequences* of brain pathways and connections, *adults spend more time making new arrangements* than forming new sequences. Learning requires energy; relearning and unlearning require even more energy. Adults must *access higher brain functions to generate the much-needed energy and unbind the old.* Adults' experience, background, and learning styles allow adults to learn new concepts (Conner, 1997–2004).

Diane Trister Dodge (1993), in her work with adult learners, notes that people generally remember 10 percent of what they read, 20 percent of what they hear, 30 percent of what they see, 50 percent of what they see and hear, 70 percent of what they say or write, and 90 percent of what they say as they do a thing. Therefore, the least effective medium for learning is verbal receiving, and the most effective is the combination of hearing, saying, seeing, and doing.

Perhaps Howard Gardner has been the most helpful in getting teachers to understand the different ways that children learn in accordance with personalities and general personal characteristics. In his theory of **multiple intelligences**, Gardner (1985; Shores, 1995) outlined eight types of intelligences that are related to the natural **learning styles** of individuals: (a) bodily–kinesthetic, (b) intrapersonal, (c) interpersonal, (d) naturalistic, (e) musical, (f) logical–mathematical, (g) visual–spatial, and (h) linguistic. Some children show a natural inclination toward drawing and understanding spatial concepts, some toward music, some toward physical activities, and so on. Just as children show these interests and "talents," so do adults. Adults' learning styles are often depicted in their chosen careers and hobbies. Architects and builders have visual–spatial talents. Individuals who garden or enjoy encounters with nature are expressing their tendencies toward naturalistic learning.

As teachers and administrators select and implement strategies or engage families in work and play with their children at home and at school, it is important to remember that the child is the common bond that links the school, community, and family. "Our understanding of parent involvement needs to be on a continuum that allows for parent participation on a variety of levels and through a wide variety of activities" (Gage & Workman, 1994, p. 77). This understanding occurs when teachers become aware of the goals that families have for their children and when they are cognizant of the mutually identified strengths and concerns of the families and the individuals who make up those families. Finally, parent involvement activities must reflect the range of specific learning styles and talents represented by adults and the general ways in which people learn. Table 9.1 outlines six types of involvement for parent–school–community relationships, detailed by Joyce L. Epstein, director of the Center on School, Family, and Community Partnerships. Each type has different challenges to tackle; different outcomes for schools, families, and communities; and different types of involvement. Some sample strategies are presented to operationalize those types of involvement for you to see the potential each may hold for a particular class or school.

Applying Selected Strategies for Partnerships

The following section expands on some of the communication strategies for sharing information and ideas with families and meeting their needs.

Family Theme Bags. Many teachers, including Jeanne Helm (1994), use theme bags as a method of involving busy families in the lives of their children at school. For the safety of younger children, these bags should be made of cloth. Helm reports that each

TABLE 9.1	Examples of Six Types of Parent Involvement Strategies

Types of Parent Involvement	Suggested Strategies
Parenting skills: ■ Child-rearing skills ■ Child-development knowledge ■ Home conditions that support school success ■ Teacher awareness of cultural diversity	*Begin* Survey or informally ask families during dismissal what kinds of workshops they might come to at school. Have a list of exciting options available that parents might just check off. *Ask More Than What* Ask where and when workshops or meetings might be held and be creative—a great place might be at a local community center rather than at school. *Who Should Lead Workshops* One of the parents whom other families admire and trust might be the best person to lead a discussion about diverse family customs or homework help tips. *Resources* Distribute multilingual brochures about community services, parks, museums, and so forth, either in paper form or on a community Web site, depending on the parents' preferred medium. *Visiting with Families* Getting to know families and their routines and customs can really help the teacher understand the ways children act in school as well as open communication for parents and teachers. Teachers can visit homes, attend community events such as fairs that many parents attend, or plan an event such as a back-to-school swim party where parents, teachers, and children can get to know each other on an informal level.
Communicating: ■ About school programs ■ About children's progress ■ About children's strengths and challenges	*Mediums* Make sure you have all contact information from each family, and ask each the best way to reach them. Don't assume all families have e-mail, and know which families "live" on e-mail. *School Bulletin Boards* If the hallway bulletin boards look the same all the time, they are less likely to be read. Change the background and decorations so important messages stand out. Have the children decorate the message board and tell

(Continued)

TABLE 9.1   Continued

Types of Parent Involvement	Suggested Strategies
	their parents so that parents might be more apt to look at something their child created.
	Solicit Funds for Home Visits/Phones A teacher's time is valuable, so extra funding for doing home visits would show that the school values this teacher role. And add more phone lines and voice-mail boxes so parents can reach a teacher when they call.
	Achievement Data and Progress Find exciting ways, such as having local high school, middle school, or community college students develop short videos or DVDs to share the school's achievement data on schoolwide successes. With technology resources more available and popular, families may tune in better to mediums other than notes home. Individual children's successes can be documented by photos as well as grades and written work.
Volunteering and attending school events: ■ Recuriting ■ Training ■ Providing support resources ■ Collaborating with businesses so parents can volunteer ■ Creative opportunities	*Matching the Parent to the Volunteer Job* Make sure there are several options available, including jobs families can do at home and on the weekend. Ask a parent for specific help to show that his or her talent is valued (e.g., ask a parent who sews to help make costumes for a classroom skit).
	Flexible Scheduling and Transportation Training for volunteer jobs should be available before school starts, during lunch hours, in the evenings, and an weekends. Some schools allow parents without cars to ride the school bus with the children.
	Resources Some businesses are flexible if a school calls to ask if parents at their business might be able to come to a training session during the day. Since high school ends earlier than most elementary and preschools do, high school students who need community service hours can provide child care for younger children of parent volunteers.

TABLE 9.1	Continued

Types of Parent Involvement	Suggested Strategies
	Family Nights Develop some parent meetings so that children and adults can participate together, such as Learning about Math Night. Set up centers in which children and families can work together to solve the problems.
Learning at home: ■ Homework ■ Practical activities that show how a school skill such as catagorizing can be used at home ■ Decision-making and problem-solving activities at home	*Establish Various Homework Supports* While some families have access to the Internet for homework helpers, other families may find a homework club or homework phone hotline a better resource. Having a school directory with families' phone numbers can be a great lifeline when children and families need to call classmates for help or due dates.
	Practical Activities at Home For younger children, one good way to reinforce skills is to send home related activities that families can engage in at home. Some simple materials that can be found at home or brought home in small plastic bags might be all the equipment needed. Finding and adding up all the shoes family members have can be a great addition problem, for example.
	Check Out Materials to Take Home Establish a school–home resource library of games, bags of books, math materials, science kits, and so forth, that can be supported with community donations. Some businesses, such as Target, donate funds to schools for just such resources. Math or word games for long car rides may take the boredom out of the ride and result in some valuable math-skill development.
	Family Nights Literacy, math, or social studies nights can be engaging if stimulating resources are available for both adults and children. A science "magic" show where experiments are amazing and then explained through pictures and diagrams or a math computer game night with lots of extra helpers to support families as they tackle the

(*Continued*)

TABLE 9.1	Continued

Types of Parent Involvement	Suggested Strategies
	computers and the math content may be fun for everyone and may carry over into home activities. Don't forget to offer food for any event. *Engaging Young Children in Some Family Decisions* While some family decisions are inappropriate for young children, involving young children in some decisions, such as which plants to plant in the garden, gives them opportunities to practice skills, such as looking at options and eliminating irrelevant information, that they will need in academics as well.
Decision making: ■ School decisions ■ Governance ■ School councils ■ Committees ■ Advocacy	*Leadership Training* While leadership comes naturally to some parents, specific training in techniques for conflict resolution, management, and Roberts Rules of Order would be important for any parent assuming a decision-making role. *Recognition and Awards* While parents who assume leadership roles and positions on committees don't expect rewards, other than knowing their son or daughter is well educated in school, award ceremonies and plaques provide a public audience for the important skills parents bring to any position or committee. *Input* Not all families have to serve in leadership roles to advocate for school policies or procedures. Schools can provide opportunities for families to have a voice in school matters such as holiday celebrations through surveys, ballot boxes, letter-writing campaigns, or e-mail voting.
Community collaboration: ■ Resources and services at school are coordinated with businesses and agencies ■ Schools can provide services to communities	*Finding the Match with Businesses* Not all businesses will be a match with every school, so locate or contact a business that has a commitment to education, a foundation with a mission to support schools, or an individual within the company that has some connection to schools (e.g., husband is a teacher).

TABLE 9.1 Continued	
Types of Parent Involvement	**Suggested Strategies**
	Partnership Publicity
	Consider ways to encourage business partners to donate to your school through recognition, such as placing a plaque next to the school entrance that lists business partner (s), or putting the business's logo and a thank-you in your school newsletter. Invite business partners to school events and mention these partners in the events' programs.
	Giving Back to Businesses
	School personnel are usually well versed in community agencies and support services for children and families. Human resource departments in companies may find their connection to a school a handy resource to call to help out an employee with family needs such as counseling services or child-care resources.

Note. Based on *School, Family, and Community Partnerships: Your Handbook for Action,* by J. L. Epstein, L. Coates, K. C. Salinas, M. G. Sanders, & B. S. Simon, 1997, Thousand Oaks, CA: Corwin Press; and *Supporting Parent, Family and Community Involvement in Your School,* by D. Davis, 2000, Portland, OR: Northwest Regional Educational Laboratory.

of her theme bags has a literacy focus reflecting the child's naturally emerging literacy. She includes an introductory letter, a journal for recording the events of the home experience, a puppet or stuffed animal, a file folder game, "what if" cards, songs and fingerplays, a storybook, and art supplies (p. 48). Such activities help family members succeed in their role as educators of children and feel like a part of the schooling experience. They also provide a point of reference for discussions in parent–teacher conferences and conversations.

Classroom Videos. Many teachers find it increasingly difficult to involve family members in the firsthand experiences of their children at school. As an alternative measure, some teachers (Greenwood, 1995) support the use of videos that, in effect, bring classroom activities to the home. This nonprint medium captures the interest of parents and can be viewed at convenient moments during a family's day. Families without videotape players at home may view the tapes at school. Greenwood, a kindergarten teacher, tapes thematic unit activities, celebrations, classroom visitors, and "author's chair" activities. The videos are checked out and accompanied by a comment sheet so that the teacher can reflect on the viewpoints of the families. As with the theme bags, the videos provide a point of interest for discussions among family members and teachers. Written parental permission is required prior to videotaping children; consent must also be obtained from program personnel.

Family Journals. Journals that travel back and forth between school and home have been successful tools for bridging gaps in communication for some teachers. Some journals include written discourse of the teacher and the parent (Harding, 1996); others also include written discourse prepared by the child (Manning, Manning, &Morrison, 1995).

Children engaging in the written aspects of emerging literacy can use "newsbooks" designed to communicate weekly with their families about school events (Manning et al., 1995, p. 34). Each child has a three-ring binder that serves as the journal or newsbook. The teacher prepares a weekly newsletter with the input of the children. The children watch as the teacher engages their input with the draft design of the newsletter on chart paper. A copy of the final newsletter is included in each child's journal. Each child also writes a personal letter to his or her family each week. Both the teacher's newsletter and the child's letter are sent home in the newsbook each week, along with paper for a parent's response. The children can share these letters with the teacher and their peers. No child is penalized because a parent has not responded. The letters and newsletters collected in the newsbook during the year as a record of events and the child's progress and interests. Teachers who use journals to communicate with families about their children's interests, fears, and daily activities gain invaluable insights concerning each family's goals and concerns for their child (Harding, 1996). Other strategies for family involvement can be found in Figure 9.3.

FIGURE 9.3	Strategies and Tips for Teachers to Involve Families

Designing a family bulletin board. Sketch a sample bulletin board that contains information from parents. (Assume that parents will be picking up their children from school.) Evaluate your design for appeal to the eye, ease with which information can be seen, and general use to families. Have a regular parent volunteer review it as well as to give you a parent perspective on the design.

"Happy-grams." Design happy-grams that use common themes for preschool programs (e.g., horses, trains, the sky, families). Sit with the children and ask them to provide some phrases of what to say in the happy messages. These can be sent home to families anytime to provide parents a welcoming message about the great ways their child is learning or interacting with others and provide a good connection between the school and home.

Themes in a bag. Consider the current thematic topic or items of interest to children in your class. Examples are colors, shapes, and bugs. In a large resealable bag, gather materials that will assist the parent in enjoying this topic at home. Include an index card with clearly printed instructions for the adult. Share this idea with a new teacher in your building to further spread the positive home-to-school feelings.

"Lights, camera, action." As part of a long-term project, videotape or collect videotapes of young children engaged in developmentally appropriate preschool activities. Write a script to accompany a portion of the videotape that enhances parent awareness of the importance of play in the developmental process. Survey families to determine if they have DVD or VHS players at home and make two or three copies of the tape in each format so these can be checked out by families as they have time or interest in viewing.

FIGURE 9.3 Continued

Parent meetings. Attend a parent meeting at another local school. Observe the physical arrangement of the meeting space. Were the parents comfortable and able to see the materials presented through audiovisuals? Did the arrangement of chairs facilitate parent participation? In what ways were parents encouraged to participate? What do you think was the outcome of the meeting? Did the purpose of the meeting seem to be met? This is a great way to get ideas for your own parent meetings.

Policy handbooks. Ask other child-care facilities if you can borrow their policy handbooks before you write your own policy statement regarding health requirements for enrolling a child in a preschool program. Compare their policies on immunization and health requirements. How are they alike, and how are they different? Can the information be easily understood by all parents? Why or why not? Draft a policy statement regarding health requirements using the other policy books' great ideas. Invite a small committee of families from linguistically and culturally diverse settings to read your draft and give you feedback before you finalize the handbook.

Creating a Web site. Work with a small group of parents to create a Web site for families in your class. Do a search of other class Web sites to get some ideas to present to the parent group. Consider what information needs to be displayed, how it needs to be displayed, and what potential links might be helpful to parents, such as the American Academy of Pediatrics, the NAEYC, the U.S. Office of Education, or the Parent Information Network. Consider—What do these sites have that seems valuable for parents? What is not helpful?

Creating a documentation display. Photograph children (with written permission) as they work on a project, either long or short term. Collect these photographs over a period of time. For some of the photos, sit down with children to write captions. Ask them to explain what they are doing and how it relates to their growth, development, and learning. Share your work as is appropriate with the children, the families, or other teachers.

Home Visits. Home visits have been a part of early childhood programs for many years. Teachers often arrange a visit to each child's home prior to the beginning of the school year or before the child begins his or her school experience. These visits provide an opportunity for parents and teachers to get to know one another without other children present, as well as to spend time together in the company of the child. Depending on the goal of the program, home visits have been included as an effective means to inform families about the program and for teachers to be informed about the child. The ultimate goal is to establish a positive relationship between the home and school (Fox-Barnett & Meyer, 1992).

The type of home visit that works best in focusing on the growth and development of the child involves a child-centered approach. During this type of visit, parents and teacher may engage in play with the child, discuss what the child will be doing at school and the role the parents may play, and basically get to know one another. The purpose of this visit is not to engage parents in filling out

When teachers come to families homes, they can build on a strong bond between children and family members they talk about in school.

forms or other administrative tasks. Although teachers do become more aware of the strengths of individual family members in parenting, it is also not the purpose of this visit to "judge" the child's home environment.

Teachers should always schedule prearranged home visits and make an attempt to visit the home when all of the adults involved in the child's care are present. Visits will need to accommodate parent work schedules. A 1-hour visit is generally appropriate.

Many teachers find it helpful to organize a home visit kit. Materials are placed into a basket or other container that can be covered. Teachers may want to include the following:

- A camera so that photographs can be taken for the children to share once in the classroom (always get permission from the adult)
- A favorite book for children
- A simple game or puzzle
- Markers and paper
- Something special to leave with the child as a reminder of the visit

During the visit, the teacher can read the book to the child. If visits are made prior to the beginning of school, the book can serve as a good transition tool for each child visited; it can then be available for reading in the classroom on the first day of school. An adult, either a parent or teacher, can encourage the child in working the puzzle, drawing, or engaging in some other favorite activity during the visit. Such activities provide a focus of discussion related to the child and occupy the child. Photographs taken during the visit can be displayed on the bulletin board or in a scrapbook at school as documentation of the visit and as another tool for easing the child's transition from home to school.

To make the most of the visit, it is appropriate for the home visitor to request that the television be turned off, that a space be set aside for using the materials with the child, and that each parent in the household can participate. The teacher can model activities with the child, involve the parents as teachers, and encourage both the parents and the child.

As you make visits at the beginning of and throughout the school year, it is important that you consider the following:

- Remember that families are of many kinds. Respect for the child dictates that the teacher remain nonjudgmental regarding family lifestyle.
- Understand that knowledge of **culture** is important in working with families. However, teachers sometimes stereotype families because of knowledge that they may obtain about specific cultures. Derman-Sparks (1989) cautioned

teachers to remember that although cultural patterns are real and affect all members of an ethnic group, families live their cultures in their own individual ways (Brinson, 2005).

- Listen to individual members of families for ideas about ways you can assist them in fostering the growth and development of their children. Encourage them to verbalize what they feel comfortable in doing with and for their children.
- Recognize the stresses placed on families, including dual careers, economic uncertainty, care for elderly grandparents, care for younger children, and information that bombards children from various media, including print, television, video games, and computer technology.
- Be prepared to work as a team member with each family.
- Be prepared to admit to family members that you may not have all the answers but that you are willing to assist them in finding appropriate resources.

In addition to the 1-hour home visit described, programs may also be home based, with the child's school program occurring in the home. Head Start provides a long-term example of such a model that exemplifies the focus on reinforcing the parent's role as the primary educator of the child (U.S. Department of Health and Human Services [DHHS], 1990). Other programs are offered as support for families with young children with disabilities. Activities prepared and implemented by home-based teachers are designed to foster the development of the child, with or without disabilities, and to encourage the parents in their role as their child's first and most important teachers and caregivers.

Displays share our families and those of others.

Some families do not want teachers to visit their home. Obviously, home visits are an impossibility for families who are homeless and for some families who live in chaos. Teachers can offer alternatives, such as visiting at a library or having a picnic in a local park. Children and families can also come to school. These alternatives provide one-on-one attention and an opportunity for enhanced communication and understanding relative to the child. As noted by Fox-Barnett and Meyer (1992), "Children who experience one hour of the teacher's undivided attention feel special and important" (p. 46). Adults may have similar feelings.

Conferences with Families. Although families should always have opportunities to schedule parent–teacher conferences, schools should schedule set parent–teacher conferences at least twice during the school year. These conferences should be a time for sharing information about the children's interests and emerging styles of learning, interesting anecdotes, and developmental progress over time in each aspect of development. During these conferences, it is important to remember that parents know their children best and that conferences are indeed for sharing. Preparing for and implementing the parent conference include the following steps: (a) compiling documentation of the child's progress that can be used as a framework for the conference, (b) setting the environment for the conference in ways that will ensure physical comfort and two-way communication, and (c) following up on parents' requests.

Preparing the Conference Portfolio. Documentation of a child's interests, developmental characteristics, and progress can be compiled in a conference portfolio. The portfolio can serve as a tool for authentic assessment and assist you as an adult in organizing your thoughts. It is one thing to be an observer of young children; most of us enjoy watching the wonderful ways children interact with their worlds. We move to another level of our development as teachers and caregivers, however, when we draw meaning from our observations of a child by relating the observed behaviors to developmental norms and to our expectations of that child. These expectations are generally based on our prior experiences with that child and children of similar age. The purpose of the developmental portfolio becomes threefold: (a) It provides you with an opportunity to learn more about the intricacies of the growth and development of the individual child; (b) it provides you with visually descriptive material that documents the child's development over time and in various situations that can be shared with the child, parents, and colleagues; and (c) it provides you with information about the types of opportunities for learning that will be developmentally appropriate for that child and be relevant to the child's experiences and learning style. These opportunities are designed to foster the child's growth, development, and excitement about learning. A growing trend is for the portfolio to be used in student-led conferencing as well. In these conferences, children fully participate in the planning, including organizing their portfolio according to items they want parents to see as great indicators of ongoing progress. Children and the teacher plan and rehearse what the child will do and show when the families come. Then, when the big night comes for the conference, the children walk the parents through the classroom and guide their parents through their portfolio. The planning and organization allow the teacher to take the role of facilitator (Austin, 1994).

A First Grade Student-Led Conference Night

Madeline (Maddy), a first grader in Ms. Chan's class, was so excited. The class had been preparing and rehearsing this week for their mid-year student-led conference night in February. In early September, the children in Ms. Chan's class invited their families to an event in which they set their learning goals, consistent with district standards. They outlined the roles of children, families, and teachers in meeting those goals and they created criteria for assessing their work—many created simple rubrics they would be using to evaluate their own and others' work. That night in September, the children also showed their families the books and resources they could use to meet those goals. Maddy's mother, Dolores, is a single parent who is very busy with her waitress job, where she sometimes works overtime, and with finding appropriate child-care for Maddy's younger sister, who just turned 4. Dolores felt she wouldn't be able to keep up with Maddy's schoolwork on a daily basis, but after having attended the goal-setting night, she felt she had an understanding of what Maddy's work would be.

In February, the class would have an opportunity to share the activities, projects, worksheets, writing, and computer skills they used to meet their goals. The evening is broken up into three 40-minute time slots with eight parents signing up for each of the three time slots. Having only one third of the 24 families in the room at the same time allows for a good flow of children and families to the animals of Florida theme-related centers—literacy, math, science, social studies, and creative arts.

Maddy first takes her mother to her desk and they sit down with Maddy's portfolio, which is neatly organized with a cover page and directions of the steps for each child and family to participate in this student-led conference. Maddy instructs her mother to read the steps out loud as they had practiced in school the day before. "Step one: review <u>Maddy's</u> September goals and have your child show you what she has been working on." After Dolores reads the goals, Maddy then takes her to each learning center and shows her work such as the Panther poem she created, the graph of the animals found in their region of Florida, the papier-mâché bat cave she created, and the math story problems she has been working on. Maddy reflects on one story problem and says, "At first when I read the problem, I didn't know whether I was supposed to add or subtract the number of oranges from the total, but then my friend Grace asked me to think about whether there would be less or more and that helped me keep working on the problem." Dolores is not only amazed with how much Maddy knows, but also how Maddy is learning to problem solve and develop self-confidence.

These young students are learning to set and meet goals, to use criteria for looking at their and others' work, and to communicate about their work. Students are able to self-critique as they develop self-confidence about their learning abilities. Parents feel more connected to their child's schooling and can more easily see their role in their child's learning.

But having a successful student-led conference night takes critical planning and skilled teachers. Last Spring, teachers visited another nearby school that used student-led conferencing and had attended a three-day summer workshop before the school year started. The principal had learned from a conference she attended that children in a nearby district had increased their parent involvement and had even raised their students' standardized test scores. At first some of the teachers were skeptical, but the other teachers who saw great potential and the value of this kind of effort persuaded their colleagues to try it. The success and parent praise of the September goal-setting meeting gave those teachers confidence in student-led conferencing. Once the principal watched excited children share successes with their families during these student-led conference nights, she knew she had made a good decision for this school community.

The Portfolio and Its Use: Developmentally Appropriate Assessment of Young Children (Grace & Shores, 1992) serves as a very helpful guide in preparing an assessment portfolio. Materials should be arranged in a three-ring binder (2-inch is usually sufficient), with sections separated by dividers. In addition to your narrative comments, artifacts used to document the various aspects of the child's development and personality will include well-organized anecdotal notes; videotapes; audiotapes;

photographs of block structures, dress-up activities, project activities, artwork, and so on; copies of dictated comments and stories; and samples of the child's writing, scribbling, or drawing. Page protectors are useful in protecting the photographs and other documentation. Pages are organized as follows:

Section I: Title Page
Section II: Observer Sign-Off Sheet
Section III: Fine Motor Development
Section IV: Gross Motor Development
Section V: Concept Development
Section VI: Language and Literacy Development
Section VII: Personal-Social Development
Section VIII: Suggested Program of Activities

Your in-depth observation of the child, conducted in the authentic environment of the classroom, yields a great deal of knowledge about the humanness of this child and his or her talents and joys. You may also discover areas that require more intense consideration. Do not ignore the talents and joys, however, because these are a vital part of the whole child. Plan for those areas as you would the child's areas of need or concern.

In planning activities, "listen" to the child—with your ears as well as with your eyes. Visualize a scaffold on the side of a building where workers are positioned at different levels. Each one's work depends on the foundation being placed by other workers. Now, substitute learning experiences in the hands of each of those workers. Children have both experiences that are designed to meet their needs today (the foundation) and experiences that will come in the future to extend their learning and to challenge them to explore and investigate the wonders of new worlds. The following is a very concrete example found in many early childhood settings:

Today, the child may be working a four-piece puzzle with knobs on the handles of each piece. We provide several of these puzzles to help strengthen skills. However, we also place on the shelf several more difficult puzzles with interesting themes to interest the child and be available for exploration as he or she becomes more interested and developmentally capable of completing them.

Documentation Panels.   While the portfolio has been used frequently in conferencing, one other form of documentation has gained recent popularity—documentation panels. Today, a number of educators are working to make learning *visible*. Visual documentation makes this possible. Several strategies involve sharing the work of children through pieces of documentation, such as photographs, drawings, and videos. Currently, many programs are having great success in assisting parents and community members to understand more about the nature of young children's learning. Teachers photograph the children at work in creating knowledge through their experiences. Such photographs, with written descriptions, are taken throughout the children's journey, featuring efforts such as short- and long-term projects.

Photographic documentation can be presented to parents on documentation panels, in albums, and in simple displays in learning centers. The daily routines of children also offer opportunities to "teach" adults about the nature of children's learning. Photographic documentation of a walk in the neighborhood might depict the discoveries along the way—a bug on the sidewalk, a squirrel feasting on a nut, an open place to run, or the experience of crossing the street.

Documentation of children working on their projects offers opportunities for teachers and parents to work together in exploring the children's learning. In their work, Bersani and Jarjoura (2002) provide such an example. After studying and analyzing the in-progress project documentation presented by teachers, parents were asked to note what they observed and what questions they had as a result of their observations. The parents and teachers then discussed possible directions for the work to take and reflected upon the meaning of the process in which they engaged as partners (2002, p. 78).

Preparing for the Conference. In addition to the preparation of the conference portfolio or documentation panels, the teacher will need to prepare the conference schedule, allotting about 30 minutes for each conference. Conferences for the purposes of developing IEPs and IFSPs will take much longer. Conferences will need to be scheduled to accommodate parents' work schedules. For a child who has two parents or more than one guardian, it is appropriate to include both parties. The physical space should be comfortable, with a table for displaying the conference portfolio. Arranging adult-size chairs around a round or oval table provides comfort and prevents the feeling of a barrier between adults that may result when the teacher sits behind a desk. Audiovisual equipment for playing audiotapes or videotapes should be set up and operable. Arrangements should be made to prevent interruptions by loudspeakers, children, or other adults (Seplocha, 2004).

Teachers preparing for a conference with a family of a child with disabilities should be cognizant of grief issues that may surface during the parent–teacher discussion. "Parental reaction to a handicapping condition is highly individualistic. Each parent will respond in his or her own way" (Gargiulo & Graves, 1990, p. 177). Teachers may encounter stages of emotional responses among families, including denial, anger, grief, guilt, and shame. These stages are often ongoing, with feelings resurfacing in reaction to changes, needs, and developmental milestones of the child (Bailey & Wolery, 1984).

Teachers will also need to be aware of cultural practices and expectations of the families participating in conferences. For example, a father may be seen as the only acceptable individual from the family unit to engage in conversation with the teacher. Teachers may also need to arrange for an interpreter if language is an issue.

Conducting the Conference. Preparing the portfolio serves as a tool in directing the teacher's observations to each child. In a sense, it demands that the teacher relate his or her knowledge of child development to the actual behaviors and experiences of each child. Therefore, by the time the conference occurs, the teacher should feel confident that he or she knows the child. Generally, however, the parent knows the child best, and the teacher must bear this in mind as the conference is conducted. The portfolio serves as a focus for describing the child's development in the context of developmentally appropriate practice and for fostering discussion about the child's interests and possible experiences for promoting ongoing development.

Greet the family members in a culturally appropriate manner. Give the parents your attention both nonverbally (eye contact and unfolded arms) and verbally. Open the conference with a positive anecdote about the child. Outline the purpose of the conference. Review the portfolio, encouraging parental input. Remember that every child has strengths and that these should be discussed first (Seplocha, 2004). Acknowledge the parents' beliefs and concerns about their child. Reflective statements such as "It sounds like you are concerned about Susan's listening to instructions" helps ensure that you have "heard" what the parent said. If you do not understand a parent's comments, ask questions for clarification of meaning. Answer a parent's questions, being honest when you do not know answers. Use terms that can be understood by the nonteaching individual; professional jargon can be intimidating and inhibit the flow of discussion. Keep the focus on discussion of the child. Close the conference with concrete suggestions for continued work with the child, such as parent–child story times and positive ways to encourage the child's independence in the context of daily activities.

Teachers are often called to participate in meetings designed to develop programs for children with disabilities. Parents may participate in meetings with as many as five or more professionals giving information about their child. When working with families who have children with disabilities, remember that these families face great challenges that may be ongoing throughout their children's lives. Showing sensitivity and **respect** for the parents' perspective of their child's disability is essential for a partnership to be formed. In many cases, the parents know more about the child's disability and progress than the teacher does because they have been so intimately involved in the child's life. End all conferences on a positive note (Seplocha, 2004).

Gargiulo and Graves (1990) made the following suggestions for teachers working with parents of children with disabilities:

- Explain terminology.
- Send the message that it is acceptable and understandable to have negative feelings when confronted with news that a child has a disability.
- Listen to the parents' needs and concerns.
- Use a two-step process when initially informing parents that their child requires special education services. After presenting diagnostic information, allow parents time to comprehend and absorb what they have been told before working together to plan intervention strategies.
- Keep parents informed by using two-way communication techniques and demonstrating respect, concern, and a sincere desire to cooperate.
- Be accountable. If you agree to provide parents with specific information, follow through on your agreement. This assists in building trust.
- Recognize that all parents will not respond in the same way to intervention strategies, depending on family structures and parenting styles. Respect a parent's right to choose his or her level of involvement.

Following up the Conference. Document the date and events of the conference. If you agreed to locate materials or resources for the family, do so in a timely fashion. Observe professional ethics by respecting the confidentiality of family–teacher communications.

Parent Meetings.

Parent meetings are held for several purposes. Orientation meetings at the beginning of the year provide information to families about the program, including curriculum events, schedules, and policies and procedures. Other parent meetings may be held for the purpose of highlighting children's activities, including plays, documented work, and parent nights to visit classrooms. Social activities provide opportunities for families to spend time getting to know one another in the context of the school environment.

The discussion of parent meetings here focuses on those meetings designed to enhance parenting skills in such a way that the growth and development of the child is reflected and nurtured and parents are supported in their roles. Even though families have issues in common with their predecessors, such as what to do when a child bites or when siblings fight, today's families have issues that are unique to this time.

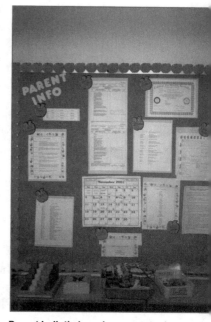

Parent bulletin boards are one tool for helping parents stay informed.

Some contemporary writers (e.g., Postman, 1985) believe that childhood is disappearing, with children and families being bombarded with information through various media, including television, video games, computer networks, movies, and print materials. Through these media, children are exposed to violence, crimes, sexual practices, and adult situations that are far beyond the developmental capabilities of their understanding. Parents often complain that their child knows far more about certain subjects than they did when they were the child's age, and more than they feel comfortable with. Today, parents ask for information about teaching children to protect themselves from strangers, help enabling children to adjust to divorce and remarriage, and help in knowing as much about computers as their 5-year-old does.

It is important to be aware of the needs of families when you plan meetings so that you can assist them in their dilemmas. Consequently, families should be surveyed with respect to topics of critical importance, convenient times for meetings, need for child care during meetings, and transportation concerns. Surveys can be both written and verbal communications between and among teachers and families. If written, surveys should be very brief. The rate of return on responses will be greater if surveys can be handed to school personnel rather than mailed back to the teacher. Parent committees can also be formed to offer topics and ideas for parent education activities.

Whether planned by parents, teachers, or a team, meetings should follow certain guidelines:

- The topic should be family focused and reflect parents' concerns.
- Each meeting should have specific goals that are shared at the opening of the meeting.

- Each meeting should be organized with an agenda that is shared with participants.
- Meetings should begin and end on time. One hour is usually an appropriate length for meetings.
- Get-acquainted activities and icebreakers should be planned, and name tags should be worn by parents and teachers.
- The physical setting should be comfortable in terms of seating, lighting, and temperature.
- Seating should afford parents an opportunity to make eye contact with several other individuals; they will be more likely to engage in conversation.
- The presentation should include time for parents to be participants and not rely solely on a lecture format.
- Family members should be given ample opportunity to ask questions.
- Depending on the focus of the meeting, community members should be invited to assist with the discussion.
- Parents should be given opportunities to evaluate the meeting at its close. Written evaluations should be simple and to the point.
- Families should be provided handouts to reinforce those points stressed during the meeting.

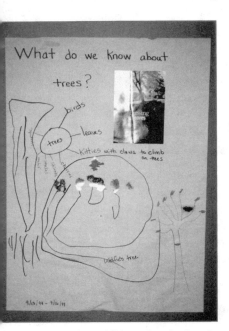

Involving children in sharing in building curriculum assists teachers in understanding their prior experiences and "home-rooted" knowledge.

If a team of teachers and parents is planning the meetings, it is important that they meet soon after each meeting to discuss its success and ways that meetings can be improved. Parents' written and oral comments are critical to this process. "Involving parents in the planning process is just another of the many ways you show respect for them and their role" (Foster, 1994, p. 80).

Volunteers. Parents and other family members, including grandparents (Latimer, 1994), can be very effective as volunteers within the classroom. Volunteers lend support to the classroom teacher while building their knowledge about child development and developmentally appropriate practice. Certainly, the Head Start model has provided many examples of the methods and successes of including family members as a part of the educational experiences of the school setting (DHHS, 1990).

In many schools, however, the term *parent volunteer* has been equated with a parent who makes photocopies, bakes cookies, organizes classroom parties, and supervises field trips. Even though these are important tasks, they do little to assist the parent in understanding what is going on in the classroom in terms of actual learning experiences or in recognizing the important role the parent plays in the education of the child. Parents are more likely to participate when they see that their involvement can benefit their child and that they are valued as a part of their child's education (Brand, 1996).

Participants in PITCH (Project Interconnecting Teachers, Children, and Homes) for Literacy used parent volunteers. Through class surveys, teachers learned that parents wanted more specific guidance and feedback from the teachers. They also wanted to know how their work as parents in the classroom was related to the teacher's curriculum goals (Brand, 1996, p. 77).

Kathleen Knowler (1988), director of the Unitarian Early Education Cooperative in Arizona, outlined eight steps to be used in orienting volunteers working in the cooperative nursery school. These can be adapted to many programs and are summarized as follows:

1. Parents are asked to visit the classroom before they enroll their child so that they can be accustomed to the hands-on experiences of the children.

2. Potluck luncheons are held prior to participation so that teachers and parents can discuss what is going on in the classroom and how the needs of the children are being met by the activities. An orientation handbook is distributed and discussed.

3. Before the beginning of school, parents are asked to participate in a workday of cleaning and organizing materials. This helps parents know where materials are located and why those locations are important.

4. A teacher makes home visits to parents before they begin their volunteer work. This gives the parents an opportunity to ask questions about their involvement.

5. Parents attend a day of class with their child so that they can be accustomed to the posted schedule and the routines followed by children and teachers.

6. After the first week, a parent orientation is held during which program participants are introduced and videos of the program are shown. Staff members engage in a panel discussion about the use of such materials as blocks or modeling clay.

7. Follow-up monthly meetings are held, with the first addressing issues of child guidance.

8. Orientation continues throughout the year via newsletters and telephone calls to parents.

Panels documenting the work of children as they "explore pets" assist families and community members in understanding the developmental process of children's learning.

Additional strategies for working with volunteers are the use of bulletin boards, file boxes of activities, and notebooks outlining daily assignments that may be conducted by volunteers. As described at the beginning of this chapter, each adult reflects particular styles of learning and interests. Teachers should be cognizant of these features and use the gifts of parent volunteers accordingly.

Decision-Making Boards and Councils. Families should always be engaged in decision making with respect to their child's care and education. Head Start is a historic example of a program that has delegated decision-making responsibility to three groups: the center committee, the parent policy committee, and the parent policy council. Both membership and leadership are democratically chosen. Each group has specific tasks and agendas. Through such efforts, family members have "ownership" in the decisions that affect the programs in which their children participate. These opportunities empower families in the care and education of their children (DHHS, 1990).

Organizations such as the PTA and the PTO have offered avenues for parents to express concerns, ideas, and talents relative to the schooling and care of children. More formal options, however, such as boards and councils, offer parents opportunities to have responsibility in the decisions that affect their children and families. Such decision making should mean "a process of partnership, of shared views and actions toward shared goals, not just a power struggle between conflicting ideas" (Epstein, 1995, p. 705).

Public school programs are also making efforts to provide more direct involvement of parents in the decision making of policies and practices in the school. In Kentucky's version, known as *school-based decision making*, each council is composed of one administrator, two parents elected by the largest PTO, and three teachers elected by the faculty. The councils make decisions in the following areas:

- Selection of the school principal from a list provided by the superintendent should a vacancy occur
- Consultation with the principal with respect to hiring instructional and noninstructional personnel should vacancies occur
- Determination of curriculum
- Assignment of instructional and noninstructional staff time
- Assignment of children to classes and programs within the school
- Schedule of the school day and week within the context of the schedule and calendar established by the local school board
- Use of school space during the school day
- Planning and resolution of issues regarding instructional practices
- Selection and implementation of discipline and classroom-management techniques
- Selection of extracurricular programs and policies regarding student participation
- Procedures for aligning programs with state standards, technology use, and program appraisal in cooperation with the local board (Lindle, 1994, p. 21)

Even though they require additional time of the teachers involved, such councils provide opportunities for members of the community to work with school personnel in making collaborative decisions that affect the lives of children. In these cases, not only are children shared, but responsibility for important decisions is as well. Involvement at this level takes time and concerted advocacy efforts to build strong partnerships with a shared commitment. See Figure 9.4 for advocacy ideas that build partnerships with diverse families.

FIGURE 9.4   Advocacy Ideas for Teachers to Build Partnerships with Diverse Families

1. Teachers should ask families more specific questions rather than general questions such as "How are things at home?" Develop some specific questions that might put families at ease and provide you with some great information about their child's strengths, preferences, and learning styles. Examples include, "What are some of Tommy's favorite books at home?" or "Where does your family like to go on vacation and what types of activities do you do as a family?"

2. Assemble a team of interested persons who can assess the current climate of parent involvement in the school and look for what impedes and what may be done to encourage parent involvement. Include on the team the principal, families with diverse cultures, school support personnel such as the guidance counselor and athletic coaches, community members from family-friendly companies, and children as applicable. See Salinas, Epstein, Sanders, Davis, and Douglas (1999) for a useful tool.

3. Work hard to establish rapport with parents who have English as a second language or who have settled recently in the community from another country. Involve them in classroom activities such as making a book for the classroom that shows typical foods, clothing, and traditions of their home country. Invite these parents to become involved in the routines of the classroom, to share books and other curricular activities with the children, and to share favorite family foods and customs with the children and other parents.

THEME 4   *in practice . . .*

Working with classmates as a team, select materials that would be used in a home-visit kit. Decide on the age of the child, types of activities that might be appropriate, order of presentation, and ways to introduce the materials to the child and family members. Role-play the home visit, rotating the persons serving as parent, visitor, and child. Discuss possible strategies for making the home visit more effective.

THEME 4   *in practice . . .*

Janet's mother is single and is caring for 6-year-old Janet and her two younger siblings. Recently, the mother has returned to college to improve her job skills so that she can support her family. Knowing how busy Janet's mother is, how can you assist her in becoming involved in Janet's school program?

THEME 4   *in practice . . .*

Children in your classroom have become excited about buses after riding on a bus to a field trip. They decide to re-create a bus and need information to get started. Think about how this project might evolve, the information that the children would need, and how their work might be documented. How could parents and community members be involved in the project itself and in reflecting on the work as presented in documentation? Work as a group to brainstorm your ideas.

SAFETY ISSUES INVOLVING THE FAMILY AND COMMUNITY

In recent years, security measures in schools have become more intense. This results from a number of factors, including:

- Custodial parents and guardians of children who fear abduction by someone seeking custody of a child
- Increased incidences of school violence resulting in deaths of teachers and students
- The September 11, 2001, attack on the World Trade Center by a terrorist group
- The ensuing anthrax infections in the United States and their effect on our mail delivery systems

Responses have included increased training for teachers and staff members regarding security; security protocol procedures; locked schools; and, most recently, new mail procedures. It is impossible for these measures not to affect communication in some ways. However, *the safety of the children is of greatest importance, and parents and school staff must use alternative strategies for including families in schools.* Buzzers attached to locked school doors serve to screen, but not lock out, parents. Mail sent from home in zipped plastic bags versus sealed envelopes serves the same purpose. Certainly, electronic mail is helpful in such times. Parents working in many schools are required to undergo criminal records checks as are our teachers. While time-consuming and sometimes cumbersome, these practices reflect our concern for the safety of our children and their teachers.

THEME 5   *in practice . . .*

Parents have asked how they can help their young children cope with tragic events like that of September 11, 2001. Go to www.naeyc.org/ece/2003/01.asp and review its statement about helping families and children with this issue. Discuss how you might deliver this information to parents.

Critical Concepts

1. The teachings of families is the foundation of children's learning in school, but teachers also realize the parent cannot replace the early childhood teacher.

2. Regardless of families' financial situation, families care deeply about their children.

3. The "common ground" or goal of both parents and teachers is to nurture children's growth and development, yet we realize that each of us brings to the learning experience our own personal childhoods, which may match or be totally different.

4. Teachers should receive preparation in ways to attend to barriers that can challenge family–school–community partnerships.

5. According to Joyce Epstein, there are six types of parental involvment (parenting, communicating, volunteering, learning at home, decision making, collaborating with the community). Each type requires unique resources and each leads to different results for families, teachers, and schools.

6. When preparing for teacher–parent conferences, gathering clear evidence of children's growth and development in all domains is critical to parents' interest and involvement. Concise developmental evidence can be organized into portfolios or documentation panels.

7. Schools should follow certain guidelines when planning family nights or meetings, such as basing the meeting on topics of relevance and interest to the families who will attend, including icebreakers, starting and ending on time, having a comfortable environment, and leaving ample time for families' questions.

8. There are multiple ways for families to volunteer their time and expertise with schools, including in areas of school or class decision making.

9. Safety has become an important issue in contemporary schools. Families and teachers can work together to implement precautionary measures for the safety of their children.

Summary Statements

✓ The parent is the child's first and most important teacher.

✓ The success of parents in nurturing their children is affected by societal issues such as political and economic concerns as well as by the personal growth and development of the individuals within the family.

✓ "Culture rules how we position our bodies, how we touch each other, what we regard as mannerly, how we look at the world, how we think, what we see as art, how we sense time and perceive space, what we think is important, and how we set immediate and lifelong goals" (Lyon, 1995, p. 51).

✓ Many cultures, lifestyles, and family practices are represented in school programs. Teachers must be cognizant of and respect such **diversity** in valuing each child.

✓ Schools, families, and communities have a **common goal**: to guide their children to adulthood. This goal is more achievable when partners have an equitable sense of equality and contribution.

✓ Schools, families, and communities must collaborate, with the focus remaining on the growth and development of the child.

✓ Communication is a key to assisting families in their work as advocates, teachers, supporters, and decision makers for their children.

✓ Many types of communication strategies are designed to provide information to parents, including newsletters, Web pages, voice mail, and e-mail.

✓ Other strategies are designed to provide parents with opportunities to engage in school-related aspects of the care and education of their children, including parent conferences, home visits, volunteering, parent meetings, and **decision-making councils**.

✓ Visual documentation assists adults and children as they reflect on the process of learning.

✓ Tools such as photographs, drawings, videos, and documentation panels help to document children's learning.

✓ A number of incidents have increased concerns about safety of children in schools, including school shootings and the September 11, 2001, attack on the World Trade Center.

✓ While door buzzers and other safety devices complicate community and family involvement, it is the safety of children that is of concern for all adults.

Research to Practice: Classroom Applications and Activities

1. The children in Ms. Anderson's kindergarten class have become very excited watching a house being built across from the school. They have watched the space being excavated, the foundation being prepared and poured, and the framework for the house being created. They have asked many questions about planning houses and the construction materials. Their interest could evolve into some type of project. How might you involve family members in a related classroom project with the children?

2. Recently, the kindergarten class at your school celebrated Mother's Day with a tea for the mothers and their children. You are a student teacher in that class. You noted that some mothers were not available to attend the tea because of their work or lack of physical proximity to their children. Discuss how you think this experience might affect young children and whether you would repeat this activity in your classroom.

3. Cheyenne's mother volunteered to work with the class of 3-year-olds 2 days per week. You were delighted to have the extra help. After several weeks of volunteering, however,

Cheyenne's mother still could not separate herself from her daughter. She was critical of her daughter's artwork, how she sat in a circle, and how she spoke to the teachers. Cheyenne was obviously not enjoying this experience. What strategies might you employ in working with this mother?

4. Dan's parents are divorced. They have joint custody, and Dan spends alternating weekends with his father. Recently, you saw Dan's father at the local grocery, and he expressed concern that he knew nothing about Dan's school life. All paperwork was sent to Dan's mother and not shared with him. As a teacher, what, if anything, would you do about this situation?

5. Four-year-old Rachel has difficulty with speech. At times, she becomes so frustrated that she points at what she wants, rather than speaking. You are preparing for a conference at which you will suggest that Rachel have a speech and language evaluation. How will you prepare for this meeting with Rachel's parents, who have indicated that she will "outgrow" this problem, and what strategies might you employ in conducting the conference?

CHAPTER 10

Assessing and Evaluating Parent–School Involvement

Issues and Strategies

Parent involvement is of basic importance to the success of all elementary school programs. For an early childhood program, it is crucial and should be a high priority.

NATIONAL ASSOCIATION OF ELEMENTARY SCHOOL PRINCIPALS, 1998, P. IV

When assessments emphasize deficits and diminished expectations for future success, we parents generally begin to look for a way to thwart these negative prognostications. At the very best, we want a miracle cure. At the very least, we want professionals to "fix" our children. . . . We believe that professionals have all the answers, and therefore, all the power.

ROCCO, 1996, P. 56

KEY TERMS

alternative assessment	developmentally appropriate assessment	formative evaluation	program evaluation
assessment	evaluation	informal evaluation	rating scales
authentic assessment	family portfolios	needs assessment	stakeholders
checklists	formal evaluation	performance based	summative evaluation
		portfolio assessment	

GUIDING QUESTIONS

1. Why is assessment of parent–school involvement important in contemporary classrooms?
2. What is the difference between assessment and evaluation?
3. What is authentic assessment and what are examples?
4. How can teachers be sensitive to multiculturalism in the assessment process?
5. What are examples of effective assessment and evaluation strategies for parent involvement in contemporary early childhood classrooms?
6. What are helpful resources for the assessment and evaluation of parent involvement?

s we have shown in earlier chapters, contemporary American families demonstrate widely varying lifestyles. The influence of divorce, remarriage, cultural diversity, dual employment, single parenthood, and other social forces has greatly affected the families who become involved in American schools. Yet, schools for young children greatly value the contributions that parents and families make in the early childhood classroom. In addition, the impact of the No Child Left Behind legislation has increased the teacher's and administrator's concerns for accountability, and this applies to positive outcomes from parent–school processes as well as from children in classrooms.

Parents have an important role in their child's development and learning, and teachers and administrators have learned that the child's success as a learner depends on parents as well as on teachers (Wortham, 2005, p. 228). Teachers report a need to better understand how to conduct needs assessments and to evaluate parent–school involvement programs. Assessment and evaluation should be an inherent part of the early childhood classroom, thus ensuring quality and good practice. This chapter focuses on the assessment and evaluation of the school–family process to determine effective strategies and plans for family involvement and how successful the strategies have been. Through assessment, the teacher, director, or other school professional can identify the specific needs of the child/parent/family population with whom he or she is working, determine what strategies may work best with them, and then evaluate the success of these strategies. Through assessment, the quality and consistency of parent involvement programs within a school setting can be strengthened, and program content and expense can be justified for continuation purposes.

This chapter on assessment and evaluation includes the following themes:

Theme 1. The rationale for developing and using parent involvement evaluation and assessment strategies is a convincing one. Understanding the importance of assessment and the evaluation process and the definitions of these two terms will facilitate the teacher's role in this important area.

Theme 2. A variety of effective methods of conducting needs assessment, authentic assessment, and portfolio assessment exist. Certain strategies are especially appropriate and effective to use in early childhood classrooms and with parent and family programs.

Theme 3. Contemporary classrooms are utilizing alternative assessment and evaluation methods that are appropriate for culturally, linguistically, developmentally, and socio-economically diverse child and parent populations. These strategies take into account developmentally appropriate assessment and evaluation approaches.

Theme 4. Teachers should be aware of and understand recommended tools and resources for assessing parent and family involvement in the educational setting. These tools vary and provide many options for teachers of younger students.

We turn now to the rationale for assessment and evaluation in parent education and involvement in early childhood programs, as well as definitions of some of the most commonly used terms in assessment and evaluation.

THE RATIONALE FOR DEVELOPING AND USING PARENT INVOLVEMENT ASSESSMENT AND EVALUATION STRATEGIES

Early childhood educators have historically valued and promoted parent involvement for its importance to children's success in school. Parents have always been active in the schools (Wortham, 2005). Examples of this belief are seen in the Head Start, Follow Through, and more recent grant-funded programs for children (Puckett & Black, 1994). According to the National Association of Elementary School Principals (1998), descriptors for the parent–school partnership include the following:

- Parents share development of the school's educational program, and so understand and support it in meetings, newsletters, conversations, and other ways; the principal and staff provide information about the developmental philosophy of the program and its goals.
- Parents are helped to increase their effectiveness in working with their children, both at school and in the home, through their involvement in the school's work and their participation in classrooms, meetings, and conferences.
- Parent concerns regarding parenting and their individual performance as parents are addressed both formally and informally—through conferences, newsletters, workshops, and in personal conversations.
- Parents are actively involved in the school site council, making decisions about the program.
- A reciprocal relationship is formed and nurtured. Teachers recognize that parents have valuable information to share about their children. All parties seek to make both school and home places where young children feel secure and enjoy success. (p. 22)

The issue of accountability never has been greater in schools, and current funding sources require that monies and other capital expenditures be justified. Furthermore, as early childhood programs proliferate and develop, it is important to measure their effectiveness to determine the need for revision, modification, expansion, or termination; thus, ongoing evaluation of programs is also necessary. Finally, issues of accountability are evidenced in the need to measure outcomes of programs for children and families.

Frequently asked questions related to program outcomes for parents and children include the following (Berger, 1991; Payne, 1994; Puckett & Black, 1994; Worthen & Sanders, 1987):

1. How were needs assessed and program outcomes determined initially?
2. What outcomes resulted from the specific educational initiative or program and were they appropriate?
3. Were the outcomes sufficient to justify the expense in money and professional time for the implementation of the program?
4. Are new outcomes suggested through the assessment data?
5. Can revisions be made that would enhance the program?
6. Are program participants satisfied with the outcomes?
7. Do the outcomes substantiate and document the need for program continuation?

Emerging Forms of Assessment and Evaluation

Although assessment and evaluation are familiar processes in school settings, a new era of observing, recording, measuring, and using information and data about program needs and effectiveness is emerging (Berger, 1991; Payne, 1994; Puckett & Black, 1994). Professionals involved in the care and education of young children are discovering new and more relevant ways of assessing the needs and outcomes of programs for children and their families. Since 1965, new approaches have emerged in evaluation, and many evaluation "models" as diverse as comprehensive prescriptions and checklists of suggestions have surfaced. The evaluation process has room for creativity; thus, early childhood teachers and school professionals should be excited and confident in their own ability to determine the most appropriate and effective evaluation techniques for their respective settings. With the emergence of more subjective, phenomenological, and qualitative approaches, the options for evaluation are limitless.

The reasons for conducting assessment and evaluation related to parents and families in school settings are numerous, and educators are discovering a variety of innovative ways to assess growth and development of students, parents, and families. Evaluation and assessment are exciting fields because of the emergence of more authentic

A new era of observing, recording, measuring, and using information is emerging.

strategies for determining programmatic success (Puckett & Black, 1994). Although the need for paper-and-pencil tests will continue to be justified, hands-on, constructive learning approaches require appropriate and suitable means of measuring the outcomes. Thus, the nature of assessment and evaluation has expanded dramatically in recent years to include not only the standardized, quantitative means of measuring but also new and more qualitative strategies that measure attitudes and feelings and that allow for a more individualized, qualitative assessment of the outcomes and products of educational programs.

Developmentally Appropriate Assessment

With the growing emphasis on accountability at both the state and federal levels, schools continue to measure the overall educational gains and outcomes from their specific programs for children. When programs are designed for younger students, ages 3 through 8 years, the issue of **developmentally appropriate assessment** is an important one, as more and more children are tested at earlier ages (Southern Early Childhood Association, 1992). Just as education professionals should be sensitive to developmentally appropriate assessment practice for children, they must also be sensitive to developmentally appropriate assessment practices for parents and families. Two recent publications of the NAEYC regarding developmentally appropriate assessments emphasize the inadequacies and dangers of inappropriate testing and assessment practices: "Guidelines for Appropriate Curriculum Content and Assessment in Programs Serving Children Ages Three Through Eight" (NAEYC & National Association of Early Childhood Specialists in State Departments of Education [NAECS/SDE], 1991) and *Reaching Potentials: Appropriate Curriculum and Assessment of Young Children* (Bredekamp & Rosegrant, 1992).

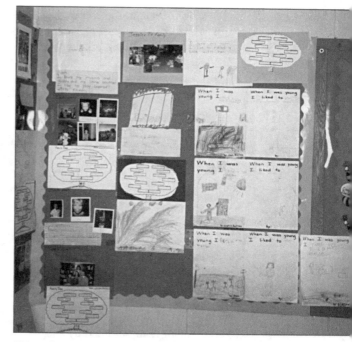

Although assessment and evaluation are familiar processes in school settings, a new era of observing, recording, measuring, and using information about program needs and effectiveness is emerging.

Developmentally appropriate assessment involves children's expression of self.

The rationale for developing assessment and evaluation strategies that are appropriate to the population of interest is driven by several forces. Concerns about the testing of large groups of students have led school professionals to develop more diverse strategies for assessing student outcomes, especially for younger children. Just as school professionals have developed a growing sensitivity to what is appropriate for the assessment of children, a need to provide more diverse means of assessing the program needs of parents and families, parent education program outcomes, and parent program evaluation has developed. Berger (1991) characterized this new emphasis on assessment as

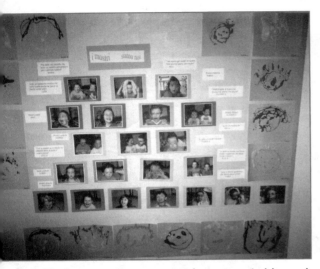

The new era of assessment is represented by such methods as authentic assessment.

> a new era of assessment . . . characterized by new kinds of tests to assess both . . . progress and program effectiveness. These "tests" include real and relevant examples of student performance, processes, and products: portfolios, journals, checklists, exhibits, and science, math, and literacy fair projects. This new era of assessment will emphasize greater collaboration among students, teachers, and parents. Its purpose will be to ensure individual competence. (p. 25)

Thus, the term *developmentally appropriate practice* (DAP) refers to identifying and using assessment and evaluation procedures that are relevant and appropriate for the culturally diverse parents and families served in school settings. For teachers to become effective in the assessment and evaluation process, they must be aware of, and sensitive to, individual family differences and take the assessment process seriously.

This new era of assessment may create discomfort for some teachers, especially those who have left the assessment and evaluation components of their educational programs to other professionals. Today's early childhood teacher needs to self-assess his or her own attitudes and skills in these areas. As school districts move to "site-based" approaches, teachers must be able to assume responsibility for this growing component of the school system. If the early childhood teacher can develop positive attitudes toward the assessment process, strengthen his or her own skills in selecting and devising appropriate assessment strategies, implement effective assessment techniques, and then use the data gathered from these processes for improved programs, then that teacher is certainly more effective and self-reliant as a professional.

The Teacher's Role in Developmentally Appropriate Assessment

According to Puckett and Black (1994, p. 27), professionals in both education and child care must do the following in the areas of assessment and evaluation:

■ Become informed consumers of tests, assessment programs, and assessment techniques.

- Beware of misapplied terminology when used to promote inappropriate practices. The term *DAP* has become widely acknowledged; however, its use to describe what authorities would consider inappropriate practice is not uncommon. Another example is the use of the term *whole language*. (An advertisement for a "whole language kit" is a bit of a giveaway of misapplied terminology. *Authentic assessment* might also fall prey to similar exploitation.)

- Accept responsibility for the growth, development, and learning of students. Finger pointing at schools in general, parents, teacher groups, central office administrators, state agencies, or legislatures as stumbling blocks to new ways of teaching and assessing does little to enhance the education process.

- Monitor trends toward national standards and actively participate in guiding those standards toward relevant and authentic assessment that can be translated into meaningful educational experiences for each child.

DEFINITIONS OF ASSESSMENT AND EVALUATION

The terms *assessment* and *evaluation* are used extensively in educational settings. We turn now to defining these terms and providing an appropriate context for the use of assessment and evaluation processes. The terms are sometimes used interchangeably, and it is important to recognize the differences between these two processes.

Assessment is used for various purposes (Wortham, 2005). Assessment can be used for diagnostic purposes, to determine appropriate classroom placement, and for program planning. **Assessment** refers to determining needs or gathering baseline data and information prior to developing and providing some kind of intervention, program, or other educational initiative. Thus, **needs assessment** is familiar to teachers and other school professionals. The goal of the assessment process is to target and identify particular outcomes and needs of the population of interest. In our case, we are focusing on the assessment of parents and families of children in early childhood school settings. Needs assessment typically is completed early in the school year to assist teachers in developing meaningful programs and communication strategies. Good assessment usually results in appropriate, focused programming that is matched to the population at hand, more desired outcomes, higher levels of parent satisfaction, and suitable baseline data from which to compare growth and gains in the population from the beginning to the end of the school year.

Evaluation, by contrast, refers to measuring the effectiveness, accuracy, success, or general positive gains of a process, educational program, or other initiative (Berger, 1991; Payne, 1994; Puckett & Black, 1994; Scriven, 1991; Worthen & Sanders, 1987). One dictionary definition of *evaluate* is, "To determine the worth of: to appraise" (*Webster's New World Dictionary*, 1960, p. 26). Evaluation will play many roles, depending on the demands and constraints placed on it (Payne, 1994). Whereas evaluation used to be primarily quantitative in nature, contemporary strategies of evaluation use more qualitative, flexible means of determining positive gains and outcomes. Evaluation can take many forms: Early childhood educators frequently associate this term with measures of parent satisfaction with some kind of parent education or parent involvement program, academic gains by a child, the effectiveness of some type of new teaching strategy or approach used by the teacher, and comparative measures of one class's performance with other classes or with some standardized measures.

Reasons for Evaluation

Brophy, Grotelueschen, and Gooler (1974) described three major reasons for conducting evaluations: (a) planning procedures, programs, products, or a combination of these; (b) improving existing procedures, products, or both; and (c) justifying (or not justifying) existing or planned procedures, programs, products, or a combination of these. It may be helpful to point out that evaluation is not the same as research, although they may have similarities. *Evaluation* is usually undertaken to solve some specific practical problem at the local level, whereas *research* is usually conducted for generalizing to a large population. Control of influential variables is generally quite restricted in evaluation studies. Research is concerned with the systematic gathering of data aimed at testing specific hypotheses and contributing to a homogeneous body of knowledge (Payne, 1994; Worthen & Sanders, 1987).

Formative and Summative Evaluation

The definitions of **formative evaluation** and **summative evaluation** are essential to this discussion. In educational settings, these two types of evaluation are commonly described and used. The goal of evaluation is always the same: to determine the worth and value of something (Scriven, 1967, cited in Worthen & Sanders, 1987). The "something" may be an object, an educational program, a curriculum unit, or almost any other entity in the educational setting (Payne, 1994). Depending on the role the value judgments are to play, evaluation data may be used developmentally or in a summary way. In the case of an overall decision, the role of evaluation is summative in nature.

By contrast, formative evaluation is aimed at improving an educational program or experience during its developmental phases. Feedback is provided to the teacher or evaluator on a continual basis so that adjustments and improvements can be made to better the program. Formative evaluation processes usually require more time than do summative evaluation procedures. Other differences are represented in Table 10.1 (Payne, 1994; Worthen & Sanders, 1987).

In early childhood settings, both formative and summative evaluation approaches are appropriate. For example, if a teacher in a new pre-K program funded by the state desires to gather ongoing feedback from parents regarding their satisfaction with, and usefulness of, the parent education/involvement component of his new class, then that teacher can ask for both qualitative and quantitative feedback from parents at strategic times during the school year. He may wish to do a needs assessment at the beginning of the year and then collect formative evaluation data at the midpoint of the year and then again at the end of the year. He may also use other strategies, such as putting a suggestion box in a convenient location for parents so that they can maintain an ongoing dialogue with the teacher throughout the school year. In addition, he can make himself accessible for telephone calls, appointments with parents, and other informal communication strategies so that he is able to maintain ongoing feedback from the parents. These strategies are examples of formative evaluation; the decision

TABLE 10.1	Differences Between Summative and Formative Evaluation	
Criterion	**Formative Forms of Evaluation**	**Summative Forms of Evaluation**
Purpose	To improve program components	To certify program utility and continuance
Audience	Program administrators and staff	Potential consumer or funding agency
Who should do it	Internal evaluator	External evaluator
Main characteristic	Timely	Convincing
Measures	Often informal	Valid/reliable
Frequency of data collection	Frequent	Limited, usually in conclusion
Sample size	Often small but varies	Usually large
Questions asked	What is working? What needs to be improved? How can it be improved?	What results occur? With whom? Under what condition? With what training? At what cost?
Design constraints	What information is needed? When?	What claims do you wish to make?

Note. Adapted from *Educational Evaluation: Alternative Approaches and Practical Guidelines*, by B. R. Worthen and V. R. Sanders, 1987, New York: Longman.

at the end of the year in terms of continuing the parent involvement component of the early childhood classroom will be based on gathering and analyzing the formative data, and on a final, summative evaluation that parents will complete at the end of the year.

EFFECTIVE ASSESSMENT STRATEGIES FOR EARLY CHILDHOOD CLASSROOMS

Needs Assessment Strategies

The first step for most teachers and other school professionals in determining programmatic and individual family needs within the ECE classroom is to measure specific needs. With U.S. schools using so many transitions and with new ECE programs and classrooms forming each fall, the real need is for teachers to learn as much as they can about the child and parent populations for the current academic year. Thus, needs assessments are typically completed in the fall, sometimes during the enrollment and orientation phase of the school year. During this time, when parents are accustomed to filling out school forms, teachers can integrate a parent and family needs assessment into the beginning-of-the-year routine. Figure 10.1 lists terms to use to describe valuable information about a family of origin.

Needs assessments can be standardized instruments, or they can be designed by the teacher for the particular parent population currently being served (Berger, 1981). We

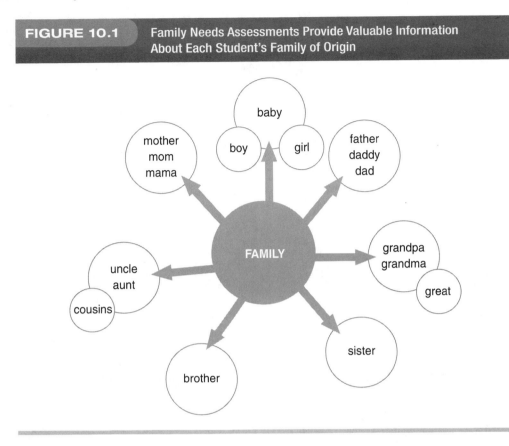

FIGURE 10.1   Family Needs Assessments Provide Valuable Information About Each Student's Family of Origin

clearly favor the latter approach. As stated earlier, part of developing appropriate assessment procedures is taking into account the particular characteristics of the population being assessed. Just as we advocate using developmentally appropriate child assessment techniques (Bredekamp & Rosegrant, 1992; NAEYC & NAECS/SDE, 1991), we also advocate designing needs assessment tools for parents that are sensitive to such demographic characteristics as age range, racial makeup, educational level, lifestyle profiles, marital and family status, socioeconomic status, and other traits that make these parents unique.

The purpose of needs assessment is to determine specific programmatic needs for a population. In this case, the target population includes the parents and families of the children enrolled in an ECE program. Needs assessments should include the following:

- Demographic information that includes the names, ages, addresses, telephone numbers, and other identifying data for that specific family and its members (mother, father, sisters, brothers, and significant others in the immediate family).
- A description of the family's lifestyle in terms of work patterns, dual- or single-earner status, and preferences for meeting times and programs for interfacing with school professionals.

- Specific types of programmatic needs (e.g., parenting skills, nutrition, study habits and skills, discipline, allowances and budgeting, communication between parents and children, sibling rivalry, intergenerational family needs, divorce and remarriage, stepparenting).
- Identification of personal needs of family members so that teachers can address specific issues related to the child in the class.
- Selection of options that are best for the family in terms of communicating on a regular basis with the teacher, principal, director, or other school professionals; this can be done by offering a menu of options such as newsletters, telephone calls at work and/or home, breakfasts, evening meetings, potluck dinners, open houses, field trips, and other avenues for communicating directly with the teacher throughout the school year.

Open-ended questions that encourage parents and other family members to express their expectations related to parent involvement, teacher–parent conferences, student outcomes, and other issues that are relevant to them are recommended. This qualitative section is quite important because it allows each family to express its own needs in a personalized way and gives the teacher some indication of the parents' writing skills and comfort level in communicating needs to the teacher. Other effective strategies for assessing the needs of parents and families in an informal way are (a) brainstorming; (b) question-and-answer sheets; (c) question boxes; and (d) innovative ways of identifying parent concerns, such as asking them to list their child's "annoyances" (annoyance test; Berger, 1981, p. 136). See Figure 10.2 for a sample family needs assessment.

Following the needs assessment, the teacher is ready to determine programmatic and individual family needs for that academic year. Information gathered from the needs assessment forms must be compiled, analyzed, and then categorized. Decision making about priorities for programs for parents; best times to schedule parent events; effective communication strategies for parents as a group and as individuals; and decisions related to the makeup of families, sibling issues, and parent–child issues can now be made. The teacher's role should be one of facilitation of parent involvement. As much as possible, the teacher should use data from the needs assessment to establish effective parent committees that will carry out the programs determined through the needs assessment survey.

On a more personal note, needs assessment information can provide the teacher with valuable information about the particular profiles of each child and family in his or her class. This information should be kept confidential. From the demographic information provided by the parents, the teacher can better understand each child in the classroom, especially as related to birth order, socioeconomic status, sibling interactions, and personal issues that confront the family.

In summary, the effective needs assessment instrument should provide much information to the teacher that will guide decision making about the parent involvement program and initiatives for the entire academic year, the best ways to communicate with parents and families, and the most effective and personalized way to communicate with each family. In addition, the teacher will have a much greater understanding of the class as a whole.

FIGURE 10.2   Sample Family Needs Assessment

CONFIDENTIAL

Teacher's name: _____

Child's name: _____

School: _____ Date form completed: _____

Directions to parents: Please complete this needs assessment so that we can address your needs throughout the school year. All information on this form will be kept confidential.

Part I. Demographic Information

I. Parent Information

   a. Mother's name and address: _____

                         Phone: _____

     Date of birth: _____ Highest grade completed: _____

   b. Father's name and address: _____

                         Phone: _____

     Date of birth: _____ Highest grade completed: _____

   c. Mother's place of employment and phone: _____

   d. Father's place of employment and phone: _____

   e. Describe ways that your workplace might be of interest to our class: _____

     _____

     _____

   f. Are you available for class visitation to share information about your place of employment, career, or other work-related information? ☐ Yes ☐ No

   g. Is your place of employment a possible site for a field trip? ☐ Yes ☐ No

   h. Explain anything about your work that would affect your schedule or preferred times for parent meetings, parent–teacher conferences, or other events involving parents: _____

     _____

     _____

   i. Special interests or hobbies: _____

     _____

     _____

     _____

   j. Any other relevant information: _____

     _____

     _____

     _____

FIGURE 10.2   Continued

Part II. Sibling Information

a. List your child's brothers and sisters:

Name	Age	School or Child Care Attended

b. Describe your child's relationship with his or her siblings, especially those brothers and sisters with whom he or she seems to have an especially close or difficult relationship:

_____

_____

_____

c. What, if any, information would you like the teacher to be aware of related to these siblings?

_____

_____

_____

Part III. Parent and Family Program Preferences

Place an X by those items that reflect your preferences in terms of scheduling activities and events for parent and family involvement during this academic year:

_____ I would like to receive regular newsletters from the teacher about my child's classroom and activities.

_____ I would enjoy attending breakfasts that provide me with more information about my child's classroom performance, parent information, and opportunities to learn more about my child's school.

_____ Evening meetings are usually easier for me to attend, if I am given at least a week's notice.

_____ I appreciate receiving telephone calls from my child's teacher regarding special events, concerns about my child, or other school-related information.

_____ I am interested in having a parent–teacher conference several times during the school year so that I can discuss issues about my child, observe his or her work in the classroom, and learn about assessment and evaluation information gathered on my child in the classroom setting.

_____ I enjoy attending meetings at school that assist me with my role as a parent. Topics I would enjoy learning more about include:

    _____ Technology in the home

    _____ Child discipline and setting limits

    _____ Nutrition and making good choices about food

    _____ Sibling relationships

    _____ Family communication strategies

    _____ Identifying special needs of my child

    _____ Divorce and remarriage

(Continued)

FIGURE 10.2 Continued

_____ Stepparents and blended families
_____ Good study habits and skills
_____ Conflict resolution
_____ Budgeting, allowance, and managing money
_____ Inclusion and understanding disabilities
_____ Intergenerational family issues and relationships
_____ Strengthening a sense of family history and identity

Other topics of interest to me:

_____

_____

_____

_____ I would be interested in volunteering in my child's classroom on a regular or occasional basis.
_____ I would enjoy going on field trips and assisting with special events in the classroom.
_____ I would be interested in serving as a parent committee chair or facilitator.
_____ I would be interested in assisting with making telephone calls or writing newsletters to inform other parents/families about classroom events.
_____ I would be interested in assisting with securing guest speakers and developing programs for parents and families to attend at the school during the school year.
_____ I would be interested in communicating with my child's classroom via the Internet or e-mail system.

Part IV. General Information

a. Explain any issues or concerns you have about your child in terms of his or her performance and adjustment to the classroom setting:

_____

_____

_____

b. In terms of your own family and parenting situation, identify and explain any issues or concerns that you would like addressed during this school year:

_____

_____

_____

c. Other comments:

_____

_____

_____

New Assessment Strategies

Assessment is in a period of transition, and a broader view of assessment has incorporated a multidimensional approach to measurement (Wortham, 2005). Less emphasis is being placed on just the outcomes of standardized tests; there is a growing trend toward more inclusive practice of assessment. **Alternative assessment** strategies now include work samples, observation results, and teaching report forms. New strategies being implemented by teachers in early childhood settings include portfolio assessment. **Portfolio assessment** is a primary example of authentic assessment. **Authentic assessment** is a standard term now used to describe any effort to assess a program, outcome, or process in a way that matches the character and type of learning process used (Berger, 1981; Puckett & Black, 1994). Authentic assessment and portfolio assessment are elaborated on later in this chapter.

In addition to evaluating and assessing programs and outcomes, we must address the unique differences of children and families in the assessment process. As the American culture blends diverse people together in educational settings, education professionals need to be sensitive to cultural differences as related to the suitability of certain kinds of programs. Through assessment and evaluation, the professional can determine which strategies are most appropriate for which populations. We must continue to address the individual differences among families as well as among children in a classroom.

With the advent of the constructivist and developmental perspectives on learning, advocated by Piaget and more recent pedagogists, assessment and evaluation have taken on new and broader meanings. If teaching strategies and beliefs about how children learn have changed, shouldn't the assessment and evaluation of these strategies also be altered? Such researchers and authors as Samuel Meisels have developed new and innovative ways of assessing the hands-on learning experiences of the child and his or her family. No longer can we as educators rely only on standardized measures to assess the outcomes and effectiveness of educational programs. We must also be able to develop individual, unique, and more qualitative strategies for assessing those kinds of programs that involve the learner in more experiential learning.

Authentic Assessment Strategies

The new era of assessment is represented by such methods as authentic assessment. The rationale and justification for authentic assessment lie in the belief that changing curriculum for children should be matched with more adaptable, appropriate assessment methods (Puckett & Black, 1994). The Goals 2000 national educational initiative focuses on teaching children to think; problem solve; become more self-reliant; and interface in a much more complex, global world. As teaching and learning strategies change, the need to assess children's work in the classroom also must change.

One response to this need is authentic assessment. According to Puckett and Black (1994, p. 4), the most desirable skills and characteristics of early learners for the 21st century include the following:

- Ability to communicate orally, in writing, and technologically
- Ability to cooperate, collaborate, and negotiate

- Ability to think critically and to solve complex problems efficiently
- Ability to view the human experience and the constantly changing world from a global perspective

These goals reflect complex human behavior, qualitative interaction among people, and sensitivity to individual and ethnic differences.

Authentic Assessment with Parents and Families

Collaboration between parents and teachers is essential for learning to be most effective for the child. The Task Force on Early Childhood Education of the NASBE (1988) described school partnerships with parents as *multilateral*, in which parents and professionals exchange information in a reciprocal process (Puckett & Black, 1994). Partnerships with parents should encourage parents to feel comfortable in their child's classroom, strengthen the parents' and their child's self-concepts, engage parents in important discussions and decisions that affect the classroom and their child, stimulate the exchange of ideas between parents and teachers, and recognize and enhance the important parent–child relationship. Teachers can assess their own attitudes and feelings about involving parents in their classrooms by using such assessment instruments as Berger's (1991, pp. 228–229), which helps teachers assess their own current parent involvement strategies and feelings about collaborating with parents.

From the stated guidelines, we are able to adapt authentic assessment strategies for parent and family involvement in the school setting. Puckett and Black (1994, p. 22) outlined the essential characteristics of authentic assessment, emphasizing that it be performance-based and related to real-life events.

Although these characteristics were designed to meet the assessment needs of young children, they are appropriate for assessing adults and programs designed for parent populations. The essence of authentic assessment is matching the assessment strategy to the context and quality of the learning experience. Thus, authentic assessment is transferable to the assessment of parents and families involved in school settings.

Authentic assessment is defined in various ways, but the following elements seem to be consistent in most definitions. Authentic assessment:

- Is **performance based**
- Focuses on defined learning objectives
- Is closely connected to teaching and learning
- Provides a broad picture of student or parent performance, learning, and abilities
- Is based on real-life events
- Uses a variety of methods for documenting individual work
- Uses work sampling and other concrete, tangible means of documentation of actual work completed
- Is sensitive to individual developmental, cultural, and gender needs and issues
- Provides a greater congruence between the individual learner and the assessment process (Berger, 1991; Maykut & Morehouse, 1994; Puckett & Black, 1994; Worthen & Sanders, 1987)

Specific areas of parent education and family involvement that lend themselves particularly well to the use of authentic assessment include the following:

- Physical development, exercise, nutrition, and general well-being of the family
- Family expressions of language and literacy, including oral histories
- Socioemotional dynamics of the family
- Family history and the development of a sense of roots
- Artistic expression and the family
- Assessment of school-based activities such as breakfasts, evening events, field trips, classroom parent centers, parent walls (described later), and almost any other parent-related activity that links the school with the parent, family, or both

Teachers who wish to engage the parents and families of the children in their classrooms can be very creative in the use of authentic assessment with parent education and family involvement programs. Authentic assessment can be applied to any population of learners. Key questions the teacher must ask at the beginning of the school year include the following:

- What knowledge (facts, ideas, concepts) will the families in my classroom gain this year?
- For each family, what is its beginning point in each of the identified programmatic areas for family involvement?
- What unique goals does each family in my classroom have?
- How will each family need my assistance to reach its goals?
- What cultural or ethnic considerations are involved in planning for these families?
- What financial or socioeconomic considerations are involved in planning for these families?
- What barriers or obstacles may exist for each family in my classroom?

Puckett and Black (1994), on the basis of an integrated review of the literature, identified learning categories as target behaviors within the following domains of evaluation:

- *Knowledge,* described as facts, concepts, ideas, vocabulary, stories, and curricular areas
- *Skills and processes,* to include physical, social, verbal, thinking, reasoning, problem solving, representational strategies, communicating, decision making, and so on
- *Feelings,* to include competence; belonging; security; self-respect; self-confidence; and feelings about others, school, teachers, and specific program initiatives for parents
- *Dispositions,* to include curiosity, friendliness, creativity, initiative, cooperation, social responsibility, and inquiry and use of new knowledge and skills

Formal and Informal Assessment

For each of the listed domains, the teacher has a wide repertoire of assessment strategies from which to choose. In some cases, formal tests and assessments may be the best choice and represent the most authentic way to conduct an assessment. In the case of parents, using standardized parent satisfaction instruments, parent decision-making instruments, or other standardized instruments designed to gather baseline data on parenting skills and attitudes may be very helpful. These instruments may be administered at the beginning of the school year, and the data can then be organized, analyzed, and used in decision making for parent education and family involvement themes and activities for the school year (see the recommended assessment and evaluation resources for teachers and parents at the end of this chapter for standardized instruments suitable for use with parent groups in school settings).

Informal assessment techniques provide greater latitude for parent expression and demonstration of skills, attitudes, and efforts. According to Puckett and Black (1994), informal strategies include performance, process, products, and portfolios. Thus, standardized, quantitative instruments are referred to as formal means, whereas informal means are more varied and subjective. Informal means must have strict criteria for use, however, and to be effective, rigorous guidelines and criteria must be written out and followed. Critics of informal assessment strategies say that it is not possible to identify specific rates of validity and reliability as is possible with formal strategies, but the goals of informal assessment are more subjective and phenomenological.

Using the needs assessment form, the teacher can begin the new academic year with an abundance of information that will guide decision making about parent involvement and family processes for each child. Thus, the early childhood teacher can tie authentic assessment to the actual planning and teaching process for the academic year. Because steps in this process are so interrelated, it is possible for the teacher to plan themes, units, and learning activities for the children that match similar themes, plans, and activities geared to the parent population, thus enhancing the connection between learning in the classroom and learning in the home.

Needs assessment and program planning for parents are not separate processes but, rather, are closely intertwined. For example, if the needs assessment information indicates that a majority of parents are seeking information about health, child discipline, financial management, and technology in the home, then the teacher can design a parent program to match these identified needs. Topics, formats for learning, timing or scheduling of events, and assessment processes can be planned at the beginning of the school year. Each event or initiative will take on its own profile and character, and authentic assessment will be reflected in the choices that the teacher makes in deciding how to evaluate the parent involvement process. There will be no right or wrong answers (except for highly technical or factual information). Instead, the teacher will assist each family in documenting its own progress throughout the school year by using a variety of assessment techniques.

Examples of Authentic Assessment with Parents and Families

Examples of authentic assessment techniques appropriate for use with parent and family groups include the following:

- *Standardized instruments* that assess parent attitudes, skills, compatibility, philosophy, discipline techniques, and so forth (often used as part of the needs assessment and for pre- and posttesting to determine program gains and effectiveness).
- *Checklists, rating scales, observational strategies* such as running records and anecdotal records, *personal interviews, time sampling,* and *event sampling,* all of which provide

the teacher or parent with multiple types of information about the child, parent–child interactions, parent behaviors, and family dynamics.

- *Individual family albums or portfolios* that include photographs of the child in the classroom, pictures from the home, photographs of parents engaged with the child at home, and pictures of the family involved in events at school.

- *Family journals* maintained jointly by parent and child. This journal requires a commitment from both the parent and the child. Each will make entries into the journal on a regular basis, such as every week, and the journal's themes will match topics or events that the child, parent, or both is involved with in the school setting, as well as self-selected family themes.

- A *family tree* that traces the child's history back three generations (longer, if feasible). This family tree can be a year-long project and can be the theme for a family night at the end of the school year, in which families bring their own family trees to share with other families in the classroom. The family tree can be enhanced with photographs of great-grandparents, grandparents, uncles, aunts, and immediate family members, including the child in the class. Parents who are more experienced in genealogy can provide ongoing support for parents who are beginners in the art of tracing and documenting family history.

- *Videotaping*, on a regular basis, of family events in the classroom or the school. For example, a theme can be chosen for each month of the school year; each family will videotape at least one segment for each theme. These videos can then be shared at a family night at school.

Family involvement themes can be documented and displayed through photographs in the classroom.

Family Involvement Themes.

Family involvement themes can include making a favorite family dish and sharing the recipe with other families, renovating some part of the home, documenting a family trip or adventure, and role-playing child–parent issues and videotaping the role-play.

The use of photography and videotaping is a

Family involvement themes can provide meaningful home–school activities for parents.

constructive way to document family activities—for example, videotaping the family engaged in a special event such as having a family reunion, planting a garden, bathing the dog, wallpapering a room in the home, washing the car, acting out spontaneous plays or pantomimes, or attending a professional ballgame or athletic event. Another example is videotaping members of the extended family, such as cousins, uncles, aunts, and grandparents. Audiotapes of children and parents reading stories together are also appropriate. The same storybook could be passed around from family to family in the classroom, and each family could have an audiotape available to share.

Finally, a classroom pet could be "adopted" by each family for a period of time (perhaps a week). During this time, the family would document its involvement with this pet. Pictures and other artifacts from this experience can be placed in a special area in the classroom or become part of the parent wall, described next.

The Parent Wall. In terms of the school classroom itself, the teacher can also use authentic assessment strategies. For example, he or she can designate a parent wall in the school. This wall becomes the parents' responsibility, and a parent committee can be appointed to plan and care for it. The parent wall should include samples of work, photographs of actual parent and family involvement in the classroom for the year, as well as current pictures that reflect the day-to-day lives of the children and families in the class. The parent wall should be large enough to accommodate numerous items and pictures. Themes can be developed for the school year, and parents can donate items for each theme. This is an example of authentic assessment because it documents the real-life experiences of young children and their parents and families as they unfold.

Children can create a special parent wall for their classroom.

The parent wall is an idea adapted from the Reggio Emilia programs of Northern Italy and is well received in programs in the United States that have chosen to use this concept of documentation of parent involvement (Edwards, Gandini, & Forman, 1993). The parent wall can include pictures from each child's home and family activities, from family events in the classroom, and from field trips or excursions that involve the children and their parents or other family members. The parent wall is a useful tool that allows much creativity. Parents delight in sharing their pictures or artifacts, and a sense of ownership and pride results from the parent wall. The parent wall provides an avenue for families to get to know each other, thus creating a stronger home–school connection for the teacher, children, and parents.

Classroom Photograph Albums. Classroom photograph albums are another example of authentic assessment in the early childhood classroom. All families and the teacher must make a commitment to this project. A large photograph album is purchased at the beginning of the school year. Parents may appoint or elect a parent committee to be in charge of organizing the album. The album evolves as the school year progresses, with each month having a particular theme selected by the parents and the teacher. Pictures of classroom events, as well as from home settings, can be included. This album becomes part of the history of the class and the teacher. Albums can be stored in secure but accessible areas so that children will develop a sense of history about other children who have been in their classroom in the past. Along with the album, a large group picture can be posted in a visible place in the classroom. As each new class enters the classroom, a large group picture can be posted and labeled. If possible, a group picture of the parents and the children, along with the teaching staff, can also be posted. Over the years, the classroom takes on a sense of permanence and history, and the children and families who have been a part of the classroom become an important part of future classes' history. This idea, too, originated with the Reggio Emilia programs.

Portfolio Assessment Strategies

Numerous schools, districts, and even states are now experimenting with the use of portfolios. In the business world, *portfolio* means the collection of stocks, bonds, and other investments a person owns or controls at a particular time—very much a picture of that individual in the eyes of other investors (Farr & Tone, 1994). Portfolio assessment is an example of authentic assessment that is becoming more popular in early childhood settings. Briefly, we provide a definition and an overview of the rationale for the use of portfolio assessment, give suggestions for developing portfolios, provide a context for their use, give an example of a parent portfolio, and discuss ways to determine their use and effectiveness.

Definitions and Rationale. In educational settings, the term *portfolio* is used to designate a collection employed to evaluate or assess something related to an individual. Portfolios are used by teachers to document their own professional experience, to evaluate personnel, and to market their skills to a prospective employer. Classroom portfolios are collections of writing and other materials that reflect the learning process and outcomes of students, parents, and other learners (Farr & Tone, 1994). The portfolio itself can take many forms, such as an expandable folder, a box, a shopping bag, or just space on a shelf. In a graduate class on creative expression in ECE, a student presented a large pizza box as an example of a portfolio container that she used in her early childhood classroom. It had been decorated by the student, and a variety of items had been placed in it throughout the school year (D. Stegelin, personal communication, 1997).

The portfolio container and its design can be a source of creative expression for the learner—in this case, the parent. Accessibility to the portfolios is essential. From the outset, creating and designing a unique portfolio is part of the portfolio assessment process. Portfolio holders should be large enough to hold a variety of materials such as art products, audio- and videotapes, drawings, photographs, and other items but be small enough to be readily stored, be sturdy enough to withstand frequent handling, and be personalized by each family and contribute to a shared understanding of that family's identity and values. Portfolio containers that have been used effectively include (a) plastic boxes for storing clothes or other household items; (b) large square boxes; (c) sturdy grocery bags; (d) corrugated boxes from office settings; (e) expandable file folders; (f) large mailing envelopes; (g) large, flat pizza boxes (unused); and (h) shopping bags with sturdy bottoms (Puckett & Black, 1994; Wortham, 2005). Portfolios must be "owned" by their users; thus, it is important to encourage parents to select their own portfolio containers and then to personalize them.

Portfolios are not new in the assessment arena, but they are being used more extensively now and for many more purposes. They are not designed to replace traditional assessment strategies; rather, they are another tool that provides more information in our goal of securing comprehensive assessment of outcomes (Farr & Tone, 1994). Portfolios make sense in many learning environments, including those for parents and families. If they are thoughtfully planned, organized, and constructed, portfolios provide valuable insight into the learning process and outcomes. For example, a random selection of 10 parent or family portfolios in an early childhood classroom will provide administrators, teachers, other parents, and school board members with a realistic measure of what has been happening in that classroom in terms of parent and family involvement. Portfolios encourage self-assessment and creative ways to document learning, integrate the total elements of a parent or family involvement program, and provide an important form of documentation. Portfolios are excellent examples of authentic assessment because the means of documenting and verifying parent and family involvement are just as open and adaptable as the projects, themes, parent events, activities, and outcomes of the parent education program itself are.

RATIONALE FOR USING PORTFOLIOS IN PARENT INVOLVEMENT PROGRAMS

- Parents learn from the portfolio, and the portfolio itself serves as instruction.
- Portfolios for parent involvement, family involvement, or both reflect the content of the parent program for a particular early childhood classroom.
- Portfolios promote the integration of language, writing, photography, visual arts, and other means of expression.
- Portfolios encourage the parents to "own" their learning process throughout the academic year.
- Portfolios provide a source for teacher–child–parent discussion and exchange of ideas.
- Portfolios keep the focus of instruction in the parent involvement program on the themes that are reflected in the portfolio itself.
- Portfolios allow creative documentation of the parent, family, and school–family dynamics throughout the year.
- Portfolios encourage family involvement and interaction; they strengthen the sense of self and a positive identity within the family.
- Portfolios promote positive teacher–child–family interactions.
- Portfolios are a creative avenue for the parents or family to document their own participation in their child's classroom events and activities.
- Portfolios provide the early childhood teacher with documentation of his or her parent or family involvement efforts.
- Portfolios can assume many forms, and they allow the creative expression of ideas among parents, children, and teachers.

Types of Portfolios

According to Wortham (2005), portfolios have become a popular trend in elementary schools in recent years, particularly in the language arts. The purpose of the portfolio defines the type of portfolio. For example, working portfolios are used to collect examples of student and parent work for future reference and evaluation. Samples are collected by both the teacher and the child, and progress notes and planning for subsequent work are important components (Gronlund, 1998). The items in this portfolio later can become part of another type of portfolio. Another type of portfolio is the evaluative portfolio, the most commonly understood type of portfolio (Wortham, 2005, p. 208). Work samples in this portfolio provide the teacher with the evidence needed to make formative and summative evaluation of progress. The evaluative portfolio is used for reporting to parents and administrators and for planning for curriculum and instruction (Barbour & Desjean-Perrotta, 1998).

Archival portfolios are passed along with the child from one year to the next, and they inform the new teacher of the child's past progress, strengths, and weaknesses (Puckett & Black, 2000). Key pieces of work are identified by the current teacher, mounted in the portfolio, and passed along to the next teacher. The archival portfolio efficently informs the "next" teacher of this child's developmental and academic milestones and accomplishments. The showcase portfolio, another common type of portfolio, is used to exhibit the child's best work. These portfolios are especially effective in communicating with parents about the child's key academic accomplishments, and they can be used for special events at the school or center, such as open houses for parents or in-house events that showcase classrooms' accomplishment.

Contexts and Uses of Portfolios with Parents and Families

Family portfolios can be maintained in virtually every early childhood classroom because of their adaptability. For parents who are not familiar with portfolios, the classroom teacher can provide a model. At the beginning of the school year, the teacher should schedule a meeting with all interested parents for the purpose of explaining the parent involvement program for the year. During this meeting, data collected from the needs assessment form (see Figure 10.2) can be shared with parents. The teacher can identify those topics or themes receiving the most votes by parents, and then the parents can work with the teacher to establish a time line and calendar of events, topics, and special activities that will involve the parents. Parents should assume a partnership perspective with the classroom teacher and be prepared to elect officers, appoint parents to special committees and roles, and facilitate the decision-making process for the parent involvement program for that year.

One topic that will need to be discussed is the documentation process of the parent involvement component of the early childhood classroom. This is the ideal time for the classroom teacher to explain the portfolio process, and having sample portfolios will facilitate this process. The teacher's initial introduction of portfolios to parents should cover the following topics:

- What a family portfolio is and what it consists of
- The purpose of family portfolios
- Who will select the items to place in the family portfolios
- What each family portfolio will look like and what the options are for decorating and creating it
- When parents will work on their portfolios
- Where in the classroom or school setting the family portfolios will be stored
- How students will assist with the family portfolios
- Who else will see the portfolios and for what reasons
- How the classroom teacher will use the family portfolios
- What outcomes the classroom teacher is looking for in the family portfolios
- How parents can use the family portfolios for self-assessment purposes

Having sample portfolios available for parents to examine will facilitate their understanding of the portfolio concept. Here are additional tips for preparing parents to work on their family portfolios:

- Have a sample available.
- Have any forms ready that you wish parents to include.
- Set up a time line for crucial elements of the family portfolio and describe how they will be used for conferencing throughout the school year.
- Encourage parents to involve their children in the planning and construction of the family portfolio.
- Have parents make covers or design special features that will make their family portfolios unique.

Farr and Tone (1994) described a basic plan that is recommended for initiating a portfolio process. An example of this basic plan, adapted for parents and families, is shown in Table 10.2.

Other specific items that can be placed in the family portfolio are self-selected family reading and writing activities; pictures drawn and captioned by members of the family; lists of stories, books, television programs, and movies that the family has shared; letters or notes from family friends or relatives; journals and self-reflections; fictional stories and imaginative writings; personal narratives; descriptions and pictures of intriguing people, places, things, and events; poems and other expressive writings; records of what the student and family members have read and written; audio- and videotapes of the student reading or of shared family literacy experiences; and student–teacher and parent–teacher conference notes (Farr & Tone, 1994, pp. 50–51). Organizing the family portfolio can include using such strategies as a table of contents (see Figure 10.3), checklists, anecdotal records, and other means of keeping the family records in a manageable yet meaningful format.

TABLE 10.2	Basic Plan for Beginning a Family Portfolio		
Activity	**Schedule**	**Parent's Role**	**Teacher's Role**
Have parents keep a journal on family activities for the year.	Make entries on a weekly basis.	Decide on format. Rotate family members. Decide on themes and topics.	Review journals. Provide monthly feedback. Give written feedback.
Develop a photograph section.	Add photos to portfolio on a monthly basis.	Arrange for camera. Rotate picture-taking responsibilities. Encourage children's participation.	Suggest photo options/ideas. Give feedback monthly.
Collect writing samples (notes, drafts, final drafts).	Add one sample per family member per month.	Decide on themes/topics. Arrange for time and materials. Encourage children's participation.	Review writing samples. Give feedback. Suggest topics for writing samples.
Develop a media section.	Set a goal for number of entries and time schedule for making entries.	Facilitate family decision making about media entries (audio-and videotaping entries).	Suggest common themes/topics. Facilitate locating of media equipment for recordings. Provide feedback.
Develop a family tree section in the family portfolio.	Set a time line for obtaining family history information.	Identify sources of information about family history: genealogy, older relatives, family Bibles, records, and so forth.	Facilitate family identification and use of genealogy information. Provide classroom materials, equipment, and table space. Provide feedback.
Have a conference with the teacher.	Establish a calendar that allows individual family conferences two times per year.	Determine preferred times for conferences.	Develop a master plan for family conferences.

Note. From *Developmentally Appropriate Assessment: A Position Paper* by the Southern Early Childhood Association, 2000 Little Rock, AR: Author. Copyright © 1992 by the Southern Early Childhood Association.

Family portfolios serve several purposes. First, they provide a mechanism for members of a family to work together toward common goals. Second, they provide a rich history of shared experiences among family members. Third, they serve as a communication tool for the classroom teacher to interact with the child, parents, and family unit. Finally, they are a form of **informal evaluation** and provide the teacher, administrators, and school board members with convincing evidence of the value of

FIGURE 10.3   Sample Family Portfolio Table of Contents

Ms. Smith's Second-Grade Class
Mars Hill Elementary School
Anywhere, USA
Academic Year: 2005–2006
Title: FAMILY PORTFOLIO: TIM ANDREW'S FAMILY
Table of Contents

SECTION I: Goals, activities, and time lines for academic year 2002–2003

- Family goals for this year, signed by family members and Ms. Smith
- Time line of planned events throughout the calendar year
- Copy of needs assessment for parents (confidential)
- Planning materials for this family portfolio
- Family journal/log for the academic year

SECTION II: Family history of the Andrews family

- Family tree of three generations
- Interviews with five older relatives (audiotapes and narratives)
- Photographs of family reunion, elder relatives, and the Andrews family this year
- History of migration from Germany to United States in 1861
- Anecdotes and artifacts from older relatives

SECTION III: Andrews family activities and events in Ms. Smith's classroom (2002–2003)

- Copies of handouts and written materials from Parent Orientation and Family Days at Mars Hill Elementary School
- Photos of Andrews family members involved at school (Parent Work Day, Halloween costume contest, Christmas party, Spring Fling, End-of-Year Festival)
- Videotape of Mr. Andrews giving a special talk to Tim's class on being a veterinarian
- Other items selected throughout the year

SECTION IV: Samples of Tim Andrews's work in second grade at Mars Hill Elementary School

- Three samples of artwork, selected by Tim
- Three samples of writing, selected by Tim
- Three samples of writing, selected by Ms. Smith
- Four samples of math/numbers work, selected jointly by Tim and Ms. Smith
- Five miscellaneous work samples, selected by Tim throughout the year
- Copies of narratives of parent conferences with Ms. Smith, twice a year
- Photos of Tim in the classroom, selected by Tim (at least 10)
- Videotape of Tim in the class play at Christmas
- Other samples to be added as the year progresses, selected by Tim and Ms. Smith (to include selected test scores, self-assessment and goal statements, teacher's notes and comments, and other evaluation information)

FIGURE 10.3	Continued

SECTION V: New friends at school

- Photos of the Andrews family with new friends at Mars Hill Elementary School
- Photos of the Andrews family's contributions to the parent wall
- Videotape of the Andrews family and their experience with the Jones family on their trip to Stone Mountain
- Photos of the field trip to the Andrews's family home for the cookout; include as many other families as possible
- Photos of the End-of-Year Festival

Note. The Andrews family selected a large three-ring binder for their family portfolio. They used the classroom video camera for videotaping family events at home, as well as the school's audiotape recorder.

parent involvement programs and efforts in school settings. Because portfolio assessment is so versatile and open ended, family portfolios are especially meaningful and appropriate. They allow the classroom teacher, parents, and child to embark on a shared adventure that strengthens the home–school connection, enhances the child's self-esteem and the family's sense of family history and identity, and allows individual creative expression.

Determining Portfolio Effectiveness

How will the classroom teacher know whether his or her family portfolio effort has been successful? Whether this year-long process has been meaningful and worthwhile may be assessed in several ways. During the school year, the teacher can gather informal, formative data on the family portfolio experience. For example, he or she can give an open-ended, qualitative questionnaire to parents during the break between fall and spring. This instrument can simply ask focused questions such as, What has been most meaningful for you in the family portfolio project? What are two strengths of this parent involvement project? What are two concerns or issues that you have about the family portfolio project? What changes would you recommend in the family portfolio process?

On an informal basis, the classroom teacher can gather feedback from parents during the fall semester regarding their attitudes about the family portfolio project. The classroom teacher can keep a list of suggestions and verbal feedback he or she has received during the first semester. Responding to parents' suggestions will please the parents involved in this project. For example, one suggestion from the fall semester might be to make the classroom available several evenings each month for parents to come to the school and add items to their family portfolios, thus allowing more flexibility and access to the school for portfolio work. Another suggestion might be to have a videocamera available for families who do not own one but who wish to include videotapes from home in their family portfolios. Keeping track of this informal feedback and then making responsive adjustments will increase the families' level of satisfaction with the project as a whole.

At the end of the school year, the classroom teacher can devise and distribute a checklist for summative evaluation purposes. This checklist should include questions that are relevant to the family portfolio experience and that relate to specific themes or projects undertaken by this group of parents. The checklist is a quantitative instrument that allows the teacher to count, average, and make future decisions based on numbers. Along with the checklist, the teacher should include an open-ended, qualitative section that allows parents to give written feedback about their family portfolio experiences and their attitudes and feelings as they conclude the school year. From these forms of formative and summative evaluation, the classroom teacher will be able to assess the quality of this experience for the families, make decisions about continuing the family portfolio project in the coming year, and then decide what changes would be good to make. The classroom teacher can also document the family portfolio experience by taking snapshots of families engaged in the portfolio construction process throughout the year, recording verbal comments made by parents and children, and using other forms of documentation that will be influential with school administrators and others who make budgetary and facility-related decisions for the school.

APPROPRIATE PARENT INVOLVEMENT PROGRAM EVALUATION STRATEGIES

Program **evaluation** has different meanings for different professionals, depending on their training and experience, as well as their individual program evaluation needs. According to Payne (1994), there probably will never be total agreement on the nature of the activities and sequence of steps in the evaluation process (p. 12). Evaluation can be informal (based on private and impressionistic information) or formal (based on systematic observations and use of data; Worthen & Sanders, 1987). Teachers use informal evaluation techniques every day as they make decisions about which textbook to use, what the destination will be for a field trip, which color of paper to use on a special bulletin board, and so forth. This section focuses on how teachers in early childhood settings can plan, implement, and improve their programs through systematic evaluation.

Each school or center has a history of how it evaluates its programs, and the final process of evaluation is dependent on several factors: time, resources, experience and knowledge of the professionals in the school setting, questions to be asked, type of program to be evaluated, and availability of resources for evaluation purposes (Payne, 1994; Scriven, 1993; Worthen & Sanders, 1987). Instead of seeking an absolute way of doing program evaluation, the early childhood professional should be creative and confident that he or she can do a good job of designing program evaluation strategies that meet the needs of the particular program of concern.

Purposes of Program Evaluation

The purposes of program evaluation are multiple. First, it provides the teacher with feedback about the effectiveness of his or her program efforts. In this case, we are concerned about the effectiveness of parent and family involvement programs. Particularly for teachers who are beginning, revising, or attempting to improve the parent and family involvement components of their early childhood programs, program evaluation is a crucial process. Second, administrators and program sponsors usually are interested in knowing the results of program evaluation. Effective programs can be replicated by other teachers, whereas ineffective program strategies can be modified or eliminated. Third, funding or granting agencies need to know about program outcomes for continuation purposes. That is why program evaluation is very important for early childhood programs that are sponsored entirely by a funding agency or that have program components funded separately. Finally, parents and families themselves benefit from knowing the effectiveness of these programs. Particularly for parents involved for the first time in their child's academic classroom setting, program evaluation outcomes and benefits can play an important role in reinforcing that their time has been well spent.

Administrators and program sponsors are interested in knowing the results of program evaluation.

According to Worthen and Sanders (1987), **formal evaluation** has played many roles in educational settings, including providing a basis for decision making and policy formation, assessing student achievement, evaluating curricula, accrediting schools, monitoring expenditure of public funds, and improving educational materials and programs. The overall goal of educational evaluation, however, is to determine the worth or merit of whatever is being evaluated (Worthen & Sanders, 1987, p. 5).

The evaluation process usually consists of several steps, including the following, which are adapted from Payne (1994, p. 13):

1. Stating program goals and evaluation objectives
2. Determining specific objectives
3. Planning suitable evaluation design
4. Selecting data-gathering methods and techniques
5. Collecting data and information for evaluation purposes
6. Processing, summarizing, and analyzing data
7. Reporting results to appropriate individuals
8. Determining program effectiveness and financial feasibility

Examples of Evaluation Tools

Evaluation of parent involvment activities and programs can be accomplished using a variety of simple, straight-forward evaluation tools. Teachers and parents are familiar with these tools because they are frequently used in the classroom.

Following is a brief discussion of checklists and rating scales. These tools provide written, objective, and measurable indicators of the successfulness of parent involvement processes.

Checklists consist of a collection of specified items that reflect the objectives of the parent involvement activity. A checklist is an outline or framework and should include these steps:

1. Identification of the skills to be included;
2. Separate listing of target behaviors;
3. Sequential organization of the checklist;
4. Record keeping (Wortham, 2005, p. 129).

Checklists are easily constructed and can be completed by the parent in a short period of time. First, the teacher should list all of the essential items that reflect both the objectives and concrete activities that are part of the activity. If, for example, a parent involvement activity consists of a series of workshops on discipline, managing homework, and parent–child communication, the teacher can construct a checklist of items that targets these workshops. The checklist might consist of 10 to 15 items, and the parent then responds to each item. The responses can be "yes" or "no," or "accomplished" or "not accomplished."

The purpose of the checklist is to measure the success of both the content and process reflected in the series of workshops. By summarizing the results of the checklist, the teacher can determine which elements were most successful and least successful and what revisions can be made for future use. The checklist can also include an open-ended question that invites the parent to provide qualitative feedback. Below is an example of checklist items:

Checklist Sample	Yes	No	Comments
1. Workshop included sufficient information about discipline for children of different ages.	___	___	_____
2. Workshops were scheduled in an accessible and convenient place and time.	___	___	_____
3. I learned effective ways to communicate with my children.	___	___	_____
4. I have successfully applied communication strategies with my children.	___	___	_____

Comments: _____
_____

Rating scales are similar to checklists but they have important differences. The checklist primarily measures whether the behavior occurred or not. In contrast, the rating scale asks the parents to indicate a qualitative judgment about the extent to which a behavior occurs. Rating scales can use numerical or verbal descriptors (inadequate, minimal, good, excellent) as the indicators of success. Using the same items as above for the series of parenting workshops, a rating scale might look like this:

Rating Scale Sample

1. Unsatisfactory	2. Below average	3. Average	4. Above average	5. Outstanding

1. Workshop included sufficient information about discipline for children of different ages.   1   2   3   4   5

2. Workshops were scheduled in an accessible and convenient place and time.   1   2   3   4   5

3. I learned effective ways to communicate with my children.   1   2   3   4   5

4. I have successfully applied communication strategies with my children.   1   2   3   4   5

Comments: _____

_____

_____

Using both the checklist and the rating scale, the teacher can determine how successful the series of parent workshops was in reaching the parent learning objectives. These tools also provide helpful information about the time, place, and format of the workshop series. Teachers can place these results in his or her own professional development portfolio to document parent involvement activities and their level of success. These tools can inform the teacher of needed changes in the workshops, remaining needs of the parents, and whether to continue or revise this parent involvement activity. Figure 10.4 provides suggestions for classroom teachers for evaluating parent involvement activities.

Who Are Stakeholders?

Stakeholders are any individuals who have a vested interest in the well-being and outcomes of a program. Most educational programs have a diverse group of stakeholders. Potential **stakeholders** in the evaluation process include several possible constituents. Scriven (1991) listed the following as potential stakeholders:

1. Policy makers and decision makers: Persons responsible for deciding whether a program is to be instituted, continued, discontinued, expanded, or curtailed

2. Program sponsors: Organizations that initiate and fund the program to be evaluated

FIGURE 10.4	Parent Involvement Evaluation Strategies for Classroom Teachers

1. **Checklists**. Teachers can design checklists for each parent involvement event or activity during the academic year. A summative checklist can be used at the end of the year. Checklists should be brief, easily understood, and time efficient to complete. Checklist items should reflect the key elements of the parent involvement activity. Responses can simply be "yes" or "no" or can be adapted to a rating scale with a Likert scale.

2. **Parent satisfaction surveys**. These surveys are brief and can be written in an objective format with a few open-ended questions. A Likert scale from 1 to 5, (with 5 being highest) can follow each question. Parents simply circle the response that reflects their level of satisfaction with certain aspects of the parent involvement event or activity.

3. **Parent conferences**. Teachers can arrange for focused parent conferences related to parent involvement activities and events, or they can integrate these questions into a parent–teacher conference that focuses on the child's developmental and academic progress. Parent conferences allow for private, one-on-one conversations and provide the teacher with helpful, qualitative feedback about the parent involvement program.

4. **Parent group interviews**. An informal but helpful way to gather parental feedback about the parent involvement program or activities is to schedule a defined time during a regular parent meeting to gather verbal feedback and encourage discussion among the parents. Teachers should establish a safe, nonthreatening environment in which parents feel free to discuss their feelings and needs related to the parent involvement program.

5. **Narrative reports**. Teachers can construct a series of open-ended questions that ask for written feedback from the parents regarding the parent involvement program components. The narrative report should be brief and not time-consuming. A good strategy is to limit the questions and responses to one page, front and back. The survey can be sent home or e-mailed for ease of return.

6. **Family portfolios**. If family portfolios are a part of the teacher's overall parent involvement strategy for the academic year, an evaluation section can be included. For example, each parent can select five products or artifacts that reflect the essence of the parent involvement experience for them for the year. In addition, the teacher can include one or two open-ended questions that ask parents to evaluate elements of the parent involvement program as well as the program overall. These items can be placed in the final section of the portfolio.

7. **Anonymous comments box**. A safe way to obtain evaluation information from parents is to set up a comments box in the classroom. Provide paper and pencils for easy use and encourage parents to leave written feedback about classroom and parent involvement activities and events. For parents who may feel intimidated by the authority role of the teacher, this is a safe way to express their concerns.

3. Evaluation sponsors: Organizations that initiate and fund the evaluation

4. Target participants: Persons, households, or other units that participate in the program or receive the intervention services under evaluation

5. Program management: Group responsible for overseeing and coordinating the intervention group

6. Program staff: Personnel responsible for actual delivery of the intervention (e.g., teachers)

7. Evaluators: Groups or individuals responsible for the design/conduct of the evaluation

8. Program competitors: Organizations or groups that compete for available resources

9. Contextual stakeholders: Organizations, groups, individuals, and other entities in the immediate environment of a program (e.g., local government officials, individuals situated on or near the program site)

10. Evaluation community: Other evaluators, either organized or not, who read and evaluate evaluations for their technical quality

Within school settings, effective program evaluation can also serve as a political tool (Payne, 1994; Worthen & Sanders, 1987). Teachers who believe in the value of their early childhood programs are frequently called on to justify or substantiate their programs or to otherwise convince administrators, funding sources, and other decision makers that the programs are of value to children and families. Thus, it strengthens a teacher's overall professional skills to be able to determine the value of his or her teaching and program efforts and to document the value of quality early childhood programs.

Program evaluation should be seen as an ongoing process, as opposed to separate and individual, discrete efforts. It is also an important mind-set for the teacher to develop: Quality early childhood programs result from ongoing and continuous documentation and improvement. If teachers can adopt a positive attitude toward the evaluation process, then they are more likely to be successful and confident in conducting evaluations with their own programs. Evaluation is a complex process because it requires a series of steps and activities that take place over a period of time.

Current Concerns and Issues in Assessment and Evaluation

According to Wortham (2005), current concerns and issues related to assessment and evaluation are several, and many are related to the increased focus on testing mandated by the NCLB. Among the most pressing issues in assessment and evaluation are the following:

- Concerns about testing children with disabilities and special needs
- Concerns about assessing young children and parents with cultural and language differences

- Concerns about testing young children who come from very different parental socioeconomic and educational backgrounds
- Concerns about testing young children in public school and Head Start programs (pp. 11–12)

The increased use of testing at all levels is an issue in American education, and the testing of very young children in preschool, Head Start, kindergarten, and early primary years is of particular concern (Wortham, 2005). The issues related to testing very young children include the effect of test taking on the child, the lack of validity and reliability of test results of very young children (Meisels, 1992), the possible misinterpretation of test results, and the risk of misapplication of test results to curriculum and instructional strategies. Another major concern is the growing diversity of early childhood classrooms and the challenge of matching assessment and evaluation instruments appropriately to the child and parent population. For example, asking a Latino child with limited English proficiency to take a standardized test in English and with different cultural concepts creates a validity issue as well as a possible stressful situation for the child. The need to create culturally and linguistically sensitive assessment tools is great. In addition, there is growing evidence that test scores are highly correlated to the parents' occupations and levels of education, location of the student's elementary school, and the family's income bracket (Wortham, 2005).

The assessment of young children with disabilities and special needs is essential if appropriate early intervention is to be developed and implemented. Thus, it is important to realize that some testing of young children is appropriate and necessary. However, the use of test scores may be used inappropriately for decisions about services, educational placements, and intervention programs (Wortham, 2005). Teachers should work closely with parents to identify appropriate assessment strategies for the young child with special needs. Parents are the primary teachers of the very young child, and parents are typically the richest source of information about the child's developmental and health progress and needs. Using several different assessment strategies is one way for teachers to verify and validate the child's developmental needs and to determine appropriate classroom interventions.

TERMINOLOGY USED IN EVALUATION

Several terms are used in the assessment and evaluation process. These terms are found in textbooks on testing and evaluation and on instruments designed for evaluation purposes. The evaluation terms and definitions listed in Figure 10.5 were derived from Wortham (2005) and Scriven (1991) and were adapted for educational programs suitable for young children. They are standard terms that teachers should be familiar with to understand evaluation processes and instruments. Figure 10.6 describes ways that classroom teachers can demonstrate sensitivity when advocating for parent involvement in their classrooms.

FIGURE 10.5	Common Terms Used in Assessment and Evaluation

Anecdotal record. A written description of an incident in a child's behavior that can be significant in understanding the child.

Anonymity. The preservation of the anonymity of respondents in an evaluation procedure, which sometimes requires great ingenuity to accomplish.

Assessment software. Software that has been developed to enable children to be assessed using a computer. Textbook publishers and developers of early childhood assessment tools make assessment software available as an option to traditional assessment tools.

Attitudes. The compound of cognitive and affective variables describing a person's mental set toward another person, thing, or state.

Authentic assessment. An assessment that uses some type of performance by a child or parent to demonstrate understanding.

Authentic measure. A test that is nearer to measuring the real ability or achievement level (or cognitive structure) than traditional tests, especially multiple-choice tests. Authentic measures are said to have more complexity, breadth, depth, or number of dimensions of performance.

Baseline. Refers to data or measures. Facts about condition or performance of subjects prior to treatment or intervention of some kind.

Behavioral objectives. Specific goals of, for example, a program, stated in terms that will enable their attainment to be checked by observation or test/measurement.

Case study method. A method at the opposite end of the spectrum from survey research, the micro end, rather than the macro end. Complements large-scale quantitative research or evaluation by providing detailed descriptions of one or more subjects.

Checklist. A mnemonic device used to gather systematic information or data about a group, learning environment, or other subject of observation. Consists of categories of descriptors that break down more complex behaviors so that observation and documentation can be done quickly and accurately.

Competency-based. An approach to teaching or training or evaluating that focuses on identifying the competencies needed by the trainee and on teaching/evaluating to mastery level on these, rather than on teaching allegedly relevant academic areas (Scriven, 1991, p. 84).

Confidentiality. Providing anonymity to participants in evaluation procedures.

Construct validity. The extent to which a test measures a psychological trait or construct. Tests of personality, verbal ability, and critical thinking are examples of tests with construct validity.

Content validity. The extent to which the content of a test such as an achievement test represents the objectives of the instructional program it is designed to measure.

Criteria. Indicators of success or merit that are included in the evaluation process.

Effect. An outcome or type of outcome.

Evaluation. Determination of the value or merit of something.

Event sampling. An observation strategy used to determine when a particular behavior is likely to occur. The setting in which the behavior occurs is more important than the time it is likely to occur.

(*Continued*)

FIGURE 10.5 Continued

Formative evaluation. An evaluation conducted during the development and implementation of an education process or program.

Generalizability. The extent to which the findings can be generalized to other populations or similar contexts. In contrast with research, of which one of its main purposes is to be highly generalizable, evaluation data often focus on the specific situation at hand. Whenever possible, however, the issue of generalizability should be included in devising meaningful evaluation strategies.

Goal-based evaluation. Any type of evaluation based on knowledge of the goals and objectives of the program, person, or product (Scriven, 1991, p. 178).

Interactive evaluation. An evaluation in which the individuals being evaluated have the opportunity to react to the content of a draft of an evaluation report.

Interest inventory. A measure used to determine interest in an occupation or vocation. Students' interest in reading might be determined by such an inventory.

Interview. A discussion that the teacher conducts with a child or parent to make an assessment.

Mean. The arithmetic average of a set of test scores.

Narrative report. An alternative to report cards for reporting a child's progress. The teacher writes a narrative to describe the child's growth and accomplishments.

Norms. Statistics that supply a frame of reference based on the actual performance of test takers in a norm group. A set of scores that represents the distribution of test performance in the norm group.

Performance-based assessment. An assessment of development, learning, or both that is based on the child's natural performance rather than on contrived tests or tasks.

Play-based assessment. Assessment for children with disabilities that is conducted through observation in play environments. Play activities can be spontaneous or planned. Play-based assessment can be conducted by an individual or through arena assessment.

Portfolio. A format for conducting an evaluation of a child or parent. Portfolios are a collection of work, teacher assessments, and other information that contribute to a picture of the child's progress.

Preassessment. An assessment conducted before the beginning of the school year or prior to any instruction at the beginning of the school year.

Project. An authentic learning activity that can also be used to demonstrate student achievement.

Rating scale. A scale using categories that allow the observer to indicate the degree of a characteristic that the person possesses.

Reliability. The consistency of measures of readings obtained in any evaluation procedure.

Rubric. An instrument developed to measure authentic and performance assessments. Descriptions are given for qualitative characteristics on a scale.

Running record. A description of a sequence of events in a child's behavior that includes all behaviors observed over a period of time.

Standardized test. A test that has specified content, procedures for administration and scoring, and normative data for interpreting scores.

FIGURE 10.5	Continued

Structured interview. A preplanned interview conducted by the teacher for assessment purposes.

Validity. A test is valid if it measures what it purports to measure. The phrase *validity of a test* (or an evaluation) really refers to the validity of a claim about its use in a certain context (Scriven, 1991).

Work sample. An example of a child's work. Work samples include products of all types of activities that can be used to evaluate the child's progress.

FIGURE 10.6	Advocacy Strategies for Classroom Teachers in the Assessment and Evaluation of Parent Involvement Programs

1. Determine the different languages and cultural backgrounds of the children and parents in your classroom; develop parent involvement assessment and evaluation tools and instruments with these cultural differences in mind.

2. Partner with a local service organization or faith-based group to provide resources and materials for the parents in your classroom. This might include clothing, shoes, linens, dishware, and other needed items.

3. Ask a professional colleague to serve as an interpreter for you as you gather baseline information about children and families at the beginning of the year. Personal interviews may be more appropriate than written needs assessments for non-English speaking families.

4. Develop parent involvement activities and events around the multicultural dimensions of your classroom. For example, potluck dinners and festivals should celebrate and include the different cultures reflected in your classroom.

5. Use authentic assessment strategies to document the parent involvement activities of your diverse classroom. Portfolios, videotapes, journals, and photography are examples of authentic assessment strategies that adapt to all cultures and languages.

6. Use simple tools for evaluating the success of individual events involving parents in your classroom as well as performing an overall evaluation at the end of the year.

7. One-page evaluation tools such as checklists and Linkert-type rating scales are easily understood; develop these tools in Spanish and other languages relevant to your classroom.

8. Consider doing end-of-the-year interviews with parents to determine their satisfaction levels with the academic year. Tape record these conversations.

9. Invite your center or building administrator to parent involvement events and involve him or her in your planning and assessment of these activities.

10. Keep your administrator informed of evolving parent issues throughout the school year, such as the arrival of new immigrant families into your classrooms, issues facing parents of children with disabilities and special needs, and your efforts to meet these individual family needs.

Recommended Resources for Parent and Family Involvement in Assessment and Evaluation

The following assessment and evaluation resources are recommended for teachers and parents:

Portfolio Assessment

Calfee, R. C., & Perfumo, R. C. (1993). Student portfolios: Opportunities for a revolution in assessment. *Journal of Reading, 36*(7), 532–537.
A survey reports rapid growth in the use of portfolios and raises concerns about their effective use.

Farr, R. (1991). Portfolios: Assessment in language arts. *ERIC Digest* (ERIC Document Reproduction Service No. ED3346093). Bloomington, IN: ERIC Clearinghouse on Reading and Communication Skills.
This is a summary of the rationale for using portfolio assessment, stressing how portfolios can serve multiple purposes, address language arts goals, and serve as authentic assessments.

Johns, J. L., & Leirsburg, P. V. (1992). How professionals view portfolio assessment. *Reading Research and Instruction, 32*(1), 1–10.
In comparing current results of an ongoing study to previous studies, researchers found that educators' familiarity with portfolios is increasing and that fewer practical problems in using them are being reported. Still, users express concerns with planning, managing, and "organizing" them.

Miller, M. L. (1992). The ins and outs of portfolios. *Communiqué, 20*(6), 3–4.
This perspective in a publication of the National Association of School Psychologists describes portfolio assessment as a viable multidimensional evaluation.

Steward, R. A., & Paradis, E. E. (1993). Portfolios: Agents of change (Have you read?). *Reading Teacher, 46*(6), 522–524.
This review of three textbooks on portfolios in reading and writing classrooms published in 1991 and 1992 recommends portfolios, but with some caveats.

Valencia, S. (1990). A portfolio approach to classroom reading assessment: The whys, whats, and hows. *Reading Teacher, 43*(4), 338–440.
This short article argues that theory, research, and instructional experiences recommend a portfolio approach to reading assessment.

Wiggins, G. (1989). Teaching to the (authentic) test. *Educational Leadership, 46*(7), 41–47.
A leading authority recommends portfolios as one form of authentic assessment, offering a descriptive example.

Performance Assessment

Brandt, R. (1992). On performance assessment: A conversation with Grant Wiggins. *Educational Leadership, 49*(8), 35–37.

Wiggins expresses concerns about assessment reforms failing because high stakes will be attached to them too soon and judgments will be unreliable. He urges educators to pay attention to task validity, score reliability, portfolio sampling, and solving problems related to generalizability.

Coley, R. J. (Ed.). (1990). Testing. *ETS Policy Notes, 2*(3).
This issue includes one article that discusses the role of testing in educational reform and one that describes work done in Connecticut in the area of student performance assessment and in two other innovative assessment programs.

Feuer, M. J., & Fulton, K. J. (1993). The many faces of performance assessment. *Phi Delta Kappan, 74*(6), 478.
Performance assessment is defined as seven common forms that include both analysis of student writing in general and portfolios.

Gardner, H. (1991). *The unschooled mind: How children think and how schools should teach.* New York: Basic Books.
An expert on understanding the development of the human mind makes an eloquent plea for educational reformation that will help students move beyond rote learning to achieve genuine understanding. Gardner makes use of what is known about human development and cognitive science, turning it into well-grounded advice that is both practical and very readable.

Hansen, J. B. (1992, April). *A purpose-driven assessment program.* Paper presented at the annual meeting of the American Educational Research Association.
This paper describes the assessment program of the Colorado Springs (Colorado) Public Schools. It includes norm-referenced, criterion-referenced, and performance-based assessment, which includes "direct writing" and portfolio assessment (ERIC Document Reproduction Service No. ED344928).

Linn, R. L., Baker, E. L., & Dunbar, S. (1991). Complex, performance-based assessment: Expectations and validation criteria. *Educational Research, 20*(8), 15–21.
This article makes a case for developing assessment criteria that are sensitive to the expectations for new assessments. It includes a list of 51 relevant references.

Moss, P. A., Beck, J. S., Ebbs, C., Matson, B., Muchmore, J., Steele, D., et al. (1992). Portfolios, accountability, and an interview approach to validity. *Educational Measurement: Issues and Practice, 11*(3), 12–21.
This article provides answers to questions related to the reporting of portfolio assessment results to audiences interested in school accountability, recommending the exploration of alternative assessments. The questions include, How can the results of classroom-based portfolio assessment be communicated outside the classroom? How might a portfolio-based assessment system be designed and implemented? How can we evaluate the merits of portfolio-based assessments?

O'Neil, J. (1992, May). Putting performance assessment to the test. *Educational Leadership, 49*(8), 14–19.
This article reports that officials in Vermont, California, Kentucky, Maryland, and other states have high expectations that performance assessments may prove as powerful a classroom influence as short-answer testing used to be.

(Continued)

Resnick, L. B., & Resnick, D. P. (1989, October). *Tests as standards of achievement in schools.*
    Paper presented at the Invitational Conference of the Educational Testing Service,
    Princeton, NJ.
The question, Can tests be both curriculum-neutral and effective means of monitoring and motivating
educational practice? is discussed. Educational reform is linked directly to assessment reform
(ERIC Document Reproduction Service No. ED335421).

Werner, P. H. (1992). Integrated assessment system. *Journal of Reading, 35*(5), 416–418.
This is a descriptive review of the integrated assessment system published by the Psychological
Corporation.

Wolf, D. P., LeMachieu, P. G., & Eresh, J. (1992). Good measure: Assessment as a tool for
    educational reform. *Educational Leadership, 49*(8), 8–13.
This article argues that portfolios are essential as tools of educational reform that will lead to
individual and internal accountability in schools.

Worthen, B., Borg, W. R., & White, K. R. (1993). *Measurement and evaluation in the schools.*
    New York: Longman.
This comprehensive examination of educational measurement covers all traditional concerns,
creating and selecting assessment for the classroom, and designing school- and districtwide
assessment programs.

Newsletters On Portfolios

Portfolio Assessment Clearinghouse. San Dieguito Union High School District, 710 Encinitas
    Boulevard, Encinitas, CA 92024.

Portfolio News. Published by the Northwest Evaluation Association, P.O. Box 2122, Lake Oswego,
    OR 97035.

Authentic Assessment with Families and Parents

Berger, E. H. (2004). *Parents as partners in education: Families and schools working together*
    (6th ed.). Upper Saddle River, NJ: Merrill/Prentice Hall.
This book contains the following two instruments:

Teacher's Attitudes About Collaborating with Parents.
A very straightforward instrument developed to assess the teacher's own attitudes about working
with parents and families (p. 124).

How Do You Collaborate with Parents Now?
A questionnaire designed to assess the current methods of collaboration used by the classroom
teacher (p. 125).

Roberts, T. W. (1994). *A systems perspective of parenting: The individual, the family, and the social
    network.* Pacific Grove, CA: Brooks/Cole.

General Assessment for Early Childhood Classrooms

Bredekamp, S., & Rosegrant, T. (Eds.). (1992). *Reaching potentials: Appropriate curriculum and assessment of young children* (Vol. 1). Washington, DC: National Association for the Education of Young Children.

Kamii, C. (1990). *Achievement testing in the early grades: The games grown-ups play.* Washington, DC: National Association for the Education of Young Children.

Leavitt, R. B., & Eheart, B. K. (1991). Assessment in early childhood programs. *Young Children, 46*(5), 4–9.

Marsden, D. B., Meisels, S. J., & Jablon, J. R. (1993). *The Work Sampling System: Preschool through grade three.* Ann Arbor: University of Michigan, Center for Human Growth and Development.

Meisels, S. J. (1987). Uses and abuses of developmental screening and school readiness testing. *Young Children, 42*(2), 4–6, 68–73.

National Association for the Education of Young Children & National Association of Early Childhood Specialists in State Departments of Education. (1991). Guidelines for appropriate curriculum content and assessment in programs serving children ages three through eight. *Young Children, 46*(3), 21–38.

Formal Rapid Assessment Instruments

For early childhood teachers interested in more quantitative and formal assessment of the parents and families in their learning settings, the following instruments may be used with the assistance of a school or community professional counselor or psychologist. These instruments are designed for programs that have structured and defined parent involvement program components, and information derived from them should remain confidential:

- Environmental Assessment Index
- Family Adaptability and Cohesion Evaluation Scale
- Family Assessment Device
- Family Functioning Scale
- Family-of-Origin Scale
- Family Times and Routines Index
- Family Traditions Scales
- Kansas Family Life Satisfaction Scale
- Kansas Parent Satisfaction Scale
- Parent–Child Relationship Survey

For additional information about these formal rapid assessment instruments, see J. Fischer and K. Corcoran, *Measures for Clinical Practice* (2nd ed., Vol. 1), New York: Free Press, 1994.

Critical Concepts

1. Assessment and evaluation of parent involvement activities and programs reflect the era of accountability and are important processes for contemporary teachers in early childhood classrooms.

2. *Assessment* refers to the gathering of baseline and needs data to develop effective parent involvement programs, whereas *evaluation* refers to the measuring of the successfulness of these activities.

3. The diversity of contemporary classrooms requires early childhood teachers to be inclusive in developing assessment and evaluation of parent involvement strategies. These tools should be sensitive to both the language and cultural diversity reflected by the parents and families who are a part of the classroom.

4. While standardized tools are still used for both assessment and evaluation, new strategies are emerging that include qualitative, performance-based methods of documenting and measuring the parent involvement process. Examples include photography, videotaping, portfolios, journaling, and other creative means of documenting parent involvement.

5. Teachers should advocate for the parents and families in their classrooms by partnering with community agencies and organizations to develop effective interventions and resources that meet the unique needs of these families.

Summary Statements

✓ A new era of assessment and evaluation in ECE now encourages the use of qualitative methods such as portfolios.

✓ Evaluation and assessment should allow for creative and individual designs to determine the value and quality of parent and family involvement.

✓ No one model for educational evaluation is best; the use of eclectic and systems evaluation models is encouraged.

✓ Accountability issues never have been greater in early childhood school settings; thus, ongoing and appropriate methods of assessment and evaluation are crucial.

✓ *Authentic assessment* is a standard term now used to describe efforts to assess a program, outcome, or process in a way that is sensitive to and matches the character and type of learning process used.

✓ National educational and advocacy organizations for young children and school-age children recommend the use of developmentally appropriate assessment and evaluation strategies for young children and their families.

✓ Early childhood teachers may feel uncomfortable with assessment and evaluation, and teachers should assess their own attitudes and aptitudes in this area.

✓ *Assessment* refers to informal and divergent ways of determining individual and parent needs, of documenting work processes and products, and of measuring program merit.

✓ *Evaluation* refers to quantitative and formalized ways of measuring program effectiveness and quality; measuring child, parent, and family outcomes; and determining whether programs should be continued.

✓ *Summative evaluation* refers to evaluation conducted at the conclusion of a program initiative, whereas *formative evaluation* refers to measures taken during developmental and ongoing phases of the program initiative.

✓ Needs assessments are administered at the beginning of the academic year or educational initiative to determine individual program needs and to establish baseline data.

✓ Authentic assessment involves the use of creative approaches, emphasizes and celebrates development and learning based on real-life events, is performance based, relates to instruction, is collaborative, and provides a broad and general picture of student learning and capabilities.

✓ *Formal assessment* refers to the use of standardized instruments, whereas *informal assessment* provides greater latitude for parent expression and demonstration of skills, attitudes, and efforts.

✓ Needs assessment and program planning for parents and families are not separate processes but, rather, are closely intertwined.

✓ Family involvement can be shaped around relevant and meaningful themes that are decided jointly between teachers and parents.

✓ Documentation of parent involvement events and activities should build on the characteristics of the building and classroom, as well as the collective skills and interests of the parents involved.

✓ A *parent wall* is a family involvement strategy adapted from Reggio Emilia programs of Northern Italy.

✓ *Family portfolios* are collections of writings, photographs, and other documentation materials that reflect the shared learning experiences of children, parents, and siblings.

✓ Portfolio assessment encourages self-directed learning, documentation of work, and shared decision making. Portfolios can assume many formats, shapes, and sizes.

✓ Each school setting has its own history of program evaluation, and each teacher should develop a meaningful program evaluation process that builds on past successful experiences and encourages new, creative evaluation approaches.

✓ Program evaluation serves many purposes in educational settings, including a basis for decision making, policy formation, student achievement assessment, evaluation of curricula, accreditation processes, monitoring of fiscal expenditures, and improvement of educational materials and programs.

✓ Assessment and evaluation instruments and tools should be selected from a wide array of available resources designed by the teacher to measure the unique aspects of his or her program and used creatively to reflect the teacher's philosophy of program development and implementation.

Research to Practice: Classroom Applications and Activities

1. As a preassessment tool, write about your own perceptions of assessment and evaluation. Think back to your early years of schooling and recall how your attitudes toward tests were formed. (*Note:* This exercise can be used as a pre- and posttest.) Write about your new perceptions of assessment and evaluation after reading this chapter.

2. Join other students in teams of two or three and develop an outline for a family

portfolio. Then, divide each team's tasks and responsibilities and create a skeleton family portfolio. Display your portfolio at a Portfolio Day in class and view each other's work.

3. Develop a resource list of assessment and evaluation instruments and resources. Categorize these items under specific topics, such as parent education, family involvement, child development, problem solving, family history and preservation, technology, human diversity, and selected curriculum areas. Be sure to include Web-based sources of information.

4. Invite a panel of five or six parents of ECE students (birth to age 8) to class to discuss their feelings, attitudes, perceptions, and concerns about parent involvement programs in school settings.

5. Create a bulletin board that explains and depicts authentic assessment. Identify the target audience for the bulletin board: parents, policy makers, other teachers, administrators, other college students, and so on.

6. Complete Berger's attitude instrument on collaborating with parents. Share the results with other students (see pp. 158–159 in Berger, E. H. [2004]. *Parents as partners in education: Families and schools working together* [6th ed.]. Upper Saddle River, NJ: Merrill/ Prentice Hall).

7. As a college class, develop a shared list of interview questions and then interview from three to five parents about their attitudes toward participating in parent and family involvement programs in school settings. Share the results of the interviews; collate the data and distribute to other class members.

8. Using a search engine, conduct an Internet search of terms related to assessment and evaluation, such as *work samples, high-stakes tests, developmental checklists, summary reports,* and *performance assessment,* and record your findings.

REFERENCES

Chapter 1

Bell, C. C., & Jenkins, E. J. (1993). Community violence and children on Chicago's South Side. *Psychiatry, 56,* 46–54.

Berger, L. M., Hill, J., & Waldfogel, J. (2005). Maternity leave, early maternal employment and child health and development in the U.S. *The Economic Journal, 115,* 29–47.

Bredekamp, S. (1987). *Developmentally appropriate practice in early childhood programs serving children from birth through age eight.* Washington, DC: National Association for the Education of Young Children.

Bronfenbrenner, U. (1979). *The ecology of human development.* Cambridge, MA: Harvard University Press.

Bureau of Labor Statistics. (2001). Unpublished data from the Bureau of Labor Statistics on marital and family characteristics from the March 2001 Current Population Survey.

Carnegie Corporation. (1994). *Starting points: Meeting the needs of our youngest childen.* New York: Carnegie Corporation.

Children's Defense Fund. (1991). *The state of America's children.* Washington, DC: Author.

Children's Defense Fund. (1996). *The state of America's children.* Washington, DC: Author.

Children's Defense Fund. (1997). *The state of America's children.* Washington, DC: Author.

Children's Defense Fund. (2005). *Child care basics.* Retrieved June 10, 2005, from www.childrensdefense.org

Clinton, H. (1996). *It takes a village to raise a child.* New York: Touchstone.

Comer, J. P. (1990). Home, school, and academic learning. In J. I. Goodlad & P. Keating (Eds.), *Access to knowledge: An agenda for our nation's schools* (chap. 2). New York: College Entrance Examination Board.

Daniel, J. (1996). Family-centered work and child care. *Young Children, 51,* 2.

Darden, E., & Zimmerman, T. (1992). Blended families: A decade review, 1979–1990. *Family Therapy, 19,* 25–31.

Drug Enforcement Agency. (1996). *Drugs of abuse.* Arlington, VA: U.S. Department of Justice.

Dubrow, N. F., & Garbarino, J. (1989). Living in the war zone: Mothers and young children in a public housing development. *Journal of Child Welfare, 68,* 3–20.

Edelman, M. W. (1992). *The measure of our success: A letter to my children and yours.* Boston: Beacon.

Edwards, C. P., Gandini, L., & Forman, G. (1993). *The hundred languages of children.* Norwood, NJ: Ablex.

Edwards, P. A., & Young, L. S. (1992, September). Beyond parents: Family, community, and school involvement. *Phi Delta Kappan, 74*(1), 74, 76, 78, 80, 85–86.

Epstein, J. L. (1988, January). How do we improve programs for parent involvement? *Educational Horizons, 62,* 58–59.

Erikson, E. H. (1950). *Childhood and society.* New York: Norton.

Everett, S. A., & Price, J. H. (1995). Students' perceptions of violence in the public schools: The Metlife survey. *Journal of Adolescent Health, 17*(6), 345–353.

Finn, C., & Petrilli, M. J. (1998, Fall). Washington versus school reform. *The Public Interest, 13*(133), 55.

Forman, G., Gandini, L., Malaguzzi, L., Rinaldi, C., Piazza, G., & Gambetti, A. (1993). *An amusement park for birds.* Available from Performanetics Press, 19 The Hollow, Amherst, MA 01002.

Glaser, R. (1985). Foreword. In R. C. Anderson, E. H. Hiebert, & I.A.G. Wilkinson (Eds.), *Becoming a nation of readers: The report of the Commission on Reading,* p. vii. Washington, DC: National Institute of Education.

Goffin, S., & Stegelin, D. (1992). *Changing kindergartens: Four success stories.* Washington, DC: National Association for the Education of Young Children.

Goldstein, J. R. (1999). The leveling of divorce in the United States. *Demography, 36*(3), 409–415.

Gonzalez-Mena, J. (2002). *The young child in the family and the community* (3rd ed.). Upper Saddle River, NJ: Merrill/Prentice Hall.

Hoyt, M., & Schoonmaker, M. E. (1991, October 15). When parents accept the unacceptable. *Family Circle, 104,* 81–87.

Klerman, J. A., & Leibowitz, A. (1999). Job continuity among new mothers. *Demography, 36*(2), 145–155.

Louv, R. (1993, July). The crisis of the absent father. *Parents, 68*(7), 54–56.

Lyon, S. (1995). What is my culture? *Child Care Information Exchange, 8,* 1.

Massey, M. S. (1998). Early childhood violence prevention. *ERIC Clearinghouse on Elementary and Early Childhood Education.* EDO-PS-98–9 [Online]. Available from http://searcheric.org

NAEYC. (1986, Sept.). NAEYC position statement on developmentally appropriate practice in early childhood programs serving children from birth through age 8. *Young Children, 5,* 4–19.

National Association of State Boards of Education, Task Force on Early Childhood Education. (1988). *Right from the start.* Alexandria, VA: National Association of State Boards of Education.

National Committee to Prevent Child Abuse. (1998, April). Child abuse and neglect statistics. Retrieved September 21, 1998, from www.childabuse.org

Olmstead, P. (1992). Where did our diversity come from? *High/Scope ReSource, 11,* 4–9.

Pear, R. (November 5, 2000). Far more single mothers are taking jobs. *The New York Times.*

Phillips, C. B. (1994). The movement of African American children through sociocultural contexts: A case of conflict resolution. In B. L. Mallory & R. S. New (Eds.), *Diversity and developmentally appropriate practices: Challenges for early childhood education* (pp. 166–182). New York: Teachers College Press.

Phillips, D. (March 1, 1995). Testimony before the Senate Committee on Labor and Human Resources. Retrieved December 29, 2005, from www.childrensdefense.org/childcare/basics.aspx

Poussaint, A. F., & Linn, S. (1997, Spring/Summer). Fragile: Handle with care. [Your Child: From Birth to Three, Special Issue]. *Newsweek, 129*(9), 33.

Powell, D. R. (1989). *Families and early childhood programs.* Washington, DC: National Association for the Education of Young Children.

Powell, D. R. (1991). Parents and programs: Early childhood as a pioneer in parent involvement and support. In S. L. Kagan (Ed.), *The care and education of America's young children: Obstacles and opportunities.* Ninetieth yearbook of the National Society for the Study of Education (pp. 91–109). Chicago: National Society for the Study of Education.

Prothrow-Stith, D., & Quaday, S. (1995). *Hidden casualties: The relationship between violence and learning.* Washington, DC: National Health & Education Consortium and National Consortium for African American Children, Inc.

Richters, J. E., & Martinez, P. (1993). The NIMH community violence project: I. Children as victims of and witness to violence. *Psychiatry, 56,* 7–21.

Rockwell, B., & Kniepkamp, J. R. (2003). *Partnering with parents.* Beltsville, MD: Gryphon House.

Ryan, M. (1992, August 30). Who's taking care of the children? *Parade Magazine,* 3–5.

Saluter, A. F. (1989). Singleness in America. In *Studies in marriage and the family.* Washington, DC: U.S. Department of Commerce, Bureau of the Census.

Shores, E. (1992). *Explorer's classrooms: Good practice for kindergarten and the primary grades.* Little Rock, AR: Southern Association on Children Under Six.

Shulman, K. (2000). *The high cost of child care puts quality care out of reach for many families.* Washington, DC: Children's Defense Fund.

Slaby, R. G., Roedell, W. C., Arezzo, D., & Hendrix, K. (1995). *Early violence prevention: Tools for teachers of young children.* Washington, DC: National Association for the Education of Young Children.

Smith, K., & Bachu, A. (1999). *Women's labor force attachment patterns and maternity leave: A review of the literature* (Working Paper No. 32). Washington, DC: U.S. Bureau of the Census, Population Division.

Stegelin, D. A. (1992). *Early childhood education: Policy issues for the 1990s.* Norwood, NJ: Ablex.

Sullivan, A. (1998). Social constructivist perspectives on teaching and learning. *Annual Review of Psychology, 49,* 345.

U.S. Department of Health and Human Services. (1990). *A handbook for involving parents in Head Start* (DHHS Publication No. 90–31187). Rockville, MD: Author.

Vygotsky, L. (1962). *Thought and language.* Cambridge, MA: MIT Press.

Vygotsky, L. (1978). *Mind and society: The development of higher mental processes.* Cambridge, MA: Harvard University Press.

Wallach, L. B. (1993). Helping children cope with violence. *Young Children, 48*(4), 4–11.

Wallerstein, J. S., & Blakeslee, S. (1995). *The good marriage: How and why love lasts.* Boston: Houghton Mifflin.

Walsh, W. M. (1992). Twenty major issues in remarriage families. *Journal of Counseling & Development, 70,* 709–715.

Zellman, G. L., & Waterman, J. M. (1998, July–August). Understanding the impact of parent–school involvement on children's educational outcomes. *Journal of Educational Research, 91*(6), 370–380.

Chapter 2

Barbour, C., & Barbour, N. H. (1997). *Families, schools, and communities: Building partnerships for educating children.* Upper Saddle River, NJ: Merrill/Prentice Hall.

Berger, E. H. (2004). *Parents as partners in education: Families and schools working together* (6th ed.). Upper Saddle River, NJ: Merrill/Prentice Hall.

Bloom, B. S. (1964). *Stability and change in human characteristics.* New York: Wiley.

Bloom, B. S. (1981). *All our children learning: A primer for teachers, parents, and other educators.* New York: McGraw-Hill.

Bredekamp, S. (Ed.). (1987). *Developmentally appropriate practice in early childhood programs serving children from birth through age eight* (Exp. ed.). Washington, DC: National Association for the Education of Young Children.

Bronfenbrenner, U. (1979). *The ecology of human environment.* Cambridge, MA: Harvard University Press.

Bubolz, M. M., & Sontag, S. (1993). Human ecology theory. In P. G. Boss, W. J. Doherty, R. LaRossa, W. R. Schumm, & S. K. Steinmetz (Eds.), *Sourcebook of family theories and methods: A contextual approach* (pp. 419–448). New York: Plenum.

Childhood. (1991). In *Great expectations* [Video]. New York: Ambrose Video.

Damian, B. (2005). Rated 5 for five year olds. *Young Children, 60*(2), 50–53.

Dave, R. H. (1963). *The identification and measurement of environmental process variables that are related to educational achievement.* Unpublished doctoral dissertation, University of Chicago.

DeMause, L. (1974). The evolution of children. In L. DeMause (Ed.), *The history of childhood.* New York: Psychohistory Press.

Epstein, J. L., Coates, L., Salinas, K. C., Sanders, M. G., & Simon, B. S. (1997). *School, family and community partnerships: Your handbook for action.* Thousand Oaks, CA: Corwin Press.

Gordon, I. J., & Breivogel, W. F. (1976). *Building effective home–school relationships.* Boston: Allyn & Bacon.

Henderson, A. T., & Berla, N. (Eds.). (1994). *A new generation of evidence: The family is critical to student achievement.* Washington, DC: Center for Law and Education.

Hunt, J. M. (1961). *Intelligence and experience.* New York: Ronald Press.

Hyun, E. (2003). The No Child Left Behind Act of 2001: Issues and implications for early childhood teacher education. *Journal of Early Childhood Teacher Education, 24*(2), 119–126.

Kentucky Education Professional Standards Board. (1995). *Interdisciplinary childhood education teacher performance standards.* Frankfort, KY: Department of Education.

Kentucky Education Professional Standards Board. (1999). *New teacher standards for preparation and certification.* Frankfort, KY: Department of Education.

Kreider, H. (2002). *Getting parents ready for kindergarten: The role of early childhood education.* Cambridge, MA: Harvard Family Research Project.

Lindle, J. C. (1994). Kentucky's reform opens doors to family involvement. *Dimensions in Early Childhood, 22.*

Morrison, G. S. (1998). *Early childhood education today.* (8th ed.) Upper Saddle River, NJ: Merrill/Prentice Hall.

Ogbu, J. U. (1988). Cultural diversity and human development. In D. Slaughter (Ed.), *Black children and poverty: A developmental perspective* (pp. 11–28). San Francisco: Jossey-Bass.

Osborn, D. K. (1991). *Early childhood education in historical perspective* (3rd ed.). Athens, GA: Education Associates.

Pianta, R. C., & Cox, M. J. (Eds.). (1999). *The transition to kindergarten.* Baltimore, MD: Paul H. Brookes.

Rideout, V. J., Vandewater, E. A., & Wartella, E. A. (2003). *Zero to six: Electronic media in the lives of infants, toddlers, and preschoolers.* Washington, DC: Kaiser Foundation.

Roopnarine, J. L., & Johnson, J. E. (1993). *Approaches to early childhood education* (2nd ed.). Upper Saddle River, NJ: Merrill/Prentice Hall.

Spock, B. (1946). *The common sense book of baby and child care.* New York: Duell, Sloan and Pearce.

Swap, S. M. (1993). *Developing home–school partnerships: From concepts to practice.* New York: Teachers College Press.

Theuvenelle, S., & Bewick, C. J. (2003). *Completing the computer puzzle: A guide for early childhood educators.* Boston: Allyn & Bacon.

Trawick-Smith, J. W. (1997). *Early childhood development: A multicultural perspective.* Upper Saddle River, NJ: Merrill/Prentice Hall.

U.S. Government (2001). HR. 1, No Child Left Behind Act of 2001. Retrieved January 7, 2002, from www.ed.gov

Wright, K., Daniel, T., & Heimelreich, K. (1999). *Building partnerships with families: A survey of parents, teachers, and administrators.* Lexington, KY: Commonwealth Institute for Parents, Prichard Committee for Academic Excellence.

Chapter 3

Anderson, L. (1992). Parent power: The developmental classroom project. In S. G. Goffin & D. A. Stegelin (Eds.), *Changing kindergartens: Four success stories* (pp. 73–98). Washington, DC: National Association for the Education of Young Children.

Bredekamp, S., & Rosegrant, T. (Eds.). (1992). *Reaching potentials: Appropriate curriculum and assessment for young children* (vol. 1). Washington, DC: National Association for the Education of Young Children.

Bronfenbrenner, U. (1979). *The ecology of human development.* Cambridge, MA: Harvard University Press.

Clinton, W. (1992). State policy related to disadvantaged and at-risk preschoolers. In D. A. Stegelin (Ed.), *Early childhood education: Policy issues for the 1990s* (pp. 21–30). Norwood, NJ: Ablex.

Comer, J. P. (1990). Home, school, and academic learning. In J. I. Goodlad & P. Keating (Eds.), *Access to knowledge: An agenda for our nation's schools* (p. xx). New York: College Entrance Examination Board.

Dye, T. R. (1992). *Understanding public policy.* Upper Saddle River, NJ: Prentice Hall.

Edwards, P. A., & Young, L. A. (1992, May). Beyond parents: Family, community, and school involvement. *Phi Delta Kappan, 74,* 72–80.

Farnum, L. (1987). Child care and early education: A partnership with elementary education. *Thrust, 6,* 19–20.

Gandini, L. (1997). Foundations of the Reggio Emilia approach. In J. Hendrick (Ed.), *First steps toward teaching the Reggio way* (pp. 14–25). Upper Saddle River, NJ: Merrill/Prentice Hall.

Gargiulo, R. M., & Graves, S. B. (1991, Spring). Parental feelings. *Childhood Education, 67*(3), 176–178.

Geiger, B. (1997). Implementing Reggio in an independent school: What works? In J. Hendrick (Ed.), *First steps toward teaching the Reggio way* (pp. 141–150). Upper Saddle River, NJ: Merrill/Prentice Hall.

Goffin, S. G. (1992). Creating change with the public schools: Reflections of an early childhood teacher educator. In D. A. Stegelin (Ed.), *Early childhood education: Policy issues for the 1990s.* Norwood, NJ: Ablex.

Gregory, B. C. (1992). The necessity of continuity between the kindergarten and the elementary school: The present status, illogical and unFrobellian. In S. G. Goffin & D. A. Stegelin (Eds.), *Changing kindergartens: Four success stories.* Washington, DC: National Association for the Education of Young Children.

Irwin, D., & Bushnell, M. (1980). *Observational strategies for child study.* New York: Holt, Rinehart & Winston.

Kagan, S. L. (1989). Early care and education: Tackling the tough issues. *Phi Delta Kappan, 70*(6), 433–439.

Kagan, S. L. (1991). *United we stand: Collaboration for child care and early education services.* New York: Teachers College Press.

Kagan, S. L. (1992). Birthing collaborations in early care and education: A polemic of pain and promise. In D. A. Stegelin (Ed.), *Early childhood education: Policy issues for the 1990s* (pp. 31–50). Norwood, NJ: Ablex.

Lazar, I., Darlington, R., Murray, H., Royce, J., & Snipper, A. (1982). Lasting effects of early education. *Monographs of the Society for Research in Child Development, 47* (2–3, Serial no. 195).

Lombardi, J. (1986). Training for public policy and advocacy. *Young Children, 42,* 65–69.

Malaguzzi, L. (1993). For an education based on relationships. *Young Children, 49*(1), 9–12.

McCormick, K. (1986). If early education isn't on your agenda now, it could be—And soon. *American School Board Journal, 41,* 69–71.

Merriam-Webster's new collegiate dictionary (10th ed.). (1993). Springfield, MA: Merriam-Webster.

Mitchell, A. (1989). Old baggage, new visions: Shaping policy for early childhood programs. *Phi Delta Kappan, 70*(9), 664–672.

Molnar, J. (1991). What good prekindergarten programs look like. *Streamlined Seminar, 9*(5), 1–7.

National Association for the Education of Young Children. (1984). *Accreditation criteria and procedures of the National Academy of Early Childhood Programs.* Washington, DC: Author.

National Association for the Education of Young Children. (2004). *NAEYC Affiliate Public Policy Toolkit.* Washington, DC: Author.

National Association of State Boards of Education. (1988). *Right from the start: Report of the NASBE task force on early childhood education.* Alexandria, VA: Author.

National Governors Association & Center for Policy Research. (1987). *The first sixty months: A handbook of promising prevention programs for children 0–5 years of age.* Washington, DC: National Governors Association.

New, R. (1998). Theory and praxis in Reggio Emilia: They know what they are doing and why. In C. Edwards, L. Gandini, & G. Forman (Eds.), *The hundred languages of children: The Reggio Emilia approach to early childhood education* (2nd ed.). Norwood, NJ: Ablex.

Riley, R. (1986). Can we reduce the risk of failure? *Phi Delta Kappan, 68,* 214–219.

Schultz, T. (1992). Developmentally appropriate practice and the challenge of public school reform. In D. A. Stegelin (Ed.), *Early childhood education: Policy issues for the 1990s* (pp. 137–154). Norwood, NJ: Ablex.

Schweinhart, L. J. (1992). How much do good early childhood programs cost? *Early Education and Development, 3*(2), 115–127.

Schweinhart, L. J., & Weikart, D. P. (1986). Consequences of three preschool curriculum models through age 15. *Early Childhood Research Quarterly, 1,* 15–35.

Schweinhart, L. J., & Weikart, D. P. (1992). The High/Scope Perry preschool study, similar studies, and their implications for public policy in the U.S. In D. A. Stegelin (Ed.), *Early childhood education: Policy issues for the 1990s* (pp. 67–88). Norwood, NJ: Ablex.

Stegelin, D. A. (Ed.). (1992). *Early childhood education: Policy issues for the 1990s.* Norwood, NJ: Ablex.

Toffler, A. (1981). *The third wave.* New York: Bantam Books.

Weikart, D. P. (1989). Hard choices in early childhood care and education: A view to the future. *Young Children, 45,* 25–30.

Chapter 4

Aboud, F. E. (1988). *Children and prejudice.* New York: Basil Blackwell.

Althen, G. (1988). *American ways: A guide for foreigners in the United States.* Yarmouth, ME: Intercultural Press.

Angelou, M. (1994). *My painted house, my friendly chicken, and me.* New York: Clarkson Potter.

Barrera, I., Corso, R. M., & McPherson, D. (2003). *Skilled dialogue: Strategies for responding to cultural diversity in early childhood.* Baltimore: Paul H. Brookes.

Battle, J. L., Black, J. K., Guddemi, M., & O'Bar, A. (1992). *Multicultural education: A position statement.* Little Rock, AR: Southern Early Childhood Association.

Bennett, L., Jr. (1966). *Before the Mayflower.* Baltimore: Penguin.

Bishop, R. S. (1988). Foreword. In D. Taylor & C. Dorsey-Gaines, *Growing up literate: Learning from inner-city families* (pp. ix–x). Portsmouth, NH: Heinemann.

Brinson, S. A. (2005). R-E-S-P-E-C-T for families. *Dimensions of Early Childhood, 33*(2), 24–30.

Bronfenbrenner, U. (1988). Foreword. In A. R. Pence (Ed.), *Ecological research with children and families: From concepts to methodology* (pp. ix–x). New York: Teachers College Press.

Bruns, D., & Corso, R. M. (2001). *Working with culturally and linguistically diverse families* (ERIC Digest No. ED455972). Champaign, IL: ERIC Clearinghouse on Elementary and Early Childhood.

Carter, M. (1995). Building a community culture among teachers. *Child Care Information Exchange, I,* 52–54.

Chan, S. (1992). Families with Asian roots. In E. W. Lynch & M. J. Hanson (Eds.), *Developing crosscultural competence: A guide for working with young children and their families* (pp. 181–258). Baltimore: Brookes.

Coles, R. (1997). *How to raise a moral child: The moral intelligence of children.* New York: Random House.

Comune di Reggio Emilia, Centro Documentazione Ricerca ducativa Nidi e Scuole dell'Infanzi. (1987). *To make a portrait of a lion (Per Fare il Ritratto di un Leone)* [Video]. Available through Baji Rankin, 346 Washington St., Cambridge, MA 02139.

Department of Early Education, City of Reggio Emilia, Region of Emilia Romagna. (1987). *I centro linguaggi dei bambini (The hundred languages of children: Narrative of the possible).* Catalog of the exhibit "The hundred languages of children," in Italian and English. Available from Assessorate Scuole Infanzia e Asili Nido, Via Guido da Castello 12, 42011 Reggio Emilia, Italy.

Derman-Sparks, L. (1989). *Antibias curriculum: Tools for empowering young children.* Washington, DC: National Association for the Education of Young Children.

Derman-Sparks, L., & Ramsey, P. G. (1993). Early childhood multicultural, antibias education in the 1990s: Toward the 21st century. In J. L. Roopnarine & J. E. Johnson (Eds.), *Approaches to early childhood education* (2nd ed., pp. 275–294). Upper Saddle River, NJ: Merrill/Prentice Hall.

Edwards, C., Gandini, L., & Forman, G. (1993). *The hundred languages of children: The Reggio Emilia approach to early childhood education.* Norwood, NJ: Ablex.

Edwards, C. P. (1986). *Promoting social and moral development in young children: Creative approaches for the classroom.* New York: Teachers College Press.

Edwards, C. P., & Springate, K. W. (1995). The lion comes out of the stone: Helping young children achieve their creative potential. *Dimensions of Early Childhood, 23,* 24–29.

Feng, J. (1994, June). Asian American children: What teachers should know. *Eric Digest* (EDP-PS-94–4). Urbana, IL: ERIC.

Ferreiro, E., & Teberosky, A. (1992). *Literacy before schooling.* Portsmouth, NH: Heinemann.

Forman, G., Gandini, L., Malaguzzi, L., Rinaldi, C., Piazza, G., & Gambetti, A. (1993). *An amusement park for birds* [Video]. Available from Performanetics Press, 19 The Hollow, Amherst MA 01002.

Forman, G. E., & Gandini, L. (1991). *The long jump: A video analysis of small group projects in early education as practiced in Reggio Emilia, Italy* [Video]. Available from Performanetics Press, 19 The Hollow, Amherst, MA 01002.

Garcia, E. E. (1997). The education of Hispanics in early childhood: Of roots and wings. *Young Children, 52,* 5–14.

Gaskins, S. (1996). How Mayan parental theories come into play. In S. Harkness & C. M. Super (Eds.), *Parents' cultural belief systems: Their origins, expressions, and consequences* (pp. 345–363). New York: Guilford.

Gilligan, C. (1982). *In a different voice: Sex differences in the expression of moral judgment.* Cambridge, MA: Harvard University Press.

Gonzalez-Mena, J. (1993). *Multicultural issues in child care.* Mountain View, CA: Mayfield.

Goodman, M. E. (1952). *Race awareness in young children.* Cambridge, MA: Addison-Wesley.

Hale, J. (1982). *Black children: Their roots, culture, and learning styles.* New York: Springer.

Hale, J. (1991). The transmission of cultural values to young African American children. *Young Children, 46,* 7–15.

Hanson, M. J. (1992). Families with Anglo European roots. In E. W. Lynch & M. J. Hanson (Eds.), *Developing cross-cultural competence: A guide for working with young children and their families* (pp. 65–88). Baltimore: Brookes.

Harris, T. T., & Fuqua, J. D. (1996). To build a house: Designing curriculum for primary-grade children. *Young Children, 52,* 77–83.

Harste, J. C., & Woodward, V. A. (1989). Fostering needed change in early literacy programs. In D. Strickland & L. M. Morrow (Eds.), *Emerging literacy: Young children learn to read and write* (pp. 147–159). New York: Springer.

Hildebrand, V., Phenice, L. A., Gray, M. M., & Hines, R. P. (2000). *Knowing and serving diverse families* (2nd ed.). Upper Saddle River, NJ: Merrill/Prentice Hall.

Joe, J. R., & Malach, R. S. (1992). Families with Native American roots. In E. W. Lynch & M. J. Hanson (Eds.), *Developing cross-cultural competence: A guide for working with young children and their families* (pp. 89–120). Baltimore: Brookes.

Jones, E., & Nimmo, J. (1994). *Emergent curriculum.* Washington, DC: National Association for the Education of Young Children.

Katz, P. A. (1976). The acquisition of racial attitudes in children. In R. P. Katz (Ed.), *Toward the elimination of racism* (pp. 125–154). New York: Pergamon.

Klein, H. A. (1995). Urban Appalachian children in northern schools: A study in diversity. *Young Children, 50,* 10–16.

Kohlberg, L. (1984). *Essays on moral development: Vol. 2. The psychology of moral development.* San Francisco: Harper & Row.

Ladson-Billings, G. (1995). Toward a theory of culturally relevant pedagogy. *American Education Research Journal, 33* (3), 465–492.

Lawrence-Lightfoot, S. (2000). Respect: *An exploration.* Cambridge, MA: Perseus.

Lynch, E. W., & Hanson, M. J. (1998). *Developing cross-cultural competence: A guide for working with young children and their families.* Baltimore: Brookes.

Mallory, B. L., & New, R. S. (1994). Introduction: The ethic of inclusion. In B. R. Mallory & R. S. New (Eds.), *Diversity and developmentally appropriate practices: Challenges for early childhood education* (pp. 1–13). New York: Teachers College Press.

McKinnon, J. (2003). *The Black population in the United States: March 2002.* Current Population Reports, Series P20–541. Washington, DC: U.S. Census Bureau.

Morrison, J. W., & Rodgers, L. S. (1996). Being responsive to the needs of children from dual heritage backgrounds. *Young Children, 52,* 29–33.

New, R. S. (1994). Culture, child development, and developmentally appropriate practices: Teachers as collaborative researchers. In B. L. Mallory & R. S. New (Eds.), *Diversity and developmentally appropriate practices: Challenges for early childhood education* (pp. 65–83). New York: Teachers College Press.

Ogunwole, S. U. (2002). *The Amerian Indian and Alaska Native population in the United States: February 2002.* Current Population Reports, C2KBR/01–15. Washington, DC: U.S. Census Bureau.

Ontake, Y., Santos, R. M., & Fowler, S. A. (2000). It's a three way conversation: Families, service providers, and interpreters working together. *Young Exceptional Children, 4* (1), 12–18.

Paley, V. G. (1992). *You can't say you can't play.* Cambridge, MA: Harvard University Press.

Phillips, C. B. (1994). The movement of African American children through sociocultural contexts. In B. R. Mallory & R. S. New (Eds.), *Diversity and developmentally appropriate practices: Challenges for early childhood education* (pp. 137–154). New York: Teachers College Press.

Piaget, J. (1932). *The moral judgment of the child.* New York: Free Press.

Piaget, J. (1983). Piaget's theory. In P. H. Mussen (Ed.), *Handbook of child psychology: Vol. 1. History, theory, and methods.* New York: Wiley.

Pipher, M. (1996). *The shelter of each other: Rebuilding our families.* New York: Putnam.

Powell, D. R. (1994). Parents, pluralism, and the NAEYC statement on developmentally appropriate practice. In B. R. Mallory & R. S. New (Eds.), *Diversity and developmentally appropriate practices: Challenges for early childhood education* (pp. 166–182). New York: Teachers College Press.

Quintero, E. (1999). The new faces of Head Start: Learning from culturally diverse families. *Early Education and Development, 10* (4), 475–497.

Ramirez, R. R., & de la Cruz, G. P. (2002). *The Hispanic population in the United States: March 2002.* Current Population Reports, P20–545. Washington, DC: U.S. Census Bureau.

Ramsey, P. G. (1986). Racial and cultural categories. In C. P. Edwards, *Social and moral development in young children* (pp. 78–101). New York: Teachers College Press.

Ramsey, P. G. (1987). *Teaching and learning in a diverse world: Multicultural education for young children.* New York: Teachers College Press.

Reeves, T., & Bennett, C. (2003). *The Asian and Pacific Islander population in the United States: March 2002.* Current Population Reports, P20–540. Washington, DC: U.S. Census Bureau.

Saracho, O. N., & Spodek, B. (1983). Preface. In O. N. Saracho & B. Spodek (Eds.), *Understanding the multicultural experience in early childhood education* (pp. 3–15). Washington, DC: National Association for the Education of Young Children.

Sharifzadeh, V. S. (1992). Families with Middle Eastern roots. In E. W. Lynch & M. J. Hanson (Eds.), *Developing cross-cultural competence: A guide for working with young children and their families* (pp. 441–482). Baltimore: Brookes.

Tabors, P. O. (1998). What early childhood educators need to know: Developing effective programs for linguistically and culturally diverse children and families. *Young Children, 53* (6), 20–26.

Taylor, D., & Dorsey-Gaines, C. (1988). *Growing up literate: Learning from inner-city families.* Portsmouth, NH: Heinemann.

Teale, W. H., & Sulzby, E. (1989). Emergent literacy: New perspectives. In D. Strickland & L. M. Morrow (Eds.), *Emerging literacy: Young children learn to read and write* (pp. 1–15). New York: Springer.

Trawick-Smith, J. (1997). *Early childhood development: A multicultural perspective.* Upper Saddle River, NJ: Merrill/Prentice Hall.

Trumbull, E., Rothstein-Fisch, C., Greenfield, P. M., & Quiroz, B. (2001). *Bridging cultures between home and school: A guide for teachers.* Mahwah, NJ: Erlbaum.

Wellhousen, K. (1996). Be it ever so humble: Developing a study of homes for today's diverse society. *Young Children, 52,* 72–76.

Willis, W. (1992). Families with African American roots. In E. W. Lynch & M. J. Hanson (Eds.),

Developing cross-cultural competence: A guide for working with young children and their families (pp. 121–150). Baltimore: Brookes.

Wolf, A. W., Lozoff, B., Latz, S., & Paludetto, R. (1996). Parental theories in the management of young children's sleep in Japan, Italy, and the United States. In S. Harkness & C. M. Super (Eds.), *Parents' cultural belief systems: Their origins, expressions, and consequences* (pp. 364–384). New York: Guilford.

York, S. (1991). *Roots and wings: Affirming culture in early childhood programs.* St. Paul, MN: Red Leaf.

Zeitlin, M. (1996). My child is my crown: Yoruba parental theories and practices in early childhood. In S. Harkness & C. M. Super (Eds.), *Parents' cultural belief systems: Their origins, expressions, and consequences* (pp. 407–427). New York: Guilford.

Zuniga, M. E. (1992). Families with Latino roots. In E. W. Lynch & M. J. Hanson (Eds.), *Developing cross-cultural competence: A guide for working with young children and their families* (pp. 151–180). Baltimore: Brookes.

Chapter 5

Baker, J. N. (1991, Summer). Beating the handicap rap [Special issue]. *Newsweek, 117*, 36–37.

Batshaw, M. L. (1991). *Your child has a disability: A complete sourcebook of daily and medical care.* Baltimore: Brookes.

Bowe, F. (2000). *Physical, sensory, and health disabilities: An introduction.* Upper Saddle River, NJ: Merrill/Prentice Hall.

Bredekamp, S. (1987). *Developmentally appropriate practice in early childhood programs serving children from birth through age eight* (Exp. ed.). Washington, DC: National Association for the Education of Young Children.

Bredekamp, S. (1988). NAEYC position statement on developmentally appropriate practice in the primary grades, serving 5- through 8-year-olds. *Young Children, 43* (2), 64–84.

Bronfenbrenner, U. (1974). *Is early intervention effective? A report on longitudinal evaluation of preschool programs* (Vol. 2). Washington, DC: U.S. Department of Health, Education, and Welfare.

Bronfenbrenner, U. (1975). Reality and research in the ecology of human development. *Proceedings of the American Philosophical Association, 119*, 439–469.

Drotar, D., Baskiewica, A., Irwin, N., Kennell, J., & Klaus, M. (1975). The adaptation of parents to the birth of an infant with a congenital malformation: A hypothetical model. *Pediatrics, 56*, 710–717.

Dunst, C. J., Johanson, C., Trivette, C. M., & Hamby, D. (1991). Family-oriented early intervention policies and practices: Family-centered or not? *Exceptional Children, 58*, 115–126.

Fallen, N. H., & Umansky, W. (1985). *Young children with special needs.* Upper Saddle River, NJ: Merrill/Prentice Hall.

Gargioulo, R. M., & Graves, S. B. (1991). Parental feelings: The forgotten component when working with parents of handicapped preschool children. *Childhood Education, 67*, 176–178.

Grant, C. U. (1982). The classroom behavior of children labeled Autistic. In P. Knoblock (Ed.), *Teaching and motivating Autistic children* (pp. 275–288). Denver, CO: Love.

Griffith, D. R. (1992). Prenatal exposure to cocaine and other drugs: Developmental and educational progress. *Phi Delta Kappan, 73*, 30–34.

Grossman, F. K. (1972). Brothers and sisters of retarded children. *Psychology Today, 5*, 82–87.

Knoblock, P. (1982). *Teaching and motivating Autistic children.* Denver, CO: Love.

Mallory, B., & New, R. (1994). *Diversity and developmentally appropriate practices: Challenges for early childhood education.* New York: Teachers College Press.

Marozas, D. S., & May, D. C. (1988). *Issues and practices in special education.* New York: Longman.

Meisels, S. J. (1986). Testing four- and five-year-olds: Response to Salzer and to Shepard and Smith. *Educational Leadership, 44*, 90–92.

Perske, R. (1973). *New directions for parents of persons who are retarded.* Nashville: Abingdon.

Public Law 94–142. (1975). The education for all handicapped children act (EHA). Section 1219.5 (Federal Register), p. 12478.

Public Law 94–142. (1975). The education for all handicapped children act (EHA). Section 6 (42 Federal Register), p. 19.

Rose, D. F., & Smith, B. J. (1993). Preschool mainstreaming: Attitude barriers and strategies for addressing them. *Young Children, 48* (4), 59–62.

Safford, P. (1989). *Integrated teaching in early childhood: Starting in the mainstream.* White Plains, NY: Longman.

Savage, S., Mayfield, P., & Cook, M. (1993). Questions about serving children with HIV/AIDS. *Day Care and Early Education, 21* (1), 10–12.

Sexton, D., Snyder, P., Sharpton, W. R., & Stricklin, S. (1993). Infants and toddlers with special needs and their families [Annual theme issue]. *Childhood Education, 69* (5), 278–286.

Solit, G. (1993, September/October). A place for Marie: Guidelines for the integration process. *Child Care Information Exchange*, 49–54.

Stoneman, Z., &Brody, G. H. (1982). Strengths inherent in sibling interactions involving a retarded child: A functional role theory approach. *Exceptional Children, 45*, 166–169.

Torrance, E. (1983). Preschool creativity. In K. Paget & B. Bracken (Eds.), *Psychoeducational assessment of preschool children* (pp. 509–520). New York: Grune & Stratton.

Vincent, L. J. (1992, Summer). Implementing individualized family service planning in urban, culturally diverse early intervention settings. *Osers News*, 29–33.

Wiegerink, R., & Pelosi, J. W. (Eds.). (1979). *Developmental disabilities: The DD movement.* Baltimore: Brookes.

Chapter 6

American Heritage Dictionary (3rd ed.). (1996). Boston: Houghton Mifflin.

Anderson, T. Z., & White, G. D. (1986). An empirical investigation of interactions and relation patterns in functional and dysfunctional nuclear families and stepfamilies. *Family Process, 17*, 407–422.

Axinn, W. G. (1996). The influences of parents' marital dissolutions on children's attitudes toward family formation. *Demography, 33*, 66–81.

Berry, J. (1978). Contemporary bibliotherapy: Systematizing the field. In E. J. Rulim (Ed.), *Bibliotherapy* (pp. 185–190). Phoenix: Orene Press.

Brazelton, T. B. (1989). *Families: Crisis and caring.* New York: Ballantine Books.

Coleman, M., & Ganong, L. (1990). The uses of juvenile fiction and self-help books with stepfamilies. *Journal of Counseling & Development, 68*, 327–331.

Darden, E., & Zimmerman, T. (1992). Blended families: A decade review, 1979 to 1990. *Family Therapy, 19*, 25–31.

Diamond, S. A. (1985). *Helping children of divorce.* New York: Schocken Books.

Dreikurs, R., & Grey, L. (1968). *Logical consequences.* New York: Hawthorn.

Fine, M. A., & Fine, D. R. (1992). Recent changes in laws affecting stepfamilies: Suggestions for legal reform. *Family Relations, 41*, 334–340.

Francke, L. B. (1983). *Growing up divorced.* New York: Linden.

Frieman, B. B. (1993). Separation and divorce: Children want their teachers to know. *Young Children, 48* (6), 58–63.

Froiland, D. J., & Hozman, T. L. (1977). Counseling for constructive divorce. *Personnel & Guidance Journal, 55*, 525–529.

Furstenberg, F. L., Jr. (1988). Child care after divorce, and remarriage. In E. M. Hetherington, E. Mavis, & J. D. Arasteh (Eds.), *Impacts of divorce, single parenting, and stepparenting on children* (pp. 245–262). Mahwah, NJ: Erlbaum.

Galston, W. A. (1996). Divorce American style. *Public Interest, 124*, 12–26.

Ganong, L., Coleman, M., & Maples, D. (1990). A meta-analytic review of family structure stereotypes. *Journal of Marriage and the Family, 52*, 287–297.

Gardner, R. (1984). Counseling children in stepfamilies. *Elementary School Guidance & Counseling, 14*, 40–49.

Glick, P. C. (1989). Remarriage: Some recent changes and variations. *Journal of Family Issues, 4*, 455–478.

Godwin, L. J., Groves, M. M., & Horm-Wingerd, D. M. (1993, Spring). "Don't leave me": Separation distress in infants, toddlers, and parents. *Day Care and Early Education, 20*(3), 13–17.

Hagan, M. S., Hollier, E. A., O'Connor, T. G., & Eisenberg, M. (1992). Parent–child relationships in nondivorced, divorced, single-mother, and remarried families. *Monographs of the Society for Research in Child Development, 57*(2–3), 94–148.

Hayes, R. L., & Hayes, B. A. (1986). Remarriage families: Counseling parents, stepparents, and their children. *Counseling and Human Development, 18*, 1–8.

Jellinek, M., & Klavan, E. (1988, September). The single parent. *Good Housekeeping, 207*(3), 126.

Keith, V. M., & Finlay, B. (1988). The impact of parental divorce on children's educational attainment, marital timing, and likelihood of divorce. *Journal of Marriage and the Family, 50*(4), 798–809.

Kosinki, F. (1983). Improving relationships in stepfamilies. *Elementary School Guidance & Counseling, 13*, 200–207.

Lindner, M. S., Hagan, M. S., & Brown, J. C. (1992). The adjustment of children in nondivorced, divorced, single-mother, and remarried families. *Monographs for Research in Child Development, 57*(2–3), 35–72.

Livingston, J. A. (1983). *Children after divorce: A psychosocial analysis of the effects of custody on self esteem.* Doctoral thesis. State University of New York at Buffalo. (UMI No. 83–26981)

Luepnitz, D. A. (1982). *Child custody; A study of families after divorce.* Lanham, MD: Lexington Books.

McCubbin, H. I., & Patterson, J. M. (1982). Family adaptation to crisis. In H. I. McCubbin & J. M. Patterson (Eds.), *Family stress, coping, and social support* (pp. 26–47). Springfield, IL: Charles C. Thomas.

McInnes, K. (1982). Bibliotherapy: Adjunct to traditional counseling with children of stepfamilies. *Child Welfare, 61,* 153–160.

Merriam-Webster's New Collegiate Dictionary (10th ed.). (1993). Springfield, MA: Merriam-Webster.

Pike, L. (2000, Spring/Summer). Effects of parent residency arrangements on the development of primary-aged children. *Australian Institute of Family Studies: Family Matters, 57,* 40–45.

Poppen, W., & White, P. (1984). Transition to the blended family. *Elementary School Guidance & Counseling, 14,* 50–61.

Sheehy, P. (1980). Family enrichment for step-families: An empirical study. *Dissertation Abstracts International, 42,* 2317A.

Sheehy, P., & Fisher, B. (1980). *Stepping together: A self-help program for stepfamilies.* Unpublished manuscript.

Smith, R. (1992). *Stressors affecting children of African American stepfamilies.* (ERIC Document ED 358 389 C 024879)

Stanton, G. (1986). Preventive intervention with stepfamilies. *Social Work, 31,* 201–206.

Strangeland, C. S., Pellegreno, D. C., & Lundholm, J. (1989). Children of divorced parents: A perceptual comparison. *Elementary School Guidance & Counseling, 23*(2), 167–174.

Visher, E., & Visher, J. (1988). *Stepfamilies: Old loyalties, new ties.* New York: Brunner/Mazel.

Visher, E. B., & Visher, J. S. (1982). *How to win as a stepfamily.* New York: Dembner Books.

Visher, E. B., & Visher, J. S. (1983). Stepparenting: Blending families. In H. I. McCubbin & C. R. Figley (Eds.), *Stress and the family: Coping with normative transitions* (vol. 1) pp. 133–146. New York: Brunner/Mazel.

Wallerstein, J. S., & Blakeslee, S. (1995). *The good marriage: How and why love lasts.* Boston: Houghton Mifflin.

Wallerstein, J. S., & Kelly, J. B. (1980). *Surviving the break-up: How children and parents cope with divorce.* New York: Basic Books.

Walsh, W. M. (1992). Twenty major issues in remarriage families. *Journal of Counseling & Development, 70,* 709–715.

Chapter 7

Adoption and foster care analysis and reporting system. (2001). Washington, DC: Children's Bureau, The Administration for Children and Families.

Barrett, K. C., Kallio, K. D., McBride, R. M., Moore, C. M., & Wilson, M. A. (1995). *Child development.* New York: Glencoe.

Bartholet, E. (1993). *Family bonds: Adoption and the politics of parenting.* New York: Houghton Mifflin.

Briggs, J. R. (1994). *A Yankelovich monitor perspective on gays/lesbians.* Norwalk, CT: Yankelovich Partners.

Brodzinsky, D. M. (1990). A stress and coping model of adoption adjustment. In D. M. Brodzinsky & M. D. Schechter (Eds.), *The psychology of adoption.* New York: Oxford University Press.

Brodzinsky, D. M., & Schechter, M. D. (Eds.). (1990). *The psychology of adoption.* New York: Oxford University Press.

Brodzinsky, D. M., Schechter, M. D., & Henig, R. M. (1992). *Being adopted: The lifelong search for self.* Garden City, NY: Doubleday.

Brodzinsky, D. M., Singer, L. M., & Braff, A. M. (1984). Children's understanding of adoption. *Child Development, 55,* 869–878.

Call, J. (1974). Helping infants cope with change. *Early Child Development and Care, 3,* 229–247.

Collum, C. (1995). Gays and lesbians should have the right to adopt children. In A. Harnack (Ed.), *Adoption: Opposing viewpoints.* San Diego: Greenhaven.

Edwards, C. P. (1986). *Promoting social and moral development in young children: Creative approaches for the classroom.* New York: Teachers College Press.

Erikson, E. H. (1950). *Childhood and society.* New York: Norton.

Evan B. Donaldson Adoption Institute (2004). *What's working for children: A policy study of adoption stability and termination.* New York: Author. Retrieved August 22, 2005, from www.adoptioninstitute.org/publications/DisruptionReport.pdf

Ferrero, E., Freker, J., & Foster, T. (2005). *Too high a price: The case against restricting gay parenting.* New York: American Civil Liberties Union.

Goyer, A. (2005). Intergenerational relationships: Grandparents raising grandchildren. *AARP Policy and Research Perspective.* Retrieved December 28, 2005, from www.aarp.org/research/international/perspectives/nov-05-grandparents.html

Harnack, A. (1995). *Adoption: Opposing viewpoints.* San Diego: Greenhaven.

Hollinger, J. H. (1993). Adoption law. In R. E. Behrman (Ed.), *The future of children: Adoption* (pp. 43–61). Los Altos, CA: Center for the Future of Children.

Kreider, Rose M. (2003). *Adopted children and stepchildren: 2000,* Census Special Reports, CENSR-6RV. Washington, DC: U.S. Census Bureau.

McGuinness, T., & Pallansch, L. (2000). Competence of children adopted from the former Soviet Union. *Family Relations, 49,* 457–465.

McKenzie, J. K. (1993). Adoption of children with special needs. In R. E. Behrman (Ed.), *The future of children: Adoption* (pp. 62–76). Los Altos, CA: Center for the Future of Children.

National Adoption Information Clearinghouse. (2000). *Adopting a child with special needs.* Washington, DC: The Administration for Children and Families.

Piaget, J. J. (1929). *The child's conception of the world.* New York: Harcourt Brace.

Rothenberg, D. (1996). Grandparents as parents: A primer for schools. Urbana, IL: ERIC Clearinghouse on Elementary and Early Childhood Education. (ERIC Document Reproduction Service No. ED 401044)

Russell, A. T. (1995). Transracial adoptions should be forbidden. In A. Harnack (Ed.), *Adoption: Opposing viewpoints.* San Diego: Greenhaven.

Silverman, A. R. (1993). Outcomes of transracial adoption. In R. E. Behrman (Ed.), *The future of children: Adoption* (pp. 104–118). Los Altos, CA: Center for the Future of Children.

Simon, R. J., Altstein, H., & Melli, M. S. (1995). Transracial adoptions should be encouraged. In A. Harnack (Ed.), *Adoption: Opposing viewpoints.* San Diego: Greenhaven.

Sokoloff, B. Z. (1993). Antecedents of American adoption. In R. E. Behrman (Ed.), *The future of children: Adoption* (pp. 17–25). Los Altos, CA: Center for the Future of Children.

Solinger, R. (1992). *Wake up little Susie: Single pregnancy and race before* Roe v. Wade. New York: Routledge.

Stolley, K. S. (1993). Adoption: Overview and major recommendations. In R. E. Behrman (Ed.), *The future of children: Adoption* (pp. 26–42). Los Altos, CA: Center for the Future of Children.

U.S. Department of Health and Human Services. (2004). *How many children were adopted in 2000 and 2001?* Washington, DC: National Adoption Information Clearinghouse. Retrieved August 22, 2005, from http://naic.acf.hhs.gov/pubs/s_adopted/index.cfm

Wasson, V. P. (1977). *The chosen baby.* Philadelphia: J. B. Lippincott (Original work published in 1939)

Wolin, S. J., & Wolin, S. (1993). *The resilient self: How survivors of troubled families rise above adversity.* New York: Villard.

Wright, K. (2001). Personal communication.

Chapter 8

Allen, L. S., & Gorski, R. A. (1992). Sexual orientation and the size of the anterior commissure in the human brain. *Proceedings of the National Academy of Science, 89,* 7199–7202.

Bailey, J. M., & Pillard, R. C. (1991). A genetic study of male sexual orientation. *Archives of General Psychiatry, 48,* 1089–1096.

Baker v. Nelson. (1971). Supreme Court of Minnesota, 291 Minn. 310, 191 N.W. 2d 185, appeal dismissed 409 U.S. 810, 93 S. Ct. 37, 34 L. Ed. 2d 65.

Baptiste, D. A. (1987). Psychotherapy with gay/lesbian couples and their children in "stepfamilies": A challenge for marriage and family therapists. *Journal of Homosexuality, 14,* 223–238.

Bozett, F. W. (1989). Gay fathers: A review of the literature. In F. W. Bozett (Ed.), *Homosexuality and the family* (pp. 137–162). New York: Harrington Park.

Bozett, F. W. (1993). Gay fathers: A review of the literature. In L. D. Garnets & D. C. Kimmel (Eds.), *Psychological perspectives on gay and lesbian male experiences* (pp. 437–458). New York: Columbia University Press.

Braschi v. Stahl Associates Co. (1989). New York Court of Appeals, W. L. 73109.

Calfia, P. (1979). Lesbian sexuality. *Journal of Homosexuality, 4,* 255–266.

Casper, V., Schultz, S., & Wickens, E. (1992). Breaking the silences: Lesbian and gay parents and the schools. *Teachers College Record, 94,* 109–137.

Cass, V. C. (1983/1984). Homosexual identity: A concept in need of definition. *Journal of Homosexuality, 9,* 105–126.

Cass, V. C. (1984). Homosexual identity formation: Testing a theoretical model. *Journal of Sex Research, 20*, 143–167.

Chan, C. (1993). Issues of identity development among Asian American lesbians and gay men. In L. D. Garnets & D. C. Kimmel (Eds.), *Psychological perspectives on gay and lesbian male experiences* (pp. 376–387). New York: Columbia University Press.

Clay, J. W. (1990). Working with lesbian and gay parents and their children. *Young Children, 45*, 31–35.

Cohen, E. (1991). Who are "we"? Gay "identity" as political (e)motion (a theoretical rumination). In D. Fuss (Ed.), *Inside/out: Lesbian theories, gay theories* (pp. 71–92). New York: Routledge.

Coleman, E. (1985). Bisexual women in marriages. *Journal of Homosexuality, 11*, 87–99.

DeCecco, J. P., & Parker, D. A. (1995). The biology of homosexuality: Sexual orientation or sexual preference? *Journal of Homosexuality, 28*, 1–27.

Espin, O. M. (1993). Issues of identity in the psychology of Latina lesbians. In L. D. Garnets & D. C. Kimmel (Eds.), *Psychological perspectives on gay and lesbian male experiences* (pp. 348–363). New York: Columbia University Press.

Falk, P. (1993). Lesbian mothers: Psychosocial assumptions in family law. In L. D. Garnets & D. C. Kimmel (Eds.), *Psychological perspectives on gay and lesbian male experiences* (pp. 420–436). New York: Columbia University Press.

Garnets, L. D., & Kimmel, D. C. (Eds.). (1993). *Psychological perspectives on gay and lesbian male experiences.* New York: Columbia University Press.

Gates, G. J., & Ost, J. (2004). *The Gay & Lesbian atlas.* Washington, DC: Urban Institute Press.

Gonsiorek, J. C. (1993). Mental health issues of gay and lesbian adolescents. In L. D. Garnets & D. C. Kimmel (Eds.), *Psychological perspectives on gay and lesbian male experiences* (pp. 469–485). New York: Columbia University Press.

Gorman, C. (1991, September 9). Are gay men born that way? *Time*, 60–61.

Hanscombe, G., & Forster, J. (1982). *Rocking the cradle.* Boston: Alyson.

Harris, M. B., & Turner, P. H. (1986). Gay and lesbian parents. *Journal of Homosexuality, 12*, 101–113.

Hildebrand, V., Phenice, L. A., Gray, M. M., & Hines, R. P. (1996). *Knowing and serving diverse families.* Upper Saddle River, NJ: Merrill/Prentice Hall.

Icard, L. (1985/1986). Black gay men and conflicting social identities: Sexual orientation versus racial identity. *Journal of Social Work and Human Sexuality, 4*, 82–92.

Jones v. Hallahan. (1973). Kentucky Court of Appeals, 73, KY.

Lackey, J. (1997). Teachers and parents define diversity in an Oregon preschool cooperative: Democracy at work. *Young Children, 52*, 20–28.

LeVay, S. (1991). A difference in hypothalamic structure between heterosexual and homosexual men. *Science, 253*, 1034–1037.

Lewin, E. (1993). *Lesbian mothers: Accounts of gender in American culture.* Ithaca, NY: Cornell University Press.

Lilly, E., & Green, C. (2004). *Developing partnerships with families through children's literature.* Upper Saddle River, NJ: Merrill/Prentice Hall.

Loiacano, D. K. (1993). Gay identity issues among Black Americans: Racism, homophobia, and the need for validation. In L. D. Garnets & D. C. Kimmel (Eds.), *Psychological perspectives on gay and lesbian male experiences* (pp. 364–375). New York: Columbia University Press.

Marvin v. Marvin. (1976). Supreme Court of California, 18 Cal. 3d 660, 134 Cal Reptr. 815, 557 P. 2d 106.

Miller, B. (1978). Adult sexual resocialization: Adjustments toward a stigmatized identity. *Alternative Lifestyles, 1*, 207–234.

Miller, B. (1979). Gay fathers and their children. *Family Coordinator, 28*, 544–552.

Miller, B. (1983). *Identity conflict and resolution: A social psychological model of gay family men's adaptations.* Doctoral dissertation, University of Alberta, Edmonton, Canada.

Miller, B. (1986). Identity resocialization in moral careers of gay husbands and fathers. In A. Davis (Ed.), *Papers in honor of Gordon Hirabayashi* (pp. 197–216). Edmonton, Canada: University of Alberta Press.

Murray, P. D., & McClintock, K. (2005). Children of the closet: A measurement of the anxiety and self-esteem of children raised by a non-disclosed homosexual or bisexual parent. *Journal of Homosexuality, 49*(1), 77–95.

Oswald, R. F., Patterson, C. J., & Kuvalanka, K. A. (2004). Same-sex marriage: NCFR fact sheet. Minneapolis: National Council on Family Relations.

Patterson, C. (1992). Children of lesbian and gay parents. *Child Development, 63*, 1025–1042.

Patterson, C. J. (2000). Family relationships of lesbians and gay men. *Journal of Marriage and Family, 62,* 1052–1069.

Patterson, C. J., & Chan, R. W. (1999). Families headed by lesbian and gay parents. In M. E. Lamb, (Ed.), *Parenting and child development in "non-traditional" families* (pp. 191–220). Mahwah, NJ: Erlbaum.

Pennington, S. (1987). Children of lesbian mothers. In F. Bozett (Ed.), *Gay and lesbian parents* (pp. 58–70). New York: Praeger.

Pillard, R. C., & Weinrich, J. D. (1986). Evidence of familial nature of male homosexuality. *Archives of General Psychiatry, 43,* 808–812.

Renshaw v. Heckler. (1986). United States Court of Appeals, (2nd Cir.) 787 F. 2d 50.

Sears, J. T. (1994). Challenges for educators: Lesbian, gay, and bisexual families. *High School Journal, 77,* 138–156.

Shon, S. P., & Ja, D. Y. (1982). Asian families. In M. McGoldrick, J. K. Pearse, & J. Giordano (Eds.), *Ethnicity and family therapy* (pp. 208–229). New York: Guilford.

Simmons, T., & O'Connell, M. (2003). *Married-couple and unmarried-partner households: 2000,* Census 2000 Special Reports, CENSR-5. Washington, DC: U.S. Census Bureau.

Smith, D., & Gates, G. (2001). *Gay and Lesbian families in the United States: Same-sex unmarried partner households.* Washington, DC: Human Rights Campaign Fund.

Stacy, J., & Biblarz, T. (2001). (How) does the sexual orientation of parents matter? *American Sociological Review, 65,* 159–183.

Strommen, E. F. (1993). "You're a what?": Family member reactions to the disclosure of homosexuality. In L. D. Garnets & D. C. Kimmel (Eds.), *Psychological perspectives on gay and lesbian male experiences* (pp. 248–265). New York: Columbia University Press.

Tasker, F. L., & Golombok, S. (1997). *Growing up in a lesbian family: Effects on child development.* New York: Guilford.

Troiden, R. R. (1993). The formation of sexual identities. In L. D. Garnets & D. C. Kimmel (Eds.), *Psychological perspectives on gay and lesbian male experiences* (pp. 191–217). New York: Columbia University Press.

Turner, P. H., Scadden L., & Harris, M. B. (1985, March). *Parenting in gay and lesbian families.* Paper presented at the First Annual Future of Parenting Symposium, Chicago.

The 21st century family. (1990, July 4). *New York Times,* pp. 1, 10.

Watts v. Watts. (1987). Supreme Court of Wisconsin, 137 Wis. 2d 506, 405 N.W. 2d 303.

Winslow, R. (1991, August 30). Study raises issue of biological basis of homosexuality. *Wall Street Journal,* p. B1.

Wisensale, S. K., & Heckart, K. E. (1993). Domestic partnerships. *Family Relations, 42,* 199–204.

Wright, J. M. (1998). *Lesbian step families: An ethnography of love.* New York: Harrington Park Press.

Wyers, N. L. (1984). *Lesbian and gay spouses and parents: Homosexuality in the family.* Portland: Portland State University, School of Social Work.

Chapter 9

Austin, T. (1994). *Changing the view: Student-led parent conferences.* Portsmouth, NH: Heinemann.

Bailey, D., & Wolery, M. (1984). *Teaching infants and preschoolers with handicaps.* Upper Saddle River, NJ: Merrill/Prentice Hall.

Bersani, C., & Jarjoura, D. (2002). In V. R. Fu, A. J. Stremmel, & L. T. Hill (Eds.), *Teaching and learning: Collaborative exploration of the Reggio Emilia approach* (pp. 66–82). Upper Saddle River, NJ: Merrill/Prentice Hall.

Brand, S. (1996). Making parent involvement a reality: Helping teachers develop partnerships with parents. *Young Children, 51,* 76–81.

Brinson, S. A. (2005). R-E-S-P-E-C-T for families. *Dimensions of Early Childhood, 33*(2), 24–30.

Clifford, R. M. (1997). Partnerships with families. *Young Children, 52,* 2.

Conner, M. L. (1997–2004). How adults learn. Retrieved August 3, 2005, from the Ageless Learner Web site: www.agelesslearner.com/intros/adultlearning.html

Davis, D. (2000). *Supporting parent, family and community involvement in your school.* Portland, OR: Northwest Regional Educational Laboratory.

Derman-Sparks, L. (1989). *Antibias curriculum: Tools for empowering young children.* Washington, DC: National Association for the Education of Young Children.

Dodge, D. T. (1993). *A guide for supervisors and trainers on implementing the creative curriculum for early childhood.* Washington, DC: Teaching Strategies.

Dorfman, D., & Fisher, A. (2002). *Building relationships for students' success: School–family–community partnerships and student achievement in the Northwest.* Portland, OR: Northwest Regional Education Laboratory.

Epstein, J. L. (1995). School/family/community partnerships: Caring for the children we share. *Phi Delta Kappan, 76*, 701–712.

Epstein, J. L., Coates, L., Salinas, K. C., Sanders, M. G., & Simon, B. S. (1997). *School, family, and community partnerships: Your handbook for action.* Thousand Oaks, CA: Corwin Press.

Foster, S. M. (1994). Successful parent meetings. *Young Children, 50*, 78–80.

Fox-Barnett, M., & Meyer, T. (1992). The teacher's playing at my house this week! *Young Children, 47*, 45–50.

Gage, J., & Workman, S. (1994). Creating family support systems: In Head Start and beyond. *Young Children, 50*, 74–77.

Gardner, H. (1985). *Frames of the mind: The theory of multiple intelligences.* New York: Basic Books.

Gargiulo, R. M., & Graves, S. B. (1990). Parental feelings: The forgotten component when working with parents of handicapped preschool children. *Childhood Education, 67*, 176–178.

Grace, C., & Shores, E. (1992). *The portfolio and its use: Developmentally appropriate assessment of young children.* Little Rock, AR: SECA.

Greenwood, D. (1995). Home–school communication via video. *Young Children, 50*, 66.

Harding, N. (1996). Family journals: The bridge from school to home and back again. *Young Children, 51*, 27–30.

Helm, J. (1994). Family theme bags: An innovative approach to family involvement in the school. *Young Children, 49*, 48–53.

Henderson, A., & Mapp, K. (2002). *A new wave of evidence: The impact of school, family, and community connections on student achievement.* Austin, TX: Southwest Educational Development Laboratory, National Center for Family & Community Connections with Schools.

Henderson, A. T., & Berla, N. (Eds.). (1994). *A new generation of evidence: The family is critical to student achievement.* Washington, DC: Center for Law and Education.

Knowler, K. A. (1988). Caregivers' corner: Orienting parents and volunteers to the classroom. *Young Children, 44*, 9.

Latimer, D. J. (1994). Involving grandparents and other older adults in the preschool classroom. *Dimensions of Early Childhood, 22*, 26–30.

Lindle, J. C. (1994). Kentucky's reform opens doors to family involvement. *Dimensions in Early Childhood, 22*, 20–22.

Lyon, S. (1995). What is my culture? *Child Care Information Exchange, 8*, 51.

Manning, M., Manning, G., & Morrison, G. (1995). Letter-writing connections: A teacher, first graders, and their parents. *Young Children, 50*, 34–38.

Postman, N. (1985). *The disappearance of childhood.* New York: Vintage.

Quint, S. (1994). *Schooling homeless children: A working model for America's public schools.* New York: Teachers College Press.

Salinas, K. C., Epstein, J. L., Sanders, M. G., Davis, D., & Douglas, I. (1999). *Measure of school, family, and community partnerships* [Teacher Survey]. Baltimore: Johns Hopkins University, and Portland, OR: Northwest Regional Educational Laboratory.

Sarason, S. (1999). *Teaching as a performing art.* New York: Teachers College Press.

Seplocha, H. (2004). Parnerships for learning: Conferencing with families. *Young Children, 59*(5), 96–99.

Shores, E. F. (1995). Howard Gardner on the eighth intelligence: Seeing the natural world. *Dimensions of Early Childhood, 23*, 5–7.

Taylor, D., & Dorsey-Gaines, C. (1988). *Growing up literate: Learning from inner-city families.* Portsmouth, NH: Heinemann.

Thorkildsen, R., & Stein, M.R.S. (1998). *Is parent involvement related to student achievement? Exploring the evidence* (Research Bulletin No. 22). Bloomington, IN: Phi Delta Kappa Center for Evaluation, Development, and Research.

U.S. Department of Education. (2000). Education for homeless children and youth report to Congress. Retrieved February 6, 2005, from www.ed.gov

U.S. Department of Health and Human Services. (1990). *Project Head Start statistical fact sheet.* Washington, DC: U.S. Government Printing Office.

Wright, K., Daniel, T., & Heimelrich, K. (1999). *Building partnerships with families: A survey of parents, teachers, and administrators.* Lexington, KY: Commonwealth Institute for Parents, Prichard Committee for Academic Excellence.

Chapter 10

Barbour, A., & Desjean-Perrotta, B. (1998). The basics of portfolio assessment. In S. C. Wortham, A. Barbour, & B. Desjean-Perrotta, *Portfolio assessment: A handbook for preschool and elementary educators* (pp. 15–30). Olney, MD: Association for Childhood Education International.

Berger, E. H. (1981). *Parents as partners in education: The school and home working together.* St. Louis: C. V. Mosby.

Berger, E. H. (1991). *Parents as partners in education: Families and schools working together* (3rd ed.). Upper Saddle River, NJ: Merrill/Prentice Hall.

Berger, E. H. (2004). *Parents as partners in education: Families and schools working together* (6th ed.). Upper Saddle River, NJ: Merrill/Prentice Hall.

Bredekamp, S., & Rosegrant, T. (Eds.). (1992). *Reaching potentials: Appropriate curriculum and assessment of young children* (Vol. 1). Washington, DC: National Association for the Education of Young Children.

Brophy, K., Grotelueschen, A., & Gooler, D. (1974). *A blueprint for program evaluation* (Occasional Paper No. 1). Urbana-Champaign: University of Illinois, College of Education, Office for Professional Services.

Edwards, C., Gandini, L., & Forman, G. (1993). *The hundred languages of children.* Norwood, NJ: Ablex.

Farr, R., & Tone, B. (1994). *Portfolio performance assessment.* Fort Worth, TX: Harcourt Brace.

Gronlund, N. E. (1998). Portfolios as an assessment tool: Is collection of work enough? *Young Children, 53,* 4–10.

Komoski, P. K. (1987). Beyond innovation: The systemic integration of technology into the curriculum. *Educational Technology, 27*(9), 21–25.

Maykut, P., & Morehouse, R. (1994). *Beginning qualitative research.* London: Falmer Press.

McGill-Franzen, A., & Allington, R. L. (1993). Flunk-em or get them classified: The contamination of primary grade accountability data. *Educational Researcher, 22*(1), 19–22.

Meisels, S. J. (1992). Doing harm by doing good: Iatrogenic effects of early childhood enrollment and promotion policies. *Early Childhood Research Quarterly, 7*(2), 155–174.

National Association for the Education of Young Children & National Association of Early Childhood Specialists in State Departments of Education. (1991). Guidelines for appropriate curriculum content and assessment in programs serving children ages three through eight. *Young Children, 46*(3), 21–38.

National Association of Elementary School Principals. (1998). *Early childhood education and the elementary school principal* (2nd ed.). Alexandria, VA: Author.

National Association of State Boards of Education. (1988). *Right from the start: The report of the NASBE Task Force on Early Childhood Education.* Alexandria, VA: Author.

Payne, D. A. (1994). *Designing educational project and program evaluations.* Boston: Kluwer.

Puckett, M. B., & Black, J. K. (1994). *Authentic assessment of the young child.* Upper Saddle River, NJ: Merrill/Prentice Hall.

Puckett, M. B., & Black, J. K. (2000). *Authentic assessment of the young child: Celebrating development and learning* (2nd ed.). Upper Saddle River, NJ: Merrill/Prentice Hall.

Rocco, S. (1996). Toward shared commitment and shared responsibility: A parent's vision of developmental assessment. In S. J. Meisels & E. Fenichel (Eds.), *New visions for the development assessment of infants and young children: Zero to three.* Washington, DC: National Center for Infants, Toddlers and Families.

Scriven, M. (1991). *Evaluation thesaurus* (4th ed.). London: Sage.

Scriven, M. (1993). *Hard-won lessons in program evaluation* (New Directions in Program Evaluation, No. 58). San Francisco: Jossey-Bass.

Southern Early Childhood Association. (2000). *Developmentally appropriate assessment: A position paper.* Little Rock, AR: Author.

Webster's new world dictionary (Concise ed.). (1960). New York: World.

Wortham, S. C. (2005). *Assessment in early childhood education* (4th ed.). Upper Saddle River, NJ: Pearson Education, Inc.

Worthen, B. R., & Sanders, J. R. (1987). *Educational evaluation: Alternative approaches and practical guidelines.* New York: Longman.